↤ KU-408-752

Geology of the country around Hitchin

The Hitchin district, covering much of north Hertford-shire and a small part of south-east Bedfordshire, straddles the north-eastern extremity of the Chiltern Hills. The central part of the area is dominated by the ever-growing conurbations of Stevenage, Letchworth and Hitchin. The eastern suburbs of Luton, including Luton Airport, cover the south-western corner. Beyond these towns the area is one of contrasting scenery which reflects the underlying geology.

The landscape is dominated by the steep north-westward facing scarp, founded on the Middle and Upper Chalk, which also forms the catchment divide between the river systems of the Ouse to the north and the Lea (and ultimately the Thames) to the south. North of the scarp is a tract of relatively flat ground founded on the Lower Chalk and Gault which rises, in the extreme north-west, to a poorly developed line of hills underlain by the Woburn Sands. South of the scarp, the dissected Chalk dip slope is covered by glaciogenic deposits, mainly till, and remnants of the Palaeogene and clay-with-flints. The scarp and dip slope are cut by the Hitchin Gap, a major north–south routeway, which is founded on an exception-ally thick, complex sequence of glaciogenic deposits in a buried valley.

The memoir describes the results of the geological survey of the district, including sections on economic geology and water supply. The account highlights the stratigraphy of the Chalk, which can now be successfully related to expanded sequences on the south coast, and also the complex interrelationship of the glaciogenic deposits proved within the Hitchin Gap, giving an insight into the development of this major feature.

REFERENCE LIBRARY
THIS COPY IS FOR REFERENCE
IN THE LIBRARY ONLY AND IS
NOT AVAILABLE FOR HOME
READING.

Cover photograph

View from Gannock Farm to the north-west. A typical scene on the Chalk scarp founded on the Chalk Rock (bright patch in field centre right). (Photograph courtesy of Brian Sawford, North Hertfordshire Museum Services.) (GS 121C)

Aerial view looking east along the scarp from over Therfield towards Reed (right centre) and Barkway (top right).

The photograph, taken in October, gives the optimum view of the area underlain by till with included Chalk rafts which give the striped tonal changes between lighter Chalk rafts and darker interposed till. (Photograph courtesy of Brian Sawford, North Hertfordshire Museum Services.)

BRITISH GEOLOGICAL SURVEY

P M HOPSON,
D T ALDISS and
A SMITH

CONTRIBUTORS

Biostratigraphy
C J Wood
I P Wilkinson
M A Woods

Structure
J M Allsop

Hydrogeology
C S Cheney

Archaeology
J J Wymer

Geology of the country around Hitchin

Memoir for 1:50 000 Geological Sheet 221
(England and Wales)

LONDON: HMSO   1996

© *NERC copyright 1996*

First published 1996

ISBN 0 11 884518 7

Bibliographical reference

HOPSON, P M, ALDISS, D T, AND SMITH, A. 1996. Geology of the country around Hitchin. *Memoir of the British Geological Survey*, Sheet 221 (England and Wales).

Authors

P M Hopson, BSc, CGeol, FGS
D T Aldiss, BSc, PhD, CGeol, FGS
A Smith, BSc
British Geological Survey, Keyworth

Contributors

I P Wilkinson, BSc, MSc, PhD, CGeol, FGS
M A Woods, BSc
J M Allsop, BSc
British Geological Survey, Keyworth

C J Wood, BSc, CGeol, FGS
formerly British Geological Survey

C S Cheney, BSc, MSc, CGeol, FGS
British Geological Survey, Wallingford

J J Wymer, MA, DSc
The Vines, Great Cressingham, Norfolk

Printed in the UK for HMSO
Dd 301325   C8   3/96

Other publications of the Survey dealing with this district and adjoining districts

BOOKS

British regional geology
East Anglia and adjoining areas, 4th edition, 1961
London and Thames Valley, 4th edition, 1996

Memoirs
Huntingdon and Biggleswade (187, 204), 1965
Saffron Walden (205), 1932*
Leighton Buzzard (220), 1994
Great Dunmow (222), 1990
Aylesbury and Hemel Hempstead (238), 1922*
Hertford (239), 1924*
Epping (240), 1987

Mineral assessment reports
No. 46   (Harlow), 1979
No. 67   (Hatfield and Cheshunt), 1981
No. 69   (Welwyn Garden City), 1981
No. 71   (Hemel Hempstead, St Albans and Watford), 1982
No. 112 (Hertford), 1982

Water supply
Water supply of Bedfordshire and Northamptonshire, 1909*
Water supply of Buckinghamshire and Hertfordshire, 1921*
Wartime pamphlet No. 20 parts 1 to 10, 1942–46*
Well catalogue for Saffron Walden (205), 1965
Well catalogue for Hitchin (221), 1970
Well catalogue for Great Dunmow & Braintree (222, 223), 1965
Well catalogue for Epping (240), 1965

MAPS

1:1 100 000
Geology of the United Kingdom, Ireland and the adjacent continental shelf (south sheet), 1991
Pre-Permian Geology of the United Kingdon (south sheet), 1985

1:625 000
Solid Geology (south sheet), 1979
Quaternary Geology (south sheet), 1977

1:250 000
Chilterns (solid geology) Sheet 51°N02°W, 1992

1:100 000
Hydrogeological map of the area between Cambridge and Maidenhead, 1984

1:50 000 and 1:63 360
Bedford (203), 1900*
Biggleswade (204), 1976
Saffron Walden (205), 1952
Leighton Buzzard (220), 1993
Great Dunmow (222), 1990
Aylesbury (238), 1923 [1990(F)]
Hertford (239), 1978
Epping (240), 1981

* Out of print, (F) photographic facsimile

CONTENTS

TABLES

ACKNOWLEDGEMENTS

NOTES

This memoir was compiled by P M Hopson from major contributions by P M Hopson, D T Aldiss and A Smith. Contributions from the following were included: J M Allsop has written on aspects of the concealed and structural geology incorporated in Chapters 2 and 7, C J Wood's work on the Chalk stratigraphy appears in Chapter 4. Contributions to the biostratigraphy, macro- and micro-palaeontology of the Gault and Chalk by M A Woods and I P Wilkinson are included in Chapters 3 and 4. R A Ellison, R W O'B Knox, C King and D W Jolley are thanked for their helpful discussions and contributions on the Palaeogene, incorporated in Chapter 5. P L Gibbard and S Boreham from the Sub-department of Quaternary Research at Cambridge University are acknowledged for their helpful discussions on aspects of the Quaternary history of the Hitchin Gap and for the pollen diagram from Todd's Green, all of which are included in Chapter 6. The note on the Palaeolithic finds in the district, in Chapter 6, is the work of J J Wymer. The hydrogeology of the district was written by C S Cheney. This memoir has been edited by Drs E R Shephard-Thorn and A A Jackson.

The completion of this survey has been assisted by many organisations and individuals. Grateful acknowledgement of financial support for mapping in the south and east of the district is made to Thames Water Authority (now Thames Water Plc). Our thanks are due to a number of quarrying concerns within the district, who have facilitated access to their properties. These include Croxton and Garry Ltd, Butterley Brick Ltd, Bedwell Park Quarry Co. Ltd and Laporte Industries Ltd. The survey was conducted under the directorship of Dr E R Shephard-Thorn (Project Manager), and Drs R G Thurrell and R A B Bazley (Group Managers).

Local government bodies have also been most helpful in supplying copies of borehole data from their archives and for other assistance. These include Hertfordshire and Bedfordshire county councils, North Hertfordshire District Council, Letchworth Garden City Corporation and Luton and Stevenage borough councils. The generous assistance of B Sawford and T James of the North Hertfordshire Museum Services and the Letchworth Museum are also acknowledged.

Several scientific collegues have been generous in making personal communications and providing access to other unpublished work. These include: Dr R G Bromley, Dr A S Gale, Professor R N Mortimore and Dr D J Wray.

Finally, our thanks are due to the land owners of the district for their cooperation in providing ready access to their property during the course of the survey.

Throughout the memoir the word 'district' refers to the area covered by the 1:50 000 geological sheet 221 (Hitchin).

National Grid references are given in square brackets; they lie within 100 km square TL unless otherwise stated.

Throughout this memoir boreholes are referred to by name (most commonly a place or prominent landmark) other than at first mention where a grid reference is also given. A listing of these boreholes, together with their unique reference number by which they may be identified in the British Geological Survey (BGS) archives, is given in Appendix 1.

Numbers preceded by GS refer to photographs in the BGS collections.

PREFACE

This memoir describes the geology of the district covered by 1:50 000 Sheet 221 (Hitchin) which extends from the eastern suburbs of Luton to the valley of the River Rib. The district is largely rural with industry concentrated on the margins of the larger towns of Stevenage, Hitchin, Letchworth, Baldock and Luton itself. It lies within the commuter belt north of London and has good rail and road links to the capital. The district is divided by the Chalk escarpment which separates the Gault clay vale from the chalk dip slope on which Palaeogene and Quaternary deposits are preserved.

One of the most important early resources of the district was flint which was first a material for tool making and then a commonly used building stone. However, significant extraction of minerals in the region did not commence until the middle of the 19th century when brick clay, agricultural lime and phosphate were exploited.

At present, the Gault is quarried for the production of bricks at Arlesey, and Chalk is worked for agricultural lime at Anstey. However, in the past, chalk (for cement manufacture) and sand and gravel (for building) were worked throughout the district. The local geology has attracted considerable interest over the years, particularly with respect to Chalk lithostratigraphy. This memoir integrates this earlier work with the large amount of additional data derived from the new survey of the district and highlights particularly the Chalk and Quaternary sequences. It is designed to be read in conjunction with the 1:50 000 scale geological map.

The memoir gives a modern synthesis of the geology of the area and will be of interest to the agricultural community and to those involved in planning, extractive industries, water supply, waste disposal and civil engineering.

Peter J Cook, DSc
Director

British Geological Survey
Keyworth
Nottingham
NG12 5GG

October 1995

ONE

Introduction

GEOGRAPHICAL SETTING

The district straddles the Chalk escarpment of the northern Chiltern Hills. The north and north-westward facing scarp overlooks the Gault clay vale and the low hills founded on the Woburn Sands beyond, whilst the gently south-eastward sloping dip slope forms part of the northern limb of the London Basin syncline. The district includes a major part of north Hertfordshire, the south-eastern extremity of Bedfordshire, around Stotfold and Meppershall, and a very small part of south Cambridgeshire near Slip End.

Physiographically, of moderate relief for south-east England, the Chiltern region stretches north-east from the Goring Gap in Oxfordshire. The extent of the Chilterns in this direction is ambiguous. Jones (1981) considers the hills to be made up of three distinct morphological areas, present on both sides of the Hitchin Gap, but others limit the Chilterns to the area from Goring to Hitchin. The three areas discussed in Jones (1981) are the high 'unbroken cuesta' from Goring to Princes Risborough, the 'middle cuesta', cut by six major wind gaps, north-east to Luton, and the topographically lower, northward facing 'cuesta' crossing north Hertfordshire (Figure 1).

The most north-easterly of the six major wind gaps, cut by the headwaters of the River Lea, crosses the south-west corner of the district, near Luton airport. Part of the 'middle cuesta' can be seen between Luton and the Hitchin Gap. North-east of this gap, the scarp becomes more subdued, due to the effects of the Anglian glaciation, but continues beyond the district into north Essex and Cambridgeshire.

The highest point in the district is in the west at Telegraph Hill (183 m above OD); from here the scarp drops towards the north-east with Therfield at 168 m above OD (Figure 1). Both prominent hills were the sites of Elizabethan pitch-pan warning beacons.

The Hitchin Gap trends south-eastward across the area from Hitchin to Watton at Stone. The gap is a complex double feature of largely glacial origin with two main arms which bifurcate northwards at Stevenage. The present-day misfit streams drain both northwards and south-eastward from the watershed in the vicinity of Stevenage.

The watershed between streams draining into the Ouse to the north and to the Lea (and ultimately to the Thames) to the south, follows a tortuous course as a result of the breaching of the scarp at the Hitchin Gap.

On the dip slope south and west of the Hitchin Gap, a deeply incised consequent drainage pattern is well developed on the Chalk bedrock. Only the lower reaches of these valleys have permanent stream flow, for example

the River Mimram which rises at Whitwell. East of the gap, the Chalk dip slope is buried beneath glacial deposits and is drained by the rivers Beane, Rib and Quin and their tributaries. Although the rivers have cut down through these glacial deposits in many places, a general north–south valley orientation has been imposed on the exhumed Chalk. Only around Walkern, in the Beane valley, where the Chalk outcrop is broad, has the south-eastward consequent drainage pattern been re-established.

North of the 'Chiltern escarpment', the north-west of the district is drained by the River Ivel and its tributaries the Flit, Hiz and Purwell. The Ivel joins the River Ouse 17 km north of the district at Tempsford. These streams are established on the relatively impervious Lower Chalk and Gault, but dry headwater valleys on Middle Chalk at the base of the scarp are seen on either side of the Hitchin Gap, around Offley Bottom and between Baldock and Therfield Heath.

The area is traversed by a number of major routeways which use the natural features of the landscape to advantage. The A1(M) and the main 'east coast' rail line utilise the Hitchin Gap to cross the Chalk escarpment. The A10 (Ermine Street) follows the Rib valley, and the A505 (Icknield Way) and Hitchin to Cambridge railway follow the scarp foot from Royston to Baldock.

The district is dominated by the towns of Hitchin, Letchworth and Stevenage, all situated within the Hitchin Gap. Hitchin, originally a medieval town at the junction of important routeways, was once the largest, but it has been outgrown by Letchworth (the first Garden City, planned in 1903) and by the 'new town' of Stevenage which expanded in the 1940s and 50s from the nucleus of Old Stevenage. Outside these urban areas, the district is rural and unspoilt. Vestiges of the 'original' beech woodland, characteristic of the poor thin soils of the Chalk, and which once covered much of the scarp and dip slope, are still found in places. South of Hitchin, the countryside is considered typical of rural Hertfordshire with brick and half-timbered houses. Thatch, weather-boarding, tile and ornate pargeting reflect the lack of durable building materials locally. This is most evident in the old churches of the district which, except for some Totternhoe Stone in the north-west, are built of flint, boulders from the glacial drift, bricks and tiles often 'quarried' from Roman dwellings, and irregular-shaped blocks of chalkstone from the Chalk. This lack of local building stone may explain why very few churches have imposing spires, but rather short, stubby towers surmounted by the characteristic 'Hertfordshire spike'. In essence, there is nothing imposing about this part of Hertfordshire. Charles Lamb, who lived for a time in Westmill near Buntingford, called it 'Hearty, homely,

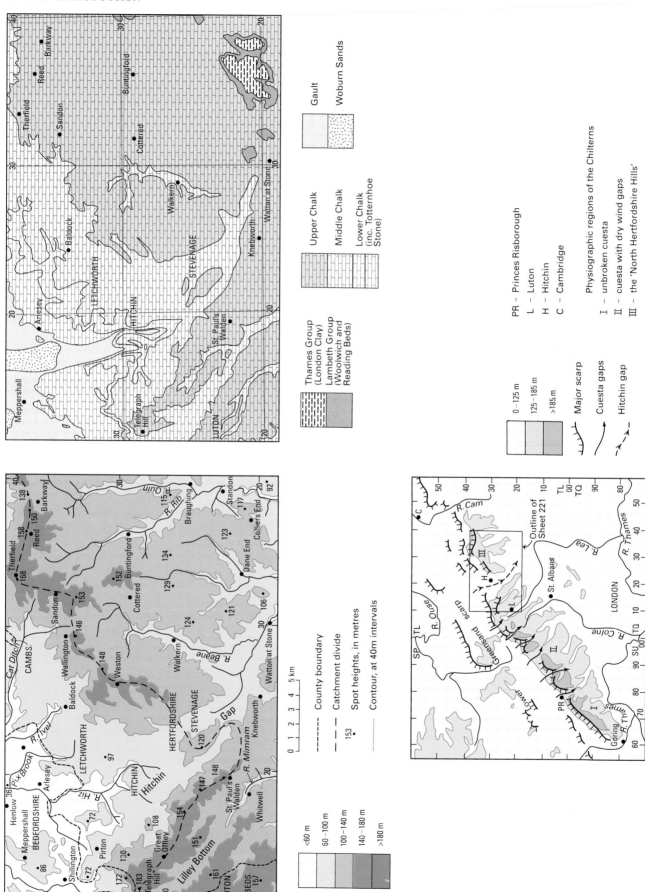

Figure 1   Physical geography and solid geology of the district and its regional setting.

loving Hertfordshire', E M Forster regarded it as 'England at its quietest; ... England meditative' and William Cobbett, a visitor to the county, penned 'what that man ever invented under the name of pleasure grounds can equal these fields in Hertfordshire!'.

HISTORY OF RESEARCH

Little on the geology of this district was published prior to the 1850s. The earliest works were concerned chiefly with the soils, and notable fossil discoveries within the counties of Hertfordshire and Bedfordshire. Reference to these works is made in the Geology sections of the Victoria County Histories for those shires (Hopkinson, 1902; Hopkinson and Saunders, 1904). A more comprehensive bibliography for Hertfordshire, citing some 370 papers between the years 1756 and 1900, some of which deal with sites within the district, is given in a series of papers in the Transactions of the Hertfordshire (formerly Watford [W]) Natural History Society (Whitaker, 1876 [W]; Hopkinson, 1886, 1903).

The district was first surveyed at the one-inch scale (1:63 360) between 1868 and 1884 as part of the 'Old Series' sheets 46NE and SE; and 47NW and SW by W Whitaker, F J Bennett, T Adams, A H Green, W Topley and W H Penning. Sheet 46NE was published as a Solid edition in 1869. Revisions and additions, including drift deposits (by A C G Cameron and A J Jukes-Browne), were incorporated in two further editions issued in 1884 and 1891. The Solid edition of 46SE appeared in 1867 followed by a Drift edition in 1898 after additions by Cameron and Jukes-Browne. The four quarters of Sheet 47 were published on a single sheet as a Solid edition in 1881 and as a Drift edition in 1884. No explanatory memoirs were published for Sheet 46, but the whole of Sheet 47 was described by Whitaker et al. (1878). Part of Sheet 47 (south of Royston) was additionally described in the memoir for Sheet 51SW by Penning and Jukes-Browne (1881). The three memoirs by Jukes-Browne and Hill (1900, 1903, 1904) on the Cretaceous Rocks of Britain refer to a number of sections within the district.

Parts of the district were resurveyed at the six-inch scale during the surveys for the Hertford (239) (1912–1932) and Biggleswade (204) (1930–1933) sheets. The areas covered by these surveys, the surveyors and the date of survey are shown on Figure 2. A substantial part of the Hitchin sheet, thus, had no large-scale coverage prior to this survey at the 1:10 000 scale. The boundaries of the 1:10 000 National Grid sheets are also shown in Figure 2.

The hydrogeological map of the area between Cambridge and Maidenhead at the 1:100 000 scale includes this district.

The concealed Palaeozoic and Jurassic rocks beneath the district are known only from the Henlow Borehole [164 356]. The geology of the concealed basement, discussed elsewhere in this memoir, is based on information from deep wells outside the district and from regional geophysical surveys.

The only published references to the Woburn Sands Formation which outcrops in the north-west of the district, are the descriptions of strata encountered in a number of water wells. A comprehensive review of the literature on the Woburn Sands, which is extensively quarried for sand and fuller's earth in the adjacent Leighton Buzzard district, is given in that sheet memoir (Shephard-Thorn et al., 1994).

The only notable present exposure of the Gault is at Arlesey [188 387]. This pit was briefly described by Jukes-Browne (1875) in a paper confirming the Cenomanian age of the Cambridge Greensand, which is also exposed at this site. The Arlesey pit was also featured in the reports of two Geologists' Association excursions led by Hill (1900, 1911). Hart (1973b), using foraminiferal evidence, determined the age of the Upper Gault at Arlesey (see below). Owen (1971, 1972) and Gallois and Morter (1982) have stratigraphically classified the Gault strata in Bedfordshire and East Anglia respectively. The Gault sequence in the Arlesey borehole (Hopson, 1992; Woods, 1992d) can be correlated with these classified sequences.

Early accounts of the Chalk in this district were confined to descriptions of the few available man-made exposures. Much of this early work was demonstrated during field visits to the district and described in a number of excursion reports in publications of the Geologists' Association and Hertfordshire Natural History Society, around the turn of the century.

Jukes-Browne (1875) summarised earlier work on the extensive 'coprolite' workings in Bedfordshire, Hertfordshire and Cambridgeshire, including a brief description of those near Arlesey. He concluded that the Cambridge Greensand was of Cenomanian age, the basal bed of the Chalk, and equivalent to the 'Chloritic' Marl (Glauconitic Marl). Hart (1973b) confirmed the Cenomanian age of this bed at Arlesey.

The Melbourn Rock and Plenus Marls in outcrops from Cambridge to the Chiltern Hills were described by Hill and Jukes-Browne (1886). The recognition of these marker horizons, and the presence of the Chalk Rock, enabled Hill (1886) to erect the tripartite division of the Chalk into Lower, Middle and Upper units, used in this district to the present day.

Henry Woods (1896, 1897) described the 'reussianum' fauna of the Chalk Rock, including localities at Luton, Hitchin, Wallington, Clothall, Reed and Barkway, within the district.

These early works on the major marker beds in the Chalk sequence of the district have been augmented more recently by Jefferies (1963) work on the Plenus Marls and by that of Bromley and Gale (1982) on the Chalk Rock. Major new stratigraphical schemes encapsulated in papers by Robinson (1986, 1987) and Mortimore (1986, 1987, 1988), based on the Upper Cretaceous sequences of Kent and Sussex respectively, have added a new impetus to the discussion of Chalk sequences throughout southern England.

The district is north of the main outcrop of the Palaeogene strata and only small outliers of the lowest beds of the Thames Group (formerly the London Clay) and the Lambeth Group (including the former Woolwich and Reading Beds) have been mapped. Brief references to

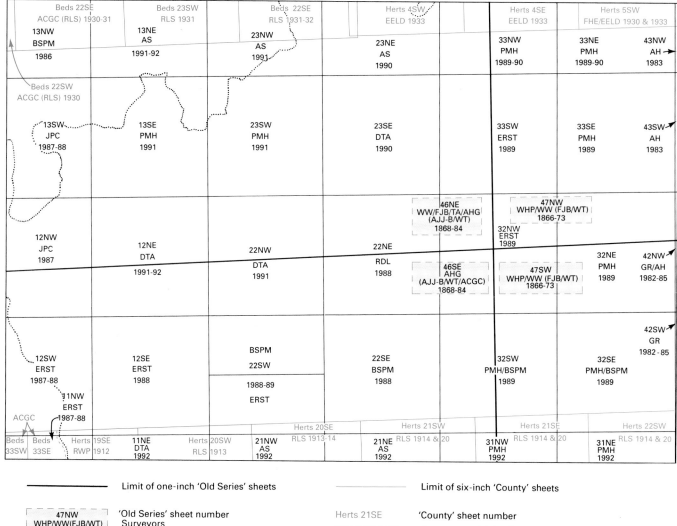

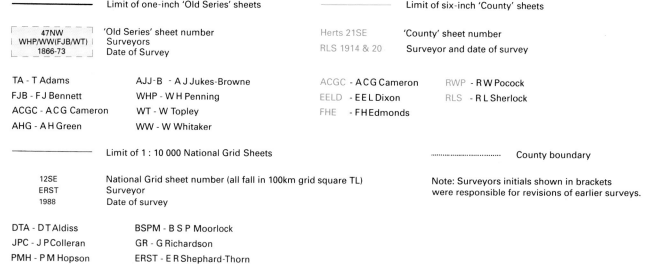

Figure 2 The component 1:10 000-scale National Grid sheets and the extent of older six-inch and one-inch surveys of the district.

the outliers at Sacombe and Collier's End were made by Prestwich (1854) and Whitaker et al. (1878). To redress this lack of information, the Dowsett's Farm borehole was sunk (Hopson, 1990) in the Collier's End outlier during the present survey (see Chapter 5).

The origin and form of the London Basin was discussed by Wooldridge and Linton (2nd edition 1955). Their synthesis of Cenozoic landscape development has since been questioned in three related papers by Moffat and Catt (1986a, b) and Moffat et al. (1986), and by other authors.

The Quaternary history of this district is closely linked to deposits and events best demonstrated at localities on the margins of the Thames Valley and in East Anglia. Much of the 19th century published work is concerned with the characterisation and distribution of the 'gravels' of the Thames Basin and their association with the Anglian till sheet. McKenny Hughes (1868) identified 'two plains of Hertfordshire and their gravels'. This early work was expanded upon at the turn of the century by Prestwich (1890), Salter (1896, 1905), Sherlock (1924) and others.

Hare (1947), erected a sequence of terraces for the Middle Thames catchment, which subsequent workers have built upon and traced through the Vale of St Albans into East Anglia (Hey, 1965; Gibbard, 1977; Green and McGregor, 1978). Rose and Allen (1977) proposed the term Kesgrave Sands and Gravels for these Early to Middle Pleistocene gravels in Essex and Suffolk. Whiteman and Rose (1992) have given a synthesis of pre-Anglian proto-Thames development and have proposed the Kesgrave Group to encompass all of the terrace aggradations found in the Thames basin and East Anglia. Gibbard (1977) has demonstrated that the youngest of these pre-diversionary proto-Thames gravels (the Winter Hill Terrace of Hare) in the Vale of St Albans was intimately associated with the early advances of the Anglian ice sheet.

Hoxnian interglacial deposits are preserved at a number of sites in the Hitchin Gap, such as Fisher's Green, near Stevenage (Gibbard and Aalto, 1977) and help to demonstrate the early existence of this landscape feature.

The relationship of the soils to the geology and geomorphology of the district has been discussed in the Soil Survey publications by D W King (1969) and Thomasson (1969) covering the Luton and Bedford, and Saffron Walden districts respectively.

GEOLOGICAL HISTORY

The early geological history of the district is reconstructed from deep boreholes, geophysical data and derived palaeogeographical reconstructions (Cope et al., 1992) from a broad surrounding region as there is little direct evidence of the strata below the base of the Cretaceous in the district.

In the early Silurian period, approximately 427 Ma ago, the region was part of a shallow sea created by a transgression from the south-east, over a landmass known as the Midlands Platform, itself formed of older Palaeozoic and Precambrian rocks. The Ware Borehole [3531 1397], immediately south of the district, proved silty limestones containing large dalmanitid trilobites and the brachiopod Meristina obtusa indicating a late Wenlock (421 Ma) age.

Towards the close of the Silurian period (early Přídolí; 414 Ma) this marine environment, as proved in the Clare [7834 4536], Soham [5928 7448], Lakenheath [748 830] and Little Missenden [SU 9009 9818] boreholes (see also Figure 3), was more restricted as the Midland Platform (the Midlands Microcraton) became re-established, and for a short time the platform was connected to the southern landmass of Pretannia (Cocks et al., 1992).

In the earliest Devonian (408 Ma), a short-lived shallow marine episode, as represented by the rocks proved in the Little Missenden Borehole, became established, but by 400 Ma the region was again emergent and a semiarid environment was established over England and Wales. It is these beds that are thought to be represented in the Henlow Borehole [164 356] in the north-west of the area.

Apart from relatively minor marine incursions from the south during the Carboniferous, the region remained a positive feature, part of the Anglo-Brabant Landmass, for some 200 Ma through the Carboniferous, Permian and Triassic periods. No rocks of this age are found in the district, any that did exist having been removed by uplift, faulting and erosion, leaving a low-relief landscape of Devonian and Silurian rocks.

At the end of the Triassic (Rhaetian 205 Ma), shallow seas separated the Anglo-Brabant Landmass from landmasses to the north-west. The regressive/transgressive fluctuations of that sea during the early to mid Jurassic (205 to 160 Ma) did not impinge on the district, but with continued transgression the shoreline of the Anglo-Brabant Landmass retreated eastwards and in late Middle Jurassic (158 Ma) to Late Jurassic (141 Ma) times shallow marine deposits were laid down in the district.

In the latest Jurassic (139 Ma), uplift and erosion removed much of the Jurassic strata formerly deposited across the region. Only thin, remnant, Jurassic sequences are proved in boreholes in the north-west of the district, presumably preserved against reactivated basement faults on the margin of the Anglo-Brabant Landmass.

In the Early Cretaceous, an emergent ridge separated the shallow marine, East Midlands Shelf in the north from the Wealden area in the south, until the Late Aptian (109 Ma). At this time, a connection (the Bedfordshire Straits) between the East Midlands Shelf and the Weald and 'Channel' basins to the south became established. The shallow marine Woburn Sands of this district were deposited in these straits. The exact margins are unknown due to erosion at the beginning of the Middle Albian.

Gradual inundation, associated with minor phases of erosion, during the Middle Albian led to the deposition of an attenuated Lower Gault marine sequence over the Anglo-Brabant Landmass. Further deepening of the sea thoughout the Upper Albian resulted in the complete submergence of the ridge across the region, and a thick, complete, Upper Gault sequence was deposited over the entire district. In the latest Albian (100 Ma), the now submerged Anglo-Brabant Landmass continued to influence deposition, and presumed movement on basement faults at this time encouraged limited erosion of the highest beds of the Upper Gault and the Upper Greensand such that the lowest Upper Cretaceous beds (the Cambridge Greensand, Glauconitic Marl) rest on different zones of the Upper Gault. The Lower Cenomanian (lowest Upper Cretaceous c.97 Ma) Cambridge Greensand contains a reworked Upper Albian fauna.

By the early Cenomanian (c.97 Ma), the open, clearer water, Chalk sea had spread throughout much of northwest Europe. Minor earth movements still influenced sedimentation early in the Upper Cretaceous, as attested by the development of arenitic chalks and hardgrounds, but by Campanian (c.75 Ma) times the Chalk sea had expanded to its maximum extent and land areas providing terrigenous materials were far distant.

Gentle folding, uplift and erosion ensued at the end of the Cretaceous and during the earliest Palaeogene prior to the deposition of the Thanet Sand, Upnor, Woolwich and Reading formations (see Chapter 5). Thus, Late Palaeogene (57 Ma) beds rest with slight angular unconformity on different Upper Chalk zones. The limited marine area within which the Thanet Sand Formation was deposited is not thought to have reached this district and the nearest known deposits attributed to the Thanet Sand Formation were proved in Gilston Borehole [4417 1349] 9 km south-east of the district. Marine conditions gave way to terrestrial/marsh/lagoonal deposition, as represented by the rocks of the Upnor, Woolwich and Reading formations. The former limit of these beds towards the north-west is unknown, but eroded outliers have been mapped in the south-east of the district around Collier's End. These outliers show that in the Early Eocene (52 Ma) the district was again submerged by a sea within which the Harwich Formation (the lower part of the Thames Group) was deposited. Again, the original extent of these marine deposits towards the north-west is unknown.

Cenozoic uplift, between 45 and 24 Ma ago, created the Weald–Artois axis, establishing the physiographic areas of the London Basin and the Chilterns escarpment, and no rocks between 40 and 8 Ma in age are known onshore in south-east England.

Remnants of shelly sands, at about 130 m above OD, on the Chiltern dip slope around Rothamsted, just to the south-west of the district, attest to a further marine inundation in the Plio-Pleistocene period (c.2 Ma ago). This limited record, and another of non-shelly glauconitic sands at Little Heath (at over 159 m above OD), would suggest that similar deposits formerly existed more widely over the south-east of the district.

In Early to Middle Pleistocene times (greater than 470 000 years before present), a major fluvial system, called the proto-Thames, flowed across Hertfordshire into southern East Anglia. Terrace aggradations of this river, on the northern limb of the London Basin syncline, are preserved at topographically lower levels (and become younger) towards the south-east. These deposits are known collectively as the Kesgrave Sands and Gravels in East Anglia. In this district only the highest (and oldest) 'Kesgrave' terrace aggradations are preserved. The Letchworth Gravel at a relatively low level in the Hitchin Gap may be related to lower 'Kesgrave' terrace levels preserved outside the district.

The over-riding of this district, approximately 470 000 years ago, by the Anglian ice sheet has modified the topography to varying degrees. East of the Hitchin Gap, itself a glacially enhanced feature, the Chalk escarpment has become subdued and buried beneath till and glacio-fluvial outwash sands and gravels. West of the gap, an essentially pre-Anglian surface surmounted by clay-with-flints is preserved.

There is no evidence to suggest that ice returned to the district after the Anglian glaciation, and for the remainder of the Quaternary the climate oscillated between temperate interglacial periods and colder intervals when periglacial processes were active. Much of the final moulding of the landscape occurred during this period with the development of solifluction and fluviatile deposits prior to the Holocene.

The present-day valley deposits of Holocene age (less than 10 000 years), basically alluvium and peat, were laid down in response to a generally relative rise in sea level.

TWO

Concealed formations

Much if not all, of the district is underlain at depth by metamorphosed Precambrian rocks of the Midlands Microcraton. Following the late Proterozoic Cadomian orogeny, this formed a stable area and was overlain by Lower Palaeozoic strata ranging from Cambrian to Silurian in age, which apparently have remained relatively undeformed. Steeply dipping Silurian sedimentary rocks, folded during the Acadian (late Caledonian) orogeny, appear to the north-east of the microcraton (Figure 5b).

In most of the district, the Silurian is unconformably overlain by thick sequences of gently dipping Devonian strata bounded by faults against the upstanding Ware 'basement high' in the south, which is probably a Variscan structure (Allsop, 1985; Allsop and Smith, 1988). The Devonian may also be faulted against basement rocks underlying the 'Charlton Axis' to the north (Figure 5b).

The Palaeozoic rocks are overlain by Mesozoic formations of the London Platform which dip very gently south-eastwards. Thin unconformity-bounded Jurassic, and Aptian to early Albian sequences are confined to the north of the district. Only later, Albian and Upper Cretaceous deposition extended throughout, presumably overlapping first onto the Devonian but directly overlying the Silurian on the Ware high. Folding and faulting of the Mesozoic sequences is minor and for the most part is thought to represent mild rejuvenation of basement structures.

Sedimentation in Palaeogene times, when the district lay in the northern part of the London Basin, was terminated by very gentle south-eastwards tilting during the Miocene.

PALAEOZOIC

Borehole evidence

Rocks of probable Palaeozoic age (?Devonian) are found in only one borehole at Henlow [164 356]. Deep boreholes in the surrounding region have also encountered Palaeozoic strata (Figure 3) and these give clues to the depth, lithology and probable age of the 'basement' rocks beneath the district. Boreholes showing that Devonian rocks, comprising mainly mudstones with some limestones and sandstones, are encountered in Ashwell [286 390] to the north, Little Chishill [4528 3637] to the east, and at several places to the south such as Little Missenden [SU 9009 9818], Bushey [TQ 1195 9577] and Turnford [3600 0444]. Red sandstone and mudstone beds at Elstow [0463 4428] to the north-west are of uncertain age, most are probably Permo-Triassic or Devonian. To the west, folded Ordovician (Tremadoc) mudstones are present at

Tattenhoe [SP 8289 3437], and Silurian (Wenlock) shales, dipping southwards at 41°, were proved at Ware [3531 1397] to the south.

Geophysical evidence

Geophysical data which can be interpreted to give an indication of the rocks at depth are also available. These data comprise regional gravity and aeromagnetic surveys together with a north–south Shell (UK) Exploration seismic reflection line (location shown on Figure 5b), deep resistivity soundings, and local gravity and magnetic surveys to the east of the district at Bishop's Stortford. Previous interpretations of the deep geological and geophysical data over a broad area have been made (British Geological Survey, 1985; Allsop, 1985; Allsop and Smith, 1988). More recently the gravity and aeromagnetic data have been included in a reinterpretation (Lee et al., 1991) using image-enhancement techniques to define the structural lineaments and geophysical anomalies more precisely. The interpretation of the concealed geology given here represents a synthesis of all the data presently available.

Typical representative physical properties of the main geological units used in modelling the deep geology are given in Table 1. The concealed sub-Mesozoic geology of the district is illustrated on the cross-section shown on the 1:50 000 geological sheet, which shows a Palaeozoic 'basement' of Devonian and Silurian rocks.

The regional Bouguer gravity anomaly and aeromagnetic maps for the district and surrounding area are shown in Figures 4a and 4b. Figure 4c shows the gravity field after removal of the effect of the Mesozoic cover, thereby revealing the density variations within the sub-Mesozoic basement rocks.

The observed Bouguer gravity anomaly map (Figure 4a) and the aeromagnetic map (Figure 4b) both show strong linear features across the area formed by gradients of the potential field which run from north-north-west to south-south-east. It is likely, however, that these features, which are discussed fully in Chapter 7, are related to different elements of the underlying structure; the gravity data are thought to relate to relatively near-surface variations of density, and the aeromagnetic data are indicative of variations in magnetic susceptibility, related to deep structures. The similarity of the trends of both sets of data suggests possible reactivation of pre-Mesozoic structures as noted in adjacent areas (Shephard-Thorn et al., 1994; Horton et al., 1994).

Superimposed on the main basement-related features shown on the Bouguer anomaly map (Figure 4a) are a number of minor anomalies, most of which are too small to isolate within the accuracy of the gravity stripping

Figure 3 Solid geology of the region with deep geology proved in boreholes and contours on the top of the Palaeozoic 'basement'.

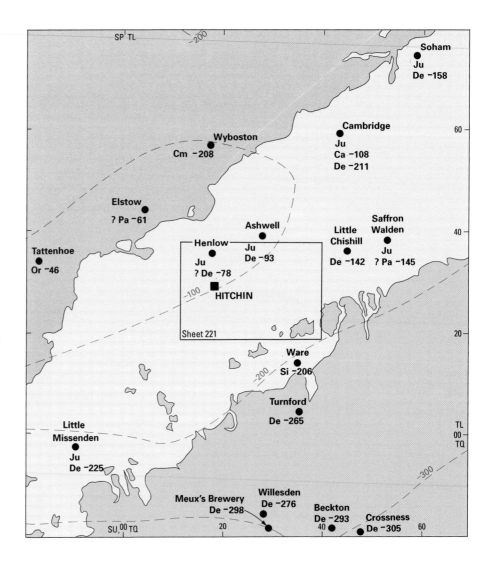

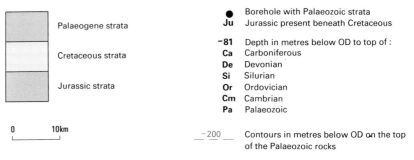

process (Figure 4c). These possess similar trends but appear from their amplitude and wavelength to be related to relatively near-surface structures, or to changes in thickness or density within the Mesozoic rocks, or the underlying low-density Devonian.

The deeper Silurian and pre-Silurian basement rocks have similar densities (Table 1) and are thought not to be responsible for the broad density variations shown in Figures 4a and 4c.

The aeromagnetic data have been processed using a variety of techniques (Vacquier et al., 1957; Smellie, 1956; Spector and Grant, 1970) to produce a map of depth to magnetic basement shown in Figure 4d. This pattern is likely to be attributable to a large magnetic body within the sub-Silurian basement (Allsop and Smith, 1988). The results have been used in combination with the gravity data, within the constraints of the data acquisition and processing, to limit the interpreted depths of sedimentary basement rocks. Thus, in areas where magnetic basement is indicated at shallow depths, the thickness of Devonian and Silurian sedimentary rocks will be restricted.

The sub-Devonian basement geology and contours on this surface are shown in Figure 5a. These should be regarded as a tentative interpretation due to the limited data available.

The sub-Permo-Triassic basement geology with contours on the underlying surface (top basement) (Figure 5b) is better controlled. Devonian rocks underlie most of the district, but Silurian rocks subcrop in the south, near Ware, on a basement ridge. This ridge separates two Devonian basins, the Luton–Cambridge Basin to the north and the London–Canvey Island Basin to the south (Allsop, 1985). The contours on the sub-Permo-Triassic surface fall from about 60 m below OD in the north-west to more than 200 m below OD in the south-east. The Charlton Axis crosses the north-west of the district. This basement feature can be traced continuously from the Oxford–Aylesbury district to the south-west (Horton et

al., 1994; Shephard-Thorn et al., 1994) and continues north-eastwards towards the south of Cambridge, where it is terminated by a major structural feature. In the district this basement ridge has little or no effect on the Bouguer gravity anomaly map. The aeromagnetic anomaly map (Figure 4b) shows only a very broad, low-amplitude feature which is likely to represent a small rise in the magnetic basement at depth.

Some anomalies in the regional geophysical data appear to coincide with major structures or variations in basement lithology; depths calculated to these features may differ according to whether gravity or aeromagnetic

Table 1 Physical properties of the main rock units (values derived from geophysical logs and laboratory measurements.

	Resistivity Ωm	Density (saturated) g cm^{-3}	Sonic velocity km s^{-1}	Magnetic susceptibility cgs × 10^{-6}
CRETACEOUS				
Chalk	c. 5–24	2.00–2.20	2.10–2.30	—
Gault	c. 20	c.2.00	c.1.7	—
JURASSIC				
Oxford Clay	c. 50	c.2.32	c.2.42	—
DEVONIAN				
general	20–40	2.49–2.52	c.2.73	—
SILURIAN				
general	10–50	2.56–2.60	c.4.60	—
Wenlock Lst.	50–100	2.66–2.70	c.4.50	—
Tuff	10–100	c.2.54	c.4.72	1353*
Diorite	c.100	2.79–2.82	c.5.35	2634*
PRE-SILURIAN BASEMENT				
non-igneous	c. 90	c.2.70–2.75	c.5.1	c.400

* Kappameter measurements on core samples from Bicester borehole.

evidence is used, indicating that the major structures identified from the gravity data may extend down to the magnetic basement.

Precambrian to Ordovician

According to recent interpretations either part (approximately the south-western half) or all of the district is underlain by the Midlands Microcraton (Pharaoh et al., 1990; Lee et al., 1990; Busby et al., 1993), a structural block of Precambrian crust overlain by relatively undeformed Lower Palaeozoic platform sequences. The Shell seismic reflection line lies entirely within the area of the microcraton and indicates reflection surfaces thought to mark the unconformity where the Devonian overlies Silurian strata, the approximate position of the Tremadoc and the top of the Precambrian. The apparent dip of each reflector is southerly. The deepest reflector appears to have been faulted (Allsop, 1985). Except at the margins of the microcraton, Ordovician strata, other than those of Tremadoc age, are absent (Pharaoh et al., 1987; 1991).

The magnetic basement, which is probably formed by Precambrian volcanic rocks (or possibly by Early Silurian rocks) (Pharaoh et al., 1991), is likely to be at depths below the surface of more than 4 km in the north-west of the area, rising to less than 1 km in the south (Figure 4d). Estimates of the depth of the source of a magnetic body at Ware (Figures 4d and 5b), based on the results of both aeromagnetic and ground magnetic surveys, indicate that it probably lies below the Silurian at only about 1.5 km depth (Allsop and Smith, 1988).

Silurian

Much of the sub-Devonian basement of the district is thought to consist of relatively undeformed Silurian rocks, tentatively identified as Wenlock, Ludlow and Přídolí in age (Figure 5a). They have not been pene-

trated by any boreholes within the district and their presence is largely inferred from the modelling of the geophysical data. They are associated with the Midlands Microcraton (Pharaoh et al., 1987; Lee et al., 1990; Busby et al., 1993) which formed a high or platform at this time.

The Silurian lies at a depth greater than 400 m below OD in most of the district, rising to 300 m below OD in the west and to 200 m below OD (c.300 m depth) in the south (Figure 5a). The relatively gently dipping Silurian strata on the platform are replaced to the west by folded and cleaved Silurian turbiditic sedimentary rocks in the north-west-trending 'concealed Caledonides of eastern England' (Allsop and Smith, 1988; Pharaoh et al., 1987; 1991; Lee et al., 1991). The nature of the boundary between these contrasting terranes is not known but is presumed to be controlled by structures formed during early Devonian (Acadian) tectonism. Its orientation is taken to be north-west–south-east, parallel to the regional trend of the eastern Caledonides. It must lie to the east of Ware, where the Silurian is in platform facies, but otherwise the position of the edge of the Midlands Microcraton near Hitchin cannot be precisely defined. Pharaoh et al. (1987, 1991) place it diagonally across the district (Figure 5b) but Woodcock (1991) and Lee et al. (1991) argue that it probably lies to the east of the area. Recent work (Woodcock and Pharaoh, 1993) has recognised four sedimentary facies in the Silurian rocks beneath East Anglia to the north-east, and a muddy shelf facies with patch reefs beneath the eastern part of this district.

Devonian

Middle and Upper Devonian strata, about 400 m in thickness, are thought to underlie most of the district. The Shell seismic reflection line suggests that the Devonian rocks have an apparent dip to the south-south-east (Allsop, 1985), and borehole evidence shows that

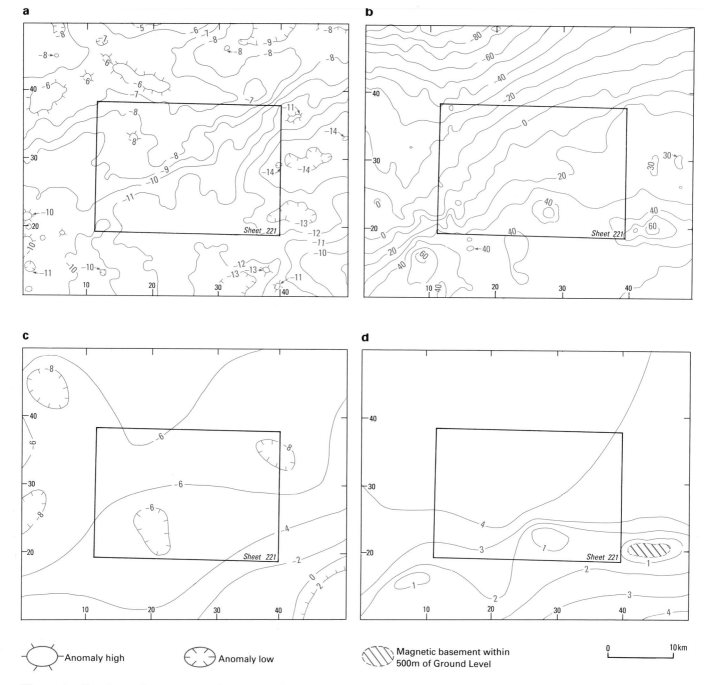

Figure 4   Gravity and aeromagnetic maps of the district.

a. Observed Bouguer gravity anomaly map. Anomalies calculated against the Geodetic Reference system, 1967, referred to the National Gravity Reference Net, 1973. Density used for data reduction 2.4 Mg/m³. Contour interval 1 mGal (1 mGal = 10 μm/s²). Based on data in the BGS National Gravity Databank.

b. Aeromagnetic anomaly map. Total force aeromagnetic anomalies in nanotesla (nT) relative to computed regional field for the British Isles. Contour interval 10 nT. Flown at 460 m barometric. E–W flight lines at 2 km spacing and N–S tie lines at 10 km spacing.

The Hitchin district forms part of the BGS UK and Continental Shelf 1:250 000 Series, Bouger gravity anomaly maps and Aeromagnetic anomaly maps: East Midlands, 52°N, 02°W; East Anglia, 52°N, 00°; Chilterns, 51°N, 02°W; and Thames Estuary, 51°N, 00°.

c. Residual gravity anomaly map to the top of the Palaeozoic basement (base Permian), after removal of the effects of Mesozoic cover. Contour interval 2 mGal.

d. Depth to magnetic basement map. Contour interval 1 km below ground level.

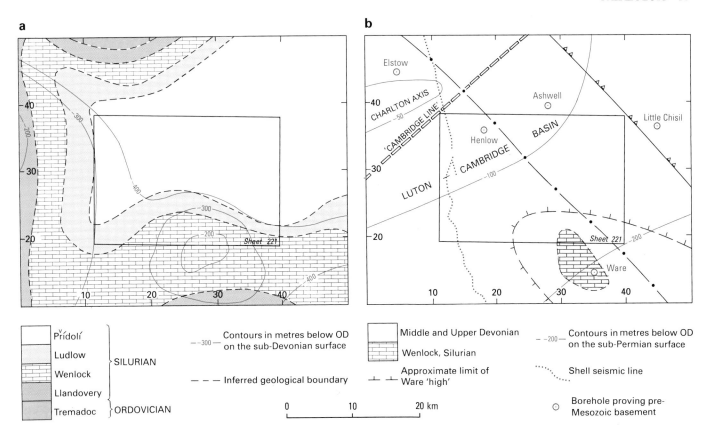

Figure 5a Pre-Devonian geology and contours on the sub-Devonian surface.

b Pre-Permian geology and contours on the sub-Permian surface.

they young towards the east. Devonian rocks occur at only about 60 m below OD in the north-west of the district but become deeper to the south-east, where they are found at 200 m below OD.

Henlow Borehole, drilled for water in 1911 to a depth of 139.0 m, terminated in 10.1 m of strata described as reddish rock and red sandy clay. These are regarded as probably Devonian in age (Smith, 1992) by comparison with the Devonian sequence proved in Ashwell Borehole, just north of the district.

Ashwell Borehole, also known as Superior Oil No. 4, provided samples which have been reliably dated. Drilled to a depth of 186.5 m in 1964, most of the borehole was open-hole but some core was recovered from the lower part. This was described by R W Gallois, and an outline log is given in Appendix 1; the macrofossil specimens were identified by D E Butler. Devonian strata were identified between 153.01–162.15 and 183.49–186.54 m depth and consist of green-grey and red-brown, calcareous, silty mudstone, bioturbated and fossiliferous in parts, and interbedded thin hard shelly limestones. Macrofossils (BGS specimens BDK 1944–2199) recorded by Butler (1975) include: brachiopods

Nervostrophia sp. cf. *Ripidiorhynchus ferquensis, Cyrtospirifer verneuili, Schellwienella* sp. and *Retichonetes armatus,* as well as lingulid, terebratuloid and spiriferacean forms; bivalves *Leptodesma* (*L.*) *disparile, L.* (*L.*) *spinigerum,* ?*Nuculoidea* sp., *Palaeoneilo constricta* and *Pseudaviculopecten* sp., and other taxa including bryozoans, a trilobite pygidium, phyllocarid crustaceans, tentaculitids and crinoid debris.

Butler (1975) noted that *R. ferquensis, C. verneuili* and *R. armatus* occurred in Frasnian strata in the Boulonnais (France). *Retichonetes armatus* is also known from the Famennian and *C. verneuili* ranges up into the Lower Carboniferous; *L.* (*L.*) *spinigerum* and *P. constricta* are known from the Frasnian or the Upper Devonian elsewhere in the British Isles. These forms may range beyond the Upper Devonian, but their occurrence in purplish mudstones yielding lingulids and phyllocarid crustaceans is reminiscent of the Upper Devonian strata proved in the Willesden Borehole [2086 8477] to the south. A Late Devonian, probably Frasnian, age was suggested for this fauna, but this was later revised to a middle or late Frasnian age (Butler, 1981) when evidence from other boreholes became available.

Deposition probably took place, during the Frasnian marine transgression, on the inner shelf, along the northern margin of a sea which covered southern England at this time.

Devonian strata once covered much of eastern England, and have been largely removed by later erosion, though they survive in several 'tectonic' basins. Thicknesses of these low-density rocks, estimated from gravity data, indicate more than 1.5 km in the Canvey Island–London Basin to the south of Ware, and, to the north, over 0.9 km of strata in each of two centres in the Luton and Cambridge areas. Silurian rocks proved in the Ware Borehole confirm the presence of a basement ridge separating the northern and southern basins. A Devonian sequence is likely to be preserved to the south-east and west of Ware, draped over the Silurian rocks where the ridge forms a less prominent feature in the Lower Palaeozoic basement surface.

MESOZOIC

Post-Variscan stabilisation and erosion in Permo-Triassic times led to the formation of the London Platform, which persisted throughout the Mesozoic. Regionally, it is characterised by very thin or absent Permian to Lower Cretaceous sequences and a reasonably thick, unfaulted Upper Cretaceous. The district lies in the central part of the London Platform as so defined (Chadwick, 1985a) although some would restrict this term to a region east and south-east of the Chilterns escarpment (e.g. Rawson, 1992). In this sense, the London Platform is part of the London–Brabant Massif (e.g. Smith et al., 1985).

The Mesozoic sequence is broken by a number of unconformities; two major unconformities separate the thin Middle and Upper Jurassic deposits from Devonian rocks below, and from the Lower Cretaceous strata above. Folding of the Upper Jurassic observed in neighbouring areas (Shephard-Thorn et al., 1994) cannot be demonstrated in this district through lack of information and its concealed southern limit is known only very approximately.

Jurassic

A global rise in sea level, accompanied by subsidence during a phase of crustal extension led to a major Early Jurassic transgression (Holloway, 1985). Much of southern England was covered by sea while a reduced London Platform persisted as land. To the north-west of the district, marine Liassic mudstones and limestones were deposited in basins to the north of the London Platform and progressively overstep south-eastwards on to the Palaeozoic rocks of the platform (Donovan et al., 1979). Thus, in Elstow Borehole (Figure 3), situated about 10 km to the north-west, a 92.3 m-thick sequence of Jurassic strata ranging from Lower Lias to Oxford Clay rests on Palaeozoic rocks.

Throughout the Middle Jurassic the area of sedimentation gradually increased. In addition to the deposition of marine beds, intermittent freshwater conditions pro-duced complex estuarine deposits. Such rocks are thought to occur in three deep boreholes in the district. The Henlow Borehole penetrated white rock, probably limestone, between 118 and 128.8 m depth, resting unconformably on rock of assumed Devonian age. Nearby, one or two boreholes at Pollards Nurseries [1616 3506] penetrated 4.5 m of probable Jurassic rocks above a final depth of 122.1 m. These beds consist of 1.1 m of hard grey shelly limestone, possibly Cornbrash, resting on 3.4 m of green clay passing down into hard blue clay, possibly Blisworth Clay. The second borehole to the south [1653 3493] proved 16.5 m of blue clay and 'rock' of probable Jurassic age which cannot be classified.

In Ashwell Borehole, on the northern margin of the district, the Middle Jurassic rocks, proved between 134.57 and 152.70 m depth, rest on Devonian basement with no intervening Liassic rocks. Jurassic strata are also present in Saffron Walden Borehole [5386 3840], to the east and in boreholes around Clophill to the west. The Jurassic strata die out to the south-east and are absent at Ware, but there are insufficient boreholes to plot the concealed southern limit of the Jurassic strata accurately.

In Ashwell Borehole (Appendix 1), specimens BDK 1754–1943 collected throughout the full thickness of the preserved Jurassic were examined (Ivimey-Cook, 1982) for macrofossils, and three samples, MPA 17884–17886, taken from near the top of the Jurassic sequence at depths of 135.03, 135.33 and 136.32 m, were examined (Cox, 1984) for palynomorphs. Lithological and palaeontological evidence taken together indicate the presence, in descending order, of the Cornbrash, Blisworth Clay, Blisworth Limestone and Rutland Formation (formerly the 'Upper Estuarine Series') resting on sandstones, siltstones and mudstones of the Grantham Formation (formerly the 'Lower Estuarine Series').

The Grantham Formation (141.02–152.70 m depth) consists of interbedded mudstones, siltstones and sandstones. The mudstones are pale grey to purplish grey, becoming dark grey to black, with much carbonaceous plant debris and minor pyrite. Sand and silt are common as wisps and lenses, and may in places infill burrows and plant root moulds. There are a few shell fragments of non-diagnostic bivalves, but the sequence is characteristic of the Grantham Formation elsewhere.

Overlying strata (138.38–141.02 m depth) are probably equivalents of the Rutland Formation, the Blisworth Limestone and the Blisworth Clay. A 0.8 m-thick bed of arenaceous shelly marl passes up into 1.6 m of greybrown, silty, shell fragmental limestone followed by 0.4 m of siltstone with wisps of fine sand. There is much fragmentary plant debris at the top, and the sparse but varied macrofauna (Ivimey-Cook, 1982) is dominated by *Modiolus* (including *M. imbricatus*) and *Placunopsis socialis*.

A possible equivalent of the Lower Cornbrash (134.57–138.38 m depth) (Ivimey-Cook, 1982) consists of a lower 2.0 m of mainly off-white, massive micritic limestone containing numerous shell fragments which suggest a Bathonian age. The upper part consists of off-white calcarenitic limestone with some thin mudstones and more silty patches. There are small silt and clay pebbles, particularly towards the top, and some clay-filled burrows. It contains only scattered bivalves which are non-diagnostic (Ivimey-Cook, 1982). Three samples yielded dinoflagellate cyst assemblages indicative of an early Callovian age and correlation with the Upper Cornbrash (Cox, 1984). Other palynomorphs include acritarchs, bisaccate pollen and trilete spores.

Sedimentation continued through the Late Jurassic with the Kellaways Formation, Oxford Clay, West Walton Formation and Ampthill Clay probably extending progressively across the district. With increased subsidence and high global sea levels (Haq et al., 1987), the Kimmeridge Clay may have overlapped all previous Mesozoic strata and extended across the London Platform, albeit much reduced in thickness (Chadwick, 1985a and b). The full extent of these Middle to Upper Jurassic strata

remains unknown, for their distribution was greatly reduced by subsequent erosion. The area of deposition declined in the Late Jurassic as global sea levels fell and uplift of the London Platform commenced. The younger Jurassic strata were eroded from the London Platform over this district to leave just a thin wedge of Jurassic beds on the northern flank of the platform, in the north-west of the district.

The northern part of the buried Hitchin Channel, which crosses the central part of the district from north to south, is deeply incised through most of the Woburn Sands near Henlow, and it is possible that it cuts down to the underlying Jurassic rocks locally. The form of the channel, however, remains poorly known hereabouts and in the absence of borehole evidence, subcrops of Jurassic strata have not been mapped in the floor of the channel.

THREE

Lower Cretaceous

The Cretaceous System is divided chronostratigraphically into two parts. The Upper Cretaceous, which equates approximately with the Chalk lithostratigraphical division, is described in Chapter 4. The Lower Cretaceous, which is subdivided into six stages, is represented in the district by the Woburn Sands and Gault formations deposited during Aptian and Albian times (Table 2).

Table 2 Relationship of Lower Cretaceous stages to rock formations (drawn to scale by age after Harland et al., 1990.

	Stage	Age Ma	Formation
Lower Cretaceous	Albian	97 / 112	Gault
	Aptian	124	Woburn Sands
	Barremian	132	Not present in district
	Hauterivian	135	
	Valanginian	140	
	Ryazanian (Berriasian)	145	

Regional palaeogeography

The limited exposure in the district has discouraged research, and an understanding of the geological history can only be gained by an appreciation of the geology of surrounding districts. This allows a regional picture to emerge, which can be applied to the district in the absence of more direct evidence. A number of regional overviews are of particular value.

The first significant attempt to describe the Lower Cretaceous rocks in England was made by Jukes-Browne and Hill (1900) in the first volume of their comprehensive memoir on the Cretaceous. The geological history was described in greater detail by Kirkaldy (1939) and later revised (Kirkaldy, 1963) in the light of research by Allen (1955, 1959) in the Weald on the sedimentology, and by Casey (1961) on the biostratigraphy. The zonal scheme based on ammonites, proposed by Casey (1961), has gained wide acceptance and proved of crucial importance in unravelling the story. The correlation of the Cretaceous rocks of the British Isles was discussed by Rawson et al. (1978). A recent atlas (Whittaker, 1985) has incorporated much additional subsurface borehole and seismic information from the oil industry into a modern interpretation of the stratigraphy and tectonics of the onshore sedimentary basins. Rawson (1992) has described the Cretaceous period in a synthesis of the geology of England and Wales, which allows the events in the district to be related to the rest of the country.

No sub-Aptian rocks are known from the district or vicinity. Shallowing seas, caused by a fall in global sea level, continued from the Late Jurassic into the Ryazanian, so that the London Platform, which then encompassed the district, persisted as an emergent land area separating two depositional provinces. To the south, material eroded from the platform, together with limestones, built up thick, fresh- and brackish-water Purbeck and Wealden deposits in the rapidly subsiding and faulted Wessex or Weald Basin which had links to the Tethyan faunal province (Casey and Rawson, 1973). Meanwhile to the north, thin, shallow-water, marine sediments, accumulating on the tectonically more stable Eastern England Shelf, had links with the Boreal faunal province. Rapid facies changes and the faunal differences between these two provinces has impeded their correlation.

In Valanginian times the London Platform, along with much of eastern England, was subjected to uplift and erosion, supplying sediments to the Weald Basin as it continued to subside. This uplift continued through Hauterivian and Barremian times (Chadwick, 1985b and c) and extended over much of the country; continuing erosion resulted in the widespread late-Cimmerian unconformity. Ruffell (1992), from a study of the Wessex Basin, has argued that a number of unconformities occur in the Lower Cretaceous representing transgressive events.

By early Aptian times, rises in sea level, coupled with the establishment of slow regional subsidence, caused a return to shallow-water marine conditions with the transgression of the 'Lower Greensand' sea. During the Lower Aptian, the Atherfield Clay and the Hythe Beds were deposited in the southern basin, which remained separated from the northern basin by the London Platform and its westward extension across the Midlands (Kirkaldy, 1963). Little or no sediment was preserved in this district, though thin *remanié* deposits at Upware to the north may record this period. As the area of deposition increased through the Upper Aptian so the separating 'Bedford Isthmus' was breached and the narrow 'Bedfordshire Straits' became established connecting the two provinces around the western end of the London Platform. Whilst the Sandgate and Folkestone Beds were deposited in the Weald, the Woburn Sands accumulated in this district. A basal conglomerate was laid down in places. Faunal exchange between the two provinces first took place during the *Parahoplites nutfieldensis* Zone, and indigenous and derived fossils of earlier Lower Aptian and Late Jurassic age are found together.

Sedimentation of mainly fine- to coarse-grained sand continued, with localised developments of fuller's earth, into Lower Albian times. A break in sedimentation, in the mid *Leymeriella tardefurcata* Zone, causes a sharp junction at the base of the *L.* (*L.*) *regularis* Subzone, expressed either as a plane of erosion, a bed of phosphatic nodules or as a change in lithology (Table 3). Above this break, a thin and variable sequence of Lower Albian sediments with a complex depositional history developed within the Bedfordshire 'Straits', forming junction beds with the overlying Gault. At Leighton Buzzard, to the west of the district, they include sandy clays with phosphatic nodule horizons and lenticular masses of Shenley Limestone, typical of a marginal marine environment (Owen 1972).

By the Mid-Albian, the main Gault transgression was established, the 'Bedfordshire Straits' were no longer recognisable, and clays were deposited over the whole area, overlapping the Woburn Sands on to the previously exposed London Platform. In this district, the Lower Gault is thin, pinching out to the east against the Palaeozoic strata. The upper part of the Lower Gault was removed by erosion before the deposition of the Upper Gault. The latter was deposited after a renewed transgression, which covered the London Platform in early *Dipoloceras cristatum* Subzone times. Marine sedimentation continued through the Albian, with periodic pauses giving rise to minor erosion surfaces, with associated phosphate and glauconite formation.

No Upper Greensand deposits of Late Albian age are known locally, having probably been removed by erosion prior to the Cenomanian transgression, the closest occurrence being in the Leighton Buzzard district to the west. In this district, the top of the Gault is truncated and gives

Table 3 Lower Cretaceous (Upper Aptian and Albian) stratigraphy in the Hitchin district. Zonation follows Horton et al., 1994) after Casey (1961) and Owen (1971, 1975, 1988a and 1988b). Not to scale.

Stage	Ammonite zone	Ammonite subzone	Formation	Lithostratigraphy
Upper Albian	*Stoliczkaia dispar*	Unnamed *Mortoniceras perinflatum* *Mortoniceras rostratum*	Gault	Upper
	Mortoniceras inflatum	*Callihoplites auritus* *Hysteroceras varicosum* *Hysteroceras orbignyi* *Dipoloceras cristatum*		Gault
Middle Albian	*Euhoplites lautus*	*Anahoplites daviesi* *Euhoplites nitidus*		
	Euhoplites loricatus	*Euhoplites meandrinus* *Mojsisovicsia subdelaruei* *Dimorphoplites niobe* *Anahoplites intermedius*		Lower Gault
	Hoplites dentatus	*Hoplites spathi* *Lyelliceras lyelli*		
Lower Albian	*Douvilleiceras mammillatum* Superzone: *Otohoplites auritiformis*	*Pseudosonneratia steinmanni* *Otohoplites bulliensis* *Protohoplites puzosianus* *Otohoplites raulinianus*		? ?
	Douvilleiceras mammillatum Superzone: *Sonneratia chalensis*	*Cleoniceras floridum* *Sonneratia kitchini* *Sonneratia perinflata*		? ? Junction Beds
	Leymeriella tardefurcata	*Leymeriella regularis* *Leymeriella acuticostata* *Leymeriella schrammeni*	Woburn Sands	
Upper Aptian (part)	*Hypacanthoplites jacobi*	*Hypacanthoplites anglicus* *Nolaniceras nolani*		Woburn Sands
	Parahoplites nutfieldiensis	*Parahoplites cunningtoni* *Tropaeum subarcticum*		

Key: Hiatus caused by non-deposition or erosion; Limestone; • Phosphate; Clay; Sand way to the Lower Chalk with Cambridge Greensand at the base.

WOBURN SANDS FORMATION

The Woburn Sands, named from Woburn to the west of this district, is the oldest Cretaceous formation present in the district. It crops out over an area of less than 1 km² near Campton in the north-west, where only the uppermost few metres come to surface, and much of the outcrop remains hidden beneath a veneer of head deposits. It is also believed to floor the northern end of the buried Hitchin Channel (Chapter 6), which crosses the district from north to south. Beneath Henlow, the concealed Woburn Sands Formation probably extends over an area of about 6 km², though the subcrop is largely conjectural and may require revision as more borehole information becomes available.

The rest of the formation remains concealed and is only known from borehole evidence. This suggests that the Woburn Sands thins out south-eastwards beneath the younger Cretaceous rocks as it overlaps the Jurassic strata on to the Palaeozoic basement (see cross-section on the 1:50 000 Hitchin (221) Sheet). It probably underlies all of the district apart from the south-east corner, but there are insufficient borehole provings to delimit the southern margin accurately.

Within the district, an unbottomed sequence of 42.2 m of Woburn Sands was proved beneath Chalk and Gault in the Fairfield Hospital [2043 3526] Borehole and it is perhaps 60 m thick in the Shefford area (Moorlock et al., 1987) in the north-west. Just to the north of the district, Ashwell Borehole proved a full thickness of 27.9 m. In the Huntingdon and Biggleswade districts (Edmonds and Dinham, 1965), recorded thicknesses range from 7.6 m possibly to 85.3 m. At Woburn, 16 km to the west of the district, the formation reaches a local maximum of at least 120 m, thinning to 20 to 30 m to the south of Ampthill. To the west of Leighton Buzzard, it dies out in places.

This variation in thickness was attributed by Rastall (1925) to a Charnian, north-west-trending, axes of uplift creating small intervening basins of deposition. Ruffell and Wignall (1990), studying depositional trends along the northern margin of the Wessex basin, have suggested that these sub-basins are wedge-shaped in cross-section along the strike, bounded on one side by a major normal or listric fault. They indicate (fig. 1) a possible major fault in the north-west of the district, downthrowing to the north and trending east-south-east from near Shillington to Hitchin, but this fault has not been confirmed by this survey. Eyers (1991) reviewing the Bedfordshire area has related Woburn Sands sedimentation to extensional tectonics.

Lithology

Attempts have been made to subdivide the formation. In pits around Leighton Buzzard to the west, Johnson and Levell (1980) recognised three units, from base to top, as follows: 'Orange Sands', 'Silver Sands' and 'Red Sands', but within the district the lack of exposure makes it hard to recognise these divisions.

The Woburn Sands give rise to light, easily leached, brown sandy soils, coloured by the ochreous yellows and browns of hydrated iron oxides, derived from the near-surface, weathered material. No significant exposures were seen within the district during this survey and the detailed lithology of the formation remains poorly known. The general nature of the rocks can, to some extent, be inferred from detailed descriptions made in neighbouring areas.

The formation is commonly encountered at some depth in water boreholes in the north-west of the district, but borehole descriptions are usually brief and may record little more than 'sand'. Unweathered beds sampled there are typically grey or greenish grey with minor limonitic yellowish brown staining.

The Woburn Sands varies from loose sand, through poorly cemented sandstone (which collapses to sand when disturbed) to more durable sandstone cemented by calcite or limonite. It consists mainly of fine- to coarse-grained, rounded, quartz sand. It may be silty and has clay wisps or seams. There are some pebbles and phosphatic nodules in parts, particularly towards the base, and minor amounts of fossilised wood and pyrite. The nodule layers represent breaks in sedimentation and active winnowing of the sea floor.

The sand fraction has some glauconite and mica, and a small proportion of heavy-mineral grains (Rastall, 1919). At Sandy, about 12 km to the north of the district, samples from near the base of the formation revealed a uniform suite showing 'an abundance of zircon, kyanite, tourmaline and staurolite, with small quantities of rutile and epidote and a few crystals of colourless amphibole and pyroxene'. Samples from Woburn, about 15 km to the west, lacked the pyroxene and amphibole. Contrary to expectations, the assemblages in these areas were of little use in determining the provenance.

Some of the clay or mudstone seams proved in boreholes in the district may consist of fuller's earth (calcium montmorillonite). This occurs within the Woburn Sands in the Leighton Buzzard district to the west (Shephard-Thorn et al., 1994), where it has been worked commercially, and may be present in this district, if only as thin impersistent seams. Typically it is a bluish grey clay, with a smooth soapy texture, which breaks down into a slurry when placed in water. It is well known for its adsorptive properties and has a wide range of commercial uses.

Unworn microscopic crystals of zircon, sphene and biotite in the fullers's earth suggest derivation from a volcanic source (Cowperthwaite et al., 1972). Glass shards, both fresh and altered, together with fragments of igneous rocks and high temperature feldspars (Jeans et al., 1977) support a volcanic origin. Analysis of fuller's earth from BGS boreholes near Woburn revealed zeolite and tridymite in one clay seam, indicating alteration of an original volcanic component (Hallsworth, 1986). Thin seams may be derived directly from ashfalls, and thicker seams are probably the result of erosion and redeposition of the ash from adjacent landmasses. The source of the volcanic material remains in doubt, though it was almost certainly beyond the present coastline; Cowperthwaite, et al. (1972) have postulated the Wolf Rock in the Western Approaches, whilst Dixon et al. (1981) suggest the southern North Sea area.

Pebbles in the Woburn Sands include a wide range of lithologies, the most numerous of which are the durable, locally derived, Jurassic and Lower Cretaceous phosphatic nodules or 'coprolites'. These are particularly important because they commonly contain dateable fossils, although the sand itself is barren. The best developed example is the 'Potton Nodule Bed' (Edmonds and Dinham, 1965), found around Potton to the north of the district where it is, exceptionally, 2 m in thickness. It was thought that such seams represented pauses in sedimentation, which allowed sea-floor currents and wave action to winnow away the finer sand grains from a considerable thickness of sands and thereby concentrate the previously dispersed heavy nodules and pebbles into much thinner layers. The nodules range from 0.5 to 8.0 cm across and are locally referred to as 'red nodules', to distinguish them from the 'black nodules' of the Cambridge Greensand. Typically, a light brown cortex conceals a darker core. Resistant ironstone pebbles are also common.

Both nodules and pebbles are worn and rounded, in contrast to the few soft angular mudstone fragments present. This suggests a high-energy environment with reworking by wave action, perhaps following a period of river action. Other less common pebbles include chert, quartz, quartzite and sandstone as well as pieces of derived Lower Cretaceous shells, ferruginous shells, vertebrate remains, and silicified wood. Calcium phosphate is present as lumps of barren phosphate or phosphatised clay, shell moulds in phosphate, phosphatised wood bored by mollusca, and phosphatised vertebrate remains.

The more exotic pebbles have been studied, from deposits outside the district, in an attempt to determine their provenance. An early study by Keeping (1880) took advantage of the extensive 'coprolite' workings in the last century to collect from and describe the phosphate-bearing strata, particularly at Brickhill, Potton and Upware to the west and north of the district. Kirkaldy (1947) re-examined these samples from sections no longer open, and made his own collections from a number of localities along the outcrop, including the Leighton Buzzard area. He reviewed the available evidence from a large area and confirmed that the older non-phosphatic pebbles of the Woburn Sands comprised mainly chert (over 55 per cent), quartz and quartzite with some sandstones. The chert includes oolitic and rhomb-bearing varieties of probable Carboniferous age as well as a porcellanous, possibly Jurassic type not noted previously. Carboniferous Limestone pebbles are noticeably absent. Many of the pebbles probably originated from the London Platform, either directly or recycled through older deposits. Some may have come from the Midlands. In either case, the source could have been eroded away entirely; thus Carboniferous chert might be derived from Carboniferous Limestone outcrops which previously covered the London Platform. A recent regional study by Garden (1991) of the pebble suites in Lower Cretaceous rocks and their provenance recognised six different assemblages and related these to tectonic activity. One assemblage, typical of the Woburn Sands and Gault of the Leighton Buzzard area, is dominated by Carboniferous shelf chert with subordinate quartz from reworked Jurassic and Cretaceous pebble beds. Ironstone and phosphates are locally common.

Sedimentary structures and palaeogeography

The lack of exposure has prevented work on the sedimentary structures of the formation within the district. They have been studied in the Leighton Buzzard district where conflicting current directions and sediment provenance have been suggested by various workers (summarised in Shephard-Thorn et al., 1994).

Large-scale, planar, cross-bedded sands are common, together with some trough cross-bedded deposits. In the Woburn Sands of East Anglia, foresets of the large-scale cross-bedding dip mainly to the south (Schwarzacher, 1953) and they are interpreted as a submarine delta formation deposited to the south of a roughly east–west-trending coast. In the Folkestone Beds (Lower Greensand) of the Weald, the current direction is from the north-west and Narayan (1963) concluded that the 'London ridge' may not have existed at that time.

Cross-bedding in sands above the main fuller's earth seam at Aspley Heath, Woburn, indicates a southerly palaeocurrent direction (Cowperthwaite et al., 1972) which is also evident from the wave shape. A placid, offshore environment of deposition is envisaged, with deltaic sand flats surrounding lagoons where influxes of volcanic ash were trapped to form the fuller's earth seams.

Johnson and Levell (1980) found evidence for bidirectional currents. The older channel-fill sands, with a dominant flood direction from the north-east, were replaced upwards by younger, estuary-mouth sands with a dominant ebb-flow direction from the south-west. Much of the cross-bedding has been attributed to subtidal sand waves. The study of clay drapes in the cross-bedded Folkestone Beds of south-east England led Allen (1982) to conclude that they were formed on large asymmetric sand waves by low-strength, but strongly asymmetric tidal currents. Bridges (1982) demonstrated an overall sediment transport direction from the north at Upware, and the north-west at Woburn. Steeply dipping sand-flow cross-strata, formed by avalanching sand down the slip faces, dominate the foresets (Buck, 1985) and range between tongue-shaped and tabular forms. Morter (1986) has attempted to show that patterns of sedimentary structures are related to transgression and regression. Thus in the Leighton Buzzard area, the transgressive base of the Woburn Sands is related to the transgression of *P. nutfieldiensis* times. The principal 'Silver Sands' occur in sandwave complexes related to the transgression in mid *Hypacanthoplites jacobi* Zone times, and the 'Junction Beds' above the mid *L. tardefucata* break (Casey, 1961) or regression are much condensed and different in character.

Biostratigraphy

Casey (1961), in his review of the palaeontology of the Lower Greensand, showed how rapid progress in our understanding of the Group was achieved in the early part of the last century by the close co-operation of field geologists and palaeontologists. Interest in these strata then declined for their generally leached and unfossiliferous nature deterred new workers. Patient work by Casey on the surviving fossils from within the hard phosphatic nodules and ironstones revealed a new sequence of ammonite forms permitting a more successful zonation of the Aptian and Lower Albian stages. With the unravelling of the succession and the improved correlation it became easier to bring together the results of other workers such as Middlemiss (1962) and Owen (1971) on the brachiopods, as interest in the Lower Greensand revived. The ammonite zonation has been further refined by Owen (1988a and 1988b) and the version given here in Table 3 follows that used by Horton et al. (1994) for the Thame (sheet 237) district.

Few fossil identifications are available for the district. An indigenous fauna of brachiopods and plant fragments has been recorded from the various sections in the Leighton Buzzard district to the west (Shephard-Thorn et al., 1994). Faunas from near the base of the unit, exposed in notable sections at Brickhill and Clophill (Cox, 1990), are indicative of the *P. nutfieldiensis* Zone, *Tropaeum subarcticum* Subzone. There are no microfossil determinations available, but calcareous foraminifera and ostracods, confirming the age above, have been described from Shefford Hardwick, just to the north of the district (Wilkinson, 1991). The ostracod faunas of the Woburn Sands of Britain are described briefly by Wilkinson (in press). At Potton, to the north, Edmonds and Dinham (1965) recorded a gastropod, bivalve and brachiopod assemblage which suggests the overlying *Parahoplites cunningtoni* Zone. An Aptian flora composed of conifer cones and driftwood has also been obtained from the nodule beds at Woburn (Casey, 1961).

Details

Two logs (courtesy of Anglian Water Services) selected from a cluster of boreholes at Meppershall pumping station provide some lithological detail, for example 40.8 m of unbottomed Woburn Sands in Borehole TL13NE/13 [1504 3706] was described thus:

	Thickness m	Depth m
HEAD		
Clay and gravel	1.4	1.4
GAULT		
Clay, hard blue with minor sand near base	32.1	33.5
WOBURN SANDS		
Sandstone, hard	0.3	33.8
Sand, coarse, lignitic	14.3	8.1
Sand, fine with thin sandstone in middle, lignitic	1.2	49.3
Sand, coarse with seam of sandstone every 0.3 to 0.4 m	4.3	53.6
Sand, green, very fine	0.3	53.9
Sandstone, dark, very hard	0.1	54.0
Sand, coarse with seam of sandstone every 0.3 to 0.6 m	15.5	69.5
Sand, coarse with trace of clay	0.3	69.8
Sandstone, hard	0.6	70.4
Sand, coarse with trace of clay	3.4	73.8
Sand, yellow	0.1	73.
Sand, with trace of clay	seen to 0.5	74.4

The adjacent borehole TL13NW/20 [1494 3705], through probably very similar strata, was described rather differently:

	Thickness m	Depth m
GAULT		
Clay, blue	26.5	26.5
Clay, blue with sand and stones	4.0	30.5
Sand, brown, coarse with some clay	0.6	31.1
Sand on very hard conglomerate	0.3	31.4
Sand, brown, coarse	1.2	32.6
Clay, dark blue with some sandy layers	2.0	34.6
WOBURN SANDS		
Sand, grey, fine with driftwood, sandstones and hard nodules	1.1	35.7
Sand, grey, fine with sandstone, some driftwood and conglomerate	3.0	38.7
Conglomerate	0.3	39.0
Sand, grey, some sandstone	2.1	41.1
Sand, grey, very coarse and fine	1.5	42.6
Sand, grey, with some sandstones	14.7	57.3
Sand, grey, with some driftwood and sandstone to base	4.3	61.6
Sand, grey, with some driftwood and clay	1.5	63.1
Sand, grey and some sandstone	4.0	67.1
Driftwood and sand	0.6	67.7
Sand, grey, fine, with some sandstone	seen to 2.4	70.1

Here the top of the Woburn Sands is placed beneath the last recorded clay, and the sandy beds above this are regarded as part of the junction beds at the base of the overlying Gault.

A number of boreholes provide evidence for the presence of Woburn Sands on the floor the Hitchin Channel. The Henlow Borehole penetrated 10.2 m of sandy clay and sandstone, interpreted as Woburn Sands, below about 107.9 m of poorly described deposits, possible drift. South of this near Lower Stondon, the Pollards Nurseries Borehole proved 26.2 m of green sandstone, sand and clay beneath 91.4 m of ?drift.

Near Arlesey, Fairfield Hospital Borehole penetrated 42.2 m of sand and sandstone beneath 104.1 m of drift, Lower Chalk and Gault. The sand was described as brown when wet, drying to a light grey, with many fragments of pyrite and fossil wood.

A British Geological Survey borehole at Arlesey [1887 3463] (Appendix 1) penetrated the Woburn Sands between 72.96 m and terminal depth at 83.49 m. The topmost 0.27 m, underlying the Junction Beds of the Gault, shows how the top of the Woburn Sands becomes cemented by the redeposition of calcite, probably leached from the overlying bed. It consists of dark brown sandstone with rounded medium- to coarse-grained quartz cemented by calcite. This rests on 10.26 m of loose sand which is greenish yellow mottled with reddish brown fine- to medium-grained quartz with some opaque minerals.

Farther east, Woburn Sands has been recorded in a number of boreholes. At Radwell for example, a borehole off Baldock Road [2308 3618] proved 27.0 m of grey sand beneath 95.0 m of Chalk and grey Gault clay. Bygrave Plantation Borehole

[2559 3655] penetrated 14.6 m of fine-grained, green sand below a depth of 137.8 m.

Just north of the district, Ashwell Borehole (Appendix 1) proved 27.9 m of Woburn Sands, of which cores from the lower 12 m were described in detail by R W Gallois. The sandstones are grey, green-grey or grey-brown, mainly hard with some calcite cement, but parts are soft and poorly cemented or loose uncemented sands. They vary from fine to coarse grained with pebbles, particularly towards the base. The sand fraction is mainly quartz, with some glauconite and mica. The sandstones are silty in part and there are a few clay wisps. Pebbles include angular mudstone and ironstone, as well as small highly polished goethite grains (millet-seed type). A thin, dark grey, silty, very micaceous mudstone near the base has poorly preserved bivalves and numerous small quartz pebbles, lenses and thin beds of coarse pebbly sand, as well as a thin bed of lignite. The basal sand has a thin plant-rich clay seam and flattened pebbles of grey silty clay.

Shallow site-investigation boreholes into the formation typically sample the weathered strata in which the iron compounds have been oxidised and ochreous brown colours predominate. The Rectory Road Borehole [1285 3817] near Campton proved:

	Thickness m	Depth m
WOBURN SANDS		
Sand, brown, very clayey silty, fine- to medium-grained, with a few iron-cemented fragments	1.4	1.4
Sand, red-brown silty, very dense, fine- to coarse-grained, with iron-cemented fragments	0.9	2.3
Sandstone, red-brown, weakly iron-cemented	0.3	2.6

The Hitchin Brewery Borehole [184 288] proved 7.0 m of Woburn Sands above terminal depth at 142 m. The top 2.4 m of olive-coloured sand rests on denser white sand.

GAULT FORMATION

The Gault, of Middle to Upper Albian age, underlies most of the district. Thin strata equivalent to the 'Junction Beds', of Lower Albian age, between the Woburn Sands and the Gault, are not differentiated on the geological map and are described here with the Gault. Some workers have included them with the Woburn Sands (Lower Greensand) on biostratigraphical grounds (Casey, 1961).

The Gault crops out in the north-west over an area of about 23 km², forming a clay vale of low to moderate relief along the foot of the Chalk escarpment. Here the Gault–Chalk junction follows a convoluted course from Aspley End in the south-west, via Shillington, Mepper-shall and Arlesey to Stotfold in the north-east. It has a tongue-like subcrop, thought to be over a kilometre wide and 5 km long, stretching southwards along the floor of the buried Hitchin Channel. Two conjectural inliers to the south of the main subcrop are mapped, in part, on geophysical evidence, and may require revision as more borehole data become available. Much of the Gault is concealed by drift, comprising principally chalky till and associated glaciofluvial deposits. Parts of the outcrop are concealed by head, and even those areas shown as drift free on the geological map may be covered by a thin layer of clayey hillwash.

The Gault dips gently beneath the Chalk, as proved in a few water boreholes in the north-western part of the district. The geological cross-section, constructed with the aid of geophysical information, shows that it falls to more than 150 m below OD in the south-east. It oversteps the Woburn Sands which pinch out in the south-east, and probably thins slightly as it overlaps directly onto Devonian 'basement'. It was deposited during Albian times (Table 3) by transgressive seas which eventually covered the whole of the London Platform.

The Gault shows less variation in thickness than the underlying Woburn Sands. Recorded thicknesses range from 47.7 m, in the Bygrave Plantation Borehole, to 73.8 m, in The Mill Borehole [2288 3592]. In the absence of core or geophysical logs, borehole records must be treated with caution. The marked change from sand at the base is easily recognised, the upper junction with the Chalk Marl at the base of the Lower Chalk is commonly misidentified. Thus, the thickness of the Gault may be exaggerated at the expense of the Lower Chalk. A thickness of 65.4 m of Gault clay with sand, phosphatic nodules and pyrite at the base recorded in the Fairfield Hospital Borehole may be a more reliable maximum than the thickness range quoted above.

Lithology

The best exposure of Gault in the district is a 15 m section, revealing the top of the formation, in the claypit operated by Butterley Brick Ltd at Arlesey [188 347]. Arlesey Borehole (Appendix 1) was drilled by the British Geological Survey alongside the pit. This is one of two boreholes (the other at Klondyke Farm [5940 7010], near Cambridge; Woods, 1992e) drilled to investigate the engineering properties of the Gault.

The borehole penetrated 57.51 m of Gault and Junction Beds (Figure 6). This lithological description of the Gault is based partly on this borehole, and partly on accounts from neighbouring districts (Shephard-Thorn et al., 1994).

Away from Arlesey pit there are only a few exposures in overgrown disused pits, some cleaned-out ditch sections and temporary excavations. Mapping relies upon extensive augering, where the descriptions are necessarily based on the weathered material within a metre or so of the surface.

Commonly the Gault gives rise to a heavy, poorly drained, dark greyish brown, clay soil, sticky when wet, but becoming hard and sun cracked in hot dry summers. Drift pebbles are commonly scattered over the surface. This soil overlies soft weathered Gault of brown, yellowish brown or greenish brown, silty clay, with some 'race' (secondary nodules of calcium carbonate), which may be mistaken for chalk clasts leading to the misidenti-fication of the weathered bedrock as till. This passes down into firmer, pale grey, silty clay or mudstone.

The Gault consists of variably calcareous mudstones and silty mudstones, usually described in boreholes as

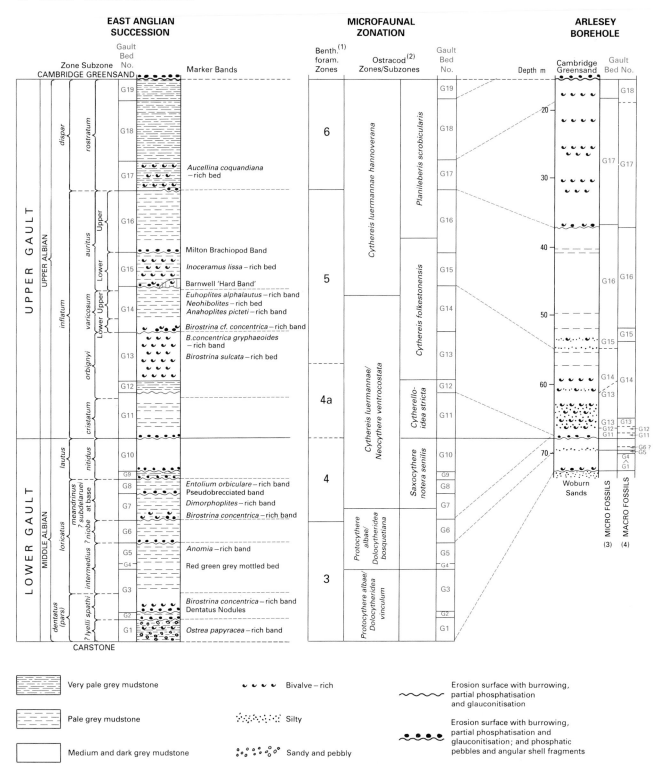

Figure 6   Relationship of the Gault sequence in the Arlesey Borehole to the standard East Anglian succession of Gallois and Morter (1982) and the microfossil zonation.

1. Benthonic foraminifera zones after Carter and Hart (1977).
2. Ostracod zones after Wilkinson (1990b).
3. Microfossil and (4) macrofossil zonation after Hopson (1992, figure 2) based on Wilkinson (1992a)
   and Woods (1992a) respectively, see also Woods, Wilkinson and Hopson, 1995.

stiff to very stiff, dark grey or blue grey, silty clay with pale grey mottling. Towards the base, a rhythmic development is expressed by weak colour banding caused by alternations of pale grey, calcareous, silty clay with darker grey, sandy, shelly, silty clay. The upper part of the formation is paler in colour and more calcareous with finely divided coccolith, foraminifera, ostracod and inoceramid debris. Sporadic, light brown, phosphatic nodules, which have grown around fossils or burrows, occur at many levels. Darker brown, polished and commonly more resistant, phosphatic pebbles are found reworked into layers. These mark erosive non-sequences when the nodules were winnowed out of the underlying beds, suffered abrasion and perhaps further phosphatisation, and were concentrated into layers on the sea bed. Some of these pebbles contain fossil fragments, which may have been derived from strata considerably older than the surrounding mudstones. It is crucial therefore to distinguish between the primary, in-situ nodules and the derived pebbles, though both are referred to as nodules or 'coprolites' indiscriminately.

There are a few fine- and very fine-grained sandy layers, and traces of selenite crystals and pyritic nodules in places. The clay, typically, appears massive because of bioturbation, but as it dries out laminated samples develop a poor fissility. Close subvertical or blocky fissuring with ochreous staining on the joint surfaces is common. The macrofauna, which is dominated by bivalves and ammonites with some gastropods and echinoids, may be abundant in fresh material but is usually weathered out of exposed sections. Here, more robust fossils, such as phosphatised remains and small belemnites, in particular *Neohibolites*, usually predominate. Microfossils are found throughout the sequence and trace fossils are common in parts. The lowest metre or so of strata are dark greenish grey and very sandy mudstone with glauconite and quartz grains as well as phosphatic and pyritic nodules.

The mineralogy was analysed (Prior et al., 1993) as part of the engineering study. Silt- and clay-size grains are in subequal proportions with generally only a trace of sand. The Gault comprises mainly calcite (31–42 per cent) and clay minerals (smectite, illite and kaolinite), with minor quartz and traces of pyrite, organic matter and siderite. Whole rock smectite concentrations show little variation with depth and range from 13 to 21 per cent. In the fraction less than 2 microns illite is fairly constant throughout at about 10 per cent and kaolinite decreases from about 60 per cent at the base to 20 per cent at the top. Conversely, smectite increases from 30 per cent at the base to about 80 per cent near the top; this increase in smectite may reflect an increase in volcanogenic input.

Stratigraphy

The first detailed stratigraphical studies of the Gault were made on coastal exposures at Copt Point, Folkestone in Kent by De Rance (1868) who subdivided the succession into 11 units (I to XI numbered top to bottom) split between the Upper and Lower Albian, based on lithology and fossil content. This concept was supported by Price (1874) who renumbered the beds up the sequence, and was later extended by Jukes-Browne and Hill (1900), to fourteen beds (1 and 1a–13) and used for regional correlation. This subdivision of the type section gained wide acceptance as a basis for description of the Gault. Recently the Gault in East Anglia, studied mainly in cored boreholes, was subdivided into nineteen beds or rhythmic units (Gallois and Morter, 1982) (Figure 6) and, herein, are referred to as Gault Beds 'G1' to 'G19'. This scheme has become the standard for the East Anglian region. Ideally, each rhythm has a burrowed erosion surface at the base, which is overlain by a lag of phosphatic pebbles and shell debris in a silty mudstone matrix, and passes up into paler grey more calcareous and less silty mudstone. Where the bed boundaries are non-sequences they may coincide with ammonite zonal boundaries: for example the boundary between the Lower and Upper Gault lithostratigraphical divisions coincides with the base of the *Mortoniceras inflatum* Zone, at the base of the Upper Albian.

The Gault has been subdivided into zones based on ammonite species (Table 3) (Spath, 1923–43). The scheme established by Spath (1923a and b) has been modified by later workers such as Casey (in Smart et al., 1966), and Owen (1972, 1975).

The macrofaunal and microfaunal zonations of the Gault have been correlated (Hart, 1973a). Both the benthonic foraminifera (Carter and Hart, 1977; Hart et al., 1989) and the ostracods of East Anglia (Wilkinson and Morter, 1981; Wilkinson, 1990b) have been used successfully for zonation. Calcareous nannofossils from the Gault at Munday's Hill, Bedfordshire have also been used to interpret the stratigraphy (Crux, 1991) and found to be in accord with Owen's (1972) ammonite zonation (Shephard-Thorn et al., 1994).

Some bivalve species are of stratigraphical significance, for example, in the genus *Aucellina* the ornament of the left valve and the inflation of the right valve umbo changes from the *Callihoplites auritus* Subzone of the *Mortoniceras inflatum* Zone, through the *Stoliczkaia dispar* Zone, and into the Lower Cenomanian (Morter and Wood, 1983).

Detailed work on the lithology and fossil content of the Gault core from Arlesey Borehole (Figure 6) has shown that the succession can be interpreted in terms of the bed sequence of Gallois and Morter (1982). The interpretation is based on lithological descriptions, together with micro- and macro-faunal studies by I P Wilkinson (1992a) M A Woods (1992a) and Woods et al. (1995) (Figure 7). These show that both the Lower and Upper Gault are present. The Lower Gault (G1 to G5 and ?G6) is condensed to less than 5 m in thickness and is separated from a much thicker Upper Gault (G11 to G18) by a marked erosion level and core loss where beds (G7 to G10) representing the upper part of the Middle Albian were not found, though a more complete Lower Gault sequence could be present. Beds G16 and G17 are much expanded, and G19, the topmost bed, is absent. This attenuation of the Lower Gault on the flank of the London Platform is illustrated in Gallois and Morter (1982, fig. 5), and it probably thins out completely to the south-east across the district. A similar, marked, Middle Albian hiatus is present in the Leighton Buzzard district (Shephard-Thorn et al., 1994).

Two geophysical logs of Arlesey Borehole are also shown in Figure 7. The Gault clay has a much higher gamma-ray value than the overlying Lower Chalk, with a distinctive 'spike' at the junction caused by the concentration of phosphatic nodules in the base of the Cambridge Greensand. There is a gradual increase in the gamma-ray value with depth, with a second major 'spike' coinciding with another nodule layer at the base of the Upper Gault (base G11). Lower values within the Gault probably relate to more sandy or silty layers. The low resistivity values within the Gault reflect the lack of water-filled pore space compared to the Lower Chalk. The magnetic susceptibility of the Arlesey core was studied using a hand held Kappameter (Raines, 1992). Four zones were recognised but these show little apparent correlation with the lithology or gamma-ray log, though a broad anomaly at 49.0–57.5 m depth coincides roughly with some harder bands.

JUNCTION BEDS

These beds have attracted considerable interest in the Leighton Buzzard district where they are associated with an unusual fossiliferous limestone, the Shenley Limestone, around Shenley Hill (Lamplugh and Walker, 1903; Lamplugh, 1922; Hancock, 1958 and 1967; Owen, 1972). They comprise a varied and condensed sequence of sands and clays with some limestones, ironstones and phosphatic nodule beds, and many internal non-sequences can be demonstrated. They are of early Albian age (upper *L. tardefurcata* Zone and *Douvilleiceras mammillatum* Superzone).

In the Arlesey Borehole 0.16 m of strata (72.80–72.96 m) are interpreted as equivalent to the Junction Beds and Shenley Limestone (Plate 1). These consist of dark red-brown, laminated, possibly haematitic ironstone, interbedded with pale yellow-brown, sandy, possibly goethitic, calcareous mudstone, containing sparse quartz pebbles and some polished quartz sand grains. In thin-section, the rocks show a variety of internal textures, including spheroidal oncolith-like growths, finely corrugated and planar laminae and complex columnar developments (Lott, 1992). Well-rounded opaque grains suggest possible reworking of ironstone laminae, and ferroan sparry calcite infilling fractures may have developed during periods of desiccation. The prominent upper reniform bedding surface and the laminated structure were considered to be typical algal mat or stromatolitic features. An intertidal environment subject to some subaerial exposure and periodic sediment influx during storms was favoured. The calcareous ironstone is in the same stratigraphical position as the Shenley Limestone of the Leighton Buzzard district, where recent detailed work on its origin has suggested a clastic-rich, carbonate infill on a wave-cut ironstone platform (Eyers, 1992). Although differing from the algal mat at Arlesey, both deposits might be expected to form in the shallow waters of this area along the margins of the 'Bedfordshire Straits'. No macrofaunas were recovered from this horizon, and the microfaunas were extremely sparse and of little biostratigraphical significance (Wilkinson 1992b).

LOWER GAULT

In the Arlesey Borehole, the Lower Gault (68.30–72.80 m depth) rests on 'Junction Beds'. At the base is a thin glauconitic sandy mudstone with polished quartz pebbles, abundant phosphatic clasts, small limonitic clasts and poorly preserved fragmentary macrofauna (Woods,

Plate 1   The 'Shenley Limestone' from the base of the Gault succession in the Arlesey Borehole [1887 3463] (see Figure 7). (GS 109S)

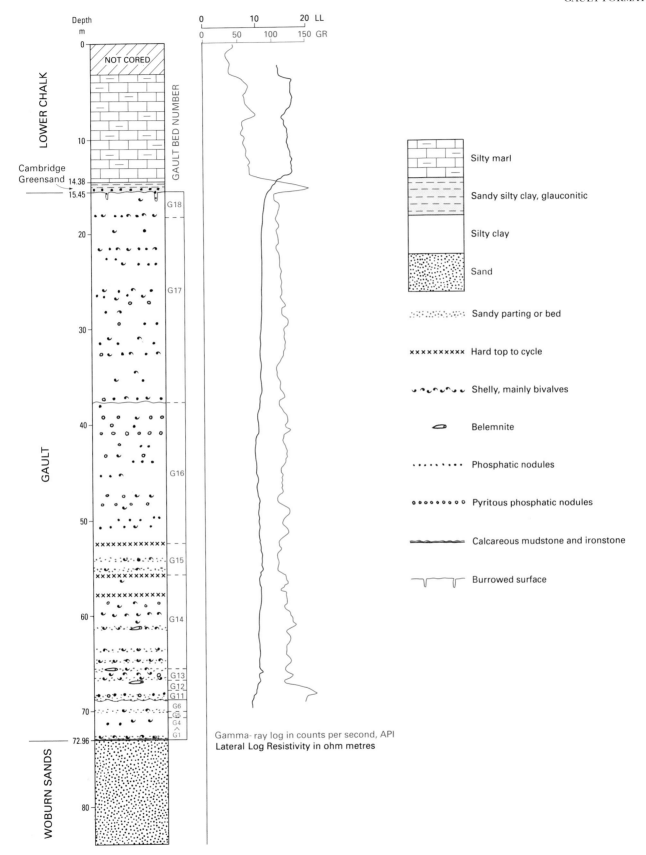

Figure 7 The Arlesey Borehole [1887 3463] graphic lithology and geophysical logs; and the relationship to the Gault Bed numbers of Gallois and Morter (1982).

1992a) suggestive of G1, G2 and G3 (Gallois and Morter, 1982). This passes up by a reduction of sand content into a grey mudstone with a richly fossiliferous horizon of the bivalve *Birostrina concentrica* associated with *Anomia* sp. and *Chondrites* trace fossils suggestive of G4 and G5. The presence of G6 is inferred from the occurrence of *B. concentrica* in a sandy, silty clay overlying a *Chondrites*-rich horizon. Thus there are representatives of the *Hoplites dentatus* and *Euhoplites loricatus* ammonite Zones. The microfaunal evidence was sparse with only long-ranging, probably Middle Albian, foraminiferal species present (Wilkinson, 1992a). The higher beds of the Lower Gault were not found, either because of a non-sequence or because of core loss, or a combination of the two.

UPPER GAULT

In the Arlesey Borehole, the Upper Gault (15.45–68.30 m depth) consists mainly of silty mudstones with some thin sandy mudstones and seams rich in phosphatic nodules. Towards the base, the macrofauna includes the radially ribbed *Birostrina sulcata* (Woods, 1992a), indicative of G11, G12 and G13. Upwards, ammonites and belemnites become more common, together with a concentrically ornamented bivalve *B.* cf. *concentrica* suggestive of G14. Bed G15 has shell fragments of '*Inoceramus*' *lissa*, and G16 has an impoverished fauna. Bed G17 is the thickest unit, consisting of a monotonous sequence of mudstones rich in the bivalve *Aucellina*. The sudden decline in the abundance of *Aucellina* at the top of the borehole core suggests this highest Gault can be assigned to G18. The microfaunal evidence (Wilkinson, 1992a) was broadly supportive of these findings, though the faunas above G14 were sparse and generally long-ranging.

Details

Campton

The site of the coprolite pit recorded by Jukes-Browne and Hill (1900, p.285) near Campton is uncertain, but probably lies just within the district [possibly at 122 380 or 121 374] (Edmonds and Dinham, 1965). Situated just above the base of the Gault, the nodule bed contained numerous ammonites which were redetermined by Spath as follows: *Anahoplites planus*, ?*Dimorphoplites alternatus*, *Epihoplites compressus* and *Euhoplites* sp. These were regarded as *remanié* fauna from several Lower Gault horizons, with the nodule seam forming the local base to the Upper Gault.

Shillington

A sample [MPA29213] collected from the top of the Gault yielded a microfauna of foraminifera and ostracods dominated by long ranging Albian–Cenomanian species (Wilkinson, 1988b). The presence of *Arenobulimina chapmani* and *A. sabulosa* are, however, indicative of the Upper Albian, benthonic, foraminiferal, zone 6 of Carter and Hart (1977). In addition the occurrence of *Arenobulimina* aff. *frankei* and *Gavelinella cenomanica* suggest the highest part of that zone.

Meppershall

The disused Meppershall Hoo brickpit, near Hoo Farm [1571 3747], revealed a 10 m face of pale marly clay, with small septaria and rusty pyrite or marcasite nodules. It yielded *Hysteroceras orbignyi* and *H. bucklandi* regarded as characteristic of the *Callihoplites auritus* Subzone of the Upper Albian (Bloom and Harper, 1938). Other fossils include a layer of crushed *Inoceramus* shells at the base and some ostracods.

Arlesey

A section in the Arlesey Brickpit [188 347], seen during this survey, exposed up to 15.0 m of stiff grey silty clay (mudstone) with beds of phosphatic nodules. At the top burrows infilled with glauconitic sandy marl extend up to 0.6 m below the base of the Cambridge Greensand.

Henlow area

Gault clay at the top of two of the Meppershall Pumping Station boreholes was described in the previous section on the Woburn Sands. Near Lower Stondon, the Pollards Nurseries Borehole [1616 3506] proved 31.7 m of Gault beneath thick drift. Farther east at Arlesey, the Hitchin Road Borehole [1899 3513] proved a full thickness of 46.6 m of Gault clay with a sandy base.

Gault clay was recorded in many of the site investigation boreholes for the Arlesey–Stotfold bypass, for example near Church End [1934 3783] along the Pix Brook proved:

	Thickness m	Depth m
GLACIOFLUVIAL SAND AND GRAVEL	1.8	1.8
GAULT		
Clay, dark grey mottled greenish brown, very silty, stiff, closely fissured with some sand and chalk gravel (cryoturbated)	1.4	3.2
Clay, dark grey mottled greenish brown, slightly silty, very stiff, thinly laminated, with iron staining on closely spaced fissured surfaces	2.5	5.7
Clay, dark grey, slightly silty, thinly laminated, with fine to medium gravel-sized brown calcareous nodules at top	seen to 16.3	22.0

One kilometre to the east upstream along the Pix Brook a borehole off Stotfold Road [2011 3710], in the top of the Gault proved:

	Thickness m	Depth m
ALLUVIUM	1.3	1.3
GAULT		
Clay, light grey, slightly calcareous silty, firm, fissured, with some sand pockets, and chalk and flint gravel (cryoturbated)	0.4	1.7
Clay, light grey mottled greyish brown, very silty, firm to stiff, closely fissured (weathered)	0.2	1.9
Clay, dark grey mottled greenish grey, silty, stiff, thinly laminated, closely fissured	2.4	4.3
Clay, dark grey, slightly calcareous, silty, stiff to very stiff, thinly bedded, closely fissured	seen to 16.7	21.0

Farther south, a 15 m-deep borehole, off Hitchin Road, Stotfold [2051 3631], had previously been logged throughout as Chalk Marl, but examination of undisturbed samples revealed about 4.5 m of grey, friable, Lower Chalk, clayey marl resting on slightly darker, stiffer, Gault clay with no sign of the expected intervening green glauconitic Cambridge Greensand in the recovered samples. Clearly such logs need to be treated with caution; the base of the Chalk is not always recognised correctly, even where there is a distinctive marker present locally.

Concealed Gault has been recorded in a number of boreholes. The borehole at the Pirton Pumping Station [1406 3181] proved 61.1 m of Gault below a depth of 30.6 m; the lower part is described as a sandy clay with coprolites. A borehole at Pirton Hall [1255 3289] was recorded as penetrating only 48.7 m. To what extent these differences are real or due to inadequacies in the logging is not known.

A similar thickness of 48.5 m was recorded in the Old Rectory Borehole at Holwell [165 330]. The Gault is 61.6 m thick at Stotfold in the Old Brewery Borehole [2191 3701], and 51.8 m at Newnham Hall [2466 3762]. The Willian Road Borehole, Letchworth [2417 3248], penetrated the top 14.9 m of the Gault, below a depth of 91.7 m.

A deep water borehole, drilled in 1831 at the yard of Hitchin (Lucas's) Brewery, Hitchin (Whitaker, 1872; Hill, 1908), was sited within the buried channel and proved 65.2 m of Gault beneath thick drift and Lower Chalk at a depth of 69.7 m or 6 m below OD. It was described simply as 'strong blue clay' and 'clay', with stones (probably phosphatic nodules) in the basal metre, and rested on Woburn Sands.

To the south-west, the Ransom's Brickyard Borehole [1873 2855] (Hill, 1908) (now part of the cemetery) proved 103.7 m of drift on Gault at about 21 m below OD. Only about 1.5 m of the Gault was penetrated, described as a 'stiff dark blue clay', and was considered by Hill (1908), not to be 'the top of the Gault'.

The Kings Walden Borehole [1546 2338] may have penetrated Gault towards the bottom at 123.4 m depth, but the base of the Chalk was not positively identified.

FOUR

Upper Cretaceous: Chalk

Strata of Late Cretaceous age, entirely in chalk facies, outcrop and are known to underlie Quaternary and Palaeogene deposits over 400 km of the district. The Chalk forms the prominent north-westward facing scarp, crossing the north-west and north of the district, and forms the south-westward sloping dip slope to the south, the northern limb of the London Basin.

The two positive features characteristic of the scarp face are attributable to more resistant beds within the Chalk sequence. These features are best developed on the scarp to the north, but can also be traced along the flanks of consequent stream valleys incised through the dip slope. These resistant beds, the Melbourn Rock and Chalk Rock, have been taken to mark the lithostratigraphical Lower–Middle and Middle–Upper Chalk boundaries respectively. Outside the region, in areas where the Chalk Rock is not strongly represented, modern lithostratigraphical schemes combine the superficially similar Middle and Upper Chalk into a single unit, the Sussex White Chalk Formation (Mortimore, 1986), or the Dover and Ramsgate Chalk formations in the North Downs (Robinson, 1986). These schemes, based on the identification of characteristic widespread marl, hardground and flint sequences, introduced a plethora of stratigraphical names which have been summarised in Mortimore (1987). Many of these characteristic sequences can be identified in the 255 m-thick Chalk sequence of this district, but the traditional scheme based on mappable horizons is used herein (Figure 8 and Table 4).

An aid in the correlation has been the regional study of characteristic geophysical responses on gamma-ray and resistivity traces from boreholes (Murray, 1986). A correlation of some representative borehole log traces within the district is given in Figure 8.

The Chalk is regarded informally to be of group status, with the Lower, Middle and Upper Chalk being of formational status; it is not formally defined as such because a stratotype has not been designated.

In the district, the Chalk outcrops span the chronostratigraphical stages of the Cenomanian, Turonian and much, if not all, of the Coniacian. There is some evidence which tentatively infers that all of the Coniacian and the basal Santonian is present in the south-east of the district. These stages are broadly represented by the Lower, Middle and Upper Chalk respectively, although the chronostratigraphical and lithostratigraphical boundaries do not coincide exactly.

A correlation of the major rock units present in the area with the accepted chronostratigraphical and biostratigraphical schemes is given in Table 4.

Lithology

The Chalk comprises predominantly soft white to off-white very fine-grained and very pure, microporous limestones with subordinate hardgrounds and beds of marl, calcarenite and flint. Chalk is composed largely of the microscopic calcareous skeletal remains of haplophycean planktonic algae (coccoliths). Other coarser carbonate material derived from foraminifera, ostracods and calcispheres, together with entire and finely comminuted echinoderm, bryozoan, coral and bivalve remains, notably disaggregated prisms of inoceramids, is present, some in rock-building proportions (e.g. the Totternhoe Stone).

In addition to this carbonate debris, five other minor constituents, of a depositional and early diagenetic origin, are present. Mud-grade material, consisting chiefly of the clay minerals illite, smectite and kaolinite, in varying relative amounts, forms an appreciable proportion (30 to 40 per cent, Destombes and Shephard-Thorn, 1971) of the marly parts of the Lower Chalk and of thin marl seams elsewhere in the Middle and Upper Chalk. Throughout the main body of the Chalk, above the Chalk Marl, the proportion of argillaceous material falls progressively until in the Middle and Upper Chalk it does not exceed 5 per cent. The geochemical signatures of individual marl seams in the Middle and Upper Chalk is proving to be sufficiently characteristic to aid the correlation of the Chiltern sequence to that of Sussex and Kent (Wray and Gale, 1993).

A coarser silt and fine to medium grade sand fraction, predominantly of detrital quartz, forms less than 1 per cent of the Chalk overall. Certain beds, most notably the Cambridge Greensand in this district, contain other stable mineral species such as mica, zircon, rutile and tourmaline (Jukes-Browne and Hill, 1903). Another minor siliceous element is derived from skeletal material such as sponge spicules and radiolaria. These are commonly replaced by secondary calcite or pyrite.

The authigenic minerals glauconite and calcium phosphate occur throughout the Chalk sequences, but are most conspicuous in winnowed and condensed horizons such as the Cambridge Greensand and Totternhoe Stone. The phosphate occurs most commonly as reworked nodules within these winnowed levels. Hardgrounds within the Chalk, for example the complex of the Chalk Rock, commonly have concentrations of glauconite and phosphate as impregnations and coatings. Much of this material is the product of early diagenesis. Finely disseminated pyrite is a common authigenic mineral in the more argillaceous parts of the sequence

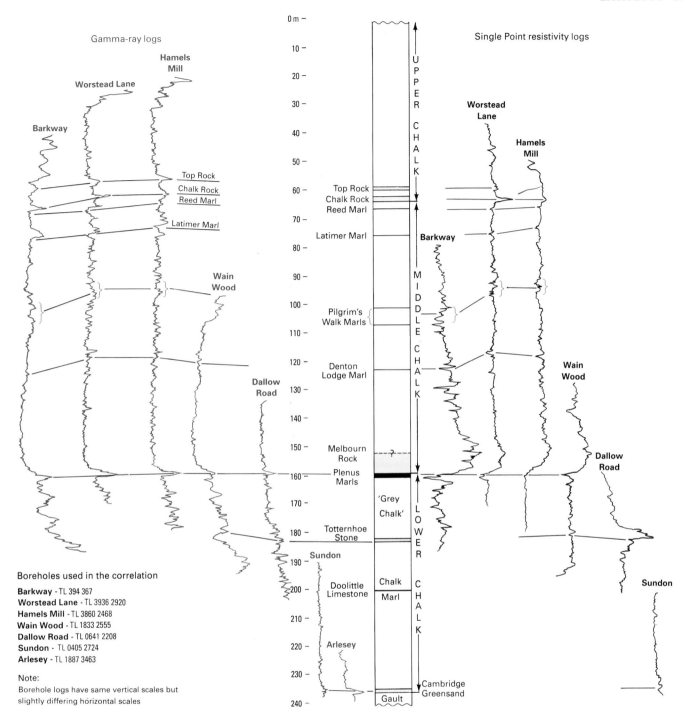

Figure 8 A correlation of selected borehole gamma-ray and single point resistivity log traces and the major lithostratigraphical divisions of the Chalk in the district.

and pyrite nodules and burrow fills are a conspicuous feature of much of the Chalk.

For parts of the Middle and much of the Upper Chalk, the most important non-carbonate constituent is flint which occurs in nodular and tabular form in seams which parallel the bedding, and also along cross-cutting joints and fissures.

Diagenesis

Two distinct phases of diagenesis can be recognised in the Chalk. An early phase, associated with interruptions in sedimentation, affected unconsolidated sediment at or just below the sea floor. A late phase was associated with deeper burial, compaction, silicification and carbonate dissolution.

Table 4   The litho-, chrono-, and bio-stratigraphical correlation of the Chalk Group within the district.

Stage	Approximate age Ma	Major lithostratigraphical units	Major lithostratigraphical markers	Biozone	Ammonite zones and subzones	Section ranges
SANTONIAN	83	UPPER CHALK		*Marsupites testudinarius*		
				Uintacrinus socialis		Anstey
	86.5			*Micraster coranguinum*		
CONIACIAN			cf. upper East Cliff Marl			Reed
				Micraster cortestudinarium		Royston School
	88.5	Top Rock / Kensworth Nodular Chalk Member		*Sternotaxis plana* (old name *Holaster planus*)		Royston Bypass
TURONIAN Upper		Chalk Rock Member	Reed Marl		*Subprionocyclus neptuni*	
	?	MIDDLE CHALK	Latimer Marl			Hitchin Station
	?		Pilgrims Walk Marl	*Terebratulina lata*		
TURONIAN Middle	?		Denton Lodge Marl			Dallow Road borehole
			Odsey Marl / Morden Flint	?	*Collignoniceras woollgari*	Walsworth Road, Hitchin
			Maiden Bower Flint			
			Aston Marl			
			Morden Rock	*Mytiloides* spp. (formerly *Inoceramus labiatus*)	*Mammites nodosoides*	Ashwell
TURONIAN Lower			Ashwell calcarenite		*Fagesia catinus*	
	90.5	Melbourn Rock			*Watinoceras devonense*	Steeple Morden
					Neocardioceras juddii	
CENOMANIAN Upper		Plenus Marls			*Metoicoceras geslinianum* (formerly *Sciponoceras gracile*)	
		'Grey Chalk'			*Calycoceras guerangeri* (formerly *Calycoceras naviculare*)	Blue / Green Lagoon
		LOWER CHALK	Jukes-Browne Bed 7		*Acanthoceras jukesbrownei*	
CENOMANIAN Middle		Totternhoe Stone			*Acanthoceras*	*Turrilites acutus*		
					rhotomagense	*Turrilites costatus*	
		'Chalk Marl'	Dixoni Limestone		*Mantelliceras dixoni*	Arlesey borehole
CENOMANIAN Lower			Doolittle Limestone		*Mantelliceras*	*Mantelliceras saxbii*	
	97	Cambridge Greensand			*mantelli*	*Neostlingoceras carcitanense*	

Early diagenesis of the Chalk in response to changing water depth, deposition rates and erosion gives rise to a variety of bedding surfaces and associated lithologies. These range from simple omission surfaces, demonstrating non-deposition, to complicated scoured, burrowed and mineralised surfaces (hardgrounds) overlying lithified chalk (chalkstone). They provide a framework of lithological markers in the Chalk sequence. The fact that many of these surfaces and lithologies are the result of basin wide changes in depositional conditions has permitted detailed regional correlations (Mortimore, 1986, 1987; Bromley and Gale, 1982; Robinson, 1986). Table 5 shows an outline of the progression in the development of hardgrounds after Kennedy and Garrison (1975a).

Late-stage diagenesis modifies the framework of Chalk lithostratigraphy created during early sedimentation. Carbonate dissolution as the result of deep burial and compaction has produced a variety of effects. In hard chalks, microstylolites are common, but in the softer chalks stylolites are absent and anastomosing residual clay seams are widespread. Where dissolution has been extensive, the softer chalk takes on a 'flaser' appearance with 'augen' of white chalk enveloped by greyish marl. The 'flaser'-like limestones described by Kennedy and Garrison (1975a) seem to be the same as the 'griotte' chalks described by Mortimore (1979).

The most conspicuous diagenetic process in the Chalk is silicification. The major product of this silicification is flint which is considered to have resulted from the segregation of silica (SiO_2), presumably derived from dissolution of original biogenic sponge material and skeletons of other siliceous organisms, notably radiolarians and diatoms, in layers, parallel to the sea floor. Flint is a chert, with a particularly well developed conchoidal fracture, which is composed of an aggregate of ultra-microscopic quartz crystals only a few microns across. It

is generally present in pure white chalks with an insignificant clay content, and is thus most prevalent in the Middle and Upper Chalk formations. Clayton (1986) suggests that this precipitation was a multi-stage process, initiated by dissolution of host carbonate and occurred 5 to 10 m below the sediment surface, at the oxic/anoxic boundary. It was aided by an excess of dissolved sulphide (initiating acid digestion) in the pore waters. Local porosity in excess of 75–80 per cent and permeability variations, particularly in response to burrowing (trace fossils are mainly *Thalassinoides* and *Zoophycos*), produced the characteristic burrow-fill form of most flint nodules. Less marked permeability resulted in tabular flint bands. Even later stage silicification and remobilisation of silica can be demonstrated by cross cutting, sheet-like bodies which line open joints and faults. The most strongly developed flint beds can be traced over large distances.

Palaeogeography and environment of deposition

The oldest chalks present in the district are of Cenomanian age. At this time, emergent land masses were present in south-west England, Wales, Scotland and Northern Ireland, and in Brittany, the Vosges, the Ardennes and the Baltic Shield. Southern Britain lay approximately 10° of latitude farther south than the present day. The Chalk accumulated on the outer shelf of an epicontinental subtropical sea of normal salinity and with little terrigenous input.

Chalk sedimentation was cyclic on a small scale, but only in the Lower Chalk, where cycles in the Chalk Marl are conspicuous, can it be easily demonstrated. Elsewhere in the succession, the lack of suitable markers or colour variations precludes the identification of these cycles. The cyclicity may reflect a linkage with the Earth's orbital cycles (Milankovitch Cycles), for example in Gale (1989).

Table 5 The development of sedimentary surfaces in the Chalk.

	Early diagenesis	Renewed deposition (early burial)	Erosion prior to burial
short pause in deposition	burrowing (principally *Thalassinoides*) in soft, unconsolidated substrate	omission surface (burrowed chalk)	scoured omission surface (burrowed chalk with calcareous arenitic lag)
longer pause in deposition	burrowing and growth of calcareous nodules	nodular chalk (variably hard chalk nodules in soft, burrowed chalk matrix)	Intraformational lag (chalk nodule conglomerate resting on bored, nodular chalk)
extended pause in deposition	continuous or semi-continuous lithified burrowed substrate	incipient hardground	true hardground; eroded chalkstone may be subsequently bored, encrusted or mineralised, or re-exposed to produce a complex hardground

The term chalkstone was introduced by Bromley and Gale (1982) and refers to the lithified substrate beneath the hardground surface.

sediment accumulation rates. These factors did not have a uniform influence over the whole area. Thick sequences accumulated in basinal areas and incomplete or condensed sequences on adjacent swells, but through time these different areas of deposition are believed to have migrated in response to movements in the Palaeozoic basement. The Chalk sequence of this district is considered to reflect deposition on the margins of the London Platform swell.

Marl seams in some parts of the Chalk, particularly the Middle Chalk, appear unrelated to sedimentary rhythms and must therefore be regarded as episodic. Their origin is not clearly understood, Wray and Gale (1993) regard them as representing an increased supply of detrital material, at times of falling sea level. Some at least may, however, represent volcanic ash accumulations analogous to the contemporaneous tuffs identified in the north German Chalk succession. As yet this relationship with vulcanicity has not been unequivocably demonstrated in southern England.

There has been much argument over the depth of the 'Chalk Sea', with early estimates ranging from 250 m (Cayeux, 1897) up to 1280 m (Jukes Browne and Hill, 1904). More recent estimates based on hexactinellid sponge assemblages (Reid, 1973) suggest a range of 200–600 m: modern sponges are most abundant and faunally diverse between these depths. Shallow-water horizons such as the rhythmically b edded Chalk Marl and the winnowed Chalk Rock indicate that deposition took place in the photic mobile zone, perhaps in water depths as shallow as 50 m. Kennedy and Garrison (1975a) suggest a range of depth for the 'Chalk Sea' of between 50 and 300 m, but deeper estimates of 100–600 m are more generally accepted. It follows, therefore, that typical white chalk is neither a deep oceanic ooze nor a deposit of shallow water origin.

In general, relative sea level rose throughout the Upper Cretaceous, until a marked fall in the Maastrichtian (Hancock and Kauffman, 1979). However, short term, possibly isochronous reversals to this progression produced regionally correlatable changes in deposition. The maximum transgression in Campanian times probably only left the highest parts of the Welsh Massif above sea level.

The sea floor, by analogy to modern equivalents, is considered to have been soft and adaptions of the fauna, particularly amongst bivalves, lend support to this argument. At winnowed horizons, where the hard substrate became exposed, encrusting organisms such as oysters became common.

LOWER CHALK

The Lower Chalk crops out in a 2–6 km-wide belt across the north-west of the district, and is known from boreholes scattered over much of the remaining area. The subcrop beneath Hitchin is displaced 4 km south by the deep incision of the buried Hitchin Channel. To the west of the channel, the outcrop is mainly drift-free; to the east, about half is hidden by glacial and more recent drift. The Lower Chalk has been divided into five informal units as follows:

Plenus Marls up to about 2.1 m	alternations of marl and marly limestones, typically with a greenish yellow colouration
Grey Chalk 15–40 m	grey chalk with some marly chalk
Totternhoe Stone 0.3–6.0 m	hard, greyish brown, calcarenite and calcisiltite
Chalk Marl 15–35 m	rhythmically bedded, off-white to pale grey marly chalk, passing down into more clayey grey marl
Cambridge Greensand up to about 0.9 m	greenish grey, sandy, glauconitic and micaceous marl rich in phosphate nodules

Both the Cambridge Greensand, at the base of the Lower Chalk, and the Totternhoe Stone, a coarser member in the middle of the unit, are shown separately where possible on the 1:50 000 geological map. The harder, Totternhoe Stone forms a slight and intermittently mappable feature on the lower part of the Chalk escarpment. No attempt has been made to map the Plenus Marls, a thin member at the top of the Lower Chalk, immediately below the feature-forming Melbourn Rock.

The uncertainty regarding the thicknesses of the units reflects the paucity of reliable data, with few boreholes penetrating the whole of the Lower Chalk; the Cambridge Greensand has rarely been recognised, and the drillers logs usually fail to distinguish clearly the Chalk Marl from the Gault. Thus, the thickness of Gault may be exaggerated at the expense of the Chalk Marl. Where available, gamma-ray logs usually show a strong signal at the base of the Chalk, caused by the concentration of phosphatic nodules (Figure 7). Similarly, the hard marker band of the Totternhoe Stone, and sometimes even the Melbourn Rock, may not have been recognised, thus compounding the uncertainty. In the absence of borehole core, the best information comes from geophysical logs, of which there are a few in the district. From the available evidence it appears that, commonly, as the Lower Chalk thins so the Middle Chalk thickens (see Chapter 7).

Note on nomenclature

Before describing these units it is appropriate to discuss briefly the terminology in use. Jukes-Browne and Hill (1903) detailed the history of the subdivision of the Chalk and from their work in the Cambridge area found agreement with the three chronostratigraphical divisions then in use in France; the Lower Chalk equates with the French *Cenomanian* stage. The top of the Lower Chalk was defined by the Cenomanian–Turonian boundary between the *Belemnites plenus* Zone and the *Inoceramus labiatus* Zone, thereby placing it at a lower level than previous schemes. The glauconitic basement bed of the Lower Chalk, known as the Cambridge Greensand in the counties of Bedfordshire, Hertfordshire and Cambridgeshire, is equivalent to the Glauconitic Marl (formerly incorrectly named the 'Chloritic Marl') of the southern counties. The age of this bed was formerly a source of confusion for the term 'Greensand', originally intended for beds between the Chalk and Gault, came to be applied erroneously to beds below the Gault. This situation was clarified in part by the adoption of the terms 'Upper Greensand' and 'Lower Greensand', the former for the younger unit, now recognised in parts as a lateral facies of the Gault. In the vicinity of Cambridge the glauconitic bed then came to be referred to as the 'Upper Greensand of Cambridge' (Sollas, 1873a and b) or the 'Cambridge Upper Greensand' (Sollas and Jukes-Browne, 1873) in order to distinguish it from the older Upper Greensand at the top of the Gault. Jukes-Browne (1875) described the correct relationship of the bed, termed simply the 'Cambridge Greensand', as the basal bed of the Chalk Marl resting unconformably on the eroded top of the Gault. It has also been called the Phosphate-bed, Nodule-bed or Coprolite-bed because of its nodule concentrations.

The use of 'Grey Chalk' and 'Chalk Marl' for the Lower Chalk above and below the Totternhoe Stone was criticised by Jukes-Browne and Hill (1900, 1903), preferring instead zones of *Holaster subglobosus* and *Ammonites* [*Schloenbachia*] *varians* respectively. It was argued that Grey Chalk and Chalk Marl had previously been interchangeable terms; that the upper part of the Chalk Marl is, in fact, a grey chalk, and the Grey Chalk passes up into a white chalk. Nevertheless, these terms have a long Geological Survey usage because of their practical utility in mapping, for example in the neighbouring Biggleswade district (Edmonds and Dinham, 1965), and in the absence of an accepted formal alternative term for the Chilterns have been retained for this memoir. These lithostratigraphical names also conform to current Geological Survey practice, which avoids the use of fossil zones (chronostratigraphical terms) for mapping purposes.

The Plenus Marls were formerly known as the Belemnite Marls or Belemnite Bed.

It can also be noted here that Jukes-Browne and Hill (1903) provided extensive faunal lists for the *A. varians* Zone (Cambridge Greensand and Chalk Marl), the Totternhoe Stone, the Chalk above the Totternhoe Stone (Grey Chalk) and the *Actinocamax plenus* Subzone (Plenus Marls). The lists include sections at Arlesey, Hitchin and Ashwell (Plate 4) in this district.

Cambridge Greensand

The Cambridge Greensand is a thin bed of pale grey marl with concentrations of dark brown phosphatic nodules and dark green or black glauconite grains. The base is erosive and sharp but irregular due to burrowing of the underlying Gault. Regionally, the base rests on different beds of the Gault, because of an important stratigraphical break, but this is not apparent at any one site. Overall, it has a greenish grey colour and forms a distinctive basal bed to the Chalk Marl. It is an excellent example of a condensed deposit.

As it thickens eastwards into East Anglia, a basic two-fold division has been recognised (Morter and Wood, 1983) in which the lower part is glauconite and phosphate-rich and contains phosphatised *Aucellina*, while the upper part lacks phosphates and is rich in non-phosphatised *Aucellina*.

It commonly crops out at the foot of the Chalk scarp and, forming no feature itself, would be easily overlooked without detailed augering. Even then, it is commonly apparent only because of the widespread former 'coprolite' workings (see Chapter 8) which have turned the ground over, bringing unweathered glauconitic material nearer to the surface. Depending upon local topography and dip, these workings may extend over a width of several hundred metres, across which glauconitic marl is detectable. In such cases the Cambridge Greensand has been mapped along the lower limit of the disturbed ground. In the last century, the coprolite workings (Bonney, 1872; Fisher, 1873; Sollas, 1873b) provided excellent sections throughout the region for study and for the collection of fossils.

When seen exposed in a working face (Plate 2), the Cambridge Greensand forms an easily recognised marker at the base of the Chalk, separating the dark to medium grey calcareous Gault clay below from the pale grey clayey marls of the Lower Chalk above, but it is often overlooked in borehole logs. When fresh, the matrix is a paste-like, pale greenish grey marl of fine calcareous coccolithic material and clay. Abundant coarser grains consisting of glauconite with traces of quartz, heavy minerals and flakes of white mica (White and Edmunds, 1932) together with phosphate clasts make up the remainder of the deposit. Acid digestion of samples from Arlesey, after removing obvious phosphate, show the deposit is composed of 41 per cent fine mud, 32 per cent coarse material (mainly glauconite sand) with only about 27 per cent soluble carbonate (Jukes-Browne and Hill, 1903).

The glauconite occurs as black, dark grey and dark olive-green, cryptocrystalline grains of fine to medium grain size. Some are the casts of foraminifera (Sollas, 1876) and may themselves contain other smaller microfossil fragments. The grains occur disseminated or concentrated by currents into 'pods' or layers, especially in the lowest 0.1 m, where they become the major component giving a sandy texture and the 'greensand' name to the unit. The glauconite dies out within about 0.9 m of the base as the Cambridge Greensand passes into the Chalk Marl. The sharp base is commonly disturbed by faunal activity, with glauconitic material infilling burrows which extend down into the top metre of the Gault.

Phosphatic nodules are also concentrated into a basal lag, ranging from 0.05 to 0.3 m thick, just above the erosion surface; the lag is thickest in hollows in the Gault surface. One or two diffuse seams occur higher in the sequence, each a few centimetres thick. Commonly, the nodules are hard, 0.05–0.15 m long, and roughly cylindrical or irregular in shape. Two types have been recognised, 'black' and 'red' nodules, also referred to as dark and pale nodules (Hart, 1973b, fig. 1). The most numerous nodules, as seen at Arlesey and northwards, are nearly black or dark reddish brown, commonly with a paler core, and similar to ironstone in appearance. The pale ones, as seen around Shillington, are a buff or pinkish brown colour throughout. In the past, they were widely known as coprolites, but few are fossilised faeces. Most are not readily identifiable; some appear to be burrow infills and a few are recognisable as phosphatised fossil casts or moulds and include rare internal moulds of cephalopods. In the Glauconitic Marl of southern England, equivalent to the Cambridge Greensand, their origin has been described in detail (Kennedy and Garrison, 1975b) and appears to be similar to present day phosphorites accumulating in glauconitic sands (Jarvis, 1992). They have a complex history of development, with cycles of burial, exhumation and mineralisation. Briefly, Kennedy and Garrison (1975b) envisage the infilling of shells and subsequent burial followed by cementation of the filling and dissolution of the aragonitic shell material. These were then uncovered by erosion and exposed on the sea floor where they were phosphatised, maybe glauconitised, and subjected to boring and encrusting organisms. Later generations of shells passed through similar cycles and each time earlier moulds were further mineralised, rebored and re-encrusted, the repetitions accounting for the varying degrees of phosphatisation and abrasion. Clumps of nodules bound together by pale brown phosphatic material also occur. Earlier ideas that the nodules were originally scattered throughout a thick Gault clay and marl sequence from which the fine-grained sediments were winnowed by sea-floor currents leaving the residual nodules and sandy material to form the Cambridge Greensand (Jukes-Browne and Hill, 1900) can thus be regarded as an over-simplification.

The association of glauconite and phosphate in sediments has only recently begun to be understood as modern examples have been compared with older deposits (Notholt, 1980; Odin and LeTottle, 1980; Notholt and Jarvis, 1990).

The Cambridge Greensand contains a *remanié* fauna of phosphatised fossils characteristic of the higher Gault and Upper Greensand, and an indigenous calcareous fauna of Cenomanian age. Formerly there was much debate over the age of the Cambridge Greensand. It was once thought that the fossils in the dark waterworn nodules represented a derived fauna from the upper part of the Gault and those in the lighter, better preserved nodules were indigenous, but this is not always the case. Casey (in Edmonds and Dinham, 1965) discussed previous work on the phosphatised fauna and found only Upper Albian forms, but concluded, on non-palaeontological grounds (and with little justification), that the deposit was probably laid down in Cenomanian times. This assumed, early Cenomanian age has been questioned by Morter and Wood (1983) who argue that the Cambridge Greensand could range from the top of the *rostratum* Subzone to basal *carcitanense* Subzone. Wilkinson (1988a) argues that where a more complete

sequence is present, the Ostracoda indicate that the basal part can be assigned to the Upper Albian.

Fossils include cephalopods, brachiopods, bivalves, gastropods, crustacea, echinoderms, corals and sponges, together with fish teeth and scales, and teeth and bone fragments of birds and reptiles, nearly all mineralised with phosphate. They are commonly pitted by boring organisms or encrusted with *Atreta*. Fordham (1874) collected about forty invertebrate and eight vertebrate species from pits in the Ashwell and Morden areas just to the north of the district, noting their inferior preservation compared to the Cambridge collections. Work by Hart (1973a) on the Cambridge Greensand at Arlesey and at Barrington [393 510], near Cambridge, has described a foraminiferal assemblage, believed to be indigenous, of Early Cenomanian age. He also noted that the nodules are commonly encrusted with juvenile oyster spat only on their upper surface, suggesting that deposition after the sedimentary hiatus was rapid enough to preserve only the young forms, and that the nodules were affected by subsequent winnowing episodes. Wilkinson (1988a) described the Ostracoda from the Cambridge Greensand south-west of Cambridge.

The Cambridge Greensand has also yielded a sparse but varied collection of both well-rounded pebbles and angular stones (Seeley, 1866; Sollas and Jukes-Browne, 1873; Jukes-Browne and Hill, 1903; Hawkes, 1943). These include Palaeozoic sandstones, quartzite and limestone as well as igneous and metamorphic rocks such as granite, schist and gneiss. They are thought to have been deposited from floating tree roots, carried into the Cenomanian sea from land masses to the west. During this survey, a few well-rounded quartzite pebbles were noted at Arlesey, probably from this bed, though none were seen in place.

Chalk Marl

Chalk Marl is the informal name for that part of the Lower Chalk extending from the top of the Cambridge Greensand to a major erosion surface at the base of the Totternhoe Stone. At outcrop, it gives rise to long gentle slopes from low wide interfluves and occupies, by virtue of the gentle topography, the greater width of the Lower Chalk outcrop. It comprises rhythmically bedded alternations of more and less calcareous marly chalk and chalky marl.

There has been much recent work on the origin of such cyclicity in sediments (Hart, 1987). Gale (1989) has demonstrated that individual cycles, or rhythms (marl/limestone couplets) can be traced over extensive areas, which suggests basinwide control of sedimentation. This in turn points to climatic control and is commonly attributed to variation in the amount of solar radiation reaching the Earth as a result of changes in the Earth's orbit.

Each cycle, typically up to 1 m thick, comprises a thicker lower part of bioturbated grey clayey marl (silty calcareous mudstone) and a thin upper part of pale grey marly chalk (argillaceous limestone). The burrowed and eroded top of each limestone marks the base of the next cycle, but where erosion has removed the limestone individual cycles are not readily apparent. In general, the lower part of the Chalk Marl is soft, medium grey and passes up through a darker less calcareous marl into a monotonous, compact, pale grey, marly chalk.

On mapping evidence, the Chalk Marl appears to be 20–25 m thick, but it may range from 15 m to over 40 m; thicknesses of 50–75 m recorded in boreholes are probably incorrect. In areas where the Totternhoe Stone exhibits an expanded 'channel' sequence (see below), such as the Green Lagoon, up to 6 m of the upper part of the Chalk Marl are absent.

The Chalk Marl weathers to a grey-brown, marly soil, up to a metre thick in places. The soil is commonly almost pebble-free, but may be littered with flint and quartzite pebbles derived from the drift. The subsoil is usually weathered, soft, pale creamy brown marl resting on pale grey to greenish grey or off-white marl with minor ochreous staining. There may be small irregular patches of whiter more chalky material in places. Traces of fish scales and shell fragments are occasionally found in auger samples. Attempts to sample the lower part by augering, usually recover disturbed marls contaminated with glauconite from the extensive nodule workings.

There are few exposures of Chalk Marl; the lowest part has often been available for study in the brickpits at Arlesey. During this survey, the lowest 8.6 m were seen in the working pit, and the nearby Arlesey borehole, situated on undisturbed ground, proved over 14 m as the surface had not been stripped off (Figure 9). The disused, flooded pits known as the Green Lagoon [198 349] and Blue Lagoon [196 345] partially expose the top few metres of the Chalk Marl, beneath the Totternhoe Stone.

Samples collected at three different levels from former exposures at Arlesey show that the insoluble residues, which are almost all in the fine clay fraction, comprise 24–46 per cent of the whole rock; the highest values are found in the middle of the unit (Jukes-Browne and Hill, 1903). The few coarse grains comprise sponge spicules, glauconite, marcasite and quartz.

Recent work on the macrofaunas show that the Chalk Marl ranges from the Early Cenomanian *Mantelliceras mantelli* Zone, *Neostlingoceras carcitanense* Subzone, in the Arlesey brickpit and borehole, up to the *Mantelliceras dixoni* Zone, in the Green and Blue Lagoons (Woods, 1992a, c and d). This is supported by the microfaunas (Wilkinson, 1992a, 1993a and c) with foraminifera suggestive of foraminiferal zones 8 to 10 of Carter and Hart (1977).

Totternhoe Stone

The Totternhoe Stone attains its maximum development in Bedfordshire and Hertfordshire, thinning both northwards and southwards. It is a distinctive, hard, gritty, calcarenitic chalk, commonly producing a feature, and forms a mappable unit separating the Grey Chalk above from the Chalk Marl below. It is generally 1.5–3.0 m thick, and lies about 20–30 m below the top of the Lower Chalk. Exposures in this district suggest that it may range in thickness from 0.5 to 6.0 m, as it does in the type area

at Totternhoe to the west (Shephard-Thorn et al., 1994; Aldiss, 1990).

In some places the Totternhoe Stone is more resistant to erosion than the soft chalk above and below, and produces a positive feature on the generally long concave slopes of the Lower Chalk. Where no feature is discernible the deposit has been mapped on its surface 'brash' or rubble. The Totternhoe Stone may be marked by a weak spring line as it separates the less permeable Chalk Marl from the Grey Chalk. It is generally considered to be the lowest level in the Chalk from which useful groundwater supplies can be extracted.

In general, the Totternhoe Stone comprises a moderately hard pale brown (khaki) or greyish brown calcarenite composed largely of fine shell debris, which imparts an abrasive gritty texture to hand specimens. In places, a layer rich in rhynchonellid brachiopods has been noted. In expanded sequences the deposit is composed of interbeds of calcisiltites, calcarenites and minor calcilutites. During this survey, the general and expanded sequences were informally described by Hopson (1992) as 'shelf' and 'channel' facies. The 'channel' sequence is known to be at least 6 m thick at the Green Lagoon where there are few rhynchonellids present, but there is a well-developed basal bed containing green and brown-coated, phosphatic nodules. Jukes-Browne and Hill (1903) described the Totternhoe Stone at Hitchin as two beds, separated by a layer of marl.

In borehole logs, the Totternhoe Stone is commonly described as silty chalk, because of the included silt and very fine sand-sized material, and it may contain small dark brown reworked phosphatic pebbles. Under the microscope it consists mainly of prisms of inoceramid shell, ostracod valves and foraminiferal tests, with dark glauconite, and minor fine detrital mineral grains of quartz and mica. A sample from Arlesey (Jukes-Browne and Hill, 1903) had an 18 per cent insoluble residue on treatment with acid.

It was formerly quarried as a poor-quality building stone, particularly in those areas where it is thickest, and a few exposures remain. It is seen more commonly as a sparse and impersistent field 'brash', or as augered samples. It gives rise to a pale brownish grey, rather clayey, soil. The fragments of bedrock are usually distinctive, being harder, brownish in colour and slightly coarser than the adjacent 'smooth' fine-grained chalk. Brash is most common where the soil cover is thin on drift-free slopes or spurs.

Grey Chalk

Following the usage adopted by the British Geological Survey for the adjacent Biggleswade district (Edmonds and Dinham, 1965), the Grey Chalk is the informal name for the upper part of the Lower Chalk, extending from the top of the Totternhoe Stone to the base of the Plenus Marls. It forms part of the Chalk escarpment below the feature-forming Melbourn Rock.

The thickness of Grey Chalk may vary from 15 to 40 m, but as the Lower Chalk is poorly described in many boreholes the thickness is difficult to determine.

The Grey Chalk is a firm, massive, blocky chalk. It is off-white or very pale grey and marly in the lower part and passes rapidly up into a less marly paler and harder upper part, the first occurrence of 'true' white chalk in the sequence in the district. Hill and Jukes-Browne (1886) recognised that this hard white chalk is thicker in the Cambridge area, and is succeeded there by a softer marly chalk, thus suggesting to them that greater erosion of the top of the Grey Chalk may have taken place in the district. At Totternhoe, in the Leighton Buzzard district (Shephard-Thorn et al., 1994), there is a thin grey-green marl a few metres above the Totternhoe Stone. It is rich in pycnodonteine oysters and some crushed inoceramids, and rests locally on a burrowed hardground, which passes laterally into a hardground containing *Ornatothyris*. The grey-green marl has been correlated with the Pycnodonte Marl of Eastern England (Gaunt et al., 1992) and probably with the basal part of Jukes-Browne's Bed 7 at Folkestone (Shephard-Thorn, 1988). This marl has not been proved in the district, but C J Wood (personal communication, 1993) recorded a hardground at Grove Mill [191 310] in the 1950s.

The Grey Chalk gives rise to a thin, light, marly, pale brown soil with a soft white angular chalk brash.

There are now few well-exposed sections in the district, but it was formerly worked at the Grove Mill quarry [191 310] (Jukes-Browne and Hill, 1903), and presumably at the Cadwell Farm pit [189 327] which now shows only the Melbourn Rock and Plenus Marls.

Jukes-Browne and Hill (1903) found that the acid insoluble residue at Hitchin (probably at Grove Mill) decreases from 9.2 per cent to 3.6 per cent in two samples, 16.7 m and 1.8 m below the Plenus Marls respectively. This fine-grained residue comprises mainly the tests of arenaceous foraminifera or their debris, together with traces of quartz. Much of the calcareous material is more finely divided than in the Chalk Marl.

Plenus Marls

The Plenus Marls form a thin but laterally persistent unit of alternating marls and thin marly limestones at the top of the Lower Chalk and are named after the characteristic fossil belemnite *Actinocamax plenus*, which occurs in the higher part of the succession. They consist of distinctive, soft, greenish grey, yellowish or buff coloured, laminated marls and firm cream to white chalk. The marl and chalk is usually interbedded, but in places the marl appears brecciated, with chalk fragments in a marl matrix or within anastomosing marl layers. Early descriptions of the Plenus Marls (Hill and Jukes-Browne, 1886; Jukes-Browne and Hill, 1903) recognised an upper and lower marl separated by a chalk. This chalk, where it took on a brecciated appearance, was termed the 'marbled rock'. More recently Jefferies (1963), in a regional interpretation of the Plenus Marls, has described eight distinct beds (Jefferies' Beds 1–8 or J1–J8) with a number of intervening erosion surfaces. In this scheme, the intercalated chalk of Jukes-Browne and Hill (1903) corresponds to J3 which, in the Chilterns, and more particularly in sections between Royston and East

Anglia, is characteristically cemented or indurated, and comparable in lithology to the basal bed of the Melbourn Rock. It is for this reason that the Plenus Marls were included in the original concept of the Melbourn Rock. Jefferies (1963) noted the persistence of the marl bands and their association with underlying erosion surfaces. He envisaged turbulent water with an increased sediment supply from rivers, following a fall in sea level; the muddy deposits accumulated as the sea level rose again. The Plenus Marls were probably deposited at a time of low sedimentation when erosion was common. Jarvis et al. (1988) and Jeans et al. (1991) also discuss the sedimentology of the Plenus Marls.

The Plenus Marls are well developed in the district. Jefferies (1963) has demonstrated a thickening along the outcrop from Swindon towards the Wash with a maximum of nearly 2.0 m at Melbourn, just to the northeast of the district; within the district they are generally about 0.5–1.8 m thick. He regarded this thickening as typical of the Turonian pattern of deposition rather than of Cenomanian deposition. However, the Cenomanian/Turonian boundary is now considered to be situated within the overlying Melbourn Rock.

The Plenus Marls occur throughout the district below the Melbourn Rock. They are rarely recognisable at the surface and have not been depicted on the geological map of the district. In boreholes they are commonly overlooked but may be recorded as grey, yellow or green marl; they are, however, readily identifiable by their strong response on geophysical logs.

The macrofauna is abundant and highly diverse compared with the underlying Lower and Middle Chalk forms. *Actinocamax plenus*, the former index fossil, is itself restricted to the higher part of the Plenus Marls.

The base of the Plenus Marls is usually marked by a burrowed erosion surface. This sub-*plenus* erosion surface has been inferred (Hill and Jukes-Browne, 1886) to cut out a varying thickness of the underlying *Calycoceras guerangeri* Zone chalk within the Chilterns, but the evidence for this is tenuous and cannot be readily substantiated.

Acid insoluble residues in samples from Hitchin varied from 19.1 per cent in the marl to 3.4 per cent in the chalk (Jukes-Browne and Hill, 1903) and comprised mainly the debris from arenaceous foraminifera with traces of quartz and orthoclase.

Details

In the following text the major exposures and boreholes sections, especially those which display more than one of the five informal rock units, are described first. Additional details are provided for each unit where appropriate.

Arlesey Brickpit [188 347] and Borehole

Arlesey Brickpit has attracted researchers over a long period. Jukes-Brown and Hill (1903) provided extensive lists of Lower Chalk fossils found at Arlesey and Hitchin but did not differentiate those found in the Cambridge Greensand from the Chalk Marl. Bloom and Harper (1938) recorded both derived fossils, the bivalve '*Inoceramus*' *concentricus* and *Belemnites minimus* and the 'indigenous' fossil *Dimyodon nilssoni* attached to the phosphatic nodules from the Cambridge Greensand (Plate 2).

The pit provides the largest exposure of the Cambridge Greensand in the district and, more importantly, an undisturbed one. It forms a consistent bed resting on the burrowed top of the Gault (see Chapter 3). The sharp basal contact seen throughout most of the exposure becomes diffuse where burrowing is intense. Phosphatic nodules are found throughout the full thickness of the bed but are concentrated at the base and in a second well-marked bed 0.39 m above the base. The basal 0.5 m of the Chalk Marl contains some glauconite and phosphatic nodules, probably reworked from this bed.

At the time of survey, the Arlesey pit [188 347] exposures, over 350 m along the eastern and southern faces, revealed an excellent section across the Chalk–Gault junction.

Plate 2 The Cambridge Greensand exposed on the eastern face of Arlesey brickpit [1878 3477]. (GS 72A)

The Gault is evident as a darker grey tone in the bottom right of the photograph below an uneven but sharp contact with the speckled (glauconite) pale greenish grey, burrowed sandy marl of the Cambridge Greensand. Two layers of phosphatic nodules occur at and slightly above the base. Hammer 0.30 m.

	Thickness m
LOWER CHALK:	
CHALK MARL	
Chalk, marly, alternating soft, dark grey and hard, pale grey beds	c.8.6
CAMBRIDGE GREENSAND	
Chalk, marly, pale greenish grey, with glauconite sand and phosphatic nodules	c.0.5–0.7
UPPER GAULT:	
Clay, stiff, grey, silty, with beds of phosphatic nodules; burrowed and sandy in top 0.6 m	seen to c.15.0

The sequence from Arlesey pit (Figure 9) compares closely with that seen in the Arlesey borehole (see also Figure 7). The northern part of the pit is now a landfill site.

The Cambridge Greensand was also recorded, between 14.38 and 15.45 m depth, in the nearby Arlesey Borehole. The microfauna (Wilkinson, 1992a) confirmed the earlier findings of Hart (1973b). Specimens reworked from the Gault are common. The benthonic foraminifera *Arenobulimina anglica, A. advena* and *Flourensina intermedia* indicate an early Cenomanian age (foraminiferal zone 8, ammonite *Neostlingoceras carcitanense* Subzone). The ostracods *Cytherelloidea globosa* and several species of *Bythoceratina* support this interpretation.

The macrofossils in both the borehole and the section were examined by Woods (1992a and d). Some were preserved as shelly material, but most were heavily phosphatised and abraded, reflecting a period of mineralisation and sediment winnowing preceding deposition. The fauna comprised: a sponge; scaphopods; brachiopods, including various species of *Moutonithyris* and terebratulids; bivalves, dominated by *Aucellina* sp including *A. gryphaeoides*; gastropods; cephalopods, including *Neohibolites* sp and *N.* cf. *praeultimus*; vertebrate teeth and bone fragments. Some of the *Aucellina* specimens had a striate umbonal region of the type regarded as diagnostic of the lower part of the bipartite Cambridge Greensand recognised by Morter and Wood (1983). The presence of *Neohibolites* forms similar to *N. praeultimus*, which in Germany appears to be wholly Albian (Spaeth, 1971), suggests that the age of the deposit could possibly range from the high Upper Albian rather than the conventionally accepted early Cenomanian.

Grove Mill

Parts of the Middle and Lower Chalk were formerly exposed (Jukes-Browne and Hill, 1903) at the Grove Mill quarry [191 310] to the north-east of Hitchin, but wrongly located by Jukes-Browne to the south-east. A modified log of the section based on notes made by C J Wood (personal communication, 1993) in the 1950s is given below:

	Thickness m
Soil and rubble	0.30
MIDDLE CHALK:	
MELBOURN ROCK (base of)	
Chalk, hard, rough, white	0.61
LOWER CHALK:	
PLENUS MARLS	
Marl, buff, laminated; irregularly interbedded with lenticular courses of hard whitish chalk (?J4–8)	0.38
Chalk, hard, smooth, white (?J3)	0.56
Marl, grey laminated (?J1–2)	0.10

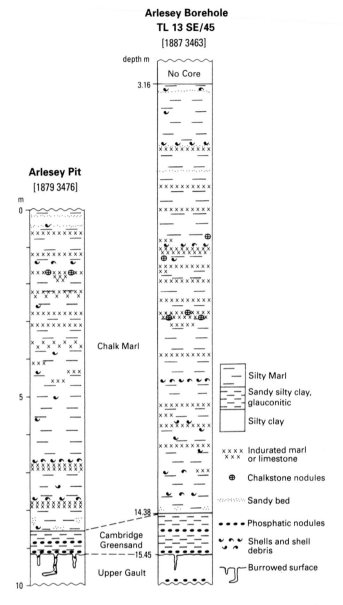

Figure 9 The Chalk Marl and Cambridge Greensand succession in the Arlesey brickpit and borehole.

GREY CHALK (Zone of *C. guerangeri*)

Chalk, smooth, blocky, greyish white	0.46
Marl, thin	0.08
Chalk, thick bedded, whitish	7.62
Chalk, thick bedded, pale grey	4.57

When this section was recorded in the 1950s, C J Wood (personal communication, 1993) noted a hardground, probably representing the *A. jukesbrownei* event in the Grey Chalk, about 6 m below the Plenus Marls. Fossils collected from this bed included *Monticlarella* sp. nov., *Ornatothyris sulcifera* and a radiole of *Hirudocidaris hirudo*. He also collected a specimen of *A. plenus*, (probably from J4) and a thin tested echinoid from the underlying *guerangeri* Zone.

Wellhead Borehole [1770 2770]

This borehole (overseen by BGS as part of a project to investigate the buried valley of the River Hiz near Hitchin) for the

NRA (Anglian Region) provided samples and a gamma-ray log for part of the Middle and Lower Chalk.

In Wellhead Borehole (Appendix 1), the Plenus Marls show a typical high gamma-ray log spike at about 4.2–5.3 m depth, suggesting that the marl recorded at 5.6–6.3 m depth could form part of the Grey Chalk rather than lowest part of an abnormally thick Plenus Marls. They appear to be similar to those seen in an exposure near Hitchin railway station [1934 2970] where hard chalkstones occur in the Plenus Marls. The Totternhoe Stone coincides with a low on the gamma-ray log. The marl at 21.2 m depth may correspond to the Nettleton Pycnodonte Marl, recorded at a similar stratigraphical position in the Totternhoe area (Aldiss, 1990).

An equivalent to the mineralised hardground recorded at about 6 m below the Plenus Marls at the Grove Mill Quarry may equate with that 8 m below them in this borehole, where there are spikes on the gamma-ray log. The hardground at Grove Mill can be correlated with the *A. jukesbrownei* Zone event or, alternatively, it may lie within the succeeding *C. guerangeri* Zone. If the *A. jukesbrownei* Zone event is marked by one of the spikes, rather than the lower marl, then its relative stratigraphical position is akin to the situation in East Anglia, Lincolnshire and Yorkshire, rather than at Totternhoe (Wood, personal communication, 1993).

Green Lagoon [1978 3486] and Blue Lagoon [1978 3444], Arlesey (Green Lagoon is the type locality of 'Aequipecten' arlesiensis)

Exposures in a pit, thought to be the Green Lagoon [198 348], south-west of Fairfield Hospital (then the county lunatic asylum), were recorded in 1884 by Jukes-Browne and Hill (1903) who demonstrated the degree of downcutting below the Totternhoe Stone. The section is given in modified form below and can be compared with the modern section shown in Figure 10.

	Thickness
	m
Soil and chalk rubble	0.91

LOWER CHALK:

TOTTERNHOE STONE

Stone, hard, brownish grey, thickly bedded with many fossils	3.05
Chalk, grey, marly, including a bed of very soft marl	1.83
Stone, very hard, sandy, with green-coated phosphatic nodules as large as walnuts	0.46

CHALK MARL

Chalk, soft, grey, sandy, passing into soft grey marl	1.98

Subsequent excavations during 1886 and 1887 showed that the base of the Totternhoe Stone was inclined at 7° towards the north-west along a 100 m section; soft grey marl beneath the Totternhoe Stone resting on a level surface of pale bluish marl, thinned northwards from 6.1 to 2.1 m. This provided clear evidence for erosion of the grey marl before deposition of a thick 'channel' sequence of Totternhoe Stone.

During this survey, the exposures of Totternhoe Stone in the Green Lagoon and Blue Lagoon (Plate 3) were re-exposed, logged and sampled for macrofaunal and microfaunal analysis. Graphic lithological logs are given in Figure 10.

The macrofaunal collection from the Totternhoe Stone at the Green Lagoon (Woods, 1992c) contains many shell fragments but relatively few whole specimens, most of which are juvenile forms. Some are darkened by incipient phosphatisation and glauconitisation, particularly the internal moulds, and

Figure 10 The Totternhoe Stone succession in the Green and Blue Lagoons, Arlesey [1978 3486 and 1978 3444 respectively].

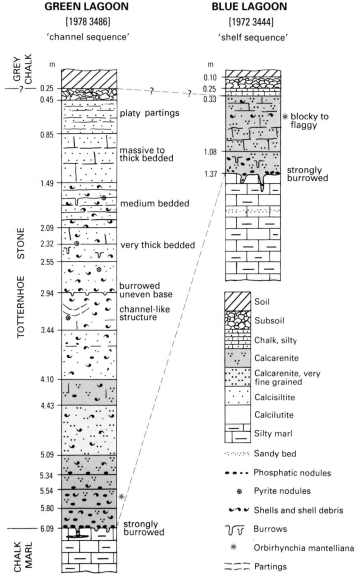

some show signs of abrasion and surface borings. The phosphatic pebble content increases towards the base of the arenitic beds where an associated increase in pycnodonteine oysters is found; the oysters commonly encrust the phosphatic clasts. These characteristics indicate reworking of the fossils, possibly with cycles of deposition, erosion and mineralisation similar to those in the Cambridge Greensand, albeit less well developed. The fauna is dominated by bivalves, particularly *Entolium* and *Oxytoma*, with some brachiopods, worms, sponges, fish, crustaceans and echinoids. The presence of '*Aequipecten*' *arlesiensis* at one horizon in the Green Lagoon section indicates that the 'channel facies' of the Totternhoe Stone incorporates material from a band equivalent to the dark fossiliferous marl seen beneath a massive prominent limestone at Folkestone (Gale, 1989, fig. 3). According to Woods (1992c) the fauna is comparable with that found at levels in the Middle Cenomanian *Acanthoceras rhotomagense* Zone of the Chalk Marl at Folkestone, probably the *Turrilites costatus* Subzone. Certain macrofossils appear to be reworked, and this faunal mixing could have continued into the early *T. acutus* Subzone. The Blue Lagoon has a thinner exposure of Totternhoe Stone (though the top in both exposures is rather ill defined) of similar age to that in the Green Lagoon (Woods, 1992c). Differences, such as the restriction of *Entolium* to one bed in the Blue Lagoon, may reflect differing conditions of deposition at the two localities. The microfauna (Wilkinson, 1993a and c) is dominated by the foraminifera *Arenobulimina anglica*, *A. advena*, *Pseudotexulariella cretosa*, *Lenticulina* sp. and *Marssonella trochus*. Together with rare occurrences of *Rotalipora reicheli*, these are suggestive of benthonic foraminiferal zone 11i of Carter and Hart (1977) in agreement with macrofossil *T. costatus* Subzone.

The thicker sequences of the Totternhoe Stone, also well displayed in the type area at Totternhoe (Aldiss, 1990), infill channels cut into the Chalk Marl, and contain a fauna derived partly from those eroded beds, possibly from progressively deeper erosion of a Chalk Marl 'shelf'. Well-developed *Thalassinoides* burrows occur at the base of the infill at the Green Lagoon. Complete specimens of the delicate bivalve *Entolium* occur in the higher part of the Green Lagoon succession, almost to the exclusion of other species.

Dallow Road Boreholes, Luton

Samples and geophysical logs from three boreholes (TL02SE/239–241) at a site less than 5 km to the west of the district, were made available by Laporte Industries Ltd after the memoir for the Leighton Buzzard district had gone to press. The core from one borehole, TL02SE/240 [0641 2208], was described by P M Hopson and the macrofossils were examined by M A Woods (1992f). A summary graphic log is given in Figure 11 for comparison with the sequences in the district. Coring commenced in the Middle Chalk, about 28.4 m above the Melbourn Rock, and proved Lower Chalk, terminating in the Chalk Marl at a depth of 76.7 m.

The macrofossil evidence (Woods, 1992f) can be summarised thus:

	Thickness m	Depth m
MIDDLE CHALK:		
Not cored	8.98	8.98
Unnamed unit: Turonian, *Mytiloides* spp. Zone s.l.	19.46	28.40
Melbourn Rock: Upper Cenomanian/ Turonian, *Mytiloides* spp. Zone s.l.	4.74	33.18
LOWER CHALK:		
Plenus Marls: Upper Cenomanian, *Metoicoceras geslinianum* Zone	0.94	34.15
Grey Chalk: Upper Cenomanian, *Calycoceras guerangeri* Zone	10.08	44.20
Grey Chalk: Middle Cenomanian, *A. rhotomagense* Zone (? *T. acutus* Subzone), ? *A. jukesbrownei* Zone and ? Upper Cenomanian, *Calycoceras guerangeri* Zone	9.66	53.86
Totternhoe Stone: Middle Cenomanian, *Acanthoceras rhotomagense* Zone, *Turrilites costatus* Subzone (with faunal reworking? in the latest *T. costatus* and early *T. acutus* Subzones	3.49	57.35

Plate 3 The Blue Lagoon, near Arlesey. (GS 72D)
View looking south-east along the face from [1980 3440] showing a typical development of the 'shelf' facies of the Totternhoe Stone. The harder prominent calcarenitic Totternhoe Stone is only c.1.0 m thick here (see scale bar and Figure 10). The top of the 'shelf' facies is indicated by M A Woods, the base is at waist height.

	Thickness m	Depth m
Chalk Marl: Lower Cenomanian, *Mantelliceras dixoni* Zone	19.40	76.75

The calcareous microfaunas, principally the foraminifera but with ostracods from selected horizons, were also examined (Wilkinson, 1993d).

The gamma-ray log shows a gradual increase in response with depth as the rock becomes more clayey, a small spike corresponding to the Plenus Marls. The resistivity log gives a large response at the Totternhoe Stone level.

CAMBRIDGE GREENSAND

Shillington–Lower Stondon

To the north-east of Shillington, the Cambridge Greensand has been traced by augering along an intricate outcrop, produced by the interaction of gentle folding, or contorted strata, with the moderate relief. The bed varies in elevation between about 60 and 75 m above OD, a much larger range than the gentle south-easterly regional dip would allow. To the east, it crops out more predictably, falling gradually from about 65 to 60 m above OD as it is traced eastwards, as a 30 m-wide outcrop, along the foot of the Chalk slope to the north of Lower Stondon before disappearing under till [158 356]. The zone worked for phosphates is about 50 to 70 m wide hereabouts.

Farther south, to the east of Lower Stondon, a small valley-bottom inlier of Gault, less than 200 m long and 60 m wide, is surrounded by disturbed Cambridge Greensand which was exposed in a recently cleaned-out ditch section [1584 3487 and 1581 3510] as 0.4–0.6 m of greenish grey marl with glauconitic sand and phosphatic nodules. Nearby, the Cambridge Greensand appears to have been worked, away from the ditch, over a 150 m wide zone.

Hitchin Channel

The Cambridge Greensand probably subcrops for 5–6 km from Lower Stondon and Arlesey to Hitchin along the western and eastern sides of the buried channel (Chapter 6). Other subcrops may occur farther south around the conjectural Gault subcrops, but the Cambridge Greensand has not been recorded in boreholes in that area.

Arlesey–Stotfold

To the west of Arlesey [181 362 and 182 358], Cambridge Greensand has been worked through two thin outliers of Lower Chalk, one with possible till cover, where the ground is much disturbed and the mapped boundaries particularly uncertain.

To the east of the River Hiz, the Cambridge Greensand can be traced from the brickpit in Arlesey [188 347] north to Church End and thence east-north-eastwards to the district margin north of Stotfold. Much of it crops out, or originally cropped out, beneath thin spreads of sand and gravel, traces of which can be found at depth where the ground has been turned over.

Concealed occurrences

The Cambridge Greensand has been recorded in only a few of the boreholes which have penetrated the Chalk–Gault junction. This is probably due to the poor logging of percussion drilled boreholes rather than the absence of the bed. A few examples are given below.

In Pirton Pumping Station Borehole, 0.15 m of dark sand was recorded below 30.0 m of Chalk Marl. Resting on Gault, this is probably the basal glauconitic sand layer of the Cambridge Greensand. At Stotfold, the Cambridge Greensand can be identified in the log of a shallow, former well shaft, near St Mary's Church [221 366] which records 7.6 m of 'soft clunch with coprolites at base' resting on 'blue clay'. At the Mill Borehole, Radwell, 0.3 m of 'coprolites and greensand' were recorded at 19.2 m depth. A similar thickness of Cambridge Greensand, with no description of its lithology, occurs in Newnham Hall Borehole. In the Bygrave Plantation Borehole, 0.8 m of greensand were recorded at a depth of 89.3 m.

CHALK MARL

In the west, the Chalk Marl occupies a large area of low ground between about 50–90 m above OD around Shillington and Pirton, extending north to Lower Stondon and south-east to

Figure 11
Graphic log of
the Chalk
sequence in the
Dallow Road
Borehole [0641
2208].

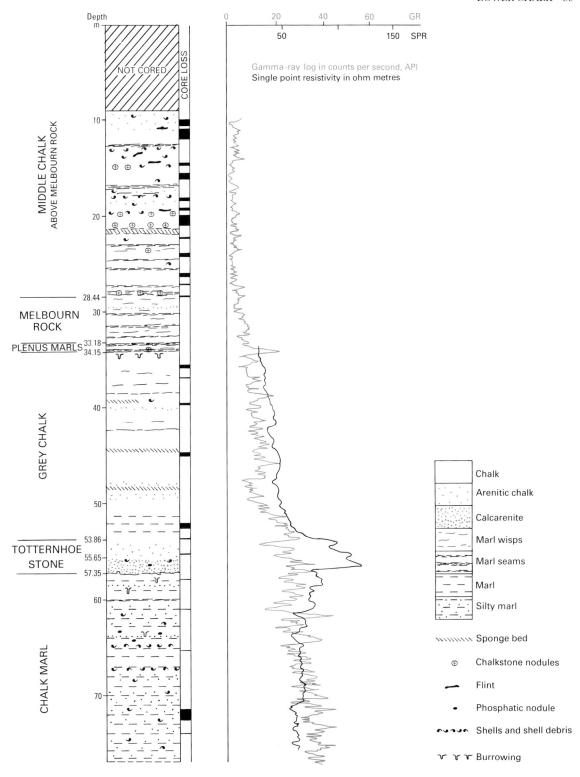

Hitchin. It probably underlies much of Hitchin, beneath thick drift within the buried channel. To the east, the outcrop is typically 2 km wide and lies at about 40–65 m above OD; it runs north-eastwards from Ickleford through Arlesey to Stotfold and Newnham.

The middle part of the Chalk Marl is not well known, as it is seen only in temporary excavations and cleaned out ditches, or as weathered samples recovered by augering.

Borehole records, particularly those from shallow site investigations, may provide useful details of lithological and geotechnical properties. For example, trial boreholes along the line of the proposed Stotfold bypass sampled much of the Chalk Marl. Descriptions given below for a borehole off Norton Road, Stotfold [2215 3617] are typical of these, though the use here of 'clay' for what is probably a marly chalk show the need for caution in interpretation:

	Thickness m	Depth m
SOIL	0.3	0.3

LOWER CHALK:

CHALK MARL

Clay, light grey mottled greyish brown, calcareous, silty, firm	0.2	0.5
Clay, light grey mottled greyish brown and orange brown, calcareous, very silty, stiff, closely fissured. Many roots and fine, white carbonate veins	1.3	1.8
Clay, light grey mottled greyish brown and orange brown, calcareous, very silty, thinly laminated, closely fissured	2.0	3.8
Clay, light grey mottled orange brown, calcareous, very silty, very stiff, thinly laminated, closely fissured	3.0	6.8
Clay, grey, calcareous, thickly laminated, very silty, very stiff, closely fissured	seen to 8.2	15.0

Deeper boreholes for water may have little more than an outline log, in which the Chalk Marl is described as chalk, chalk marl, marl or clay, making it difficult to differentiate the unit. For example, the Pirton Pumping Station Borehole, which commenced about 9 m below the Totternhoe Stone, records 30.0 m of Chalk Marl with Cambridge Greensand at the base.

Letchworth

In the Letchworth area, the William Road Borehole proved the full thickness (61.3 m) of Lower Chalk but only a skeletal log is recorded:

	Thickness m	Depth m
Loamy soil	0.30	0.30

MIDDLE CHALK:

Chalk	3.66	3.96
Chalk and flints	0.61	4.57
Chalk	22.86	27.43
Chalk (lumpy) ?Melbourn Rock	1.52	28.95
Chalk, grey, hard. Melbourn Rock	1.53	30.48

LOWER CHALK:

Chalk, putty (soft)	27.43	57.91
Chalk, grey (hard)	33.83	91.74

GAULT	14.94	106.68

Hitchin

Although several boreholes penetrated the Lower Chalk near Hitchin, probably only one of these proved its base. In the Hitchin Brewery Borehole, 46 m of 'whitish marl' and 'light-coloured clay' above the Gault were classified as Lower Chalk (Whitaker, 1872). Two boreholes west of Oughton Head, [1890 2980] and [1591 2982], commencing 10 m below the Melbourn Rock, recorded about 38 m of 'chalk' on 'blue clay' previously assigned to the Gault, implying a total thickness for the Lower Chalk of only 48 m. It is more likely that the 'blue clay' is part of the Chalk Marl.

TOTTERNHOE STONE

The Totternhoe Stone has been traced across the north-western part of the district. It forms an outcrop 20–50 m wide,

near the foot of the Chalk escarpment, generally at heights of 50 to 95 m above OD. Near Pirton, it is seen in an overgrown and partially backfilled, 8–10 m-deep pit [158 326]. The poor exposure shows brownish grey to brown, very silty, fine sandy, chalk with burrows and ochreous staining on the south-east side. When ploughed, the adjacent field is littered with Totternhoe Stone brash, reportedly the spoil from stone extraction in the late 1940s to repair bomb damage to Pirton church. The depth of the pit, and the blocky nature of the cobble-sized brash, suggest that here the stone was extracted from a thick 'channel' sequence.

Nearby field brash indicates the presence of the thinner 'shelf' facies of the Totternhoe Stone, along an almost imperceptible feature, such as west of New Wrights Farm [154 325] and north of the Icknield Way near Punch's Cross [154 305].

Totternhoe Stone subcrops under drift in the Hitchin Channel, but it has rarely been recognised in boreholes. It is inferred to be about 30 m below the base of the Melbourn Rock.

To the east of the channel it is exposed in a small pit 120 m west of Cadwell Crossing [187 317]:

	Thickness m
TILL	
Clay, yellowish brown, stony, silty, chalky	0.6
LOWER CHALK:	
Chalk, white	0.8
TOTTERNHOE STONE	
Chalk, soft, pale yellowish brown, silty, with darker brown burrows	1.6

South of Cadwell Farm, brash of the Totternhoe Stone is seen in a depression, possibly a former pit, above a spring-fed watercress bed at [192 321]. To the north of the farm [188 326 to 192 330], minor faults with throws of about 5 m can be recognised, from their effects on the outcrop pattern. Overgrown watercress beds here [188 326] show limited exposures of off-white to brownish grey, firm to hard blocky, burrowed and shelly silty chalk. It can be traced northwards by its intermittent arenitic brash which is best seen at about 55 m above OD, on a valley spur [196 337], as a wide expanse of very hard, silty, sandy chalk rubble with included phosphatic and marcasite nodules. It is exposed in the disused quarries of the Green and Blue Lagoons to the west of Letchworth (see above).

GREY CHALK

The Grey Chalk outcrop forms a narrow belt west of the buried Hitchin Channel, with the exception of two small outliers around Pirton. Within the buried channel the subcrop has been proved in places by boreholes. To the east of the Hitchin Channel the outcrop broadens but is concealed by drift in many places.

In the Holwell area, the thickness of the Grey Chalk is estimated at about 15 m, from mapping.

The former exposure at Grove Mill has been described above. At Cadwell Farm [1889 3274], a roadside pit, described below (Figure 12), now has only 0.7 m of Grey Chalk exposed beneath the Plenus Marls. The foraminiferal assemblage (Wilkinson, 1993b) contains planktonic forms such as *Dicarinella hagni*, *Rotalipora greenhornensis*, *R. cushmani* and *Praeglobotruncana stephani* as well as *Hedbergella brittonensis*. Benthonic forms include *Arenobulimina advena*, *Gavelinella intermedia* and *G. baltica*. Together, these confirm a late Cenomanian age of this chalk, probably in the upper part of benthonic Zone 13 (Carter and Hart, 1977) or UKB7 (Hart et al., 1989).

A borehole near Radwell off the old A1 road [2337 3636], in Grey Chalk, may have penetrated the Totternhoe Stone at its base:

	Thickness m	Depth m
SOIL	0.3	0.3
LOWER CHALK:		
Chalk, soft, clayey at top, passing down into medium hard, greyish white chalk, with ironstaining on joints	9.7	10.0
Chalk, medium hard, yellowish grey-white with ironstaining on horizontal surfaces	2.9	12.9
Chalk, hard, dark grey, passing down into greyish white, massive chalk	seen to 4.0	16.9

The upper part of the Lower Chalk was sampled in two recent percussion boreholes on the industrial park between Letchworth and Baldock. These uncored boreholes produced relatively poor samples but a number of marker beds were identified in hand specimen and from geophysical logs. Both boreholes commenced above the Melbourn Rock, in the Middle Chalk, and proved Plenus Marls above Grey Chalk and Totternhoe Stone. Up to 30.5 m of Grey Chalk was proved in the borehole off Avenue One (Letchworth Obs. 1) [2318 3299]:

	Thickness m	Depth m
Made Ground	4.80	4.80
MIDDLE CHALK:		
Chalk, white, very shelly, becoming hard and non-shelly below 12.00 m	12.20	17.00
MELBOURN ROCK	2.00	19.00
LOWER CHALK:		
GREY CHALK Chalk, off-white, soft to firm, very fractured, with sponge remains and very hard chalks. Becoming off-white to pale grey, marly chalk with more common marl seams at depth	30.00	49.00
TOTTERNHOE STONE Chalk, firm to hard, pale greyish brown, silty chalk, with rare shells	2.00	51.00
CHALK MARL Marly chalk, soft to firm, greyish brown	6.00	57.00

A major marl seam in the Grey Chalk at 35.8 m depth is overlain by extremely hard silty chalk with shell fragments which may be correlated with the Jukes-Browne Bed 7.

Temple End water supply borehole near Hitchin [1723 2760] proved 4.8 m of chalk rubble, classified as the Middle Chalk, and then 39.6 m of Lower Chalk. The Lower Chalk consists of 30.2 m of 'chalk with layers of hard chalk', underlain by 0.9 m of 'very hard chalk or upper greensand' which is tentatively interpreted here as the Totternhoe Stone. This passes down into 8.5 m of 'chalk marl, becoming clayey and dark in colour'. The identification of Totternhoe Stone in borehole samples can be difficult and its recorded position in this and other borehole logs should be treated with some caution.

The Offley Bottom Borehole [1607 2886], commencing 2 m below the Melbourn Rock, proved 46 m of Lower Chalk. In downward succession it passed through 25.2 m of 'chalk varying in hardness', 2.1 m of 'fractured crumbly chalk' (probably the Totternhoe Stone) and 17.7 m of 'light grey chalk marl becoming darker with depth'.

In the Wain Wood Borehole [1832 2555] the base of the Middle Chalk at 63.7 m depth, as indicated by gamma-ray and resistivity logs, cannot be correlated with changes in hardness recorded in the brief lithological log. These geophysical logs also indicate the top of the Chalk Marl at 88.7 m, giving a combined thickness of 25 m for the Grey Chalk and Totternhoe Stone.

At least 33.5 m of the Lower Chalk were penetrated in the Wymondley Bury Borehole [2213 2712]. The lithological log records 'chalk marl', 'hard chalk (Totternhoe Stone?)', and 'grey chalky marl'; the resistivity and gamma-ray logs suggest that the base of the Middle Chalk is at 61.5 m depth and confirm that the borehole passed through the Grey Chalk into the top of the Chalk Marl, but the Totternhoe Stone cannot be identified with certainty.

In Ashwell (Plate 4), just outside the district, a disused quarry [2697 3945], which has been partly backfilled, has a well-

Plate 4   Ashwell quarry [2687 3945]. (GS 70M)

The junction of the Plenus Marls and the Melbourn Rock (see also Figures 12 and 13). The brightly coloured Bed 6 of Jefferies (1963) is the prominent bed (marked B) in the lower middle of the photograph. The junction with the overlying Melbourn Rock is shown by the arrow (A) below the hard nodular chalk. Ruler 1.0 m.

exposed section of Melbourn Rock described in detail below (Figure 13). At the base, 0.7 m of massive, soft, white, jointed chalk with a few marly pockets and wisps yields sparse fish scales and inoceramid shell fragments form the top of the Grey Chalk just beneath the Plenus Marls. Jukes-Browne and Hill (1903) described a thicker section, possibly from this quarry, with over 11 m of Lower Chalk consisting mainly of whitish blocky chalk overlain by softer greenish chalk.

PLENUS MARLS

The Plenus Marls crop out across the north-western part of the district immediately beneath the Melbourn Rock, but are only rarely exposed.

Cadwell

A small roadside pit [1889 3274], 350 m north of Cadwell Farm and east of the main railway line, exposes 1.77 m of the Plenus Marls, the thickest sequence seen in the district, as well as most of the overlying Melbourn Rock (Figure 12). This lies within a fault-bounded block and the section is intensely faulted and weathered, enhancing the rubbly appearance of the Melbourn Rock. Minor flexures disturb the marl seams. The Plenus Marls, 1.37 m thick, were formerly exposed during widening of the Great Northern Railway cutting at Cadwell (Hill and Jukes-

Browne, 1886). This may refer to nearby sidings on the opposite side of the road. Here the compact white chalk (?J3) was replaced by 'marbled rock', greyish in colour with patches of white, containing abundant broken shells. These included the following fossils (names revised to current usage): *Terebratula semiglobosa*, *T. biplicata* [presumably *Ornatothyris* spp.], *Rhynchonella plicatilis* [*Orbirhynchia multicostata*], *Ostrea vesicularis* [*Pycnodonte*] and *Belemnitella plena* [*Actinocamax plenus*]. According to Wood (1993) this fauna is a mixed *remanié* accumulation of elements from both the lower (*O. multicostata*, *Pycnodonte*) and higher (*A. plenus*) faunal assemblages of the Plenus Marls. The anomalous occurrence, in sections at Hitchin and localities to the north-east, of terebratulids may represent a local development of a shallow-water-facies fauna, such as that found associated with the *jukesbrownei* event at Totternhoe Quarry (Shephard-Thorn et al., 1994) and at the base of the former Grove Mill Quarry. At this locality the normal thickness proportions of the Plenus Marls are reversed with the 'upper marl' (?J4–8) being thicker than beds J1–3 inclusive. A former quarry west of Wilbury Hill, the site of which is also uncertain, showed 1.06 m of Plenus Marls (Jukes-Browne and Hill, 1903).

Norton

A small overgrown and degraded pit [2344 3482], south of Norton Bury, has small exposures of hard to very hard, blocky

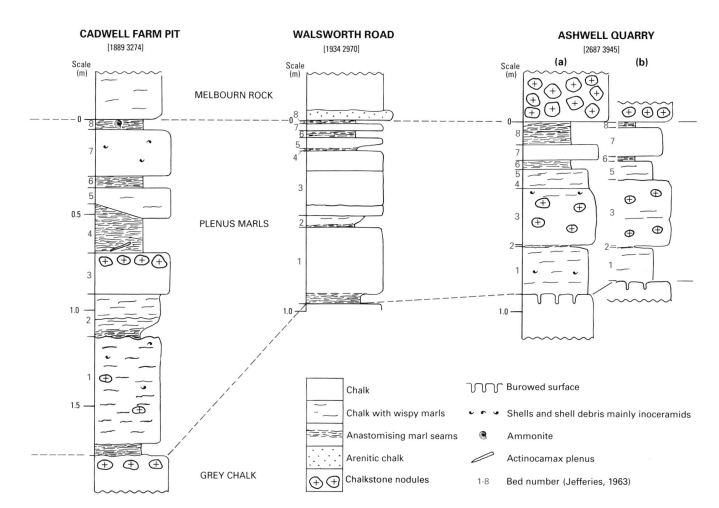

Figure 12 The Plenus Marls exposures at Cadwell Farm, at Walsworth Road (Hitchin) and Ashwell Quarry showing the Jefferies (1963) Bed numbers.

fractured chalk of the Melbourn Rock overlying soft, pale yellow, faintly laminated, marly chalk of the Plenus Marls.

Hitchin

To the south of Pirton Road [1717 2875], west of Hitchin, Plenus Marls were seen unusually as field brash on the steep slope. A temporary excavation [1934 2970] at Walsworth Road, near Hitchin Station, revealed 0.96 m of Plenus Marls (Figure 12). Bed J3 is intensely indurated and composed of hard nodular chalk and splintery chalkstone, comparable with the basal bed of the Melbourn Rock; beds J4–8 are condensed, to 0.16 m.

The quarry section at Ashwell, located just outside the district [2687 3945], was described and collected during this survey, in 1992. It provides a good exposure of the Plenus Marls (Figure 12a; Plate 4) as detailed below. A second section (Figure 12b), exposed in 1993, shows both the lateral variation in the exposure and the practical difficulties of defining the different bed boundaries consistently. Seven separate units have been recognised and equated with Jefferies Beds 1–8. The basal unit, J1, rests on the burrowed top of the Grey Chalk and consists of 0.22–0.30 m of marly chalk. This is separated from the 0.25–0.35 m of white massive chalk forming J3 by a thin marl parting, J2. Bed J3 is not noticeably indurated here and passes laterally into a nodular 'marbled rock'. Bed J4 is either very thin or poorly represented, and it is likely that it is largely incorporated into the conglomeratic J3. Bed J5 forms a 0.10 m-thick, yellowish white, marly chalk which in places has an argillaceous base (possibly part of J4) which rests directly on the conglomeratic top of J3. It is overlain by 0.02–0.05 m of yellow chalky marl, J6. Bed J7 consists of 0.08 m of yellowish white chalk followed by 0.10–0.15 m of yellowish brown marl, Bed 8. Samples collected from the basal bed (Woods, 1992b) yielded the brachiopod *Orbirhynchia* sp. (cf. *O. multicostata*) and bivalves *Pycnodonte* sp., *P.* (*Phygraea*) *vesiculare* and *Inoceramus pictus*? confirming Plenus Marls (J1–?2), Upper Cenomanian, *M. geslinianum* ammonite zone. As at Cadwell Farm, the conglomeratic J3 contains a mixed fauna, here comprising *Monticlarella jefferiesi*, *Ornatothyris* sp. and *A. plenus* (Wood, 1993).

The Plenus Marls have been recognised in a number of water boreholes in the southern part of the district by their characteristic gamma-ray response.

MIDDLE CHALK

The Middle Chalk crops out on the scarp face, from near Smiths End [395 380] in the east to Telegraph Hill [118 287] in the west, in dry valleys, mainly in the south-west of the district, within the Hitchin Gap, and as an inlier in the River Beane valley around Walkern [295 265]. The width of the outcrop varies considerably as a reflection of this intricate pattern, but also in response to the thickening of the Middle Chalk from west to east, and the development of a secondary, lower, scarp, surmounted by Melbourn Rock, east of Letchworth. Rock head contours at the base of the drift in the Hitchin Gap also suggest that the Middle Chalk is present in subcrop as far to the south-east as Hook's Cross [280 206] near Watton at Stone.

Within the district, the Middle Chalk thickens from about 60 to 70 m in the west near Luton, to approximately 95 to 100 m, north and west of Buntingford, in the east. Large exposures are rare, with most former quarries having been backfilled as the urban areas expanded. Much of the detailed stratigraphy has been derived from quarry and section descriptions closely adjacent to the district, most notably those at Ashwell [2697 3945], Steeple Morden [300 405, 301 388], Royston School Quarry [364 405] and the Royston Bypass Cutting [373 410].

The Middle Chalk consists mainly of white, pure, massively bedded chalk, in marked contrast to the grey marly Lower Chalk. With the exception of the Melbourn Rock at the base, the succession contains no distinctive mappable units. Detailed descriptions of sections, rock cores and the interpretation of geophysical well signatures demonstrate the variability of the Middle Chalk. However, some marker horizons, mainly thin marls and flint bands, have been noted in boreholes and sections enabling correlation with sequences in adjoining areas to be made.

Generally the formation comprises, from the base, the following broad lithological units: the Melbourn Rock (c.2–7 m), shell-detrital chalks (c.10 m), and massively bedded chalks with marl and nodular flint courses (c.75–85 m).

Melbourn Rock

The Melbourn Rock, 2–7 m thick, at the base of the formation, forms a strong positive feature on which a heavy soil brash of rubbly hard chalk is often developed. It consists of hard to very hard, off-white, blocky fractured chalk with marl wisps and few fossils. Accentuation of the marl partings gives weathered quarry faces a knobbly appearance.

The Melbourn Rock was originally defined as 'several thin beds of yellowish laminated chalk with layers of marl, separated by courses of hard rocky chalk, the whole having a maximum thickness of 10 feet' (3.05 m) (Penning and Jukes-Browne, 1881). In an earlier paper, Jukes-Browne (1880) stated that the Melbourn Rock had been named after Melbourn in Cambridgeshire, but as originally conceived this included the 'Zone of *Belemnitella plena*' (named the Actinocamax plenus Marls by White, 1909), the Plenus Marls of modern usage.

Hill and Jukes-Browne (1886) redefined the Melbourn Rock by excluding the Plenus Marls and considered it to be the basal bed of the Middle Chalk. In this paper, and in their subsequent regional synthesis (Jukes-Browne and Hill, 1903), they recognised that the Melbourn Rock could be divided into two (a lower white and a higher yellow unit) and also that the type Melbourn sections were relatively thin (maximum 2.28 m). They noted that the sections at Ashwell and Hitchin Station were thicker (2.40 and 3.05 m) and presumably more complete than the original type locality, and that the Melbourn Rock graded up into the "*Rhynchonella cuvieri* Zone" (i.e. fossiliferous beds characterised by *Orbirhynchia cuvieri*). Of the sections quoted by Jukes-Browne and Hill in the type area, only that at Ashwell still exists. It is difficult, however, to compare the present section (Figure 13) with their original measurements and it is uncertain where they drew the upper limit of the Melbourn Rock.

The Ashwell section must be regarded as the only available stratotype for the Melbourn Rock. The most appropiate level at which to draw the top of the Melbourn Rock in this section, based on mapping criteria, would be at the top of the 'flaggy bed' (see details), at the change from relatively hard, flaser bedded, indistinctly nodular chalk below to massive bedded white chalk above. This possibly corresponds to the top of the higher (yellow) portion of the original type concept of the Melbourn Rock.

The Melbourn Rock is also exposed at Cadwell Farm pit [1889 3274] and in a temporary trench section at Steeple Morden Plantation Quarry [300 405]. It was previously exposed at Grove Mill [191 310] (see Lower Chalk details and Jukes-Browne and Hill, 1903), in the Hitchin Station railway cutting and in a temporary section (1992) at Walsworth Road, Hitchin [1934 2970].

The Melbourn Rock of the district includes within it the base of the Turonian stage as represented by the entry of *Mytiloides spp.*. Evidence given below suggests that the Melbourn Rock covers the highest part of the ammonite zone *Metoicoceras geslinianum*, as well as the *Neocardioceras juddii*, *Watinoceras devonense*, *Fagesia catinus* and possibly up to the base of the *Mammites nodosoides* Zone.

Shell-detrital Chalks

Above the Melbourn Rock, there are approximately 10 m of white, shelly, crisp to firm chalk with minor beds of chalkstone and some very shelly chalk (shell-detrital chalks composed principally of *Mytiloides spp.*). These deposits are well exposed at both pits at Steeple Morden, at the top of the beds exposed at Ashwell and in the Hitchin Station railway cutting. They span the *Mammites nodosoides* and the basal part of the *Collignoceras woollgari* ammonite zones and most, if not all, of the *Mytiloides spp.* zone of the traditional zonal scheme.

A number of marker horizons within the shell-detrital chalks have been identified in the Chilterns during recent surveys (Wood, 1993), and these aid regional correlation of this part of the sequence. Three metres above the 'flaggy bed' at Ashwell, chalk between two marl seams ('the Ashwell top marls') contains a high diversity inoceramid assemblage including *Mytiloides columbianus s.l.*, *M. aff. hattini* and *Inoceramus cf. apicalis*. This level has been tentatively correlated with the Gun Gardens Marls of the Sussex sequence (Mortimore 1986). The lowest of these marls is also equated with the informally named 'basal marker marl' at Steeple Morden. In the chalk, 0.65 to 0.70 m above the 'basal marker marl', conspicuous shell debris yielded small examples of *Mytiloides labiatus* and *Inoceramus cf. apicalis*.

At Steeple Morden, some 2 m above the top of the Melbourn Rock, a bed approximately 0.5 m thick occurs, which is the coarsest and most shell-detrital chalk in the district. During the early stages of this survey it was referred to as the 'false Melbourn Rock', because the operators terminated quarrying at this level in the belief

that it was the Melbourn Rock itself. The bed is here formally named the Morden Rock (Plate 5). It is highly fossiliferous and yields common *Orbirhynchia*, *Conulus* and *Discoides*, in addition to rock-forming quantities of *Mytiloides cf. mytiloides*. Within this bed two serpulid encrusted *Mytiloides* fragments were found suggesting a broad correlation with the *Filograna avita* bioevent (Gale et al., 1993) of the South Coast succession (Wood, 1993). The entry of *Mytiloides mytiloides* in flood abundance is an important bio-event within the *Mammites nodosoides* Zone.

Immediately above the Morden Rock is a 0.05 m marl. This shell-detrital chalk/marl couplet can be traced throughout the northern and central part of Steeple Morden Plantation quarry. It has been noted in trench sections in the south of that pit, and the more southerly Station Quarry.

A group of three marls marks the lower limit of the main flint bearing succession at Steeple Morden. The topmost marl is the best developed and is stained brown in places. It is presumed to correlate with the informally named 'Aston Marl' (Wood, 1993) at Ivinghoe–Aston Quarry [SP 960 176] (south of the Leighton Buzzard district), where it is overlain by the shelly 'Maiden Bower Flint', first recognised at Totternhoe (Shephard-Thorn et al., 1994). Only sparse small finger flints, although similarly of a shelly nature, are developed at this level at Steeple Morden.

The top of the shell-detrital chalks is marked by the lower of a pair of marls. The upper marl is usually the best developed, and is here formally named the Odsey Marl (Table 4). A conspicuous more-or-less continuous, nodular shelly flint, including fragments and three-dimensional valves of *Mytiloides cf. mytiloides*, is developed below this pair of marls and is here formally named the Morden Flint (Plate 5). The Odsey Marl is also recognised in the Hitchin Station railway cutting section. In southern England, the upper limit of the shell-detrital chalks falls near the base of the Middle Turonian *Collignoniceras woollgari* Zone (Wood, 1993). The sequence between the 'Aston Marl' and the Odsey Marl can be readily identified in the Chilterns and North Hertfordshire by its shelly character, but the flint seams are so variable in occurrence as to provide only local markers.

Shell-detrital chalks and shelly flints are commonly identified in soil brash, a short distance above the outcrop of the Melbourn Rock, but the diffuse nature of the upper boundary has precluded the delimitation of this part of the Middle Chalk on maps.

Terebratulina lata **Zone Chalk**

Above the shell-detrital chalks the remainder of the Middle Chalk comprises 75 to 85 m of white, massively bedded, sparsely fossiliferous chalk with thin marl seams, hardgrounds, sponge beds and semi-porcellanous horizons. The lower and upper parts of this sequence also contain regular courses of nodular flint. Some of the marl seams are readily identifiable on geophysical traces from boreholes and these aid regional correlation (Murray, 1986). Only minor exposures are known within the district and these are not easily placed within the

Plate 5   Examples of the Morden Rock and Morden Flint at the Steeple Morden Plantation quarry [300 405]. Hammer 0.30 m. (GS 70Q, GS 70U)

sequence. Most of the detailed descriptions given here are of necessity from nearby exposures in adjacent districts, including: the upper part of Steeple Morden quarry [298 402], the Royston Bypass Cutting [372 410] and Royston School Pit [364 405] in Royston. These cover parts of the *Terebratulina lata* Zone but none of the sections can be demonstrated to overlap. The Reed Pit [3595 3704] no longer exposes much of the highest Middle Chalk (including the type Reed Marl), and details of this part of the section is included with the description of the Upper Chalk exposed there (see Upper Chalk).

Four regularly spaced marker marls (or marl complexes) have been identified within the *T. lata* Zone of this region (Table 4). They are in ascending order, the Denton Lodge, Pilgrims Walk, Latimer and Reed Marls (Murray, 1986). The Royston Bypass Cutting exposed approximately 36 m of beds including two marl complexes equated with the Denton Lodge and Pilgrims Walk marls. These have been tentatively correlated with the New Pit Marls (in part) and the Glynde Marl complex, respectively, of the south coast in Sussex. The Royston School Pit exposes a total of 12.4 m, which includes

the 0.10 m-thick Reed Marl. This is correlated with the Caburn Marl of the Sussex successions and the Twin Marls of the East Anglian successions (Mortimore and Wood, 1986). The Latimer Marl (equated with the Southerham and Mount Ephraim marls), the Reed and Pilgrims Walk marls, are not exposed in this district but are recorded on several wireline logs.

The Latimer Marl is well exposed (but there termed the Mount Ephraim Marl) in the pit near Great Chesterford [507 429] in the Saffron Walden district to the north-east. This marl is known to contain the large foraminifera *Coskinophragma* in abundance, a key biostratigraphical marker in marl correlation throughout southern England (Mortimore and Wood, 1986). The upper 30 m of the Middle Chalk is well exposed in the Kensworth Quarry [017 197] to the west of this district (Shephard-Thorn et al., 1994).

Macrofossil zonation of the Middle Chalk

The base of the Turonian, represented by the first appearance of *Mytiloides* spp., is within the Melbourn

Rock. The Cenomanian age of the lowest part of the Melbourn Rock is indicated by the occurrence of *Inoceramus* ex gr. *pictus* and *Sciponoceras*, including *S. bohemicum anterius*. The occurrence of common *Sciponoceras* at Ashwell and other localities in the Chilterns, and comparison with the Cenomanian/Turonian sequence at Eastbourne, Sussex, suggest that the *Metoicoceras geslinianum* Zone extends up into the Melbourn Rock of this district. This zone was previously considered to terminate at the top of the Plenus Marls. The key to the correlation between north Hertfordshire and southern England lies in the recognition of the entry of *Orbirhynchia* at, or just below, the variably calcarenitic base of the 'flaggy bed' at Ashwell and Steeple Morden. In the absence of ammonites in this district, this calcarenitic development, associated with the entry of *Fagesia catinus* in the south coast succession, can be used to recognise the base of the correlative international *Psuedaspidoceras flexuosum* ammonite zone. The base of the *Mammites nodosoides* Zone has not been positively identified in north Hertfordshire, but it is provisionally inferred to fall at the thin flaser marl at the top of the 'flaggy bed' at Ashwell. Thus, the stratotype Melbourn Rock can be inferred to cover the ammonite zones of topmost *M. geslinianum*, *Neocardioceras juddii*, *Watinoceras devonense*, *Fagesia catinus* and possibly up to the *Mammites nodosoides* Zone (Table 4) although none of the zonal indices has been recognised from the Chilterns or north Hertfordshire.

The basal Middle Chalk succession, from the top of the Plenus Marls to the highest bed of shell-detrital chalks, has been traditionally referred to the *Inoceramus* (correctly *Mytiloides*) *labiatus* Zone (Table 4). The remainder of the Middle Chalk is referred to the *Terebratulina lata* Zone, whose base is drawn at the first appearance of the zonal index. These traditional zones are thick and insufficiently refined for detailed correlation. It is likely that, for the lower part of the Middle Chalk at least, a finer zonation based on inoceramid faunas and related to the standard ammonite zones, will be introduced in the near future.

The use of *Mytiloides labiatus* as a zonal index for the lower part of the Middle Chalk is inappropriate for several reasons. The first appearance of the genus *Mytiloides*, which can be taken to indicate the base of the Turonian stage, occurs within and not at the base of the Melbourn Rock. There is no agreement amongst specialists as to species concepts within *Mytiloides* from this part of the succession, nor is it entirely clear how *M. labiatus* relates to other species assigned to the same genus. *Mytiloides labiatus*, as generally understood, appears to have a rather restricted stratigraphical range, and probably appears only in the lower part of the interval from first occurrence of the genus to the top of the shell detrital chalks. The higher part of this interval is characterised by *M. mytiloides* and related forms. In recognition of these problems, the somewhat unsatisfactory term 'Zone of *Mytiloides* spp.' has been used in recent years for the shell-detrital chalks, low in the Middle Chalk. The next higher zonal index of the traditional scheme, *T. lata*, occurs a short distance above the base of the overlying, relatively massive chalks, and is perhaps diachronous.

The entry of *Terebratulina lata* in southern England is a little above the abrupt lithological change from shell-detrital chalks with *Mytiloides* to massive poorly fossiliferous chalk. Elsewhere this lithological change corresponds to the lowest occurrence of flint and the appearance of poorly preserved *Mytilodes subhercynicus* and *Collignoniceras woollgari* (Mortimore and Pomerol, 1991). In north Hertfordshire, the lithological change comes just below the Odsey Marl, a metre or so above the Morden Flint as seen in the Steeple Morden quarries. The base of the *T. lata* Zone has not so far been recognised at either the Steeple Morden quarries or the Hitchin Station railway cutting sections although the index fossil was recorded from the quarry adjacent to Hitchin Station (Jukes-Browne and Hill, 1903). However, by comparison with southern England, it can be inferred that the greater part of the succession above the Odsey Marl falls in this zone. The apparent absence of *T. lata* from the lower part of this succession in the district may reflect a diachronous first appearance of this taxon, for there is evidence from farther north in East Anglia and in Lincolnshire that this bio-event occurred later in the north than in the south (Wood, 1993).

Details

This section commences with the description of the seven major sections from which the framework for the lithostratigraphy of the Middle Chalk of this district is derived, and also includes descriptions of selected small exposures and borehole sections.

Of the seven major exposures only two, both in Hitchin, fall within the district, the remainder being to the north just within the Biggleswade district (Sheet 204). The minor exposures are often difficult to place accurately within the sequence due to the lack of suitable marker horizons and the paucity of faunal elements, particularly in the *T. lata* Zone.

Ashwell

The only well-exposed, permanent section of the Melbourn Rock is at Ashwell [2697 3945] and this site, following the loss of the original site at Melbourn itself, must now be considered as the stratotype. A detailed section, with informal bed names is shown in Figure 13. Approximately 8 m of beds are exposed, from the base of the Plenus Marls to well above the Melbourn Rock.

The Ashwell site is believed to be the same as that described by Jukes-Browne and Hill (1903, p.464), a description repeated by Edmonds and Dinham (1965) who noted that the top of the section also contained abundant '*Inoceramus labiatus*'. The pit has now been backfilled to just below the level of the Plenus Marls and forms the garden of the bungalow adjacent to the site.

The lowest bed of the basal chalkstone unit of the Melbourn Rock contains *Sciponoceras* sp. and is inferred to correlate with the basal bed at Eastbourne which contains *Metoicoceras geslinianum*. The top of the nodular chalks beneath the 'flaser bed' is variable in thickness, presumably reflecting a period of scour and erosion. A comparable development is seen in the pit at Sewell [SP 995 224], near Totternhoe (see Shephard-Thorn et al., 1994) and in the temporary exposure off Walsworth Road, Hitchin [1934 2970]. This marked lithological change between the nodular cemented chalkstones and the flaser-bedded unit above, probably represents a non-sequence with the Ceno-

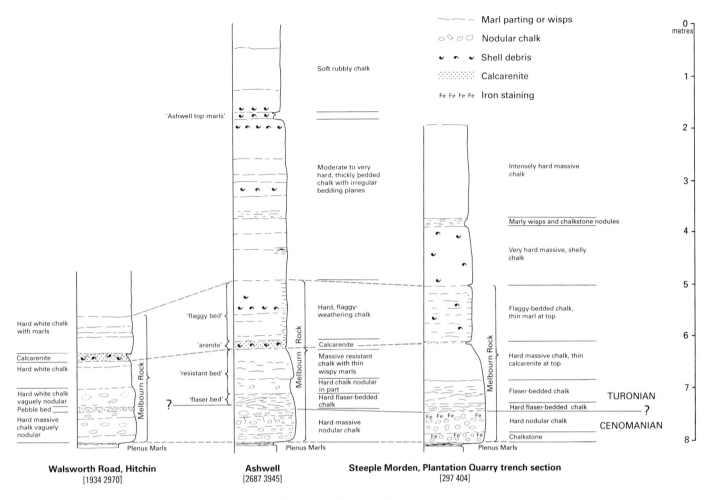

Figure 13 The Melbourn Rock exposures at Walsworth Road, Hitchin, at Ashwell and at the Steeple Morden Plantation Quarry.

manian–Turonian boundary being inferred to fall within the hiatus.

The 'arenite' bed, (strictly calcarenite) at the base of the 'flaggy bed' marks the entry of *Orbirhynchia*; this bio-event noted between the Holywell Marls 2 and 3 on the south coast (Gale et al., 1993) is known to mark the entry of *Fagesia catinus*.

The top of the hard flaggy-weathering, poorly fossiliferous bed above (the 'flaggy bed') marks the the upper limit of the Melbourn Rock as identified during field mapping. The chalk between the 'Ashwell top marls' is highly fossiliferous yielding a high-diversity inoceramid assemblage as noted above. The marls can be tentatively equated with the Gun Gardens Marls 1 and 2 of Mortimore (1986). They are also tentatively suggested to be equivalent to the 'basal marker marls' at Steeple Morden Plantation quarry.

Steeple Morden Plantation and Station Quarries

The two quarries, just to the north of the district, each expose up to 25 m of beds within the lower part of the Middle Chalk (Figures 13 and 14). They are being operated at present for high purity whiting. The most northerly of the pits (the Plantation Quarry [298 402]) was described in Jukes-Browne and Hill (1903) and referred to as the Morden Grange Plantation. The section was reproduced in Edmonds and Dinham (1965) with the additional comment, 'A chalk pit [296 401] in Morden

Grange Plantation shows smooth white chalk overlain by 5 to 6 feet (1.52 to 1.83 m) of nodular chalk; these beds dip north-east at 5° at the western end of the pit and are horizontal at the eastern end'. The section recorded is as follows:

	Thickness
Soil and chalk rubble	4 ft (1.22 m)
Bedded white chalk with few flints	20 ft (6.10 m)
Tough yellowish rocky chalk	1 ft (0.30 m)
Rather soft chalk with scattered flint and a course of finger-shaped flints 10 feet (3.05 m) down; *Galerites sub-rotundus, G. castanea, Rhynchonella cuvieri, Terebratula semiglobosa* and *Ptychodus*	12 ft (3.66 m)
and in the lower level:	
Chalk between two layers of flint	3 ft (0.91 m)
Tough yellowish chalk full of *Inoceramus mytiloides* dipping eastward	15 ft (4.57 m)

A number of points were noted by Jukes-Browne and Hill (1903) which can be related to the structure and lithologies seen today. Firstly the quarry appears to be situated in a syncline and corresponding anticline of low amplitude, plunging slightly south-eastwards, and low dips to the north-west, north-east and south-east can be seen within the present pit. Secondly a *mytiloides* bed (the Morden Rock) is seen at the

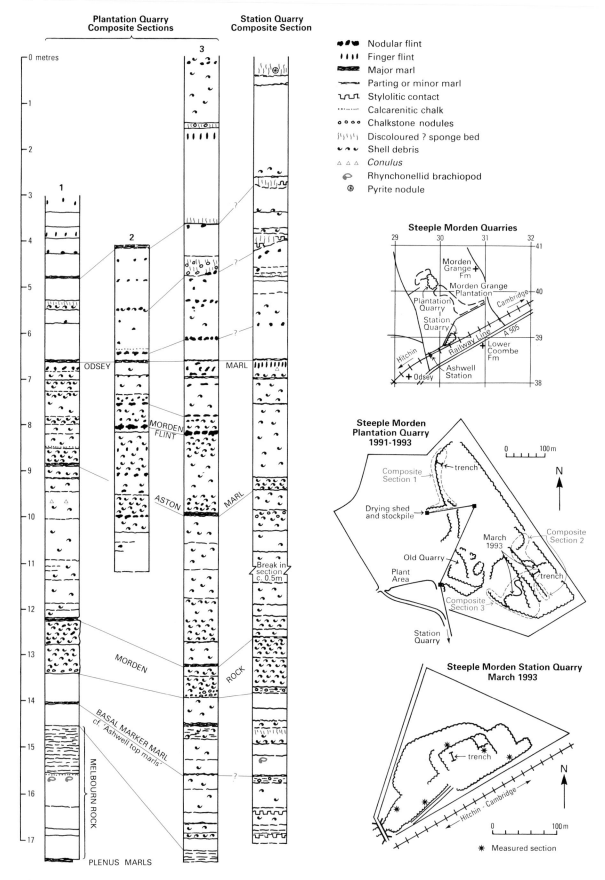

Figure 14 The correlation of beds above the Melbourn Rock in composite sections from the Steeple Morden quarries.

base of the succession today, and thirdly the mention of *Ptychodus* teeth suggests correlation with one of the higher sponge beds within which shark and ray teeth are concentrated.

South of the Plantation Quarry a cut and fill tunnel (made in 1991) [3004 3878] to carry a conveyor under a farm track in preparation for an extension to the workings (the Station Quarry), showed the following section within the Middle Chalk.

	Thickness m
White soft rubbly chalk becoming blocky with depth. Sparsely fossiliferous (mainly brachiopods) throughout. Impersistent rusty staining 0.9 m from top. Thin marl parting on stylolitic contact 0.16 m from base	2.10
White crisp blocky chalk stained pale yellow around ?sponges. Some fragmentary shell debris and stylolitic marl partings throughout. Incipient chalkstones in places	0.15–0.33
White massive well-jointed crisp chalk. Thin marl partings poorly developed	1.33+

These beds are equivalent to the higher beds at the Plantation Quarry. At that time the operators reported that the Melbourn Rock (possibly the Morden Rock) was at depths of 17 m in boreholes at the Station Quarry site.

Visits were made to the Station Quarry [301 388] in 1992 and 1993 subsequent to the mapping of the area in 1991, to record new exposures as the pit was developed. A composite diagram of the sequence exposed is shown in Figure 14.

During the investigations at these two quarries, three trial trenches were dug by the operators to aid the correlation. One of these in the northern part of Plantation Quarry exposed the Melbourn Rock and underlying Plenus Marls allowing correlation to be made with the Ashwell section. The other trenches, one in each of the two pits, both terminated just above the predicted position of the Melbourn Rock after having passed through the very hard shell-detrital Morden Rock. They permitted a closer correlation between the northern and southern parts of the Plantation Quarry and the sections exposed at the Station site.

In Plantation Quarry examination of the weathered faces of the most northerly sections has resulted in the recognition of several lithological and biostratigraphical marker horizons (Plate 5) in the lower part of the succession above the Melbourn Rock. These have proved crucial in the interpretation of other sections in both quarries at Steeple Morden and are named in the figures.

Two separate successions can be identified in the northern and southern parts of Plantation Quarry respectively. The northern succession is condensed and flintless up to the level of the Odsey Marl immediately below which inconspicuous small finger flints are developed. The somewhat expanded southern section is highly flinty from the level of the 'Aston Marl' to the Odsey Marl with several variably developed flint bands, of which the Morden Flint (Plate 5) is the most important and most consistently developed. The succession in the southern Station Quarry is comparable to the 'flintless' northern part of the Plantation Quarry although fortuitously the development of the Morden Rock (Plate 5) can be identified in all three successions. The change from the 'flintless' to 'flinty' sequences in the Plantation Quarry is relatively abrupt across an approximately east-west line, this differentiation presumably results from either structural control or the presence of seafloor mounds of the Etretat type (Kennedy and Juignet, 1974).

Walsworth Road, Hitchin

This section [1934 2970], which was logged during the early stages of development of the site on the south side of Walsworth Road, is now completely obscured. It consisted of very hard, off-white or pale yellowish grey, poorly fossiliferous chalk, verging on chalkstones. The beds are nodular in part with thin flaser-like marl partings. This succession, attributed to the Melbourn Rock for the most part, rests on a complete Plenus Marls sequence (Figure 12). The section is highly fractured throughout, but approximately 2.3 m of the Melbourn Rock were seen. The outline correlation of this section with those at Ashwell and Steeple Morden is shown in Figure 13. The principal correlation, relating to the identification of the basal 'arenitic' chalk with *Sciponoceras*, and the calcarenitic chalk beneath the flaggy shelly chalks above which rhynchonellids occur, were noted.

Hitchin Station Railway Cutting

This exposure [196 295] was first described by Hill and Jukes-Browne (1886) and given in expanded form by Jukes-Browne and Hill (1903).

1903 description:
'The best section of the *Rhynchonella cuvieri* zone is in the cutting and quarries by the side of the line south of Hitchin Station. The quarries are carried down below the level of the line, and are sometimes worked down to the bottom of the Melbourn Rock. The succession is as follows:

	Thickness
Soil and chalk rubble	4 ft (1.22 m)
Firm whitish chalk with *Galerites subrotundus*, and a layer of flints at base	6 ft (1.83 m)
Firm whitish chalk with much *Inoceramus* shell, *Galerites subrotundus* and *Rhynch. cuvieri*	14 ft (4.27 m)
Harder white chalk with *Rhynch. cuvieri*, *Inoceramus mytiloides* and *Terebratula semiglobosa*	10 ft (3.05 m)
Hard white nodular chalk with the same fossils, and also *Discoidea minima* and *Cardiaster pygmæus*	10 ft (3.05 m)
Very hard nodular yellowish rock with *Rhynchonella cuvieri*, top of Melbourn Rock	4 ft (1.22 m)

Below this there is said to be hard, nodular, greenish-grey rock about 6 feet (1.83 m) thick, making the whole about 50 feet (15.24 m) (actually 54 feet or 16.46 m) thick, but as the highest bed is rather soft homogeneous chalk, and neither Rhynchonellæ nor Inocerami are common in it, the layer of flints may be regarded as the top of this zone.'

The description indicates that the succession ranges from the top of the Melbourn Rock into the shell-detrital chalks of the *Mytiloides spp.* Zone and probably into the base of the *T.lata* Zone as indicated by the loss of inoceramids up-sequence at the level of the flints.

Three sections were measured during the present survey (Figure 15) when only the uppermost 8.3 m of the original section was still available for inspection. The top of the shell-detrital chalk is marked by a rusty stained anastomosing marl, the Odsey Marl of Steeple Morden. One of the flint bands recorded recently must correspond to that noted in the 1903 description.

The shell-detrital chalks with flints broadly correlate with the southern 'flinty' succession at the Steeple Morden Plantation Quarry and therefore also represent the basal part of the Middle Turonian *Collignoniceras woollgari* Zone. The base of the

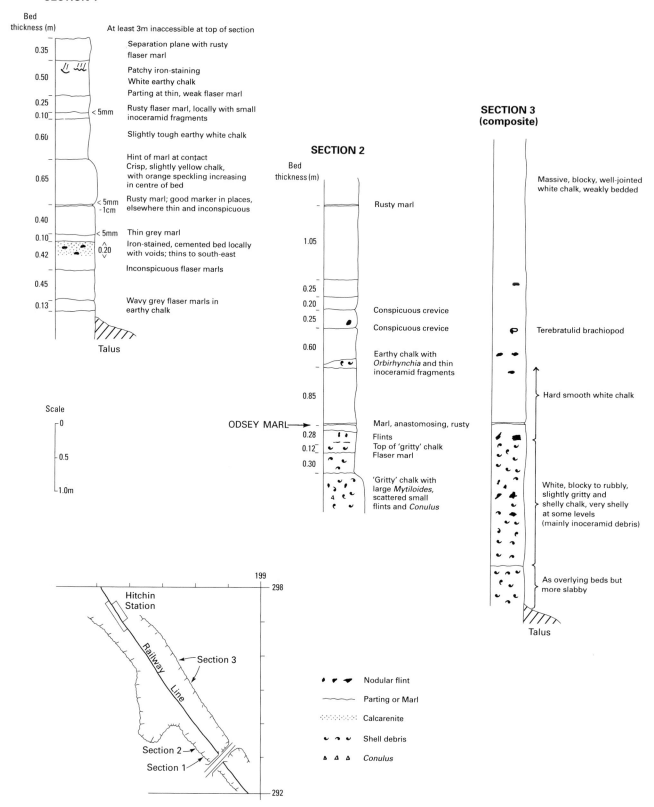

Figure 15   A correlation of three measured sections in the lower part of the Middle Chalk in the Hitchin Station railway cutting.

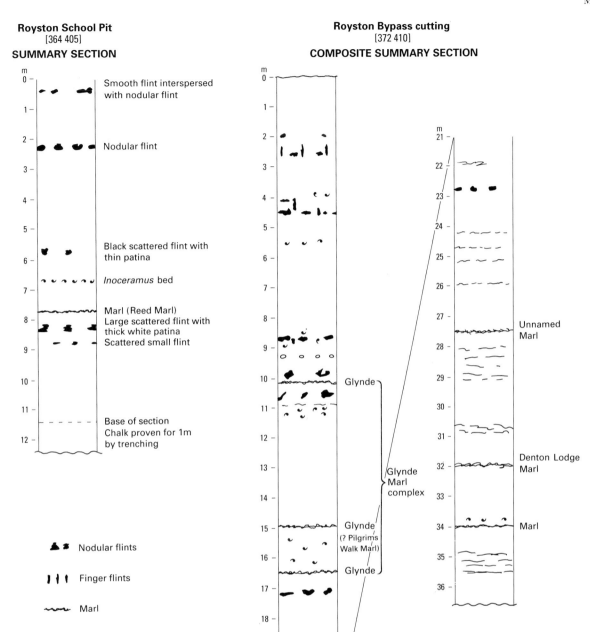

Figure 16 Outline lithological logs of the upper part of the Middle Chalk for the Royston Bypass cutting and for the Royston School Pit.

suceeding *T. lata* Zone would be expected to occur above the shelly chalks in this section but the level of entry of the zonal index is not known, although Jukes-Browne and Hill (1903) recorded *T. lata* from the 21 m or so of beds exposed in an adjacent quarry [1955 2939] (see minor details).

Royston Bypass Cutting

This section [373 410] was shown in outline by Mortimore and Wood (1986) where it is related to sections in both the

southern and East Anglian Chalk provinces. A composite section (R N Mortimore and C J Wood, personal communication, 1991) is shown in Figure 16. The attribution of the marls in this section to the named marls of the local succession must be regarded as highly tentative at present.

Royston School Pit

This small overgrown pit [364 405] (Figure 16) is the only local exposure where the Reed Marl can still be seen (the Reed Marl is now obscured at the stratotype to the south). The base of the Chalk Rock (the base of the Upper Chalk) is in some doubt here but may be represented by the band of black scattered flint above the *Inoceramus* bed. Bromley and Gale (1982) state about the Reed Marl....'In north Hertfordshire, where the Chalk Rock is represented only by a single hardground, this is underlain at some distance by a marl. At Reed (type locality) the marl lies about 2 m below the nodular representative of the Chalk Rock' (see Upper Chalk details for a description of the Reed pit).

Other details

A number of small but significant exposures were recorded during the recent survey. They are arranged here, as far as possible, in stratigraphical order from the base.

Temporary sections were noted during mapping on the Letchworth industrial estate. The sections were topographically one above the other and together show about 12 m of beds within the lower middle part of the Middle Chalk ranging approximately between 19 and 31 m above the base of the Melbourn Rock.

Off Avenue Two [2339 3272] and approximately 93 m above OD

	Thickness m
Topsoil/Till	0.80
Chalk, off-white, fractured, crisp, with *Inoceramus* fragments	2.30
Chalk, white, rubbly, with pale grey marls; 3 cm marl at base. Bed varies in thickness along face	0.07–0.30
Chalk, off-white, blocky, with ochreous sponge beds 0.3 and 0.6 m from top	2.80
Ochreous sponge bed	0.10–0.20
Chalk, off-white, fractured	2.55
Sponge bed, strongly developed, ochreous, marly wisps at base	0.17–0.25
Chalk, off-white, blocky, fractured	0.20+

Off Avenue Two [2333 3285] at approximately 85 m above OD

	Thickness m
Topsoil/Till	0.50
Chalk, off-white, very broken	0.36
Marl, grey, poorly developed in places	0.01–0.03
Chalk, off-white, fractured, with a course of small finger flints in the middle of the sequence	0.82–0.95
Chalk, off-white, blocky, fractured, finger flints in basal 10 cm	0.66
Chalk, white, blocky	0.20+

Both these sections are stratigraphically above the beds seen in Letchworth Obs 1 and 2 boreholes [2318 3299, 2336 3328] (see Appendix 1).

The higher parts of the Middle Chalk are seen in the disused quarry beside Hitchin Station, although much obscured by debris and vegetation and highly fractured. A face in the south-west corner of this quarry [1955 2939] exposed about 8 m of apparently flintless white chalk. The base of this face is approximately 4 m above the general level of the made ground in the floor of the pit. This quarry was described in Jukes-Browne and Hill (1903): '.... a good section of its (the *T. lata* zone) lower beds are exposed in Mr Ransome's quarry near the railway station, which is a continuation of the section given on p.464; above the beds there noted there is about 70 feet (21.34 m) of

soft white chalk with few scattered flints, but no regular layer of flints, except that near the top of the underlying zone. *Galerites subrotundus* and large *Terebratula semiglobosa* are common, with *Terebratulina gracilis* var. *lata*, *Ptychodus decurrens* and other fossils'.

A temporary section in the Middle Chalk was opened at the site of a new road bridge near Blakemore [2082 2723] during construction of the Little Wymondley bypass. This exposed 5 m of firm white chalk, below about 86 m above OD, with two conspicuous marl seams at the level of the bypass. The position of the base of the Middle Chalk at 32 m above OD in a nearby borehole (near Wymondley Bury [2150 2702]), together with structural contour plots for the base of the Upper Chalk, suggest that these marls are about 40 m below the Chalk Rock and 50 m above the base of the Melbourn Rock. The marls may thus be equivalent to the Pilgrims Walk Marls.

A small quarry south of Little Wymondley [2133 2709] exposed about 2.5 m of blocky white chalk with a tabular flint. Jukes-Browne and Hill (1903) recorded some 4.6 m of 'soft white chalk, with a band of grey marl and a layer of flints above it; *Spondylus spinosus*, *Inoceramus cuvieri*? and *Terebratula semiglobosa* occur here.' This marl would have been at between 90 and 95 m above OD, and therefore some 60 m above the base of the Melbourn Rock and is unlikely to be equivalent to that exposed at Blakemore.

A pit near the top of the Middle Chalk, at Lannock Farm [241 306], and noted for the occurrence of the very rare heteromorph ammonite *Metaptychoceras smithi*, was backfilled in 1963.

In 1989 an old chalk pit at Mill Hill [3010 3482] showed the following section, approximately 5 m below the base of the Chalk Rock:

	Thickness m
Chalk, weathered, blocky	0.60
Flint, band of large black nodules	0.15
Chalk, blocky	0.60
Flint, band of small scattered nodules	—
Chalk, blocky	0.60
Flint, double band of black burrowfill nodules with thin white cortices. Ochreous traces of sponges in intervening chalk	c.0.20
Chalk, blocky	0.60
Nodules of harder chalk with traces of sponges scattered in a thin band	—
Chalk, blocky, massive	1.60

The beds were more or less horizontal, and were displaced by a minor fault throwing down about 0.2 m to the north-west. No marl seams were observed.

At Wigmore Bottom [123 223], large excavations for a new building cut through about 6 m of clay-with-flints, with major solution pipes beneath, to reveal a chalk sequence from just above the Chalk Rock to about 8 m below its base. The section was as follows:

	Thickness m
UPPER CHALK including Chalk Rock (see Upper Chalk details)	1.7–1.8
MIDDLE CHALK	
Chalk, blocky, white, traces of bedding	c.5.00
Marl, olive-grey to grey-green (Latimer Marl)	0.13
Chalk, blocky, white with band of black flint nodules and tabular flint (up to 25 mm thick)	

	Thickness m
0.8 m below top, and scattered nodules 1.8 m below the top	3.00+

The Latimer Marl was seen to be displaced by minor faults in the sides of the excavation.

A temporary excavation for a new building [1135 2085], in a subsidiary dry valley down which Kimpton Lane descends from Luton airport, revealed the following section across the Middle/Upper Chalk junction in 1988:

	Thickness m
UPPER CHALK including Chalk Rock (see Upper Chalk details)	c.4.50
MIDDLE CHALK	
Chalk, rubbly nodular with trace of marl at base (possibly Reed Marl)	0.90
Chalk, massive, blocky with band of black flint nodules 1.5 m below the top	c.4.50
Latimer Marl, greenish grey marl	c.0.10
Chalk	1.00
Flint, nodules with incipient tabular band	0.05
Chalk, massive	1.00+

Several small pipes filled with clay-with-flints were noted, as were oblique joints and fissures parallel to the bedding, apparently injected with brown silty clay. The strata have a low dip of 1 to 2° in a northerly direction.

In the extreme south-west of the district exposures in the railway cutting east of the River Lea, now overgrown, were noted by Pocock in 1912 (field slip, Bedfordshire 33SW). At one point [1129 1966], he recorded a thin wavy marl band just below the Chalk Rock (1.2 m below the top of the cutting), with a thin tabular flint 0.6 m lower. This is probably equivalent to the Reed Marl noted at Wigmore Bottom and Kimpton Lane.

Just north of the district, a number of small temporary exposures were noted which show sections within the middle part of the Middle Chalk succession.

At Lower Coombe Farm petrol station [3091 3886], at approximately 76 m above OD, a sequence which is probably equivalent to the highest part of the Steeple Morden Station Quarry exposure was seen. The description below has been compiled from a face in chalk and an immediately adjacent excavation for new fuel tanks. Neither exposure is now visible.

	Thickness m
Topsoil	0.20
MIDDLE CHALK	
Chalk, white, crumbly, becoming more competent to base	2.78
Chalk, yellow-stained, white, massive (?sponge bed); rare white patinated flints 70 mm from base	0.56
Chalk, white, jointed, blocky	0.13
Chalk, white, with pale grey anastomosing irregular marls; individual seams of marl 1 to 4 mm thick	0.07
Chalk, white, crisp, blocky	0.23
Pale grey anastomosing irregular marls as above	0.07
Chalk, white, jointed, blocky, hard to firm with rare small (<50 mm) black flints 0.10 m from top, and a thin 1 to 2 mm wispy marl 0.77 m from top	1.00+

Topographically higher than the beds at the Station Quarry and half a kilometre east of Thrift Hill is an exposure [3255

3825] excavated for a new rifle range. The top of the sequence is at approximately 94 m above OD.

	Thickness m
MIDDLE CHALK	
Chalk, white, crisp, with flint bed at surface	1.80
Marl, grey, laminated with fine white ?burrows at base	0.07
Chalk, white, crisp, blocky, sparsely fossiliferous, yellow-stained ?sponge in upper 0.10 m	1.41
Marl, grey, laminated with diffuse upper boundary	0.03
Chalk, white, crisp, blocky, with stained ?sponge seam and bed of Inoceramus fragments between 0.4 and 0.5 m from top. Flint bed at base	1.85+

The marls here are between 60 and 70 m below the Chalk Rock on the scarp to the south and may thus correlate with the Denton Lodge Marls.

Two sections, [3222 3937, 3228 3938], at Kings Ride, to the north of the rifle range also show a sequence of chalks and marls. These are some metres higher in the succession and thus likely to be equivalent to the Pilgrims Walk/Glynde Marls seen in the Royston Bypass section.

	Thickness m
MIDDLE CHALK	
Chalk, off-white, firm, massive, with blocky jointing	0.95
Chalk, off-white, with anastomosing wispy pale grey marl seams, each 1 to 2 mm thick	0.05
Chalk, off-white, soft to firm, massive, with large blocky fracture. Some shell fragments	0.50
Marl, pale grey	0.02
Chalk, off-white, firm, massive, some bedding shown by horizontal discontinuities, ?marl partings	1.08
Marl, pale grey, well developed, with wispy base	0.02
Chalk, off-white, firm, massive, with rare shell debris	0.78+

	Thickness m
MIDDLE CHALK	
Chalk, off-white, blocky, becomes massive with depth. Wispy marl seams at top and 0.80 m from top	3.65
Marl, pale grey, well-developed, with wispy base	0.02
Chalk, off-white, blocky, with some shell fragments	0.96+

Minor faulting with throws of 0.10 to 0.15 m effects the upper part of the second section at Kings Ride, but the well-developed lowest marl is the same in both sections.

UPPER CHALK

The Upper Chalk forms the crest of the Chilterns escarpment and underlies much of the south and east of the district and has been removed by erosion from the bottom of some of the dry valleys in the Chiltern Hills and from most of the Hitchin–Stevenage Gap.

The Upper Chalk dips gently south-eastwards and is overlain on an eroded surface by Palaeogene deposits and the clay-with-flints (Chapters 5 and 6). This erosion surface also dips south-east but at a slightly lower angle, so that the preserved thickness of the Upper Chalk increases to a local maximum of about 70 m beneath the Palaeogene deposits in the south-east of the district. The north-westwards thinning of the Upper Chalk is exaggerated where the base of the clay-with-flints locally slopes towards the escarpment (Chapter 7) and in many places along the scarp edge very little of the Upper Chalk remains. In addition, the clay-with-flints is commonly let down into solution hollows in the Chalk, typically of cylindrical or funnel-like form, which are generally up to 10 m in diameter.

The base of the Upper Chalk is taken at the base of the Chalk Rock Member (Table 4) which, in this district, comprises up to about 2.5 m of chalkstones and nodular chalks, with one or more mineralised hardground surfaces. The Chalk Rock is overlain by several metres of hard chalks and chalkstones, which include the Top Rock (up to 1 m thick), the highest indurated bed in the Chalk of the Chilterns. This is a condensed succession in comparison with that of the Sussex coast, and it is followed here by up to 65 m of massive white chalks with discontinuous bands of nodular or tabular black flint and sporadic thin marl seams. Fossils are abundant at certain levels in the Upper Chalk, most notably in the Chalk Rock.

These strata can be seen in a number of small disused quarries at the level of the Chalk Rock and in a single large active quarry (at Anstey) in the higher beds. There are numerous other small sections but these cannot easily be placed stratigraphically or correlated with each other. Little lithological information has been noted for any of the boreholes in the Upper Chalk in the district, but geophysical logs have been recorded for a few, all in the east. The Top Rock and the Chalk Rock are both marked by coincident peaks on resistivity and gamma-ray logs. A marl seam, apparently marking the base of the *Micraster coranguinum* Zone, and an overlying unit of marly chalks can probably also be recognised on resistivity logs, although in the absence of lithological records this cannot be confirmed.

Stratigraphical nomenclature and correlation

Bromley and Gale (1982) described the Chalk Rock of southern England in some detail, assigning it formational status. However, Gale et al. (1987) revised this, naming it as a member of their 'White Chalk Formation', which corresponds to the combined Middle and Upper Chalk formations of this memoir. Gale et al. (1987) also treated the Top Rock as a member, but here it is given the status of a bed.

By analogy with recently proposed lithostratigraphical classification schemes for the Chalk of southern England, all the cemented chalks occurring near the base of the Upper Chalk in the Chilterns area could be treated together as a member, comparable with (although not directly equivalent to) the Lewes Nodular Chalk Member (Mortimore, 1986). Subdivisions such as the Chalk Rock would then have the status of 'beds'. However, the Chalk Rock has already been defined separately as a distinctive unit (Bromley and Gale, 1982) and it is delineated on relevant BGS geological maps (whereas the Top Rock can be mapped only locally). The Chalk Rock is therefore treated as a member herein.

The beds between the Chalk Rock and the Top Rock have not previously been named in the Chilterns, but are now included in the Kensworth Nodular Chalk Member (see below). In southern England, Gale et al. (1987) refer to equivalent beds as the lower 'leaf' of their St Margaret's Member (equivalent to the Lewes Chalk of Mortimore, 1983, 1986). The Top Rock of the Chilterns, described as 'the lithified horizon that terminates the nodular unit overlying the Chalk Rock' (Bromley and Gale, 1982), is also included with the 'Kensworth Nodular Chalk Member'.

The Chalk Rock is present throughout the Chilterns and can be traced into Dorset, but looses its identity in the basinal sequences to the north (Northern Province) and to the south-east (Anglo-Paris Basin). The Chalk Rock as seen in the district comprises only the top hardground suite of Bromley and Gale (1982) and is presumed to equate with the higher parts of the Kingston Beds in the Lewes Nodular Chalk Member in Sussex. The Top Rock of the Chilterns also represents a condensed sequence of beds in the higher part of the Lewes Chalk, probably including those from the Navigation Hardgrounds up to the Light Point Hardgrounds (Mortimore, 1986; Mortimore and Wood, 1986; Wood, 1990). The Kensworth Member is thus equivalent only to part of the Lewes Chalk.

The base of the Chalk Rock (and therefore of the Upper Chalk) is conventionally taken to coincide with the base of the *Sternotaxis plana* (previously *Holaster planus*) Zone (Rawson et al., 1978). In practice, the base of the *S. plana* Zone lies slightly above the base of the Chalk Rock (*sensu* Bromley and Gale, 1982) as it occurs in north Hertfordshire (Table 4) (Wood, 1990). Much of the higher Turonian has been condensed within the Chalk Rock, but the highest part of the *S. plana* Zone is represented by the beds between the top of the Chalk Rock and the base of the Top Rock (Bailey et al., 1983; Mortimore and Wood, 1986; Wood, 1990).

In the district the base of the succeeding Coniacian Stage and of the *Micraster cortestudinarium* Zone (which are not necessarily coincident — Rawson et al., 1978) can both be placed at the base of the Top Rock (Table 4), which represents a condensed lower part of the *M. cortestudinarium* Zone (Wood, 1990; Bristow, 1990). The higher part of the *M. cortestudinarium* Zone occupies about 20 m of the Upper Chalk above the Top Rock, but at least 25 m of the youngest Cretaceous strata preserved in the district belong to the *M. coranguinum* Zone, in the Middle and Upper Coniacian, probably extending into the basal part of the Santonian.

Chalk Rock

The Chalk Rock (Table 4) is a complex of nodular chalks and chalkstone beds. The latter are capped by mineralised hardground surfaces which developed on the contemporary sea floor during breaks in sedimentation (Kennedy and Garrison, 1975a; Hancock, 1989). Of the six laterally extensive major hardgrounds recognised in the Chalk Rock (Bromley and Gale, 1982), only the highest and most widespread, the Hitch Wood Hard-

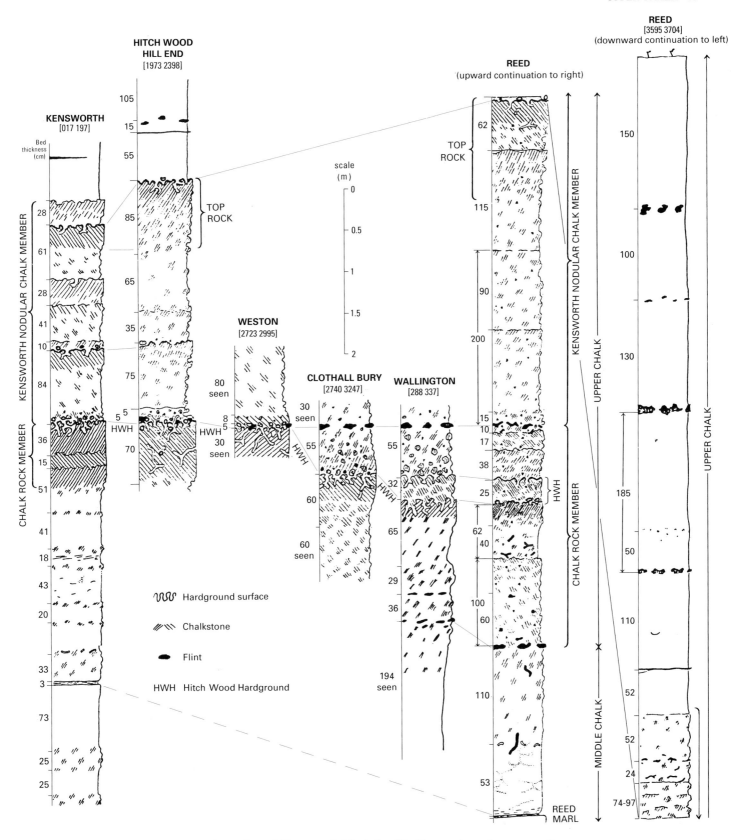

Figure 17 Sections in the Chalk Rock and Kensworth Nodular Chalk members demonstrating the expansion of the sequence from west to east across the district. Based on field notes by R G Bromley (October 1978) and by R G Bromley, A S Gale and C J Wood (1981) and kindly made available for this memoir.

ground with its overlying pebble bed, is present in north Hertfordshire. Traced eastwards, within the district this hardground divides into two subsidiary surfaces (Figure 17) and further surfaces appear just above it within the pebble bed. The local development of the Chalk Rock varies between 0.6 and about 2.5 m in thickness.

At outcrop on the lip of the Chilterns escarpment, the Chalk Rock typically gives rise to a well-defined, positive, topographic feature associated with locally voluminous spreads of fossiliferous rubbly brash in ploughed fields. Occurrences on the sides of the dip-slope valleys are similar but are more commonly obscured by colluvial cover, particularly on east- or north-facing slopes.

The Hitch Wood Hardground is characteristically a complicated, highly convolute surface mineralised by both phosphate and glauconite. Both the surface and the underlying bed of pale brownish or yellowish grey chalk-stone (intensely indurated chalk, *sensu* Bromley and Gale, 1982) are penetrated by thalassinoid burrows which are largely infilled by soft, rather powdery chalk. Dark to pale brown, or green mineralised pebbles, up to about 20 mm in diameter, occur immediately above and below the hardground surface and in some instances can be shown to have fallen into the burrows. The chalkstone also encloses dark green to black glauconite grains and pyrite nodules up to 40 mm in diameter. Fine, black, manganiferous speckling occurs but is likely to be a product of weathering.

The chalkstone passes gradationally downwards through partially indurated to rather nodular chalks, usually with a rather indistinct lower limit, against the normal uncemented chalk beneath. Where the Hitch Wood Hardground divides in the eastern part of the district, additional chalkstone beds appear beneath the subsidiary hardground surfaces.

The Hitch Wood Hardground is overlain by a bed of indurated chalk containing glauconitised and phosphatised pebbles. It is this horizon that yields the superbly preserved mineralised internal moulds (steinkerns) and external moulds, some preserving fine shell ornament, of originally aragonite-shelled molluscs (notably ammonites, but including gastropods, scaphopods and bivalves). This is the '*reussianum* fauna' of the older literature, named after the heteromorph ammonite *Hyphantoceras reussianum* which is a characteristic component. Corals, sponges, brachiopods, calcitic bivalves and echinoids are also present.

Where the Hitch Wood Hardground is present, Bromley and Gale (1982) place the top of the Chalk Rock at a distinctive flint nodule horizon which lies on the hardground or a short distance above it, at the top of the pebble bed. The flints partly or wholly within this bed preserve the features of trace fossils, particularly *Planolites* and *Chondrites*, and appear carious (rough, 'decayed', cavitated surface), but even those immediately above it tend to be rindless and grey in colour. Bromley and Gale (1982) take the lithological base of the Chalk Rock to be the lower limit of hardening beneath the lowest hardground surface that is present in any particular section; this is an unsatisfactory criterion. In some sections, a flint nodule horizon close to this limit forms a convenient marker (Figure 17).

The type section of the Hitch Wood Hardground was described from a small roadside chalk pit below Hill End Farm [1973 2398], near Hitch Wood, in the west of the district, where the Chalk Rock is about 0.7 m thick (Bromley and Gale, 1982, fig. 13). To the east, it undergoes a marked expansion (Figure 17). At Weston [2723 2995] (as in the type section) the Hitch Wood Hardground appears as a single well-phosphatised surface with traces of glauconitisation. Green and brown mineralised pebbles occur at this hardground surface and a flint layer immediately above it. This can be described as the 'Hitch Wood facies'. A similar hardground surface occurs at Clothall Bury [2740 3247], but it is separated from the overlying flints by some 0.55 m of nodular chalks containing small phosphatised pebbles, i.e. the pebble bed has thickened.

At Wallington [288 337], the Hitch Wood Hardground is divided into a lower 'Green Hardground' separated from an upper 'Brown Hardground' by about 0.30 m of chalkstone (Figure 17). This is the 'Reed facies'. The colours refer to the relative predominance of glauconitic and phosphatic mineralisation, respectively. The lower hardground yields the more abundant and diverse fauna, including some very well-preserved sponges. Most of the fossils are preserved as unmineralised moulds in pale chalkstone which contains pale green glauconitised pebbles. By contrast, fossils from the upper hardground are phosphatised clasts, and include ammonites from a younger biostratigraphical assemblage. The greatest local expansion is seen at Reed [3595 3704], where additional hardgrounds and chalkstone beds have appeared, presumably by the further division of the Green and the Brown Hardgrounds, which are more weakly mineralised than at Wallington (Figure 17; Bromley and Gale, 1982, fig. 13). Further details of these sections are given below.

This expansion (increase in the lithostratigraphical complexity) of the Chalk Rock is accompanied by an increase in overall thickness from 0.6 m in the south-west of the district to 1.2 m at Clothall Bury and 2.5 m at Wallington and Reed. Thickness estimates from field survey of unexposed sections in the east of the district range up to 5 m. This increase continues eastwards to the M11 motorway cutting near Great Chesterford [TL 50 40] (C J Wood, written communication, 1993). There is also an increase, from west to east, in the thickness of the Middle Chalk across the district. The thickening of the Chalk Rock is suggestive of a transition from a platform to a slope facies. Preliminary studies of the Chalk Rock in field brash suggest that the change from the platform facies to the slope facies could occur within a zone a few hundred metres wide at Clothall [27 31] consistent with some element of structural control on Chalk sedimentation.

Kensworth Member

The Chalk Rock is overlain by nodular chalks and chalkstones with further hardgrounds. These strata are included here in the newly defined Kensworth Member, which extends from the top of the Chalk Rock to a little above the Top Rock (Figure 17). The proposed holo-stratotype locality is at Kensworth Quarry [017 197], near Dunstable, described by Bromley and Gale (1982, fig. 13), Wood (1990) and Shephard-Thorn et al. (1994), where the hardgrounds above the Chalk Rock are best developed. The section exposed at the Reed Pit [3595 3704] (see details) is proposed as a parastrato-type.

In the west of the district, the interval between the top of the Chalk Rock and the base of the Top Rock is about 2 to 3 m and is also about 3 m where exposed at the Reed Pit. However, geophysical logs from boreholes elsewhere indicate that it increases to about 6 m in the east of the district, and estimates from field survey of unexposed ground suggests that it may reach 10 m in places. Although these beds are sparsely fossiliferous, the bivalve *Spondylus spinosus* is locally common just above the Hitch Wood Hardground, for example at Hill End chalk pit [1973 2398] (Wood, 1990).

Nodular chalks with relatively weakly developed hard-grounds can occur for a short distance above the well-mineralised hardground of the Top Rock, for example at Kensworth (Wood, 1990; Shephard-Thorn et al., 1994) and Reed (Figure 17).

The Top Rock, uppermost of the well-cemented beds above the Chalk Rock, is a group of hardgrounds which pass laterally into nodular chalk (Bromley and Gale, 1982). In this district it comprises a particularly hard chalkstone bed, 0.3 to 1 m thick, capped by a glauconi-tised convolute hardground scattered with glauconitised clasts. At Reed, there is a second, less well-developed, unmineralised, hummocky hardground within the Top Rock (Figure 17).

The Top Rock is exposed in very few places and in most occurrences it is seen only as soil brash in ploughed fields. It is most typically composed of a very hard, uniform fine-grained chalkstone, with a very pale pinkish hue in places, and lacks the fine porosity apparent in the Chalk Rock. In further contrast, the Top Rock contains no grains of glauconite or other dark-coloured mineral, although small green glauconitised pebbles do occur (Wood, 1990). As in the Chalk Rock, however, there is manganese speckling on joint surfaces and pyrite nodules are present in some localities. The Top Rock contains fewer fossils than the Chalk Rock, although sponges, small terebratulid (*Concinnithyris*) and rhyn-chonellid (*Orbirhynchia*) brachiopods and shark's teeth are present. However, at the Redbournbury Quarry [123 103], 8 km south of the district, the Top Rock chalk-stones have yielded a *remanié* assemblage of inoceramid bivalves, including *Cremnoceramus? waltersdorfensis han-novrensis* and *C? rotundatus*, which characterise the lower part of the *M. cortestudinarium* Zone as developed in southern England (Wood, 1990). Fractures tend to pass through the fossils, unlike the Chalk Rock, in which calcitic fossils tend to separate from their matrix when the rock is broken.

The Top Rock has been mapped only near Kings Walden [158 238], Clothall [2903 3066], Therfield [323 371] and Reed [373 372]. It can be detected on the available geophysical borehole logs and is suspected to

be present in some other areas, but could not be traced systematically. It may be weakly developed or obscured by superficial cover where it has not been mapped.

Upper Chalk above the Kensworth Member

Above the Top Rock, the sequence is composed mostly of massive, soft to firm white chalk, with courses of nodular or tabular flint at intervals, and at least one per-sistent marl seam. Regionally, the upper limit of the Chalk is defined by the sub-Palaeogene erosion surface, but in much of the district this has been modified by solution or erosion during the Quaternary. The greatest remaining thickness of these beds (about 65 m) is in the south-east of the district, but some 48 m is present near Barkway in the north-east.

Much of the sequence above the Top Rock belongs to the middle and upper parts of the *Micraster cortestudinar-ium* Zone, but east of the Hitchin–Stevenage Gap at least the lowest part of the succeeding *M. coranguinum* Zone is also present and there is a single record of Santonian macrofaunal elements, from the middle of the *M. coran-guinum* Zone, at a pit in eastern Stevenage (p.62).

A prominent marl seam exposed in the Anstey Quarry [395 329] is inferred (Wood, 1991) to correlate with the Upper East Cliff Marl of the standard east Kent succession, which marks the base of the *M. coranguinum* Zone (Bailey et al., 1983). It can be argued (see details) that this must lie between 19 and 39 m above the Top Rock. The presence of *M. coranguinum* Zone chalks has also been indicated for three pits north and north-east of Stevenage (see details). Each of these could lie within 25 m of the base of the Upper Chalk, albeit in that part of the district where the Chalk Rock is most condensed.

Out of a total of 70 m for the Upper Chalk in the district, the thickness of *M. coranguinum* Zone chalk preserved beneath the Palaeogene could therefore approach 45 m, although it might be as little as 25 m.

Details

Details of the Upper Chalk of the district are described here, firstly those locations where the Chalk Rock or Top Rock occur, starting in the west and south, followed by locations which expose the beds above the Top Rock.

EXPOSURES OF THE CHALK ROCK AND THE TOP ROCK

In the past, numerous small chalk pits were opened at the level of the Chalk Rock and Top Rock, but all are now degraded and several have been completely backfilled. No complete sections of the Chalk Rock were seen during the recent resurvey of the district, but several had previously been re-excavated and studied in detail by Bromley and Gale (1982) and their collabo-rators.

Luton Hoo Railway Cutting

The section noted by Jukes-Browne and Hill (1904) 'south of Luton, and half a mile north of Chiltern Green Station' was in the railway cutting in the extreme south-west of the district [113 195].

As recorded in 1894 this section comprised:

	Thickness
UPPER CHALK:	
Soft, white chalk with many flints	24 ft (c.7.2 m)
Hard, compact, cream-coloured chalk-rock with green-coated nodules	2 ft (c.0.6 m)
Lumpy, greyish white chalk, with a few scattered flints, many Micrasters	11 ft (c.3.3 m)
Hard, compact, cream-coloured chalk- rock with green grains and green-coated nodules	2 ft (c.0.6 m)
MIDDLE CHALK:	
Chalk with marl seams and scattered flints	27 ft (c.8.4 m)

An extensive faunal list was presented. From these descriptions, it is clear that the lower of the two beds of 'chalk-rock' (sensu Jukes-Browne and Hill, 1904) is the Chalk Rock as presently recognised and the higher is the Top Rock. Saunders (1890) also described the section, presenting a faunal list and noting that the two beds are 'often faulted'.

Kimpton Lane

In 1988, a temporary excavation for a new building beside Kimpton Lane, near Luton airport [1135 2085], revealed the following section:

	Thickness m
UPPER CHALK:	
Chalk, white, rubbly, weathered	c. 1.5
Top Rock; hard chalkstone, slightly greenish, weathered	0.4
Chalk, blocky, weathered	c. 2.0
Chalk Rock; very hard chalkstone, rubbly	up to 0.6
MIDDLE CHALK:	
Chalk with marl seams and flints	c. 7.5 m

This and the previous locality are very close to the temporary section at Luton [109 204] figured by Bromley and Gale (1982, fig. 13) which is a short distance to the west of the district.

Wigmore Bottom

In 1988, temporary excavations for a new building just to the east of Luton at Wigmore Bottom [123 223] revealed the following section beneath about 6 m of clay-with-flints:

	Thickness m
UPPER CHALK:	
Chalk, white, blocky	c. 0.8
Chalk Rock; very hard nodular chalk, much burrowed, phosphatised in part, nodules with glauconite coatings on upper surface	0.9–1.0
MIDDLE CHALK:	
Chalk with marl seams and flints	c. 8.0

Temple Dinsley

This locality was recorded by Jukes-Browne and Hill (1904) as 'an old quarry near Temple Dinsley House'. The house is on the east side of Preston village, and this description could refer to the quarry that lies some 300 m farther to the north-east [1840 2507]. They observed two bands of 'Chalk Rock' each about 1.5 m thick, separated by a band of 'lumpy chalk' up to 2.4 m thick. This implies that both the Top Rock and the Chalk Rock were seen, but neither was exposed during this survey.

Preston

Jukes-Browne and Hill (1904) noted that a small quarry beside the road, about 1 km north-east of Preston [1881 2516], exposed a section of about 1.2 m in the lower part of the Chalk Rock, which was highly fossiliferous. The quarry is now degraded and no significant exposures were seen during the survey.

Hill End

The exposure at the Hill End Pit, near Hitch Wood [1973 2398], 5 km south of Hitchin, is the type locality for the Hitch Wood Hardground (Bromley and Gale, 1982, fig. 13). In spite of its small size, it is also famous as a fossiliferous locality, most notably for the impressive ammonite fauna which is generally very well preserved and also very varied, including some rare forms (Woods, 1896, 1897; Billinghurst, 1927; Reid, 1962; Wright, 1979; Kaplan et al., 1987). The site is now a reserve maintained by a local natural history society although little of the geological sequence formerly exposed is visible.

According to unpublished field notes by R G Bromley (held at BGS Keyworth), dated 1978, the Chalk Rock is 0.7 m thick at Hill End, but this does not include a 50 mm bed with fossils and mineralised chalk pebbles, just above the flint layer on the Hitch Wood Hardground. A thin chalkstone bed capped by a minor hardground occurs 0.80 m above the Hitch Wood Hardground, this within a 2 m interval of nodular chalk (yielding the ammonite *Pseudopuzosia marlowense*) which passes up into the Top Rock (c.0.7 m). The Top Rock is also capped by a well-developed mineralised hardground. About 1.6 m of the overlying white chalks with flints was also seen (Figure 17).

Nonmineralised, indigenous specimens of *Micraster cortestudinarium*, of a type indicative of a relatively high level within the *M. cortestudinarium* Zone, occur in the Chalk immediately overlying the Top Rock (Wood, 1990).

Lannock Farm

Jukes-Browne and Hill (1904) gave a faunal list for a locality at this farm (Lannock Manor Farm), which lies about 1 km west of Weston [2480 3042], but the exact position of the exposure is not now known. The chalk pit (now backfilled), beside the road at Lannock Hill [240 305], lay below the level of the Chalk Rock, as do other known pits in the vicinity.

Weston

A small chalk pit 0.6 km east of Weston [2723 2995] once exposed about 1.2 m of nodular chalk overlying about 0.3 m of 'very hard compact rock with a layer of green-coated nodules at the top' (the Chalk Rock), passing down into 'tough nodular chalk with some scattered flints' (Jukes-Browne and Hill, 1904). This section was also figured by Bromley and Gale (1982, fig. 13) and is summarised in Figure 17. The BGS collections include a specimen of the ammonite *Hyphantoceras reussianum* (the characteristic fossil of the *reussianum* fauna) from this locality.

Clothall Bury

A small chalk pit beside a minor road, north-west of Clothall Bury Farm [2740 3247] once exposed the Chalk Rock, where it is just over 1 m thick (Bromley and Gale, 1982, fig. 13). Only one hardground surface is present. This is well phosphatised but traces of glauconitisation are present, especially on the 'boss-tops' (the hardground surface between the burrows). Bromley (unpublished field notes, 1978, held at BGS Keyworth) records that phosphatised pebbles and fossils continue to just above the flint (Figure 17). He also notes that the interval between the hardground and the flint yielded *Coscinopora*, '*Ventriculites*', *Septifer*, *Cardita*, gastropods and a giant nautiloid.

This chalk pit still exists but no significance exposures were seen at the time of this survey.

Clothall

Jukes-Browne and Hill (1904) mentioned the Clothall Bury Pit 'north-east of ... the church', but also recorded a section in another quarry 'half a mile west-south-west of the [Clothall] church', as follows:

	Thickness
Hard chalk with many flints of various sizes and shapes	4 ft (c.1.2 m)
Hard nodular chalk, rough, lumpy, and cream-coloured with many fossils, a few scattered flints and small pieces of light brown phosphate	5 ft (c.1.5 m)
Irregular layer of soft dusty yellowish chalk	9 in (c.0.2 m)
Chalk consisting of hard lumps in a softer matrix	4½ ft (c.1.4 m)

The description of 'hard nodular chalk' clearly refers to the Chalk Rock, but the location of the section is now in doubt.

Quickswood

A former chalk pit [2752 3272] a few hundred metres to the north-east of the Clothall Bury pit, between Quickswood House and the adjacent minor road, also exposed the Chalk Rock, but by 1978 it had been backfilled and restored. Unpublished BGS field records (c.1888) note that this pit exposed 'soft chalk with flints', below which was about 1 m of the Chalk Rock (base not seen). Bromley (unpublished field notes, 1965) observed that (as at Clothall Bury) the upper (brown) hardground seen at Wallington was apparently not present.

The BGS collections from Quickswood include specimens of the brachiopods *Cretirhynchia cuneiformis*, *Orbirhynchia reedensis* and the large form of the echinoid *Micraster leskei* (Woods, 1993). These suggest an horizon equivalent to the higher part of the Kingston Beds (Lewes Chalk) of Sussex (Mortimore, 1986) and so were probably collected from the Chalk Rock. A specimen of *Micraster precursor* (sensu Drummond, 1983), which is characteristic of beds in the *S. plana* Zone above the Kingston Beds, was presumably collected from above the Chalk Rock.

Kingswoodbury

There is a small exposure of the Top Rock in the north-western face of a chalk pit, about 2 km south-east of Clothall [2903 3067]; rubbly showings of off-white chalkstone contain scattered green glauconitised pebbles up to a few millimetres in diameter, and sparse thin bivalve shell fragments. Fragments of the Top Rock can also be found in soil for up to 100 m on either side of the pit.

Wallington

The chalk pit 'about a third of a mile north-west of Wallington Church' noted in 1884 by Jukes-Browne and Hill (1904) can

still be seen just south of a minor road, west of the village [288 337]. The section is figured by Bromley and Gale (1982, fig. 13) and in more detail in Figure 17. Here, the Chalk Rock is about 2.5 m thick, and the single hardground seen at Clothall Bury and to the west has divided into two (Figure 17). Although the chalk pit still exists, only part of the section was visible during this survey.

Bromley (unpublished field notes, 1981) observed that below the upper flint the Chalk consists of chalkstone penetrated by a network of cylindrical *Thalassinoides* burrows (10 to 18 mm diameter) infilled by soft powdery chalk. Small phosphatised chalk pebbles (less than 5 mm) occur up to the level of the upper flint, and their abundance and size-range increases downwards towards the Brown Hardground. The larger fragments are mostly steinkerns. Fossils are abundant at the hardground, particularly immediately beneath it.

Below the Brown Hardground, the chalkstone is more massive, containing less distinct *Thalassinoides* than above, and the size, abundance and degree of phosphatisation of fossils decreases downwards. Nevertheless, pale phosphatised fossils, 20 to 40 mm in diameter, still occur on the top of the Green Hardground. Moulds of aragonitic fossils are also present. This strata between hardgrounds also contains dark green angular clasts of phosphate up to about 10 mm diameter. These are not noticeably concentrated towards the Green Hardground. Glauconitised clasts also occur above the Brown Hardground but are sparser and paler.

The Green Hardground is well glauconitised on the boss-tops, revealing *Entobia* and other borings in section, but otherwise the green mineralisation is pale. Weakly mineralised fossils, fossil moulds and a few dark green or dark brown pebbles occur only within 0.10 m below the hardground. Some 0.30 m below the hardground, the degree of induration reduces to that of nodular chalk and about 0.60 m below there are only isolated nodules. At 0.65 m below the Green Hardground there is another bed of splintery chalkstone, although without a clear upper surface or any green or brown mineralisation. Chalkstone and nodular chalk then continue down to the lower flint.

The base of the Chalk Rock could conveniently be taken at this lower flint (2.3 m below the upper flint), or at a sparser line of flints some 0.36 m above it (making the Chalk Rock only 1.9 m thick) but literal application of Bromley and Gale's (1982) criteria would place it about 0.53 m below the lower flint, where the chalkstone nodules first appear (2.8 m thick).

At the base of the exposed section, in the Middle Chalk, there is an horizon of large inoceramid fragments, which probably correlates with a similar layer seen 0.83 m above the Reed Marl at the Reed Pit.

Therfield

A pit about 0.9 km north-north-east of Therfield Church [3388 3785] in a zone of glaciotectonic disturbance (Chapter 6) shows most of the Chalk Rock dipping northward at 15°, with the flint nodules marking the base resting on chalk of the *T. lata* Zone (Jukes-Browne and Hill, 1904; Bromley, 1967).

Jukes-Browne and Hill (1904) noted that another pit, 'half a mile south-west of the church', shows the Chalk Rock to be nearly horizontal, but its location is unknown.

Reed

The Reed Pit, which is 1 km north of the village [3595 3704], is well known as the type locality for the Reed Marl and for the inclination of the Chalk within a glaciotectonic thrust slice

c.1.5 m

Plate 6   Reed pit [3595 3704]. The thin Reed Tabular Flint (indicated by R G Bromley) is approximately 1.5 m above the omission surface (arrowed) that marks the top of the Kensworth Member (see also Figure 17). (GS 114)

(Plate 6). This contains a complete section from the Reed Marl, a marker bed below the Chalk Rock in the *T. lata* Zone (although this was not exposed at the time of the survey) to above the Top Rock (Figure 17) (Bromley, 1967; Bromley and Gale, 1982, fig. 13; Whitaker et al., 1878; Jukes-Browne and Hill, 1904, p.236). The grey Reed Marl is overlain by some 0.83 m of grey to greyish white chalk containing grey *Thalassinoides* burrows. That is capped by an horizon of inoceramid shell debris and burrow-fill flints, above which the chalk gradually becomes nodular, passing up to the base of the Chalk Rock. The Middle Chalk above the Reed Marl and below the Chalk Rock has yielded *Sternotaxis plana* and *Micraster corbovis* of *lata* Zone type.

The Green and Brown Hardgrounds which represent the Hitch Wood Hardground at Wallington occur at a similar distance from each other at Reed, although they are more weakly mineralised. However, two further, albeit unmineralised, surfaces appear between the Brown Hardground and the 'upper flint', which at Hill End and Weston rests on the Hitch Wood Hardground. At Reed, the 'lower flint' seems to mark the limit of significant cementation and is taken as the base of the Chalk Rock, which is here about 2.5 m thick. The Reed Pit is the type locality of the rhynchonellid brachiopod *Orbirhynchia reedensis*, found in the Chalk Rock, and it is the only locality where the Chalk Rock has yielded the brachiopod

Kingena elegans, which essentially belongs to the Northern Province of the English Chalk.

At Reed, the Kensworth Member is 5 m thick, of which the Top Rock makes up 1 m. The 8.5 m of flinty chalk above the Top Rock contains fragments of the inoceramid *Cremnoceramus* sp., indicating the higher part of the *M. cortestudinarium* Zone (Wood, 1991). There is no definite lithostratigraphical or biostratigraphical evidence for overlap between the Upper Chalk sections exposed at Reed and at Anstey (see below).

Barkway

The section at Barkway Pit, which is 1 km north of the village church [3815 3664], shows at least two glaciotectonic thrust slices, each containing the Chalk Rock (Chapter 6) which dips northwards at about 60°. The Chalk Rock fauna at this locality has been summarised by Whitaker et al. (1878) and the section mentioned or described by Jukes-Browne and Hill (1904), Bromley (1967) and Bromley and Gale (1982).

Pinner's Cross

Descriptions of the Chalk Rock at Pinner's Cross, near Smith's End (where it dips northwards at about 40°), by Whitaker et al. (1878) and Jukes-Browne and Hill (1904) presumably refer to an old chalk pit adjacent to a minor road 0.15 km south of Smith's End [4010 3747].

Anstey

In spite of minor normal faulting, exposures in most of the various faces of the large, currently active quarry at Anstey [395 329] can be correlated to provide a total composite section of about 17.2 m of Upper Chalk. Some 18 to 20 discrete horizons of flint occur in this strata, ranging in character from more or less persistent tabular flints to large nodular flints (at one level with downward extensions) and scattered small flints. A bed of large nodular flints underlain by 3 m of flintless chalk provides a useful marker in the middle of the section. A bed rich in inoceramid bivalves occurs about 0.8 m above the lowest exposed level, and macrofossils (particularly *M. cortestudinarium*) are relatively common at other horizons, except within 6 m of the top of the section. A 20 mm-thick marl seam is present 1.6 m below the top of the section (Hopson, 1990, fig. 1).

Macrofossil assemblages from the lower part of the section up to 6 m below the top are strongly suggestive of the higher part of the *Micraster cortestudinarium* Zone, an assignment which is supported by evidence from the foraminiferal assemblages in two samples from 5 and 14.7 m below the marl seam, respectively (Wilkinson, 1990a; Wood, 1991). Two samples, taken from the marl seam and from about 1 m above it, yielded foraminifera indicating beds in the latest *M. cortestudinarium* Zone at the oldest (Wilkinson, 1990a). Indeed, the absence of *Reussella kelleri* in both samples suggests that they belong in the basal part of the succeeding *M. coranguinum* Zone (Wood, 1991).

Taken together, the observations at Anstey suggest that the marl seam can be correlated with the Upper East Cliff Marl, the higher and more persistent of a pair of marl seams seen in the Kent coastal succession, which marks the base of the *M. coranguinum* Zone (Bailey et al., 1983). This is equivalent to the Shoreham Marl 2 of Sussex (Mortimore, 1986; Wood, 1991).

The absence of conspicuous fragments of large, thick-shelled inoceramid bivalves (*Platyceramus, Volviceramus*) from the beds above the marl seam suggests that only the extreme basal part of the *M. coranguinum* Zone is present. The inoceramid assemblages from below the marl seam are difficult to interpret, but are not directly comparable with those seen above the Top Rock at Reed and suggest an even higher level in the *M. cortestudinarium* Zone (Wood, 1991). There is no definite lithostratigraphical evidence for overlap between the 15.5 m of *M. cortestudinarium* Zone chalk exposed below the marl seam at Anstey and the 8.5 m of chalk exposed above the Top Rock at Reed (Figure 17), so the total thickness for this zone is apparently not less than 24 m.

Moreover, the structural contour plot of the base of the Upper Chalk (Figure 31) suggests that this surface could lie as much as 30 m below the bottom of the Anstey Quarry. Assuming that at Anstey there is (as at Reed) about 6.3 m of strata between the base of the Chalk Rock and the top of the Top Rock, the Top Rock could therefore lie about 24 m below the base of the section at Anstey, with the higher, non-condensed portion of the *M. cortestudinarium* Zone being 39 m thick in total.

On the other hand, interpretation of a resistivity log for a borehole at Nuthampstead [4142 3517], which is about 3 km north-east of the Anstey Quarry, suggests that the marl seam marking the base of the *M. coranguinum* Zone is only about 19 m above the Top Rock. This implies that the Top Rock lies only a few metres below the Anstey section (Wood, 1991) and that there is some overlap between the sections seen at Anstey and at Reed.

Standon

Exposures in a degraded quarry beside the River Rib east of Puckeridge [3961 2290] show some 3.9 m of white well-jointed chalk with five courses of nodular flints. One of these, about 1 m from the base of the section, is associated with a bed of iron-stained, semi-porcellaneous chalk containing inoceramid fragments. This bed yielded foraminifera indicating the *M. coranguinum* Zone (Wilkinson, 1990b).

Aston

A former chalk pit, about 1 km east of Aston [2845 2285], exposed some 4 m of Upper Chalk in a faulted section. A prominent marl seam near the base of the section possibly equates with that seen at Anstey, which is taken to mark the base of the *M. coranguinum* Zone. Two irregular lines of flint occur about 1 and 2.2 m above this marl. Another marl seam is present about 1 m above the upper flint. Specimens of *Micraster spp.* occur within about 0.3 m above the upper flint.

Discontinuous sections, in the roadside bank opposite this quarry [286 228] and for 150 m north-eastwards towards Benington, exposed Chalk with the inoceramid *Platyceramus*, confirming that both this section and the quarry lie within the basal part of the *M. coranguinum* Zone.

A temporary section just south-west of the crossroads near the site of the Aston Pit [2840 2260], and which is topographically lower than and presumably stratigraphically below it, yielded macrofossils (including the bivalve *?Cremnoceramus* as well as *M. cortestudinarium*) indicating the *M. cortestudinarium* Zone (Woods, 1993, p.36).

Benington

A roadside section immediately south of Benington Church [297 235] exposed Chalk containing abundant *Platyceramus*, indicating a position low in the *M. coranguinum* Zone.

Nine Acre Spring

A small pit on the south-west side of Nine Acre Spring ('spring' is a local term for a small wood), which is 2.5 km south of Weston [2641 2762], exposed some 4 m of soft white chalk with a sparse nodular flint course. The lower beds in the pit are affected by subvertical fracture zones up to 1 m wide, and oblique tabular flint sheets are present. Bromley (unpublished field notes, 1965, held at BGS Keyworth) suggested that this pit, and another beside a minor road about 800 m to the north-east [270 280], exposed chalks of the *M. coranguinum* Zone. Structural contours for the base of the Upper Chalk (Figure 31) indicate that both sections are within 25 m of the base of the Upper Chalk.

Chesfield

According to Culpin (1921), chalks exposed in a pit at Chesfield [2480 2790] had been assigned to the *M. coranguinum* Zone (no authority quoted) but he felt that they lay too close to the Chalk Rock for this to be so. In fact, these exposures are likely to be some 25 m above the Chalk Rock and so, in view of the findings at Anstey and at Nine Acre Spring, could indeed extend into the *M. coranguinum* Zone, particularly as they lie within the area of the Hitch Wood facies of the Chalk Rock, where the sequence is most condensed.

Almond's Hill

The Almond's Hill Pit, in the east of Stevenage [243 255], was observed in 1884 by Jukes-Browne and Hill (1904) when it exposed a total of about 21 m of soft white chalk with numerous layers of flint. They inferred that the Chalk Rock lies some 20 m below the lowest beds in the quarry.

The BGS collections include 5 specimens from this locality assigned to *Gibbithyris ellipsoidalis*. If this identification is correct then, based on the range of this species in southern England (Bailey et al., 1983; Mortimore, 1986), an horizon a short distance above the base of the Santonian, in the middle of the *coranguinum* Zone, can be inferred (Woods, 1993, p.35).

Other localities

BGS Technical Reports describing the geology of parts of the district record sections of the Upper Chalk above the Top Rock west of Lodge Farm, Dane End [3355 2088]; north of Sacombe Green Road [3370 1969] (within the *M. coranguinum* Zone, but not the lowest part); 400 m south of Sacombe Hill Cottages [3220 1921]; and south of Rushden [3098 3083]. Each comprises soft or firm white chalk with courses of grey or black flint.

These reports also note similar occurrences of the Upper Chalk above the Top Rock west of Chesfield [2430 2785] (probably in the higher part of the *M. cortestudinarium* Zone); WSW of Chapel Farm, Whempstead [3105 2125]; SE of Whempstead [3245 2057]; north of Braughing [3998 2552]; east of Westmill Bury Farm [3728 2720]; north of Westmill Bury Farm [372 278]; east of Barwick Ford [3880 1880]; in a road cutting, SW of Sacombe [3250 1882]; 2 km SE of Whitwell [1972 1997]; 1.5 km north of Cottered [3171 3050]; in the stream-bed of The Old Bourne, east of Wood End, [337 260 to 335 252]; 1 km west of Rushden [2911 3184]; and near Well Wood, 1.5 km west of Watton at Stone [2830 1917].

FIVE

Palaeogene

The district is north of the main outcrop of the Palaeogene beds of the London Basin. Small outliers, for the most part concealed beneath glacial deposits, have been mapped in the south-east of the district eastward from the River Beane. These outliers form part of a train of small isolated deposits in central Hertfordshire which trend in a west-south-west direction, parallel to the main outcrop (Figure 18). The former extent of the Palaeogene beds to the north-west is not known, but their distribution is indicated by the distribution of the derived clay-with-flints (see Chapter 6).

The Palaeogene beds present within these outliers, as proved in the Dowsett's Farm Borehole [3806 2079] (Figure 19), fall within the Palaeocene and Eocene. They are represented by the Upnor, Woolwich and Reading formations of the Lambeth Group and the lowest part of the Thames Group following the proposals of Ellison, Knox, Jolley and King (1994). The Thanet Sand Formation, which underlies the Upnor Formation in the Gilston Borehole [4417 1349] to the south-east (Figure 18) (Hopson, 1979; IGS, 1978), is not represented in the Dowsetts Farm Borehole. It is probably absent in this district (Hopson, 1982), except for possible remnants preserved within solution pipes and hollows in the Chalk.

Onshore in the United Kingdom, the position of the Palaeogene stage boundaries is imprecise, because of the lack of significant biostratigraphical markers in the generally unfavourable lithofacies, and there is a lack of international agreement on the definition of those stage boundaries. Evidence from the deep sea record and a consensus of opinion amongst biostratigraphers suggests that the Palaeocene/Eocene boundary is best placed at the base of calcareous nannoplankton Zone NP10 (Table 6). Berggren et al. (1985) summarised the magneto-stratigraphy of the Palaeogene, and correlated a time-scale to planktonic micropalaeontological schemes erected by various authors (Table 6). The recognition of the NP9/NP10 zonal boundary onshore in the United Kingdom has proved difficult due to the lack of marine sequences and disconformities at the critical interval. However, Knox and Morton (1988) recognised two phases of Palaeogene volcanic activity in the North Sea Basin; representatives of the younger phase can be identified onshore in East Anglia (Knox and Ellison, 1979), and the older phase in north-east Kent (Townsend and Hailwood, 1985). This allows an indirect correlation of the onshore sequences with nannoplankton-rich sequences in the eastern Atlantic, where attenuated pyroclastic phases are also present (Knox, 1984).

Thus, the NP9/NP10 zonal boundary falls in the hiatus between the Woolwich and Reading formations and the Harwich Formation (Table 6). The lower zonal boundary between NP8/NP9 falls in the hiatus between

the Thanet Sand Formation and the Upnor Formation (Knox, 1990).

Various schemes have been invoked for the classification of the Palaeogene in southern England since the classic papers by Prestwich (1850, 1852, 1854). Whitaker (1866, 1889) summarised these and other early works and erected a primarily lithostratigraphical scheme, which remained in use with only minor amendments well into the second half of this century. Hester (1965) added significantly to the understanding of the lithofacies and palaeogeography of his 'Woolwich and Reading Beds'

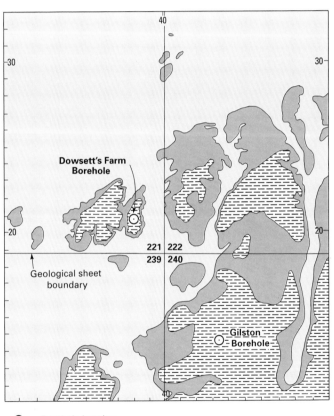

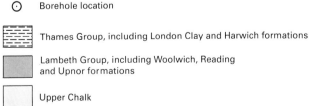

Figure 18 The distribution of the Palaeogene outliers of the district in relation to their mapped occurrences on the Great Dunmow (222), Hertford (239) and Epping (240) geological sheets.

Table 6 Micropalaeontological schemes for the Palaeogene compared to the magnetic polarity timescale (after Berggren et al., 1985) and the lithostratigraphical scheme of Ellison et al., 1994.

Age (Ma)	Magnetic polarity		Foraminifera		Calcareous nannoplankton			Dinoflagellates		Chrono-stratigraphy	Lithostratigraphy	Boreholes
54	Chron C23	N / N	P8	*Morozovella aragonensis*	CP10	NP12	*Marthasterites tribrachiatus*	D8	*Charlesdowniae coleothrypta*	EOCENE / EARLY / YPRESIAN	Thames Group — London Clay Formation	Dowsetts Farm TL32SE38 3806 2079 · Gilston TL41SW35 4417 1349
55		N						D7b	*Dracodinium variolongi-tudum*			
56	C24	N / N	P7	*Morozovella formosa formosa*	CP9	b NP11	*Discoaster binodosus*	D7a	*Dracodinium similis*			
57		b	P6	*Morozovella subbotinae* · *Morozovella edgari*		a NP10	*Marthasterites contortus*	D6b · D6a	*Wetzeliella meckelfeldensis* · *Wetzeliella astra*		Harwich Fm	
58		a	P5	*Morozovella velascoensis*	CP8	b / a NP9	*Discoaster multiradiatus*	D5	*Apectodinium hyperacanthum*		hiatus — Reading Fm / Woolwich Fm / Upnor Fm (Lambeth Group)	
59	C25	N	P4	*Planorotalites pseudo-menardii*	CP7	NP8	*Heliolithus riedeli*			PALAEOCENE / LATE / THANETIAN	hiatus — Thanet Sand Fm	
60					CP6	NP7	*Discoaster gemmeus*					
61	C25	N			CP5	NP6	*Heliolithus kleinpelli*	D4 / D3	*Cerodinium speciosum*	SELANDIAN	Ormsby Clay Fm ?	
62		b / a	P3	*Planorotalites pusilla pusilla* · *M. angulata*	CP4 · CP3	NP5 · NP4	*Fasciculithus tympaniformis* · *Ellipsolithus macellus*					

Sequence proved in boreholes

(the Lambeth Group). A lithofacies-depositional environment model (Ellison, 1983), drawing on the results of the BGS mapping throughout south-east England, demonstrated that the interrelationships proposed by Hester (1965) were in fact more complex in detail. Ellison proposed a model with shallow-marine sediments to the east of the basin and lagoonal clays in the west separated by an offshore sand barrier.

In a major review of the stratigraphy of the London Clay and associated deposits, King (1981) proposed a revised lithostratigraphical classification (Table 7) based on the recognition of five major transgressive/regressive cycles; each cycle is marked by a basal pebble lag or glauconitic bed. An early transgressive event marks the base of his Oldhaven Formation and the overlying London Clay Formation is subdivided into units A to E, with the lowest unit further divided into A1 to A3. The base of A2 corresponds with the base of the *Wetzelilla astra* Zone and hence was considered to be the basal Eocene transgression. The maximum marine transgression is considered to have been during the deposition of unit B.

A comparison of the lithological schemes of various authors and their relationship to the most recent scheme proposed by Ellison et al. (1994), and also adopted in this descriptive memoir, are given in Table 7. However, the lithostratigraphical terminology adopted during the mapping between 1988 and 1991 was based on nomenclature used in recent BGS publications for adjacent areas. Thus, Palaeogene deposits of the Lambeth Group and the lower part of the Thames Group described here are equivalent to the Woolwich and Reading Beds (including the 'Bottom Bed') and the London Clay (including the 'Basement Bed'), respectively, shown on the accompanying map.

These essentially lithostratigraphical schemes have been utilised in biostratigraphical correlations by a number of authors (Costa and Downie, 1976; Costa and Müller, 1978; Jolley and Spinner, 1992; Keen, 1978; King, 1981; Martini, 1971; Murray et al., 1989.

The deposits of the Palaeogene were laid down during a period when climatic conditions were significantly warmer than the present day. The mean annual temperature estimates show an increase from warm temperate conditions during the deposition of the Thanet Sand Formation to fully tropical conditions when the London Clay Formation was deposited. The London Clay Formation is noted for its extensive tropical biota, characterised by the *Nipa* palm (mangrove) floral association (see Collinson, 1983).

The heavy minerals of the Palaeogene sand of southeast England (Morton, 1982) indicate that detrital minerals within the London basin were derived from two distinct sources. The constituent sands of the Thanet, Woolwich and Reading formations, and those within the Thames Group, indicate derivation from the Scottish Highlands, presumably by southward longshore drift

Table 7 A comparison of the lithological schemes previously used to describe the Palaeogene sequences of the Hitchin and adjacent districts with that proposed by Ellison et al., 1994.

Whitaker, 1889	Cooper, 1976	King, 1981		Ellison, Knox, Jolley and King, 1994 and this memoir	
London Clay	Upper London Tertiary Group — London Clay Formation	Thames Group — London Clay Formation: E, D, C, B, A3		Thames Group — London Clay Formation	
		A2 Walton Member			
		Swanscombe Member A1			
Basement Bed		Tilehurst Member		Harwich Formation	
Oldhaven Beds	Lower London Tertiary Group — Oldhaven Fm. inc. London Clay Basement Bed and Blackheath Pebbles Member	Oldhaven Formation — Herne Bay Member			
Blackheath Beds		Blackheath Beds			
Woolwich and Reading Beds	Woolwich and Reading Beds	Woolwich and Reading Beds		Lambeth Group — Reading and Woolwich Formations	
				Upnor Formation	
Thanet Sand	Thanet Formation	not defined		Thanet Sand Formation	
				Bullhead Bed	

along a basin margin lying to the west of the present outcrops. The sands of the Upnor Formation and some beds in the upper part of the Woolwich and Reading formations are derived from a landmass south of the basin, for example the Armorican and/or the Ardennes–Rhenish Massif.

LAMBETH GROUP (PALAEOCENE)

This group comprises the Upnor, Woolwich and Reading formations. Their relationship to the facies scheme of Hester (1965) are shown in Table 8.

In south-east England, the Upnor Formation rests disconformably on the Thanet Sand Formation such that, towards the west and north-west, it oversteps progressively older beds. In this district, the Thanet Sand Formation is absent or confined to solution pipes into the Upper Chalk. However, there is some evidence to suggest that the basal pebble lag of the Palaeogene may be a composite deposit in places within the district with elements of both the basal 'Thanet' Bullhead Bed (of large, nodular, green-coated flints) and the pebble lag (well-rounded black flints) at the base of the Upnor Formation incorporated into a single horizon. For example, at Arbury Wood [304 208], a line of large nodular green-coated flints and red and black coated well-rounded chatter-marked flints rest on the Chalk and can be traced on either side of a minor valley 150 m west of the wood. The same composite nature may also be invoked for the deposits which fill solution pipes in the Chalk, for example at Sacombe Green [338 196]. These occurrences indicate that deposits of the Thanet Formation were formerly more extensive and that the present margin, to the south-east of the district, is the result of erosion prior to and during the Upnor Formation transgression.

The base of the Upnor Formation in this district is marked by a pebble bed, dominated by well-rounded black, red and patinated 'chatter marked' flint pebbles, but with some small green-coated (glauconite) nodular flints and rare white quartz. These pebbles are usually set in a clayey sand matrix, but in places it is bound with stiff brown silty clay. The pebble bed is generally 0.2 m thick, but beds up to 0.91 m have been recorded in the district (Whitaker et al., 1878; and see Details).

The Upnor Formation, approximately 3 m thick in the Dowsett's Farm Borehole, comprises clayey, silty, fine sand and sandy, clayey silt with glauconite and discrete seams of stiff silty clay. The beds are mainly of a pale grey, pale yellow and greenish yellow colour but are mottled in bright red and dark green in places. In analyses of the Upnor Formation ('Bottom Bed'), Hope MacDonald (1965) demonstrated that glauconite forms up to 4 per cent of the light mineral fraction of the sand.

Above the basal pebble bed, the Upnor Formation contains discrete layers of well-rounded, black, flint pebbles. These pebble horizons may be no more than a single pebble in thickness and probably represent short-term fluctuations in the westward encroachment of the sea.

The grading and mineralogy of the Upnor Formation and the Woolwich and Reading formations were discussed by Bateman and Moffatt (1987), who referred to an unspecified site in the Colliers End outlier. Their results show that the Upnor Formation tends to be texturally and mineralogically more diverse than the overlying Woolwich and Reading formations, and suggest that this is due to reworking during the short-lived transgressive event represented by the Upnor Formation. Morton (1982) also regarded the deposit as mineralogically distinct but suggested this was the result of a southerly provenance. Morton's results show the non-opaque heavy minerals to be dominated by zircon (50–60 per cent) with subordinate proportions of tourmaline, staurolite, kyanite and rutile.

The boundary between the Upnor Formation and the overlying Woolwich and Reading formations is usually taken at the first upward break from a dominantly sandy lithology to one dominated by clay. This break is commonly marked by a pebble bed, 'upper conglomerate' of Bateman and Moffat (1987), which has been identified (24.40 to 24.50 m depth) in the Dowsett's Farm Borehole.

The Woolwich and Reading formations (undivided) are represented in this district by approximately 6 m of interbedded, stiff, waxy clays and clayey, silty, fine sands; all are highly colour mottled (Plate 7). All of the beds belong to the 'Reading Type' facies, as designated by Hester (1965, fig. 4), who regarded the deposits as fluviatile or partly deltaic in origin. The essentially terrestrial origin of these deposits, within marsh, tidal creek and

Table 8   The relationship between the Palaeocene schemes of Ellison et al. (1994) and Hester (1965).

Ellison et al. (1994)		Hester (1965) facies	lithostratigraphy
Lambeth Group	Reading Formation Woolwich Formation	fluviatile, partly deltaic facies lagoonal or estuarine facies	Reading Beds Woolwich Beds
	Upnor Formation	marine facies	Bottom Bed
	Thanet Sand Formation	marine facies	Thanet Beds

subaerial dune environments, was first propounded by Hawkins (1946). In reassessing the facies distribution of these beds, Ellison (1983) considered that the mottled clays, sandy clays and sands (which make up the 'Reading Beds' of Hester) were deposited in brackish-water lagoons. The bright mottling and clay content are the result of desiccation, weathering and pedogenesis during subaerial exposure in a tropical environment as proposed by Buurman (1980) (Plate 7).

THAMES GROUP (EOCENE)

Only the lowest part of this group is present in the district and it is apparently limited to the Colliers End outlier. Beds equivalent to the Harwich Formation and the lowest part of the London Clay Formation have been proved in the Dowsett's Farm Borehole (Table 7, Plate 7).

In Dowsett's Farm Borehole, the Harwich Formation (14.87 to 18.44 m) is represented by dark greenish grey and olive green, heavily bioturbated, glauconitic, clayey, fine sandy silt with discrete thinly laminated, silty clay and silty sand seams and with some thin shell beds. This unit has been tentatively identified in the borehole as representing the Swanscombe Member of King (1981).

The beds, between 15.25 to 18.35 m depth, include the foraminiferids *Epistominella* sp., *Guttulina* spp. and *Protelphidium* sp. and the ostracods *Cyamocytheridea* sp. nov., *Cytheretta nerva*, *Clithrocytheridea faboides* and *Cytheridea unispinae* (C King, personal communication, 1993). The association of *C. nerva* and *C. unispinae* is diagnostic of division A1 of King (1981). The unit also contains poorly preserved molluscs attributable to *Arctica* sp. and *Panopea* sp.

In the north-east of the London Basin, outside this district, volcanic ash beds have been recognised in the thicker sequence attributed to the Harwich Formation (Knox and Ellison, 1979). These were regarded by King (1981) as being within his laterally equivalent Swanscombe Member. The ash horizons have not been identified in this district due either to nondeposition or more likely to erosion, prior to the deposition of the Walton Member (Table 7). They have, however, been noted in the Great Dunmow (Lake and Wilson, 1990) and Sudbury (Pattison et al., 1993) districts to the east.

In Dowsett's Farm Borehole, the London Clay Formation (2.16 to 14.87 m) consists of silty clays (Figure 18), the upper part of which is weathered, cryoturbated and contains thin secondary ironpan. King (personal communication, 1991) regards the beds between 4.02 to

Plate 7   Representative cores of the Harwich (a 'London Clay') and Reading (b) formations from the Dowsetts Farm Borehole [3806 2079], Colliers End. (GS 111BB, GS 111CC)

a

Base 9.52 m

b
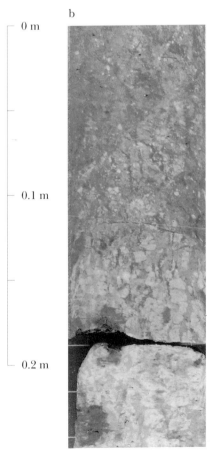
Base 24.40 m

14.87 m depth to be within his Walton Member (A2). This member is characteristically a pale to dark grey, clayey silt to silty clay, with partings and laminae of very fine sand and silt and abundant lignitic debris in part. These pass up into homogenous stiff silty clays of the unnamed 'A3' unit between 2.16 to 4.02 m. This bed, although partly decalcified, yielded the agglutinating (non-calcareous) *Ammodiscus cretaceus* which confirms the 'A3' correlation, and a total thickness for the Walton Member in this district of 10.85 m.

King (1981) identified four lithofacies in the 'London Clay' which he linked to different depositional environments. Two of these lithofacies have been identified in the Dowsett's Farm Borehole. The clays, silts and silty clays are the product of slow deposition in a low-energy marine setting with probable water depths of between 20 and 200 m; they are strongly bioturbated, but upward-coarsening cycles can be identified. The pebble beds represent very slow to interrupted sedimentation, usually associated with glauconite and eroded surfaces in a well-oxygenated, possibly shallow-water environment.

Details

Few exposures of Palaeogene rocks were noted during mapping of the district. To aid the interpretation of the rocks found at outcrop, Dowsett's Farm Borehole was drilled in 1990, sited to sample the thickest part of the sequence, in the largest outlier, around Collier's End. This borehole (Figure 19) proved a total of 25.24 m of beds attributable to the Palaeogene and included a significantly thicker sequence of the 'London Clay' than had been estimated from the field mapping.

Apart from shallow ditch sections, only one exposure was noted during the survey, in contrast to the numerous small sections seen during the original survey in the 1860s to 70s.

In the top of an old chalk pit [3173 1943], 400 m west of Sacombe Hill Cottages, the following section was seen:

	Thickness m
GLACIOFLUVIAL DEPOSITS	0.55
UPNOR FORMATION	
Sand, bright yellow and orange-brown, mottled, silty, clayey, very fine to fine, with a bed of well-rounded black and rare reddish black flints at base	0.21
Sand, clayey, very fine to fine, yellow, mottled orange and red, with well-rounded black flints at base	0.38
Sand, clayey very fine to fine, yellow	0.21
Sand, clayey, with green-coated finger and small nodular flints throughout	0.45
Sand, clayey, very fine to fine, pale yellow	0.27
Clay, reddish brown, waxy, with small angular green-coated flint pebbles on uneven base	0.15
UPPER CHALK	
Chalk, soft, white, jointed, with seams of nodular flints. Beds much obscured by talus	6.00+

A number of sections were noted in the outliers around Sacombe, Colliers End and Braughing by Whitaker et al. (1878) (the modern nomenclature is shown in brackets). For example, an exposure 'half a mile (805 m) east of Sacombe Pond' (possibly just within Sheet 239 to the south) showed '... six feet (1.83 m) of mottled clay and sand with two lines of pebbles...'; these are attributable to the Upnor Formation. A

further note, presumably relating to the same section, states '... at the bottom of the Reading Beds (Upnor Formation) there are green-coated flints'.

Within the Colliers End outlier, a section 'at the kiln ... just south of the village (Colliers End) and east of the High Road' [?371 202] showed the following beds:

	Thickness
(Woolwich and Reading formations)	
Brown clay with race, especially in one layer	8 ft (2.44 m)
Black clay	about 3 ft (0.91 m)
(Upnor Formation)	
Light coloured clay and red mottled clayey sand with flint pebbles 3 inches (0.08 m) at bottom	about 2 ft (0.61 m)
Light-grey bedded sandy clay, red mottled, except in lower part which is more sandy	over 7 ft (2.13 m)
Very small flint pebbles and green-coated flints in greenish clayey sand ('Bottom Bed') resting evenly on the chalk	about ¾ ft (0.23 m)
Upper Chalk	
Chalk with flints	seen

The sequence above agrees closely with that described from the Dowsett's Farm Borehole.

A further section was also noted nearby, 'on the western side of the High Road, opposite the kiln' [369 203].

	Thickness
(Harwich Formation)	
Brown finely bedded sandy clay and loam	nearly 10 ft (3.05 m)
Brown clayey sand ('Basement Bed')	4 ft to water (1.22 m)

The locations of these two sections were tentatively identified during this survey, but both are now overgrown and degraded.

Three boreholes drilled as part of the sand and gravel assessment of the Hertford area (1:25 000 sheet TL31) penetrated beds of Palaeogene age; descriptive logs for these boreholes are given below. Additional details on grading and the overlying drift deposits are given in Hopson and Samuel (1982) and in the records held in the National Geosciences Records Centre at Keyworth.

TL31NW/12   [3221 1970]   Near Sacombe Hill Farm
Surface level 106.1 m above OD

	Thickness m	Depth m
Till	1.1	1.1
LAMBETH GROUP (READING (base of), and UPNOR FORMATIONS)		
Clay, sandy, silty, pale grey, orange-brown mottled; becomes sandier to base	0.3	1.4
Sand, medium- and fine-grained, with less than 5 per cent of small rounded flint pebbles, orange-brown mottled brown, with pale grey silty seams to base	0.5	1.9
Sand, silty, fine- to medium-grained, with a trace of fine, rounded, black, flint pebbles; pale grey, brown and orange-brown mottling	2.4	4.3
Sand, very clayey, stiff, pale greenish grey, with brown and orange brown mottling	0.7	5.0
Sand, silty, fine-grained to sandy silt, pale grey and brown mottled. Fine, well-rounded,		

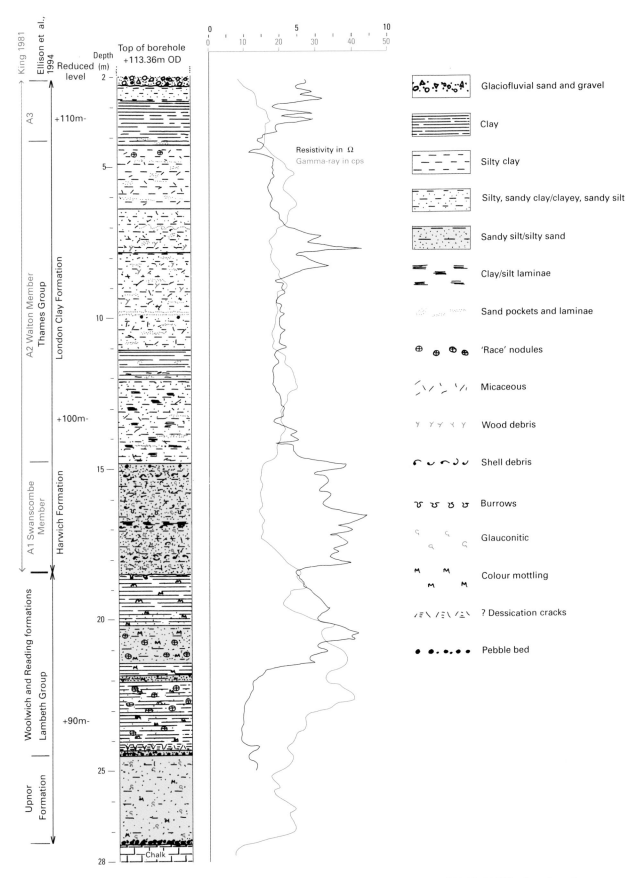

Figure 19 Graphic and geophysical logs for the Dowsett's Farm Borehole [3806 2079], showing the relationship of the strata to the lithostratigraphical schemes of King (1981) and Ellison et al. (1994).

	Thickness m	*Depth* m
flint-pebble seam at 5.0 m; becomes pale grey from 5.4 m	1.5	6.5
Pebble bed of fine to coarse, rounded, flint pebbles in pale grey sandy silt matrix	0.1	6.6

Upper Chalk

Chalk, soft, white, with flint nodules	0.4+	7.0

TL31NW/19   [3424 1940]   Near Sacombe Green
Surface level 113.1 m above OD

	Thickness m	*Depth* m
Till	8.8	8.8

LAMBETH GROUP (READING (base of), and
   UPNOR FORMATIONS)

Sand, very clayey, fine- to medium-grained, stiff orange-brown with grey and black mottling	0.2	9.0
Clay, silty, brown and grey, mottled with black staining; orange mottles from 9.5 to 9.7 m	0.7	9.7
Clay, stiff, brown, with black staining	0.3	10.0
Sand, silty, fine-grained to fine sandy silt, pale pinkish brown, mottled yellow-brown, orange-red and purple. Green, pink and red mottling from 11.1 m. Fine, well-rounded, black, flint pebbles at base	1.9	11.9
Sand, silty, fine-grained, pale greenish grey, mottled purplish brown and red, becoming more silty and clayey to base	2.2	14.1
Clay, silty, stiff, greyish green, mottled orange-brown, with some rounded black flints	0.6	14.7
Clay, silty, fine sandy, packed with fine to coarse, well-rounded flints	0.2	14.9

UPPER CHALK

Chalk, soft, white, with flints	0.4+	15.3

In both the boreholes the division between the Upnor and Reading Formations is unclear, and particularly in TL31NW/12 where numerous pebble beds have been noted. In borehole TL31NW/19 the base of the Reading Formation is probably marked by the pebble bed at 11.9 m.

TL31NE/1   [3590 1968]   Near Standon Green End
Surface level 110.0 m above OD

	Thickness m	*Depth* m
?Till	2.1	2.1

THAMES GROUP (?LONDON CLAY FORMATION)

Silt, clayey, soft, grey, mottled brown	0.4	2.5
Silt, fine sandy, greyish brown with lenses of grey sticky clay and orange-brown silty sand	1.9	4.4
Silt, clayey, stiff, dark grey	0.5	4.9
Clay, bluish grey to dark grey, stiff	0.9+	5.8

In borehole TL31NE/1, the sequence is difficult to classify, but its height above OD suggests that it probably represents the Walton Member (A2) of the London Clay Formation.

A series of trial boreholes for the A10 trunk road improvement scheme, provide a north–south traverse through the Colliers End outlier and penetrated the Palaeogene rocks in a few places. An abridged log of the deepest of these boreholes is given below.

TL32SE/43   [37676 21235]   North-west of Dowsett's Farm
Surface level 106.65 m above OD

	Thickness m	*Depth* m
Till and glaciofluvial sand and gravel	10.60	10.60

LAMBETH GROUP (READING (base of), and
   UPNOR FORMATIONS)

Silt, clayey, very sandy, firm, light grey mottled brown and orange-brown	1.30	11.90
Silt, very clayey, stiff, light grey mottled brown, orange-brown occasionally purple red. Becomes very sandy below 14.50 m	3.80	15.70
Silt, sandy, with a little subrounded fine flint gravel, firm light grey	1.50	17.20
Clay, very silty, sandy, very stiff, with much subrounded fine to coarse flint gravel, light grey	0.40	17.60

UPPER CHALK

Chalk, off-white, fractured, weathered	7.70+	25.30

The junction between the Upnor and Reading formations is probably at 14.50 m, where there is a notable increase in the sand content of the deposits. The pebble bed which is usually present at this level, has not been recorded in this borehole.

SIX

Quaternary

There is a gap of approximately 50 million years in the geological record of this district; deposits of the late Palaeogene and Neogene, of the Tertiary epoch, and part of the Early Pleistocene are absent. The Quaternary of southern England covers the time span from approximately 2.3 to 2.47 million years ago to the present day. The Quaternary includes the Flandrian (or Holocene), representing the last 10 000 years, and the earlier Pleistocene covering the remainder of the period. The Pleistocene is further divided into Early (Lower), Middle and Late (Upper) divisions (see Table 9).

At the type site in southern Italy, the base of the Pleistocene is placed at the level of the Olduvai palaeomagnetic subchron event which is now dated between 1.67 and 1.87 million years ago (Harland et al., 1990). This supersedes earlier dates of 1.72 to 1.88 Ma (Shackleton and Opdyke, 1976; Berggren et al., 1980). Most researchers working around the southern North Sea, however, prefer to accept an earlier age limit for the Pleistocene at approximately the Gauss/Matuyama magnetic reversal (Table 9). This event is dated at 2.47 million years ago, significantly older than the stratotype.

Table 9 The age, magnetic polarity and correlation of the British Pleistocene stages.

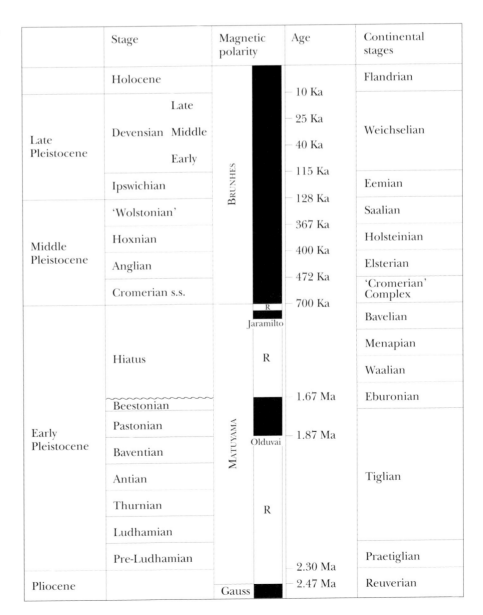

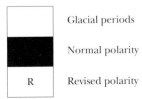

Glacial periods

Normal polarity

R Revised polarity

Thus defined, the Pleistocene includes those deposits which record pronounced palaeoenvironmental and palaeoclimatic changes (Šibrava, 1992).

The sequence of British Quaternary stages (Mitchell et al., 1973) depends greatly upon successions in East Anglia to the east of the district. The Early Pleistocene stages are based largely on studies of the biota preserved in the Ludham (West, 1961; Funnell, 1962 and Norton, 1967) and Stradbroke (Beck et al., 1972) boreholes. The youngest part of the Early Pleistocene and much of the Middle Pleistocene are known from coastal exposures in Suffolk and Norfolk (Reid, 1890; West, 1980 and Banham, 1971). The Hoxnian (West, 1956 and Turner, 1970) and Ipswichian (West, 1957) interglacial stages are both named from localities in East Anglia; the intervening Wolstonian cold stage (about which there is much debate as to its true age) has its type site in the Midlands (Shotton, 1953). The type site for the Devensian is at Four Ashes in Staffordshire (Shotton, 1977).

These Quaternary stages were formally correlated in Mitchell et al. (1973) but a more recent concensus view of Early and Middle Pleistocene correlation between Britain and Holland is given by Gibbard et al. (1991). A digest of that scheme and others for the remainder of the Quaternary, together with palaeomagnetic data and approximate timescale are given in Table 9. The succession of deposits proved within the district and adjacent areas are given in Table 10.

The Quaternary of East Anglia is composed of a complex and varied sequence of largely unconsolidated deposits, reflecting deposition in different environments and climatic conditions. The Quaternary history is characterised by Early Pleistocene warm and cold marine and fluviatile deposition, followed by glacial and interglacial oscillations up to the present day. The deposits of the glacial and interglacial periods (particularly those of Anglian age) are widespread throughout the region and they largely conceal the earlier Pleistocene deposits.

Within this district, there is no evidence of Early Pleistocene marine deposits, although shelly, iron-cemented sands have been found at Rothamsted, 6 km to the south (Dines and Chatwin, 1930). Fluviatile deposits of the former courses of the Thames, of Early Pleistocene age, have been mapped in the south-east of the district in the vicinity of Braughing [395 250].

The Middle and Late Pleistocene are represented by deposits of glacial and interglacial origin. They are mainly associated with the Anglian glaciation, when an ice sheet covered much of the British Isles, as far south as a line from Bristol to London. This glacial period, which occurred between 400 000 and 472 000 years before the present, is the only part of the Pleistocene represented by glaciogenic deposits within the district. The southern margin of the Anglian glaciation is found in the Vale of St Albans, just to the south of this district, where a complex sequence of interleaved glaciofluvial, glaciolacustrine and glacial deposits occurs (Gibbard, 1977). Similar deposits can be traced northwards into the district, within the Hitchin/Stevenage Gap, and to a lesser extent into the Rib/Quin valley. These complex ice-marginal sequences are apparently not represented on the dip slope of the Chilterns where a simpler till and glaciofluvial sand and gravel stratigraphy has been mapped.

The Hoxnian interglacial is represented by lacustrine deposits preserved in kettle-hole like depressions in the Anglian deposits within the Hitchin/Stevenage Gap. This indicates that this major feature was sustantially in its present form during the waning stages of the Anglian glaciation.

Subsequent ice sheets did not reach the district, but considerable remoulding of the landscape occurred during the post Anglian period. Periglacial and fluviatile deposits relating to these post-Anglian times are found within this and adjacent areas (particularly the Thames Valley).

The Flandrian may be regarded as the present interglacial, and covers the period from the end of the Late Devensian glacial (the Loch Lomond readvance), at between 11 000 to 10 000 years BP to the present day. Previous interglacials are characterised by biota which show pre-, early-, late- and post-temperate zones (Turner and West, 1968); Flandrian deposits in southern Britain are known to cover the first three of those zones and we are thus climatically in the acme of the present interglacial period.

In this district, the deposits of the Quaternary fall into three groups. Firstly, those of a residual and fluviatile origin formed prior to the Anglian glaciation and whose original geomorphological expression has been greatly modified; secondly, the Anglian glacial deposits, which rarely retain their original landforms, and thirdly the post-Anglian deposits which are the product of mass-movement and fluviatile processes acting mainly upon the Anglian glacial deposits. The generalised relationships between the Quaternary deposits is shown in Figure 20.

PRE-ANGLIAN

Clay-with-flints

The clay-with-flints is typically composed of orangish brown or reddish brown clays and sandy clays containing abundant flint nodules and pebbles. It is generally less than 10 m thick, and occurs as a dissected capping overlying the Upper Chalk, on interfluves of the Chilterns dip slope, or, very locally, overlying the Middle Chalk at the top of the main escarpment. In the district, particularly in the east, much of the clay-with-flints has been covered by glacial deposits or removed by glacial erosion.

The clay-with-flints was derived mainly from thin basal Palaeogene deposits by periglacial and pedological processes during the Quaternary, but also incorporates some residue from solution of the underlying Chalk and minor additions of Quaternary sediment (Catt and Hodgson, 1976; Catt, 1983, 1986). The base of the deposit thus approximately corresponds to the sub-Palaeogene transgression surface, which dips very gently to the south-east (Chapter 7). The clay-with-flints could be expected to pass gradationally into the Palaeogene deposits in the south-east of the district (cf. Bateman, 1988), but in the area where this transition would occur (east of the

Table 10 The Quaternary deposits of the Hitchin district and their relationship to deposits in adjacent areas.

Stage	Deposits of the Hitchin district	Adjacent districts		
		Thames Valley	Vale of St Albans	East Anglia
Flandrian	Peat Alluvium	Alluvium		
Devensian	Dry valley deposits River terrace deposits Coombe deposits Head ?Alluvial fan	Lower Floodplain Terrace		
Ipswichian		Upper Floodplain Terrace		
Wolstonian	Coombe deposits Head Alluvial fan	Taplow Terrace Lynch Hill Terrace		
Hoxnian	Hitchin brickearth	Boyn Hill Terrace		
Anglian	Glaciofluvial deposits Glaciolacustrine deposits Till Deposits of the Hitchin Gap	Black Park Terrace Winter Hill Terrace	Smug Oak Gravels Eastend Green Till Moor Mill Laminated Silts Westmill Upper Gravel Ware Till Walton Road Laminated Silts Westmill Lower Gravel	Lowestoft Till Barham Sands and Gravels Barham Arctic Structure Soil
Cromerian s.s.	Letchworth Gravels			Valley Farm Rubified *sol lessivé*
Hiatus				
Beestonian	Kesgrave Sands and Gravels (Westland Green Gravels)	Gerrards Cross Terrace Beaconsfield Terrace Satwell Terrace Westland Green Terrace Stoke Row Terrace		Kesgrave Sands and Gravels
Pastonian				
Baventian				
Antian				
Thurnian		Nettlebed deposits	Pebble Gravels	'crag'
Ludhamian			'crag' at Rothampstead	
Pre-Ludhamian				
	Clay-with-flints			

Hitchin Gap) the clay-with-flints has been eroded or covered by the extensive glacial deposits (Figure 31c).

However, where structural contours for the clay-with-flints can be constructed, they show considerable variations from a simple south-east-dipping surface, principally where the base of the deposit slopes down into the larger valleys and towards the Chalk escarpment (Figure 31). This is more likely to reflect mass movement during the Quaternary than unevenness in the pre-Palaeogene surface. For mapping purposes, the point at which clay-with-flints, formed by essentially vertical redistribution of material, passes into head, deposited by lateral mass movement, is judged by geomorphological criteria, but these have not necessarily been applied consistently throughout the district.

Shallow, circular depressions, usually 10 to 50 m in diameter but exceptionally up to 80 m, are locally common on, or close to, the clay-with-flints outcrop. They are taken to mark the sites of buried solution pipes penetrating the Chalk surface. These pipes typically range up to

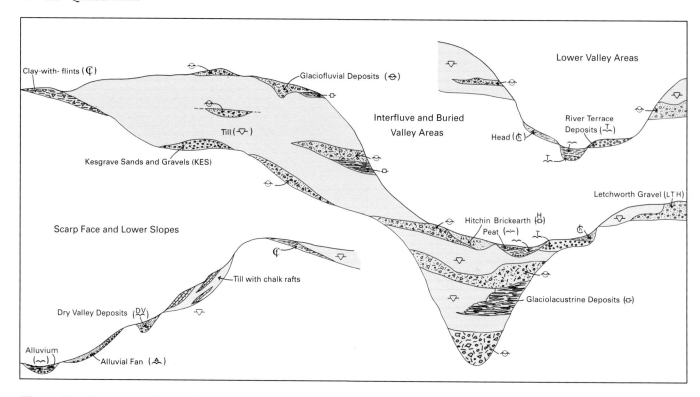

Figure 20 The generalised relationships between the Quaternary deposits of the district.

about 10 m in diameter and 10 to 15 m in depth, but larger and compound examples occur. The clay-with-flints has been let down into the solution pipes as they formed, so that flint clasts in the clay tend to be aligned parallel to their walls. In some instances, recognisable remnants of the Palaeogene deposits are also present in the pipes. Brown silt and clay can be found at several decametres depth in boreholes in otherwise undisturbed Chalk, having infiltrated down joints.

The old cockpit at Quickswood, east of Baldock [2754 3296], is of similar area to some of the surface depressions, although it is somewhat deeper than is typical. It seems probable that an existing hollow was adapted for this purpose by the former occupants of the old Quickswood House, which previously stood nearby.

Yellowish brown silty clay, commonly used for brick-making in the past, was laid down where water accumulated in surface declivities, but these deposits are generally hidden beneath stony head and are included with clay-with-flints on the maps (Shephard-Thorn, 1993, fig. 2; Shephard-Thorn et al., 1994).

The thickness of the clay-with-flints can vary considerably over short distances because of the solution pipes. For example, one of a series of site investigation boreholes, south-east of Baldock near Newfield Hill, Weston [2530 3234] proved Chalk beneath 0.7 m of clay-with-flints, but another borehole close by [2532 3234] penetrated 10.9 m of sandy clay and clayey sand before reaching the Chalk. Outside the solution hollows, boreholes indicate a general thickness for the deposit of about 5 m, rarely exceeding 10 m.

The composition of the clay-with-flints is quite variable. The matrix is typically a stiff, often waxy, mottled reddish, orangish or yellowish brown clay, with black manganiferous staining, but in some places it is silty or sandy. Minor deposits of sand and pebbly sand are also included locally. These probably represent lithological variation in the parent Palaeogene formation.

Flint occurs as complete or broken nodules, as more or less angular pebbles and gravel, or as well-rounded pebbles. Many of the nodules have been deeply patinated (bleached) and many are stained reddish brown or black by iron and manganese oxides and hydroxides. Some of the angular fragments are likely to be products of in-situ shattering by weathering, but others probably have been incorporated by cryoturbation from overlying glacial sediments. Some of the larger fragments display the shallow pitting arising from prolonged exposure to frost. The well-rounded pebbles are characteristic of certain Palaeogene deposits from which they were derived. They normally display short arcuate superficial fractures ('chatter-marks') formed in their littoral depositional environment (Gibbard, 1986). In places, the clay-with-flints consists entirely of such pebbles packed together with a clay matrix. Exotic quartzite pebbles occur sporadically with the flints, as do fragments of sarsen (Palaeogene sandstone with siliceous cement) and 'Hertfordshire pudding-stone' (well-rounded flint pebbles in a siliceous matrix).

In a few areas, such as near Clothall [2748 3205] and south-west of Rushden [2936 3045], blocks of hard, pale-coloured, porcellaneous limestone resembling calcrete are found in the soil close to the base of the clay-with-flints. Some of these blocks enclose small flint nodules, some display small angular voids or internal lamination and some comprise recemented limestone breccia. This material is distinct from the chalkstones within the lowest part of the Upper Chalk (Chapter 4), but its origin is not known (Aldiss, 1991).

The practical difficulties of augering in stony ground precluded the delineation of lithological variations in the clay-with-flints. Further difficulties arise in distinguishing some glaciofluvial deposits from the sandier facies of the clay-with-flints, unless the former contain obvious chalk or erratic detritus, and in classifying deposits where the clay-with-flints may have been redistributed by glacial processes.

In an area north-west of Preston [16 25], the clay-with-flints includes deposits of mottled orangish brown and pale grey or greyish brown clay, some silty or sandy, locally streaked with the more typical reddish brown clay, and usually containing only flint gravel, sparse angular pellets of chalk and rare pebbles of quartz and quartzite. This is regarded as a relatively undisturbed portion of the original Palaeogene deposits, albeit having incorporated some material from overlying glaciofluvial deposits and fragments of the underlying Chalk by cryoturbation (Aldiss, 1992a).

Between Stevenage, Walkern and Weston, there seems to be a gradational passage from clay-with-flints to thin reddish brown clays with a sparse content of flint which occur at the fringes of some till outcrops and overlying the Chalk. These are thought to represent reconstituted basal till, probably derived from the clay-with-flints. Boreholes at Wedgwood Way, Stevenage [262 268], showed the presence of reddish brown silty clay with flint and chalk clasts near the base of the till sequence.

In some places in the south of the district, for example around Sacombe Green [341 196], where both the Palaeogene strata and the till are thin and have been affected by cryoturbation, a reddish brown flinty subsoil develops which resembles the clay-with-flints, particularly where the till has been decalcified. The presence of erratic material and of angular flint sand grains indicates the glacial origin of such deposits.

In some areas, for example just to the west of Wallington [290 338] and south-west of Rushden [29 30], there are enclaves of the clay-with-flints in chalky till, but some of these may be large rafts within the till rather than inliers.

Details

The clay-with-flints is generally seen only in small temporary exposures or in boreholes, and good sections are rare in the district.

Excavations for a large building at Wigmore Bottom [123 223], in 1988, revealed a number of large solution features with infills of 'brickearth' (Shephard-Thorn, 1993, fig. 2). The internal relationships are quite complex: the clay-with-flints seems to have been let down initially into a solution pipe as it developed, and continuing subsidence involved possible reworked remnants of Palaeogene deposits. Laminated silty brickearth accumulated in two phases, firstly while subsidence was active and then after it had ceased. This brickearth is apparently waterlain but is believed to contain an appreciable proportion of wind-blown silt (loess). The whole sequence is covered by stony clay head, derived from the clay-with-flints up-slope.

A trial soakaway pit excavated at Luton airport [1227 2131] in 1988 revealed the following section in the clay-with-flints. The Chalk was not seen.

	Thickness m
MADE GROUND	up to 2.5
Clay, yellow-brown with flints, grey mottled due to gleying	up to 1.0
Clay, yellow-brown and grey, mottled	up to 2.0
Clay, sandy, pale grey-brown	up to 1.0
Clay, sandy, yellow-brown	up to 3.0

Thicknesses were estimated. It seems that the pit had been excavated in the 'brickearth' fill of a solution collapse feature.

An example of a relatively thick clay-with-flints sequence described in some detail is given by the record for the borehole near Hornbeam Spring [2432 1921], on the line of the A1(M) near Knebworth:

	Thickness m	Depth m
Soil, sandy clay	0.2	0.2
CLAY-WITH-FLINTS		
Clay, brown, sandy, with gravel and flint boulders	0.5	0.7
Clay, firm, light brown, mottled, silty	3.3	4.0
Clay, very stiff, red-brown, mottled, becoming sandy with depth and containing gravel and flint cobbles	4.2	8.2
Clay, very stiff, dark brown, peaty, sandy	0.6	8.8
UPPER CHALK		

Organic material has not been found in the clay-with-flints and the description notes 'peaty' clay just above the chalk. This description probably refers to manganiferous staining.

Kesgrave Sands and Gravels

Deposits assigned to the Kesgrave Sands and Gravels are limited to the south-east of the district around Braughing [395 250] and Dassels [393 273]. Similar deposits are more extensive in the Great Dunmow district (Sheet 222) to the east.

The term Kesgrave Sands and Gravels was first proposed by Rose, Allen and Hey (1976) and was fully described by Rose and Allen (1977). At that time the term was reserved for quartz- and quartzite-rich sandy gravels and pebbly sands which were considered to be the product of a single terrace aggradation of a former Thames drainage system (the proto-Thames) which crossed East Anglia from the Vale of St Albans towards Ipswich and thence northward to Norwich.

Rose and Allen considered the Kesgrave deposits to be of Beestonian age, based on the superposition of the Valley Farm Rubified *sol lessivé* which is the remnant of a soil formed during the warm Cromerian stage.

This simple picture has been significantly modified by further research, so that now a number of terrace aggradations, preserved on the northern limb of the London Basin, have been delimited within the Kesgrave deposits. These proto-Thames deposits have been correlated with the terrace sequence of the Middle Thames identified by Hare (1947) and later correlated regionally by Sealy and

Sealy (1956), Green and McGregor (1978), Green, McGregor and Evans (1982) and by Gibbard (1977, 1983, 1985). Whiteman and Rose (1992) have proposed a nomenclature for all of these ancestral Thames terrace aggradations, and the term 'Kesgrave' has been used as a group name (Table 11). The British Geological Survey uses the term Kesgrave Sands and Gravels on the maps in East Anglia in a formational sense, as first defined, that is it includes all of the quartz- and quartzite-rich sub-Anglian sands and gravels of proto-Thames affinity.

Gibbard (1977) identified quartz- and quartzite-rich gravels in the Vale of St Albans which he termed the Westmill Upper and Lower Gravels. These gravels, which he equated with the Winter Hill Terrace of the Middle Thames catchment, also contain some nondurable pebble species which he regarded as being derived from the advancing Anglian (Lowestoft) ice sheet. Thus he regarded the Westmill Lower Gravel as the last proto-Thames terrace aggradation, before the Thames was diverted to its present more southerly course. The Westmill Upper Gravel, which rests on the Ware Till, reflects a short-term, glaciofluvial event prior to the advance of the main Anglian ice sheet, which deposited the Eastend Green Till (Gibbard, 1977). The glaciofluvial deposits, mapped on the southern edge of the district, may include beds of sand and gravel equivalent to the Westmill Upper and Lower gravels of Gibbard (1977) in the area to the south.

The Kesgrave Sands and Gravels shown on the Hitchin sheet correlate, by their relative height above Ordnance Datum, to the gravels described and mapped around Westland Green by Hey (1965); they were further discussed by Lake and Wilson (1990). The 'Kesgrave' deposits of this district thus represent one of the earliest terrace aggradations of the proto-Thames.

In general, the deposits comprise pebbly sands and sandy gravels with a low silt and clay content. The gravel fraction (greater than 4 mm) is mainly of fine-grade material, with some coarse gravel and rare cobbles usually concentrated in a basal lag. The gravel-grade material is mainly of angular and well-rounded flint, in subequal proportions, which amounts to 60–65 per cent of this grade overall. Rounded quartz and quartzite, in the ratio of 2:1, accounts for between 30 and 35 per cent of the gravel with minor proportions of sandstone, ironstone, igneous and metamorphic rocks. In the 4 to 8 mm fraction there is a marked increase in the quartz and quartzite content and a decrease in flint content.

The sand fraction is medium with fine grade and minor amounts of coarse grade. It is composed largely of subrounded to subangular quartz grains, with some of angular medium- and coarse-grade flint. The heavy mineral content is low; it includes zircon, rutile and tourmaline. This is in marked contrast to the heavy mineral suite of the glaciofluvial sands and gravels (discussed later) and can be a useful means of separating superficially similar sand and gravel deposits associated with the Anglian glaciation and earlier events.

Details

There are no large exposures of this deposit within the district; quartzose gravels were noted, incorporated into solution features in the Chalk in a small pit north of Braughing [3993 2552] and in a ditch section [4005 2695] on the margin of the sheet, east of Dassels. Elsewhere the deposit was recognised on the occurrence of a quartz-rich gravel brash in the soil.

Letchworth Gravel

This 'quartzose' sandy gravelly deposit was recognised for the first time during this survey (Smith, 1992a). It occurs at surface over an area of less than 1 km² to the northwest of Letchworth (Figure 21), from which it takes its

Table 11 Ancestral Thames stratigraphy and nomenclature of Early and Middle Pleistocene age (after Whiteman and Rose, 1992).

Group	Formation	Member Middle Thames	Essex/Suffolk	Lithology	Palaeogeography	Stage UK	Continent
	Maidenhead	Black Park Terrace		Flint-dominated	Thames diverted to its present southerly course	Late Anglian	Late Elsterian
Kesgrave	Colchester	Winter Hill (Lw.) Terrace	Lower St Osyth Wivenhoe	Flint with quartz and quartzite (ratio 4f:lqtzite)	Thames confined by the Cotswold escarpment reworking Sudbury Fm. far-travelled material	▲ Early Anglian ⁞ Cromerian to Pre-Pastonian ▼	▲ Elsterian to 'Cromerian' Complex ▼
		Winter Hill (Up.) Terrace Rassler Terrace	Ardleigh Waldringfield				
	Sudbury	Gerrards Cross Terrace Beaconsfield Terrace Satwell Terrace Westland Green Terrace Stoke Row Terrace	Moreton Bures Stebbing Westland Green	Flint with much quartz and quartzite (ratio 2.5f:lgtzite)	Thames headwaters draining west Midlands beyond Cotswold escarpment		▲ 'Bavelian' Complex Menapian Waalian Ebouronian ▼ Late Tiglian
	Nettlebed	Nettlebed deposits		Flint only	Thames catchment confined to London Tertiary basin		

name. It is best seen around Fairfield Hospital [204 353], on the eastern side of the Hitchin Gap, where it caps a low flat-topped hill rising to about 70 m above OD. Smaller spreads to the south are found on both sides of the Pix Brook where it is also overlain by the till.

There are no natural sections available for study and an auger hole near Fairfield Hospital [2048 3540], is designated the type section; the surrounding mapped outcrop for some 250 m, is taken as the type area.

The base of the deposit in the type section is at about 66.5 m above OD. Elsewhere gravels mapped at surface have a fairly flat base at about 62 to 66 m above OD; it is likely that these slight differences are caused, at least in part, by a feather edge of downwash and soil creep material.

The Letchworth Gravel comprises pebbly sands and sandy gravels, rich in rounded quartzite, quartz and sandstone pebbles, which enable it to be readily distinguished from the flint-rich Anglian glaciofluvial gravels. In parts it has a reddish brown medium- to coarse-grained sandy matrix which gives a characteristic orange-brown very sandy pebbly soil.

The origin of the Letchworth Gravel remains unresolved, and the subject of continuing investigation (Smith, in preparation). The lack of obvious glacial indicators, such as chalk and Jurassic limestones or fossils, suggests that it is not a glaciofluvial gravel associated with the nearby till. It rests unconformably on the Lower Chalk and is not directly overlain by younger drift around Fairfield Hospital. Farther south, it appears from the mapping to be overlain by chalky drift (assumed to be Lowestoft Till), though superposition of till on the gravels could not be proved by hand-augering, and it is therefore regarded as pre-Anglian in age (Hopson, 1992).

Its relatively high clay content may be the result of illuviation, suggesting that it remained near the surface undergoing alteration for some time prior to burial by the till. Additional evidence for this may be found on the flints, most of which have a thick yellow cortex indicating a long period of weathering, suggesting that they are 'old' flints eroded out of the Chalk a long time ago and probably predate the chalky till, whose contained flints usually have a relatively thin whitish cortex.

The non-flint pebbles and the red sandy matrix are similar to the suite of deposits related to the Baginton Lillington Sands and Gravels of the Midlands (Shotton 1953), which some authors now regard as pre-Anglian in age (Rose, 1991). Thus it is probably of comparable age to the Kesgrave Sands and Gravels, postdating the clay-with-flints and predating the Anglian glacial drifts.

The available evidence suggests that the gravel is in situ and of Midlands derivation. It could be a pre-Anglian glaciofluvial deposit, but no such glaciation has yet been identified. More likely, it is a fluvial deposit laid down by a pre-Anglian stream draining southward from the Midlands Baginton–Lillington catchment area, and following a valley through the Chalk scarp along the line of the Hitchin Gap, into the Thames Basin–Kesgrave terrace sequences. There it can be correlated tentatively, on the basis of elevation above OD, with the latest (and lowest) deposits of the Colchester Formation (Whiteman

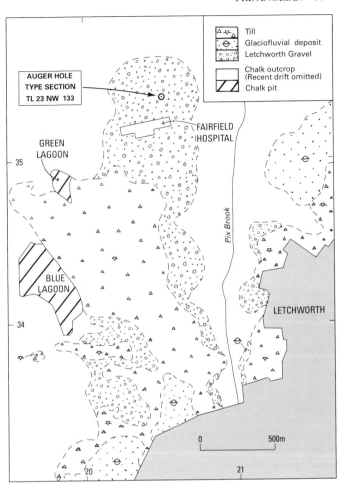

Figure 21 The distribution of the Letchworth Gravel.

and Rose, 1992), of the Kesgrave Group, which immediately predates the deposition of chalky Lowestoft Till of the Anglian glaciation. In terms of composition, the high quartzite and quartz content together with a still significant flint content is intermediate between those of the Upper and Middle Thames regions.

Details

Much of the ground close to the Fairfield Hospital buildings has been disturbed and care was needed in the selection of a type section. A site was chosen in a field [2048 3540], judged to be the highest easily accessible point likely to give the maximum thickness of undisturbed deposit. A pit dug by hand and deepened by hand-auger successfully penetrated the full thickness of the Letchworth Gravels (see Appendix 1). Samples were collected for grading and further analysis (Smith, 1992). This type section showed that 3.55 m of mainly clayey and very clayey, gravel and sandy gravel rest on soft, puttied Lower Chalk. Nearby, the borehole at the hospital itself [2043 3526] proved 2.1 m of drift, assumed to be gravel. Apart from possible occurrences in solution hollows the deposit is probably no more than 3 to 4 m thick.

Pebble counts on the (8 to 32 mm) gravel fractions of two surface samples and five samples collected from the auger hole show about 60–80 per cent durable quartzose components, comprising rounded pebbles of quartz, quartzite and sandstone with about 15–25 per cent subangular flints. The fine gravel fraction (+ 4 to − 8 mm) is particularly rich in ironstone which can form as much as 20 per cent. Minor Jurassic shell fragments and limestone pebbles are found at the base of the deposit; originally they may have occurred throughout the deposit but have been largely destroyed in the decalcified part by percolating groundwaters. Their survival, immediately above the Chalk bedrock, may be attributed to carbonate saturation of the groundwater in this zone.

The full log for the type section, at [2048 3540] is shown in Appendix 1.

ANGLIAN

The sequence consists of till, glaciofluvial deposits (mainly sands and gravels) and glaciolacustrine deposits; these are discussed under separate headings, below. In addition, two major facies are described, consisting of the complex associations of these lithologies, relating to two contrasting ice-front situations. Firstly, the 'glacio-tectonic' deposits of the Barkway to Therfield area occur where ice movement has been impeded by the Chiltern escarpment, leading to bedrock rafting and redeposition. Secondly, the buried channel sequences of the Hitchin Gap and other areas occur where ice lobes have found preferential advancement along pre-existing valley systems (which they may also erode) or where subglacial erosion has resulted in thicker than normal sequences.

Perrin et al. (1979) considered the Anglian deposits of Lowestoft (the main Anglian ice advance) type to be characterised by high, opaque, heavy-mineral suites in the generally low fine sand contents. Non-opaque mineral species also contain considerable amounts of non-durable heavy minerals such as kyanite. This is in marked contrast to the underlying Letchworth Gravel and Kesgrave Sands and Gravels, with low opaque and high resistate heavy-mineral suites. The differences in the heavy-mineral suites can be a useful indicator where reworking has occurred.

Till

The till of this district is considered to be entirely related to the Anglian glaciation and has been termed variously the Chalky Boulder Clay or Lowestoft Till. It is the major and most widespread of the Anglian deposits of this district.

The term Chalky Boulder Clay was introduced by Harmer (1902) who applied it to the blue-grey chalky clays found over the monotonous plateau in East Anglia; this district represents the south-western extremity of that plateau.

Boswell (1931) demonstrated that the Chalky Boulder Clay contained two tills which he termed the Chalky-Jurassic and Upper Chalky Boulder Clay. Subsequently, Baden-Powell (1948, 1950) and West and Donner (1956) distinguished the two tills of Boswell as the Lowestoft and Gipping tills. This was based on their internal differentiation and stone orientation, and they considered them to be the product of two glaciations. The work of Perrin,

Rose and Davies (1979) demonstrated that there was no basis for distinguishing two glaciations. They suggested instead, that the East Anglian plateau till represented a single glacial event, with differences in lithology and stone orientation being simply attributed to ice-streaming within a complex ice sheet. They used the term Lowestoft Till to cover all of the Chalk and Jurassic-clay-rich tills in East Anglia; this concept has been generally accepted since.

The lithological characteristics of the Lowestoft Till were comprehensively expounded by Perrin et al. (1979), and by more recent workers investigating the stratigraphy of the Anglian Till (?ice) margin, for example Cheshire (1983) in the Vale of St Albans and Whiteman (1987) in central Essex. Although these studies were made outside the district, they give a general indication of the lithology of the till around Hitchin; indeed, with the exception of the buried glacial channels, the till exhibits a remarkable lithological consistency throughout East Anglia.

In the Vale of St Albans, Gibbard (1977) identified two tills related to the Anglian glaciation, the Ware and Eastend Green tills. The Ware Till, he believed, represents an early south and south-eastward advance through the Hitchin Gap, and the later Eastend Green Till represents the main ice advance over the Chiltern chalk scarp to the north. The relationship of these tills to those identified in the Hitchin Gap is given in the description of the buried channel sequences (see below).

For the most part, the till of the district is an unsorted, matrix-dominant, stony clay of lodgement type, derived from source rocks of Jurassic and Cretaceous age entrained as the Anglian ice advanced in fan-like fashion from the area of the Wash.

The till encompasses variations of this lithology resulting from different genetic processes acting upon the entrained debris within the ice sheet; thus, ablation, solifluction, subaqueous sedimentation and shear-stress deformation have produced local differentiation within an otherwise structureless sequence. These differences are most commonly associated with the 'channel' or 'valley' sequences which acted as conduits for subglacial drainage.

The unweathered till is mainly a blue-grey or dark grey, massive, stony, chalk-rich, sandy, overconsolidated silty clay. The most abundant clasts, accounting for 50 to 60 per cent of the total, are of chalk, and range in size from boulders to granule grade (and below). They are predominantly rounded and vary from relatively soft to very hard; the latter commonly show striae. Other common clasts are flint (both angular and well-rounded), quartz, quartzite and sandstone. More rarely, Jurassic and Cretaceous fossils and rocks, Carboniferous Limestone and a variety of igneous and metamorphic rock types are found. Clasts of considerable size have been found on the till and a number have achieved some 'notoriety' such as that in Royston town centre (a gritstone) or the finer-grained quartzite used as a monument to Vincenzo Lunardi, at the site of his landing near Sacombe End [3642 1979], after the first manned balloon flight in England in 1784.

In places, particularly near the base of the till, the entrainment of large volumes of locally derived material greatly affects the appearance of the till, so that the boundary can become obscure. This is particularly prevalent where the Anglian ice has overridden the clay-with-flints or Palaeogene deposits.

At the surface, the till is decalcified and weathered to a yellow-brown, stony clay soil. Deeper within the weathered zone, the till becomes yellow-brown mottled pale grey around surviving chalk pebbles. It is this layer which is most frequently seen after deep ploughing or in drainage ditches. The depth of weathering varies considerably depending on a complex inter-relationship of factors, which include mineralogy, climate, groundwater levels, drainage conditions and the incidence of vegetation. Over much of the outcrop, however, the weathered zone rarely exceeds 1.5 m.

Within the 'channel' sequences, there are some true lodgement tills which conform to the description above, but flow-banded tills are more common. The latter are pale grey, chalky and very silty, grading into lacustrine silts and clays, in places. These tills in places contain few exotic clasts, the majority being of chalk or flint; the clasts are generally smaller, ranging only up into the lower end of the coarse gravel (16 mm) grade. They are believed to be the product of high-density mass movement and aqueous sedimentation and as such conform to the descriptions of flow- and waterlain-tills.

The channel sequences are not confined laterally by vertical sides as suggested by Woodland (1970). Slopes in excess of 45° can be demonstrated at some localities on the sides of these channels, but in general the confining slopes are much lower. This factor is crucial in the current interpretation of these channel sequences. It now seems likely that there is no 'cut off' point between the 'channel' and 'plateau' sequences (as would be the case in Woodland's tunnel valleys), but that one grades laterally into the other, albeit over a limited width. The inter-relationship of the till with the glaciofluvial and glaciolacustrine deposits is complex; sands and gravels, and structureless stone-free silts and clays are found beneath, within and above the till. This presumably reflects their original environment of deposition within or adjacent to the Anglian ice sheet. The complexity is greatest within the channel sequences, but it can also be seen within the plateau area.

The till appears to be thickest within the Hitchin Channel sequence where a number of discrete beds have been proved (see discussion later). The generally poor descriptions of glacial deposits in borehole logs throughout the district preclude an accurate assessment of thickness. In the channels, the aggregate thickness of till may be considerable but generally, in boreholes, where till can be separately identified, individual beds rarely exceed 10 m. Within the Hitchin Channel, the Henlow Borehole [164 356] proved 107.9 m of glaciogenic sediments, but the beds are poorly described in the borehole log. Estimates of till thickness over the plateau, based on mapping, suggest a range between 10 and 20 m east of Stevenage, but farther east, in the vicinity of Walkern and Buntingford, boreholes show a maximum thickness of between 25 and 40 m. For example, in boreholes at Walkern Park Farm [3151 2474] and Bury Farm, Wyddial [3741 3171], 27.4 and 39 m, respectively, of 'boulder clay' were recorded. The till thickens to the east of the district (Horton, 1988); it is at least 30 m thick over the plateau and reaches a maximum of 38.1 m at Meesden Hall [4384 3247].

Large exposures of till are rare but the upper weathered zone is commonly exposed in drainage ditches. In the past, the till was exploited on a small scale for brick and tile manufacture and for the 'liming' of 'light' agricultural land; only a few overgrown and degraded exposures remain.

Glaciofluvial deposits

These deposits have been mapped extensively within the major valleys and in patches across the plateau. They have been proved as sheet-like and irregular-shaped bodies in close association with the till. The sediments were deposited as proglacial outwash and within subglacial and englacial streams. They are highly variable in thickness, lateral extent and composition. The deposits range from fine, clean, cross- and planar-bedded sand to structureless, clay-bound cobble gravel (or hoggin); most commonly they fall within the pebbly sand and sandy gravel range.

The suite of pebbles within these deposits closely reflects those found within the till, with the proviso that glaciofluvial transportation has tended to remove much of the softer chalk and other nondurable clasts so that flint becomes the dominant component.

In general terms, deposits found beneath and above till are low in chalk clasts and rich in flint, quartz and quartzite; those within till are commonly chalky and appear to grade laterally into glaciolacustrine deposits and till.

The deposits have been worked from a number of small pits, commonly less than 5 m deep; large-scale extraction is limited to the thicker deposits associated with the channel sequences. The generally variable distribution, relatively high clay, and deleterious pebble content have tended to limit their use as aggregates and they are presently of limited economic importance in this district.

The cohesiveness of the sands and gravels depends mostly on their clay and silt content, but in places some are cemented by secondary iron-minerals (ferrocrete). In a few places, sands and gravels cemented by calcrete-like material or by sparry calcite occur as blocks. These occur near the base of the till, for example south of Wellhead [1753 2739] and in the pit at Holwell [1676 3200] (Bloom and Wooldridge, 1929).

In the Vale of St Albans to the south, Gibbard (1977) noted the existence of the Westmill Upper and Lower Gravels. The Upper Westmill Gravel is intercalated between the Ware Till and Eastend Green Till, and therefore represents a truly Anglian deposit, equivalent to at least part of the succession encountered along the southern margin of this district and within the channels of the Hitchin and Rib/Quin valleys. He also considered

Plate 8 An 'ice-push' stucture in glaciofluvial deposits within the Hitchin Channel at the Holwell pit [1668 3215]. (GS 120U)

The direction of movement is from left to right (north to south). Note the small- scale faulting at the base of the structure indicating that part of the sequence at least must have been in a frozen state at the time. Approximate scale shown.

the Westmill Lower Gravel (the youngest, pre-diversionary, proto-Thames terrace) to be Anglian in age and on this basis it probably received an influx of pro-glacial outwash via the Hitchin Channel (Gibbard, 1977, fig. 16b).

The existence of ice in close proximity to sand and gravel accumulations can also be demonstrated by a number of structures regarded as the result of ice push. Examples were noted at Holwell [1668 3215] in the Hitchin Channel (Plate 8) and near Dane End [3294 2079] and by ice wedge casts noted by Gibbard (1977) at Moor Mill Quarry [143 025] south of this district.

Glaciolacustrine deposits

The glaciolacustrine deposits are commonly associated with the channel sequences; elsewhere, only very limited outcrops have been noted. The deposits are typical of quiet-water accumulation. They are composed of fine- and very fine-grained sandy silts and silty clays with rare stones (?dropstones) and are commonly finely laminated. In places, the deposit is highly calcareous with sand- and silt-grade chalk grains.

At surface, the deposits are oxidised to a pale yellowish brown colour, but at depth, in boreholes, within the Hitchin Channel, the deposits are dark grey to greenish grey fine sandy silts with included thin chalky waterlain tills and clayey sandy gravels. In some specimens, collected within otherwise undisturbed and laminated sequences, the silts are severely disturbed and disrupted by 'slumping' (Plate 9). The origin of these slumped units within otherwise undisturbed sediment may be attributed to periodic erosion and sediment collapse, ice ploughing or post-burial slumping of wet and/or frozen sediment instigated by the wasting of included buried ice.

The minor occurrences encountered on the plateau are generally thin as shown by many small degraded pits, commonly only 2 to 3 m deep. These pits provided the raw material for brick and tile manufacture in the past.

It can be difficult to be certain if individual occurrences of fine-grained sediments of this type should be correctly attributed to lacustrine or to fluvial deposition. In general, where sequences of fine sand, silt and clay are extensive and thick, locally up to 25 m in the Hitchin Channel, and have been mapped as a separate unit, they have been classified as glaciolacustrine even though some may have been deposited in subglacial standing water. Conversely, thin occurrences closely associated with sands and gravels probably represent quiet-water fluvial accumulation (i.e. overbank or abandoned channels).

Within the Hitchin Channel, two major sequences of glaciolacustrine sedimentation have been identified from boreholes and are believed to represent deposition in 'finger lakes' in front of the ice margin during pauses in advance or retreat phases of the Anglian ice. The duration of these phases are not known and it is not even certain that the two sequences represent only the development of two separate lakes. Indeed, elsewhere and particularly in the upper reaches of the Rib/Quin valleys, the distribution of glaciolacustrine deposits seems to indicate deposition only during the waning of the Anglian ice sheet and probably represents a considerable number of small temporary lakes separated in space and time.

Details

The details shown here represent a selection of the more important exposures found throughout the district. Many more are described in the Technical Reports for individual 1:10 000 geological sheet areas (given in Appendix 2). Because of the close interrelationship of the three major glaciogenic deposits, the details are given by area, starting in the south-west of the district.

SOUTH-WEST OF THE HITCHIN GAP

The mapped outcrop pattern of the glaciogenic deposits in the area of Lilley Bottom, the Mimram valley and its dry tributary to the north, shows that they occupy a channel, or channels, cut into the Chalk. The River Mimram and tributary have partly exhumed these channels, but locally [196 193] the Mimram has been diverted to the south and has cut a new channel in Post-Anglian times.

There is little information which shows the maximum depth of the channel. From the local absence of till and of any glacial deposits on the interfluves, it seems unlikely that the buried channel was formed as a tunnel-valley, beneath a cover of ice. The long-profile of the channel is therefore assumed to slope consistently towards the south-east. It is also assumed that the cross-profile resembles that of the present-day dry valleys, or is more 'U-shaped'. It therefore seems that the base of the channel is unlikely to be deeper than about 70 m above OD anywhere in the Kimpton area.

Constructed contours on the base of the glaciofluvial deposits suggest that the greatest thickness remaining in the Kimpton area is preserved around [190 198] and is unlikely to exceed about 30 m.

A small estate quarry [1923 2197], south of St Paul's Walden Church, showed a 5 m face, 25 m wide, in 1988. At the top, 1.5 m of dark brown, sandy, decalcified gravel with an irregular base rests on up to 2 m of brown, sandy, flat-bedded, fine to medium gravel with flint, chalk and 'Bunter' pebbles. In the west, this overlies Chalk. Elsewhere, it rests on 0.5 m of coarse gravel with flint, sarsen and 'Bunter' quartzite cobbles, up to 0.25 m by 0.10 m in size. This gravel passes down into 1.0 m of brown sandy flint gravel with chalk, which overlies Chalk bedrock.

Till occurs as the filling of subglacial valleys near Stopsley Holes Farm [156 248] and between Kingswalden Bury [161 235] and Frogmore [171 160]. The field relationships at Frogmore suggest that it is deeply cut, and may contain over 30 m of till and associated deposits, although there are no confirmatory borehole records.

Glaciolacustrine deposits have been identified only near High Heath Farm [204 189], where they occur within the glaciofluvial deposits. They consist mainly of stoneless, bedded silts and silty clays, and are up to about 12 m thick.

No exposures of these glaciolacustrine deposits were seen, and they are known entirely from hand-auger samples. They are covered by rather sandy or gravelly soils, which are locally impenetrable to augering, and which seem to be derived from the interlayered glaciofluvial deposits. This pervasive cover of sandy gravelly soil and head limits the confidence with which these deposits could be mapped.

Notwithstanding the problems of delineating these fine-grained deposits precisely, it seems from their mapped outcrop pattern that they form a thick lens within the glaciofluvial sands, divided by at least one interdigitated bed of fine- to medium-grained sand. The outcrop pattern suggests that this lens could reach 12 m in thickness.

EXPOSURES IN THE HITCHIN CHANNEL

Only exposures showing relatively thin sequences related to the infilling of the channel are discussed here. Borehole evidence showing the interrelationship of the various units in the channel are given in the subsequent section on buried channels.

Vicarsgrove Pit [178 276]

The only remaining section is at the north end of the pit. The upper part of this face is in till (3.5 m attributed to the Vicarsgrove Till, see below). It seems to decrease in thickness to the west and south, tending to wedge-out against the side of the channel, and to the east it apparently passes laterally into bedded glaciolacustrine deposits. Beneath this till were exposed 3 m of laminated silts and clayey silts, with bedded sands and thin sandy gravels, all conspicuously rich in chalk fragments, together with clasts of flint and other exotic lithologies. The deposit is reported to continue downwards for at least another 10 to 12 m. A lower, massive till, seen elsewhere in the pit, is composed of dark grey, pebbly, silty clay, altered to pale grey and brown at its top and base. This is tentatively correlated with the Maydencroft Till (see below).

The beds at the Vicarsgrove Pit 'dip' at about 20° to the north and some of the beds thicken in that direction, suggesting that they were deposited on a slope. Alternatively, the deposit might have been tilted by collapse after melt-out or intraformational erosion, or as a result of ice-push. Bloom and Wooldridge (1930) observed 'step-faulting' in bedded glaciofluvial sand and gravel in this pit and it also appears in a photograph published in Bloom (1934). Some of the bedding surfaces are gently undulating, some of the beds are graded, while others (either silt or gravel) enclose sand lenses up to 0.05 m thick. A few pebbles occur in the laminated silts and these are probably drop-stones.

The largest of the old workings on Thistley Farm [1897 2656] exposes 2 m of pale brown, laminated, slightly sandy, clayey silt, with a few thin beds of fine sand. There is some minor contortion of the laminae, which are otherwise very regularly, plane-bedded. This deposit continues down for at least 1 m, and is part of an extensive glaciolacustrine deposit, which is both overlain and underlain by glaciofluvial deposits. With increasing clay and gravel content, it seems to pass laterally south-west into the till. It wedges out to the east, where there is an elongated lens of similar deposits at a slightly lower level.

In the Willian area, within and marginal to the confines of the channel, trending northward from Stevenage to Letchworth, glaciolacustrine deposits occur at outcrop in four localities, in association with the other lithologies of the Anglian sequence.

The deposits here are similar to those in the Hitchin Channel with the exception that wherever they were tested around Willian they were highly calcareous. In form, the two most extensive outcrops to the north and south of the Willian Road near to the Letchworth golf course [217 310] appear to infill a saucer-like depression which was later filled by till and glaciofluvial deposits.

The deposits are believed to represent localised accumulation in small quiet-water bodies during relatively quiescent periods of channel infill.

Only one exposure of these deposits was found during the survey in a freshly cleaned drainage ditch on the Letchworth golf course [2156 3096] where 1.05 m of brown, sandy, silty, friable clay with some flints (head) was seen to overlie at least 0.85 m of pale yellowish brown, very finely laminated, very fine to fine sandy silt.

Details of a gravel pit beside the Ash Brook [probably either at 207 272 or at 204 271] are given by Bloom and Harper (1938). The glacial gravel is more than 12 m (40 feet) in thickness and dips north-west towards the adjacent valley.

A gravel pit referred to by Culpin (1921) and Priest (1921) as the 'Tail' pit, east of Little Wymondley, is probably still discernible [220 275]. The gravel contains more numerous erratics of crystalline lithologies (such as mica-schist, feldspar porphyry, gneiss, basalt and andesite, some inferred to be of Scandinavian origin), and Carboniferous, Jurassic and Cretaceous rocks, than the gravel in a pit at St Ippollitts (possibly the one mentioned in the previous paragraph), where the erratics are mostly of Jurassic origin. Erratic pebbles, which can be seen in soil of the surrounding areas, support this observation. Priest (1921) also reports that a basalt boulder (presumably an erratic) up to 0.7 m in diameter was seen beside the road in Little Wymondley.

A gravel pit at Mill Hill, near Almshoe Bury [203 257], was visited by Bloom (1930), who recorded 4.6 m of reddish clay and rolled flints, well bedded at the top, overlying pebbly clay and sand, with the Chalk exposed at the base.

A shallow pit, north-east of Great Wymondley [2240 2904], seen during this survey exposed 1 m of orange-brown, sandy gravel with lenses of fine to coarse sand, some gravelly or clayey, and dipping towards the west. The gravel contains rounded and angular flint pebbles, many *Gryphaea* and some other erratics, up to 20 cm in diameter.

A 5 m section, in the north-east corner of Elms Yard [2135 2753], exposed bedded sand and gravel, including some bouldery gravel, thin silts, a 0.5 m bed of brown and grey pebbly clay and several metres of clean, yellowish brown sand. The pebbles and boulders are composed of flint and erratic rock-types and include a block of Jurassic limestone up to 0.5 m across.

The bypass cutting on the east bank of the Ash Brook [203 276] exposed bedded glaciofluvial deposits, overlapping till, onto the Chalk. These deposits vary considerably from pale brown silts, through fairly clean, orangish or yellowish brown sands to pale brown, chalky, gravelly sands, reddish brown, clayey, gravelly sands and sandy gravels with angular to rounded flint pebbles, rounded chalk and erratic pebbles and cobbles up to 0.3 m in diameter.

South of Holwell, two exposures [1668 3215 and 1676 3200] in a partially backfilled complex of pits showed up to 14 m of very variable sands and gravels.

At the smaller of the two pits [1668 3215], a sequence of up to 10 m of sands and pebbly sands overlain by clayey, sandy gravel was seen. The small pit is entirely occupied by an over-

turned structure (towards the south) which is regarded as the result of ice push from the north (Plate 8).

The larger pit to the south [1676 3200] shows a sequence of sand and gravel on till, which overlies a further sequence of sands and gravels. The upper unit (buried beneath dumped till) is an orange-brown, very clayey, medium to coarse pebbly sand approximately 1.5 to 2.0 m thick. The base of this unit is uneven as the result of postdepositional cryoturbation into the underlying till. The pebbles in this upper unit are predominantly of angular flint.

The intermediate till unit is a bluish to purplish grey, silty clay with the usual suite of erratic rocks. In places, the till takes on a distinct purplish hue and contains derived septaria, up to 0.8 m across, associated with a marked increase in fossil fragments. The deposit is between 3 and 4 m thick and has a sharp planar erosive base.

On the west and south faces of the larger pit at Holwell, the lower sand and gravel unit is divided into three. Immediately below the till, bedded, pebbly sands and sandy gravels between 1.5 and 2.5 m thick occur. The bedding is planar and of low angle. These rest, with an even but erosive base, on a very clayey, coarse gravel bed with no internal structure. The lithological character of this bed suggests derivation as a mudflow, a flow till or a turbid flash-flow deposit. The 'mudflow' bed is between 0.8 and 1.2 m thick with a slightly undulating base. It cuts across the cross-bedding and microfault structures of the underlying sequence. The lowest part of the sequence is pale yellowish brown, fine- to medium-grained sand with pebble stringers and thin beds of fine, sandy, dark brown clayey silt; it is up to 6.5 m thick, increasing towards the north. The cross-bedding structures suggest flow towards the south. The sequence has been affected by small-scale faulting, presumably as a result of loading by ice (or its release) of the frozen deposit prior to the deposition of the 'mudflow' bed.

On the east face of this exposure, the 'mudflow' and topmost sand and gravel beds dip across the face, and are eventually cut out towards the north by the overlying till. The lower sequence increases in thickness expands to some 14 m, and becomes much more gravelly towards the north of the pit, where the deposit comprises a clean, cross-bedded, fine to coarse gravel with sand interbeds. It is this sequence which is incorporated into the ice-push structure 100 m to the north-west. The basal metre or so of the till is faintly laminated and in places includes thin interbeds of gravelly brown, very chalky clay. Where the 'mudflow' and topmost sand and gravel have been removed, the top of the underlying sand is secondarily cemented into a thin, pale yellow, gravelly calcrete.

At Hoo Farm an overgrown, 5 m-deep pit [1535 3735], in the top of a low ridge, previously showed ferruginous flint gravel with some ironstone and sand. Further to the north-east, the deposit was worked to a depth of 6 m in the former Meppershall Hoo gravel pit [1565 3755] (Bloom and Harper, 1938, pl. 28). It consists of very variable, bedded, coarse- to very coarse-grained sand with scattered stones becoming silty and marly in parts or passing into silty clay. Cross-bedding, with a northerly dip of 35°, was noted by Sherlock, in 1931, on his 6-inch-scale field slip. Bloom and Harper (1938) noted the bedding and erratics, and regarded the deposit as clearly of glacial origin. They supposed that it might occupy an oval depression in the Gault (which was exposed in the base) formed by a subglacial stream. Certainly, the deposit is flanked to the north-west and south-east by Gault and probably infills a small incision cut in the bedrock at the margin of the Hitchin buried channel.

Beyond the western margin of the Hitchin buried channel, near Stondon Manor [151 355], an irregular spread of sand winds its way downslope from 75 to 65 m above OD. It is poorly exposed in the mostly overgrown faces of the partly backfilled 4 to 8 m-deep pit [1535 3535]. It consists of pale brown, loose, clean, medium-grained sand with no pebbles. Immediately to the south of the pit, chalk occurs at the surface showing that the sand is deposited in a steep-sided hollow or channel cut into the bedrock.

South-east of Stevenage towards Watton at Stone, a number of exposures related to the Hitchin Channel were seen; the most notable are described below. Two pits at Pound Farm, Datchworth [262 193 and 262 191] are 3 to 4 m deep and up to 250 m across. The latter shows degraded faces of 2.0 m of orange-brown, medium, pebbly sand. The former may be the larger Holterns pit referred to by Salter (1905). He described 3.0 m of stratified gravel with sandy and clayey patches, piped into the Chalk in places, with the gravel consisting chiefly of rounded and green-coated flints, and 'Bunter' quartzite, quartz, 'Hertfordshire conglomerate' and sandstone. Sherlock (1919a) described 4.3 m of bedded gravel from one of these pits, possibly the southern one, in which clay pockets and bands were left as unworked mounds on the floor of the pit. In addition to the gravel components listed by Salter, he noted also the presence of Liassic limestone. The deposit rests on Chalk, forming, in one place, a chalk pinnacle, with no intervening Palaeogene beds as previously mapped here.

NORTH AND EAST OF THE HITCHIN CHANNEL

Letchworth

A temporary exposure in a gas pipeline, 250 m north-north-east of Norton Church [2325 3465], showed the following section:

	Thickness m
Till, yellowish brown, becoming mottled grey, silty clay with chalk pebbles and some flint; quartz and Jurassic fossil debris. Very clayey, chalky flint gravel (up to 0.4 m) interbedded within the till over a short distance at the north-east end of trench	up to 2.5

The only other notable exposure north of Letchworth is in a heavily overgrown and degraded ravine-like section created by the outfall from a major land drain in the north-east corner of the Green Lagoon. It shows a section, up to 5 m, of chalky, yellowish brown, silty clay which becomes very chalky towards the base. The contact with the underlying Chalk was not exposed.

A shallow, 1.5 m deep pit at Bygrave Common [254 352], is apparently situated on a very thin till cover resting on Chalk. However, the bottom always stayed damp and when the farmer attempted to drain the hollow by digging a hole in the base, yellow chalky clay was found to a depth of 3.5 m. Close by, Chalk bedrock was seen to rise steeply to near the surface, and it seems probable that the till here infills a solution hollow; certainly the Chalk surface beneath the till is highly irregular in places.

In the Ashwell district and the south-eastern part of the Stotfold district, glaciofluvial sand and gravel is found on the hill tops or upper slopes, at 75 to 95 m above OD, on the edge of, and partly underlying, the discontinuous till sheet, for example at Odsey [289 384], north of Pembroke Farm [278 383, 273 376], near Bygrave [265 367] and Radwell [245 355]. All of these have been sporadically worked in small pits, which now have little exposure. The deposits are variable in lithology and irregular in shape, and only pockets of thicker, and hence more desirable, sand or gravel have been extracted. They indicate a typical thickness of only 2 to 3 m, in contrast to estimates from the mapping; commonly the deposits are draped

downslope for 5 to 10 m, probably as little more than a gravel veneer, though this is usually difficult to prove as they are mostly too stony to auger through.

Larger gravel spreads, on ground less than 50 m above OD underlie, the villages of Stotfold, Church End (north Arlesey), Henlow and Clifton. Around Spinney Farm [22 38], sand and gravel was deposited in a fan of material at the 'mouth' of the Cat Ditch, where it leaves its confined valley [234 380], extending westwards for 2 km across the Lower Chalk on to the Gault. To the north-east, it thins out rapidly but westwards it merges with similar deposits of the River Ivel and Pix Brook.

Walkern

A small pit [2958 2727], north-east of Walkern, exposed 2 m of cross-bedded, sandy gravel with subrounded to subangular pebbles of flint and subrounded clasts of quartz, limestone and sandstone. Interbeds of chalky sand were seen to be penetrated by decalcified pipe structures. A larger pit [2995 2790] to the north was reputedly 6 m deep, and more material was extracted from tunnels beyond the working face.

Weston

Immediately to the west of Wallington, where it directly overlies the Upper Chalk, the till contains a large component of material derived from the clay-with-flints. Some auger samples consist of orangish brown clay or sandy clay with flint pebbles. Small numbers of black-stained, well-rounded flint pebbles (derived from Tertiary sediments, and typical of the clay-with-flints) are present in the soil, but erratic pebbles also occur there. Furthermore, the flints in the clay itself are not conspicuously red-stained (as is usual in the clay-with-flints), and the clay also contains a variable proportion of chalk pebbles.

The gravels extending south-east from Clothall form low hills, but the most obvious field indication of their presence is the associated very stony, sandy soil. Springs occur at the base of these deposits. Although the gravels have been worked at several places, the only exposure seen was in a disused pit [2838 3006], which shows about 1 m of gravelly sand.

Watton at Stone to High Cross

Where the till overlies the Palaeogene deposits, it contains appreciable quantities of reworked clay and well-rounded flint pebble material of Palaeogene origin. In places, therefore, the boundary between till and the Palaeogene strata is diffuse. A further complication can arise where both the Palaeogene and till strata are thin and affected by cryoturbation; in this situation the soils and subsoils take on characteristics very akin to those of the clay-with-flints particularly where the till component is itself fully decalcified. In these circumstances, the sparse occurrence of reworked fossil material or coarse, angular, flint sand is the only means by which the till and clay-with-flints lithologies can be differentiated. Outcrops of this type of material, classified in this case as till, have been mapped north and north-east of Woodhall Park School [317 189], around Sacombe Green Farm [341 196] and south-west of Salmonsley Wood [356 191].

The only notable exposure of till was seen in excavations which were made to increase the size of, and to amalgamate the three lakes at Sacombe Lake [336 186]. The many exposures here, which were quickly degrading and flooded as the lake filled, show a variable thickness (approximately 0 to 2 m) of weathered, yellow-brown, mottled, pale grey, silty, chalky clay grading down into dark grey, silty clay with chalk pebbles. Discolouration of this lower, essentially unweathered material was seen along fissures to the full depth of the temporary exposures. A maximum thickness of 3 to 3.5 m of till was seen during low water conditions in March 1992.

A clear section of glaciofluvial deposits was seen in Round Wood [388 192], north-east of Barwick Ford, on the River Rib. Up to 3 m of interbedded sand and sandy gravel is being extracted for the maintenance of farm tracks. The material is principally fine- to coarse-grade flint gravel and quartz sand matrix, with interbeds of chalky, fine- to medium-grained quartz sand. The gravels also contain some quartzite, sandstone, fossil debris (mainly *Gryphaea*), well-rounded flint, and rare igneous and metamorphic clasts. The bedding structures suggest the sand and gravel was deposited from water flowing towards the south and south-south-west along the line of the present Rib; this and the relatively high, nondurable chalk content suggest that deposition probably occurred from a nearby ice front (or ?valley glacier) along a precursor of the Rib valley at the waning of the late Anglian ice sheet. The underlying glaciolacustrine deposits in this area further suggest that initial deposition might well have taken place in a marginal 'finger' lake.

Buntingford, Puckeridge and Dane End

A few notable exposures, generally within deep drainage channels, are detailed below.

A ditch section, 300 m north-north-west of Gaylors Farm, Westmill [3628 2727] exposes up to 4 m of pale yellow brown, very chalky clay, intimately associated with a coarse angular flint and rounded chalk clay-bound gravel. Till occurs within, above and below the gravel over some 30 m of section; the gravel is typical of englacial deposition, being very chalky and structureless.

An exposure 300 m east of Westmill Bury Farm [3737 2719], in the back face of a cut and fill platform, excavated for new farm buildings, showed:

	Thickness m
Till	
Clay, yellow-brown, mottled grey, chalky, silty	1.7
Glaciofluvial deposits	
Gravel, with chalk and flint, pockets of sheared/ folded fine chalk sand	1.2
Upper Chalk	
Chalk, white, fractured, with flints	0.4+

A river bluff, near New Bridge on the A10 [3823 2580], showed the following section through glacial deposits within a glacially over-deepened valley. The deposits between the tills are typically englacial in origin.

	Thickness m
Till	
Clay, yellow-brown, becoming grey, stiff, silty, with many pebbles and some cobbles of flint and chalk	1.5
Glaciolacustrine deposits	
Silt, dark to pale grey, laminated, fine, sandy	0.4
Glaciofluvial deposits	
Gravel, coarse angular flint and rounded chalk grains, with brown, clayey, sand matrix	0.3
Till	
Clay, pale grey, silty, with much rounded chalk material	0.6

A stream section, 400 m west of the Old Rectory, Aspenden [3504 2826], up to 3 m deep in places, shows a very variable thickness of angular flint and chalk gravel of coarse to cobble grade, in a sandy clay-bound matrix (glaciofluvial deposits), resting on an uneven surface (with up to 2 m of relief) of pale to dark grey, silty, stiff clay with many chalk and some flint pebbles (till). To the east, downstream, a section on a meander bluff shows only till.

A steep river bluff, 350 m north of Aspenden Bridge, Buntingford [3640 2891], on the River Rib, east of The Watermill artificial channel, shows a complicated sequence of glaciofluvial deposits and glaciolacustrine deposits resting on an uneven surface of till. The following is a representative section:

	Thickness m
Head	
Sand, clayey, very stony, with an earthy texture. Uneven base	up to 1.1
Glaciolacustrine and glaciofluvial deposits	
Interbedded, laminated silts and fine pellet, chalky, sandy gravel with basal cobble gravel	up to 1.2
Till	
Clay, brown becoming greyish yellow-brown, very silty, packed with rounded chalk pebbles	up to 3.2

To the south of the above section, the interbedded silts and gravels grade into a coarse to cobble grade flint gravel.

Two further sections showing till are given below.

Stream section, 100 m north of Corney Bury, Buntingford [3569 3092]:

	Thickness m
Head	
Clay, dark yellow-brown, sandy, silty, pebbly, with an earthy texture	0.3 to 1.0
Glaciofluvial deposits	
Gravel, fine to coarse, highly variable angular flint and rounded chalk, with clayey, chalky sand matrix. Uneven base	0.2 to 1.6
Till	
Clay, pale grey, mottled yellow- brown, stiff, silty, with rounded chalk pebbles	up to 1.4

Stream section, 400 m north-west of Brick Bridge [3022 3146]:

	Thickness m
Head	
Clay, pebbly, sandy, silty, with earthy texture	up to 0.6
Glaciofluvial deposits	
Gravel, with fine to coarse angular flint and rounded chalk, in calcareous medium to coarse, very clayey, dark yellow-brown matrix; cobbles of flint at base	0.6 to 1.3
Till	
Clay, very pale grey, very silty, with rounded chalk pebbles	up to 0.6

Within the valley of the River Quin, between Green End [393 254] and Hare Street [390 295], glaciofluvial deposits are principally composed of angular and nodular flint with a dark brown, sandy and very clayey matrix. It appears to be a thin basal bed of sand and gravel resting on till. Similar deposits of very stony clay/very clayey gravel, some identified as till because of their excessive clay content, are mapped east of Buntingford [367 289], north of Aspenden [355 292] and around the transmitting station [377 254] south of Westmill.

Glaciofluvial deposits are excavated on Brookfield Common [3294 2079], in a small spur-top pit, and used for the maintenance of farm tracks. The pit exposes between 3.5 and 4.0 m of matrix-supported, fine- to cobble-grade gravel in yellow-brown medium to coarse sand. The gravel consists predominantly of flint, but has some quartz and quartzite, and some stringers of fine chalk gravel throughout. It becomes more clayey with depth. Some bedding, which is evident from included sand seams and chalk gravel beds, demonstrates that the whole sequence is severely cryoturbated (?folded) with some vertical beds.

Near Park Covert [3173 2368], Benington, old much degraded pits show between 6 and 9 m of apparently decalcified glaciofluvial sand and gravel. Small exposures show fine to coarse gravel with cobble stringers in an orange-brown medium to coarse sand matrix.

A large area of ground with many old diggings, west of New Bridge on the A10, showed one good section [3780 2595] of interbedded fine chalky gravel and coarse to cobble grade flint gravel. Within the 7.5 m of sands and gravels are a number of thin coarse sand to fine gravel seams, which are extremely chalky in places.

A pit at Haley Hill [3719 2841], near Buntingford showed up to 2.5 m of yellow-brown and brown very chalky, fine gravel overlying coarser sandy gravel. The gravel is predominantly well-rounded chalk with flint and rare quartz and quartzite in a medium to coarse quartz and flint sand matrix. This pit was first noted by Whitaker et al. (1878, p.34) who described 'a large block of conglomerate' more correctly called a ferrocrete. A block of dark purplish brown clast supported ferrocrete fitting this description was visible at the time of this survey.

Cottered and Rushden

Near Lodge Farm, one [3195 3120] of several small pits at the margin of the till sheet exposed up to 2 m of yellow-brown, fine to medium, sandy gravel with scattered flint cobbles and large horned flint nodules. The gravel is mainly of flint and chalk with 'Bunter' quartzite, quartz, pink sandstone and *Gryphaea* shells. South of Lodge Farm, these deposits rest directly on clay-with-flints and to the west on Upper Chalk, suggesting that they occur in a channel at or near the base of the till.

Barkway and Therfield

A temporary exposure, created during the excavation for an ornamental pond at Gannock Farm [317 354], showed up to 1.5 m of yellow-brown chalky till with an irregular (?piped) base resting on dark reddish brown clay-with-flints. A maximum of 1.8 to 2 m were seen during the survey but it was reported that the pond was excavated to a depth of 12 feet (3.66 m) in 'red clay and flints' without touching chalk.

In the area between Barkway, in the east, and Stump Cross [319 370] in the west (7 km), the till incorporates exceptionally large rafts of chalk. The rafts were mapped in a band some 500 to 1000 m wide along the scarp face. They can vary from little more than a seam of crushed chalk a few decimetres thick up to 10 to 15 m of stratified competent chalk characteristically formed of the hard Chalk Rock and Top Rock.

They are still exposed at the Reed and Barkway pits which are discussed below.

Glaciotectonics of the Barkway and Therfield area

The area south of Royston in north Hertfordshire has long been known to contain exposures which show Chalk dipping at high angles contrary to the regional dip of the Upper Cretaceous in this western part of East Anglia.

The existence of these exposures was noted by Penning (1876) and subsequently quoted as evidence for a 'flexure' in the Chalk in the memoirs for the 'Old Series' one-inch sheet 47 (Whitaker et al., 1878) and quarter sheets 51SW and 51NW (Penning and Jukes-Browne, 1881). This view was repeated by various authors up to the turn of the century (Jukes-Browne and Hill, 1903, 1904; Hopkinson, 1902; Anon, 1883). The limited north to south extent of these anomalous dips was attributed by these authors either to a limiting fault north of the exposures or to a corresponding (presumably tight) syncline which had subsequently been eroded away. The recent mapping did not prove the existence of either of these structures.

The occurrence of till intimately involved with the Chalk at some localities was regarded as evidence of the '... sliding down of beds...' (Penning and Jukes-Browne, 1881, p.67) or '... trickled from above...' (Bonney, 1906) on the steep scarp.

The debate as to the origin of these high dips was significantly expanded by Woodward (1903a, b and c) who proposed that they were the result of the rafting of large bodies of chalk by glacial action. This was strongly opposed by Bonney (1906) who could not conceive the idea of firstly the existence of 'land ice' nor, if it did exist, of its capacity to move such large rafts of Chalk. This view was not, however, held by most of his contemporaries. The sites east of Barley were later discussed by White and Edmonds (1932) and by Jones (1938). The latter, in a report on a field meeting to the Barkway and Reed pits south of Royston, commented '... The conclusion seems clear that the disturbances are of Pleistocene age...'. The pits at Barkway and Reed were again briefly described by Bromley (1966) in a field meeting report dedicated primarily to the description of the Chalk of the district.

In subsequent work by Bromley and Evans, and published as part of the Geologists' Association Guide (Blezard et al., 1967), they demonstrated that the Chalk sequences identified on bio- and lithostratigraphical grounds were repeated and divided one from another by thin, impersistent partings of chalky clay of undoubted glaciogenic origin. The, then heavily overgrown, pit at Great Chishill was discussed by Horton (1988). During the mapping which preceded Horton's report, individual Chalk rafts were not identified, suggesting that this occurrence is a single raft of limited lateral extent.

This survey, at 1:10 000 scale, has demonstrated the distribution of these deposits to be more extensive than originally envisaged, and has shown that up to eight chalk raft/till couplets are stacked against the Chalk scarp. This new evidence supports the glaciotectonic thrusting proposals of Woodward and Bromley, and also the emplacement model proposed herein.

Under favourable farming conditions, these rafts can be clearly recognised on the ground, and in aerial photographs of various dates, held by Hertfordshire County Council. These photographs, taken during periods when the ground was fallow, show arcuate, pale toned structures which coincide closely with the ground mapping (see also Frontispiece herein). The slight mismatch between ground observation and aerial photography interpretation in some places can be attributed to the inclusion of exceptionally chalky till and chalk 'mylonite' at the margins of the rafts, which give rise to equally pale tones on the photographs. These discrepancies have, for the most part, been tested by augering in the field. Satellite images also show these features, albeit at lower resolution.

Rafts of transported Chalk have been mapped during the survey of sheets TL33NW and TL33NE. They occur in a zone about 7 km by 1 km along the scarp face and brow between Stump Cross in the west to Barkway in the east. The rafts do not significantly overtop the Chalk scarp to the south, where a normal till sequence rests on in situ Chalk and, in places, remnants of clay-with-flints (Figure 22).

In-situ Chalk Rock, was determined during the field mapping, shows a broad north-west-trending anticline in the Chalk, with its crest just west of Therfield. South of Stump Cross [TL 319 366], the Chalk Rock crops out at about 130 m above OD, rising to 150 m above OD west of Therfield. Towards the east from Therfield, the Chalk Rock falls progressively so that between Reed and Barkway it is at an elevation of about 125 m above OD, at Barley 105 m above OD and at Great Chishill 95 m above OD (outside the district to the east). With only one minor exception, the Chalk rafts composed principally of Chalk Rock are resting on, or significantly above, the in-situ Chalk Rock, thus demonstrating unequivocably their up-scarp movement.

The deposit is considered to be entirely glaciogenic, and the included Chalk rafts are taken simply as large erratics within the till sequence. At least eight rafts, separated by till, have been identified in the vicinity of the Barkway and Reed pits, but elsewhere only a single raft may be incorporated into the till. The chalk rafts are principally composed of the nodular Chalk Rock with contiguous chalk of the *T. lata* Zone below and the *S. plana* Zone above. The exposure at Reed also includes a higher hard chalk bed, the Top Rock, which can be mapped sporadically along the scarp elsewhere in the district.

The rafts can be up to 600 m across and between a few decimetres to 15 m thick. In the thinner rafts, and along the margins of the larger rafts, the chalk is extremely rubbly and some may consist only of 'mylonitised' chalk within the till.

The only exposure which shows more than one Chalk raft, separated by till, is at Barkway [3816 3664]. The 'clay gall' previously noted by Woodward (1903a) in a pit at Reed [3595 3704] is no longer visible. At present, the pit shows Chalk with steep northward dips, and only a single raft, 15 m in thickness.

The one substantial exposure of till interposed between Chalk rafts at Barkway is essentially a little-modified Lowestoft Till, and reports of other such sub-stantial occurrences describe chalky clays with all the characteristics of this till. Less substantial 'till' seams noted in the literature are apparently modified, and augering has shown that there is a gradation from rubbly chalk to unadulterated till at the margin of the chalk rafts in a few places. However, the till at Barkway shows no such modification or shearing either marginally or internally, leading one to suspect that the Chalk rafts were generally incorporated into the nose of an advancing ice sheet, and transported above the basal shear zone. Surface augering supports this view and, with the exception of the minor gradational margins noted above, contacts between till and Chalk raft are sharp, and in one area at least are near vertical (e.g. west of Reed Pit).

It is postulated (Hopson, 1995) that the mechanism of emplacement was controlled by four factors, which prevailed only in the area between Stump Cross and Great Chishill. These are:

the scarp between these two localities was aligned east to west, perpendicular to the movement of ice;

the Chalk Rock formed a secondary scarp feature below that formed by beds some 25 to 35 m higher in the Upper Chalk;

the Reed Marl, beneath the Chalk Rock, acted as a plane of decollement on which the rafts were initially thrust;

the jointing pattern in the Chalk of this area offered the weakest configuration to the advancing ice.

A number of authors, for example Van der Wateren (1985), Ringberg (1983), Banham (1975), Croot (1987) and Ehlers et al. (1986), have identified areas where large rafts of frozen drift and bedrock have been incorporated into till sequences. All have invoked the incorporation of these blocks along thrust planes within the quarrying zone of an advancing ice lobe, following the model summarised by Christiansen and Whitaker (1976) from work by Clayton and Moran (1974).

A similar process is suggested herein (Figure 22) with the added complication of a second compressional event as the raft laden ice impinged on the major scarp south of the site of excavation.

This incorporation process is preferred to the somewhat simpler model of push in advance of the ice, since this would have undoubtedly created a more chaotic distribution, if not overturning of some of the rafts, which is not observed in this area.

It is envisaged that ice impinging against the scarp-foot in the Chalk Rock was locally under compression. As the ice overtopped this feature, the resultant pressure release was sufficient to freeze the ice onto the substrate and large masses of Chalk thus frozen to the base of the ice were then incorporated along shear planes within the ice as it advanced. This is similar to lee side plucking as suggested in Boulton (1979) but on somewhat a grander scale than he envisaged. These plucked masses took up a 'piggy back' attitude within the ice as it advanced.

This heavily laden ice impinged against the second major scarp to the south where 'lodgement' of the rafts and interposed tills took place in a compressional envi-

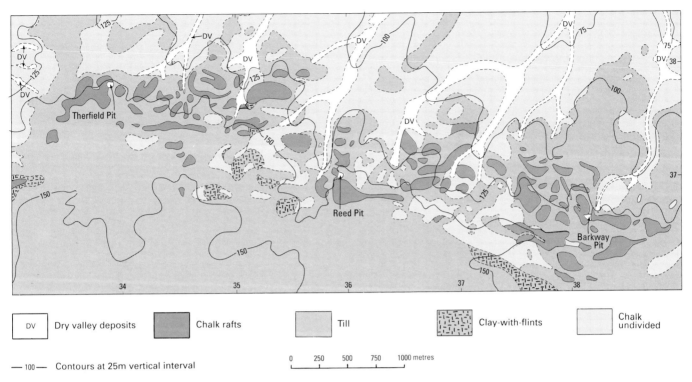

DV Dry valley deposits   Chalk rafts   Till   Clay-with-flints   Chalk undivided

—100— Contours at 25m vertical interval

0 250 500 750 1000 metres

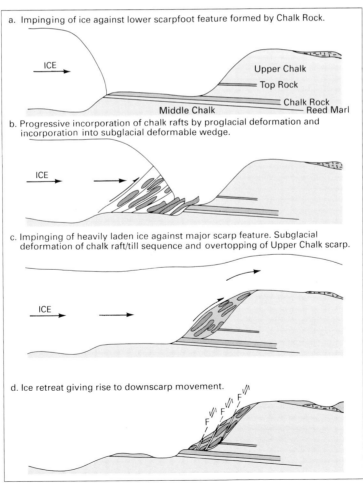

a. Impinging of ice against lower scarpfoot feature formed by Chalk Rock.

ICE →

Upper Chalk
Top Rock
Chalk Rock
Reed Marl
Middle Chalk

b. Progressive incorporation of chalk rafts by proglacial deformation and incorporation into subglacial deformable wedge.

ICE →

c. Impinging of heavily laden ice against major scarp feature. Subglacial deformation of chalk raft/till sequence and overtopping of Upper Chalk scarp.

ICE →

d. Ice retreat giving rise to downscarp movement.

F F F

Figure 22 The distribution of Chalk rafts within till between Therfield and Barkway and a simple model for their emplacement.

ronment. On further southward movement of the ice sheet, it overrode both the lodged material (which protected the remaining in-situ Chalk Rock) and the major scarp top itself. This phenomenon adequately explains why large Chalk rafts are not found south of the scarp top.

Finally, on deglaciation, some downscarp movement within the raft/till deposits resulted in minor normal faulting as seen in the Barkway pit.

Some minor features observed during the surface mapping can be attributed to small-scale variations in the method of incorporation of the Chalk rafts into the ice. The rafts were probably in a frozen condition when plucked from the substrate, and their internal stratification has therefore been substantially preserved despite their rubbly appearance. Previously lodged till, frozen to the substrate, would have been incorporated at this time as well, giving rise to the unsheared till/chalk couplets such as that seen in the Barkway exposure. They were probably transported encapsulated in ice some distance above the base of the ice sheet and suffered little subsequent shearing.

On the other hand, chalk incorporated into the sediment-laden basal deformation zone of the ice sheet would have suffered constant shearing, abrasion and 'mylonitisation', giving rise to the gradational chalk to till lithologies when finally lodged against the major scarp.

Within the transported Chalk rafts, the fracturing resulting from freezing and thawing are reflected in the shattered rubbly appearance of the chalk and the fractured flint seen in exposures today.

Buried glacial channels

The ice-sheet which advanced into the district during the Anglian glaciation presumably further eroded the existing escarpments and valleys and apparently created some new drainage channels. The Anglian glacial deposits largely smothered this new land surface, tending to infill or 'bury' both the pre-existing and the newly formed valleys.

Many of the valleys existing before the glaciation persisted as channels draining meltwater from the ice sheet. Whereas in most of the district the glacial sequence consists mainly of a fairly homogeneous sheet of lodgement till, with minor glaciofluvial sands and gravels, the sequences laid down in these channels are characteristically heterogeneous. They have a much greater proportion of glaciofluvial deposits commonly associated with glaciolacustrine deposits, both of which are interbedded with tills of a variety of types. Indeed, the abundance of sand and gravel within the channels which drained the ice sheet may account for the general paucity of outwash materials associated with the till outside the channels (Lake and Wilson, 1990).

As these complex, channel-fill sequences include a greater proportion of sandy, relatively uncompacted deposits, and because they are thicker and are more likely to have contained rafts of 'dead' ice, the channel-fill tends to settle more than the regional till sheet. It is also more permeable. Postglacial drainage therefore often follows lines of preglacial or synglacial drainage. Exceptions occur where valleys were blocked by till or by ice, forcing drainage diversion.

The channel-fill sequences have thus commonly been dissected by postglacial erosion. This was most rapid during periglacial conditions which prevailed at the end of the Anglian and during subsequent cold periods. Erosion seems to be concentrated on the north and east sides of valleys, presumably where solar radiation removed snow cover most rapidly. In many of the present valleys in the Chilterns the remaining glacial (and periglacial) deposits lie on the south and west sides, while the postglacial channel has cut sideways into the Chalk (Ollier and Thomasson, 1957; Thomasson, 1961). The deepest part of the preglacial channels may remain buried.

Examples of six types of glacial channel can be identified in the district (Figure 23).The most numerous, Type 1, follow those preglacial valleys which were approximately radial to the ice sheet. They have probably undergone relatively little modification by glacial erosion (Brown, 1959). This type is represented by channels in the valleys of the Quin, Rib, Beane, the Old Bourne and, in the Hitchin–Stevenage Gap, by the Stevenage Channel. There are two possible examples of radial englacial drainage channels which apparently do not follow pre-existing valleys, Type 2. Both examples lie between the headwaters of the River Beane and the Chalk escarpment.

Channels of Type 3 are also radial to the ice sheet, but were deeply eroded during the glaciation and are steep-sided. They do not necessarily mark preglacial drainage lines. The Hitchin Channel and some of its tributaries, including the Ash Brook Channel, are of this type. In places, the floor of the Hitchin Channel was eroded to as much as 100 m below the present land surface, below present-day sea level.

There is one example of each of the other types, all west of the Hitchin–Stevenage Gap. Deposits from a tangential, ice-margin channel, Type 4, occur between Offley Grange and Pirton. The valley of the River Mimram, and Lilley Bottom approximately follow an ice-margin channel of hybrid type, Type 5. This lay at the limit of glaciation, and sections of the pre-glacial channel have been blocked by till so that drainage was diverted into newly eroded valleys. Type 6 is represented by a portion of the Lea Gap. This lay beyond the maximum extent of glaciation but contains thin glacial outwash deposits.

Buried channels of Type 1 and 3 are common in East Anglia, occurring in most, if not all, of the larger river valleys (Woodland, 1970; Mathers and Zalasiewicz, 1986; Lake and Wilson, 1990). The glacial sequences in these channels are of considerable economic as well as scientific interest. The river valleys tend to be lines of communication and settlement and associated construction projects often have to contend with difficult ground conditions on the thick, heterogeneous channel-fill sequences, parts of which are weak or permeable. Furthermore, sand and gravel resources are concentrated within the channel-fill sequences. The pits left after extraction of aggregates may be used for waste disposal, with further potential for planning problems and the threat of groundwater contamination. The buried channels are hydrogeologically important because of their permeable fill, but also because they commonly mark water-bearing fracture zones in the underlying Chalk (Woodland, 1970; Barker and Harker, 1984) (Chapter 8).

The nature and distribution of the glacial channel-fill sequences in the district are known mostly from field surveys together with borehole records. During this survey, five boreholes to investigate the Hitchin Channel just south of Hitchin were drilled by the British Geological Survey with financial support from the National Rivers Authority (NRA) (Aldiss, 1992a). These were supplemented by five geophysical traverses using gravity or electromagnetic methods, also with NRA support (Chacksfield and Raines, 1992). A similar but smaller geophysical survey had previously been carried out on a shallower section of the Hitchin Channel at Langley (Figure 23), where there was some control on the interpretation from existing borehole records (Raines and Chacksfield, 1991).

Each of the buried channels of the district is described below, starting with those east of the Hitchin–Stevenage Gap, then dealing with those within the Gap, and finally with those to the west. General descriptions of the types of deposit found within the glacial channel-fill sequences have already been given.

BURIED CHANNELS IN THE EAST OF THE DISTRICT

Channels of Type 1 The presence of buried glacial channels in the valleys of the Rivers Rib, Quin, Old Bourne and Beane (Figure 23) is shown by the subcrop pattern at the base of the Anglian sequence, which slopes into the preglacial valleys, and by the nature of the complex infilling sequence, which is dominated by glaciofluvial deposits, interbedded and intergradational with glaciolacustrine silts and tills. The few boreholes in these valleys show that the base of the glacial sequence is, at most, 10 to 20 m below the surface of nearby alluvium, with the deepest levels typically slightly to the west of the present valley axis. There is no firm evidence that the form of the preglacial valleys has been greatly modified by erosion during the Anglian.

As observed by Brown (1959), it is likely that the River Rib leaves the line of its preglacial valley south of Standon [393 212] but her proposal that the buried channel then extends south-east is not borne out by this survey. These suggest that the buried channel turns south-south-west and is rejoined by the present-day river a few hundred metres downstream.

Just to the south of the district, near High Cross, a borehole near Haven End [3753 1840] in the catchment of the River Rib passed through two tills (the upper 10 m thick, the lower 3 m), both underlain by a few metres of glaciofluvial deposits (Hopson and Samuel, 1982). An exposure of about 3 m of interbedded sand and gravel in the Rib buried channel sequence, probably corresponding to the upper layer of glaciofluvial deposits in this borehole, occurs north-east of Barwick Ford [388 192]. This displays cross-bedding structures indicating southwards flow. This upper layer of glaciofluvial deposits passes laterally into glaciolacustrine silts exposed in the Rib valley nearby. These are taken to mark a small proglacial lake formed immediately after retreat of the ice, or perhaps as a result of drainage obstruction by the ice.

To the north, only one till seen with the glaciofluvial deposits in the glacial channels of the Rib and the Quin, but other outcrops of glaciolacustrine deposits appear, marking the position of a series of small proglacial lakes formed at progressively higher levels up both valleys.

Glacial sequences in the valleys of the Old Bourne and its tributaries comprise fairly extensive glaciofluvial deposits interbedded with till, but there is no information about their thickness. No glaciolacustrine deposits were identified there.

In the valley of the Beane, north of its confluence with the Stevenage Channel (Figure 23), the glacial sequence comprises mostly till with some glaciofluvial deposits and a few small outcrops of glaciolacustrine deposits. There is little evidence to support suggestions that this valley was deeply incised by Anglian erosion (Brown, 1959; Woodland, 1970). The presence of a deep buried channel at Walkern is indicated only by two old and seemingly unreliable borehole records: the 'Victoria Brewery, Walkern' [287 257] records some 60 m of drift over Chalk, and Walkern Mill Borehole [2858 2545] records about 9 m of boulder clay above a further 20 m of undescribed material. Even if parts of the channel do reach such depths, they must be of very limited extent, because to the south near Aston [28 23] the Chalk occurs at or very near the surface in the bottom of the Beane valley.

Between Walkern and Cottered, glaciofluvial deposits emerge from beneath the till as a sheet cutting down through the clay-with-flints and dividing within two discrete steep-sided channels south-west of Cottered [310 285]. A borehole at Cromer Windmill, Ardeley [3031 2857], within the more northerly of these channels, proved 9 m of sands and gravels above the Chalk. The Bury Grange Borehole in the southerly channel [3017 2764] proved 9.8 m of drift above the Chalk.

Brown (1959) postulated that preglacial drainage channels carried the headwaters of the Beane south-east into the Old Bourne. Recent mapping of the base of the Anglian shows that this is unlikely to have been so.

Channels of Type 2 A series of isolated patches of sandy gravel within the till near Sandon [323 345] extends southwards to Broadfield Lodge Farm [320 315]. There sandy gravel also occurs below the till, partly in a poorly defined channel which cuts out the underlying clay-with-flints to rest on the Chalk. This is the best example in the district of a possible englacial channel and did not follow a pre-existing drainage line. There is no link between these deposits and those seen south-west of Cottered, but they could have formed parts of the same drainage system.

In another channel of Type 2, south of Clothall [268 316], glaciofluvial deposits cut out the clay-with-flints to rest on the Chalk. These deposits may be continuous,

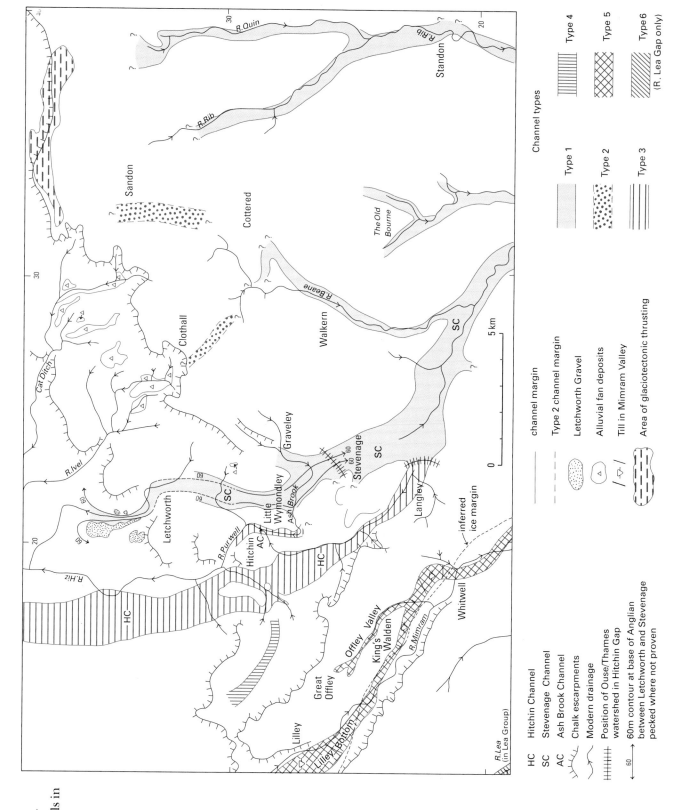

Figure 23
Distribution of
buried channels in
the district.

beneath the till, with glaciofluvial deposits 2 km to the south-east [281 301]. These two may make an englacial channel draining into the Beane valley area.

BURIED CHANNELS IN THE HITCHIN–STEVENAGE GAP

Configuration of the channels   There are two major buried channels within the Hitchin–Stevenage Gap; the Hitchin Channel, which was deeply incised during the Anglian glaciation (Type 3), and the Stevenage Channel, which was not (Type 1). Both have several short tributary channels. The smaller Ash Brook Channel, which lies between them, is also incised (Type 3) (Figures 23 and 24).

The presence of a deep, drift-filled channel at Hitchin was first deduced by Hill (1908, 1912), mainly on the basis of borehole records. Woodland (1970) proposed that the major drift-filled channels of East Anglia, including some of those in the district, originated as tunnel-valleys ('rinnentaler') formed by subglacial erosion, following a suggestion of Boswell (1914). Although Cox (1985) questioned the applicability of this interpretation to some of Woodland's examples in Norfolk, the Hitchin Channel shares all the major characteristics of tunnel valleys found in Europe.

The Elsterian (Anglian) drift-filled valleys of north Germany and Denmark are typically some tens of kilometres long (up to at least 70 km), but fairly straight and commonly less than 1 km wide). Channels branch and intersect in an anastomosing network, but on a regional scale are arranged radially to the area which was covered

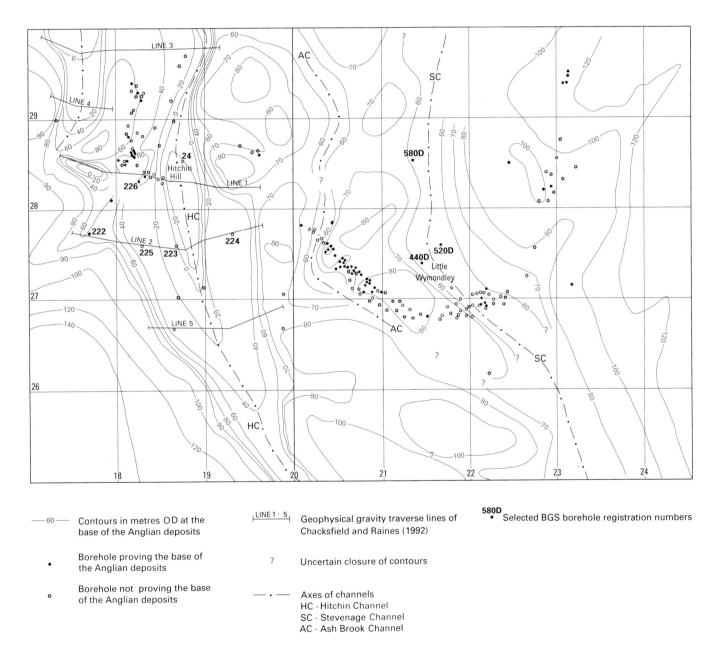

—60—	Contours in metres OD at the base of the Anglian deposits
•	Borehole proving the base of the Anglian deposits
o	Borehole not proving the base of the Anglian deposits

⊢LINE 1 - 5⊣	Geophysical gravity traverse lines of Chacksfield and Raines (1992)
?	Uncertain closure of contours
—·—	Axes of channels HC - Hitchin Channel SC - Stevenage Channel AC - Ash Brook Channel

580D
• Selected BGS borehole registration numbers

Figure 24   Contours marking the base of the Anglian deposits in the Hitchin channel.

by the ice sheet. They do not necessarily follow any pre-existing feature in the bedrock. The sides are relatively steep and the floors are typically fairly flat; the channels are a hundred metres or more deep. The long profile is not consistently graded, and closed depressions may occur in the floor of the channel. The sedimentary infill is dominated by waterlain sands, gravels, silts and clays, in large upward-fining cycles. There is relatively little till, especially in the deeper parts, but it may occur at the channel margin (Grube, 1983; Ehlers et al., 1984).

It is envisaged that tunnel valleys are formed and largely infilled during large torrential outbursts of subglacial meltwater accumulations (Woodland, 1970; Ehlers et al., 1984). Wingfield (1990) argues that formation and infill of subglacial channels occurs very rapidly, during meltwater outbursts of catastrophic proportions. Ehlers et al. (1984) observe that under a hydrostatic head of ice, sediment-laden water can be forced upwards, forming closed hollows in the channel floor. Where the water escapes at the ice front, the end of the tunnel valley can be marked by a step in the floor of the channel (Woodland, 1970; Ehlers et al., 1984).

Contours on the base of the Anglian deposits in the district (including inferred contours in areas where the deposits are thought to have been removed by subsequent erosion) have been constructed from outcrop patterns, geophysical profiles and borehole evidence (Figure 24). In some sections of the Hitchin Channel the outcrop patterns and borehole evidence show that the channel-fill sequence lies on an eroded surface of Chalk, which slopes more steeply than 1 in 4. The occurrence of such steep slopes at the channel margin is supported by the interpretations of local gravity surveys, although these are very sensitive to the value adopted for the small density contrast between the sands in the channel and the Chalk forming its walls (Chacksfield and Raines, 1992).

The Hitchin Channel is presumed to be a continuation of the buried channel beneath the River Ivel, north of the district. This passes through the ridge formed by the Woburn Sands at Sandy [17 48] and can be proved beneath the Ouse valley at least as far north as Huntingdon, some 40 km north of Hitchin (Edmonds and Dinham, 1965; Horton, 1970).

At Henlow, in the north of the district, the channel-fill sequence is at least 108 m thick, resting on presumed bedrock at more than 50 m below OD in the Henlow Borehole [164 356]. Thick glacial sequences have also been proved at Holwellbury [1653 3493], Ickleford [1823 3169] and Hitchin, most notably at Ransom's Brickyard (now part of the town cemetery) near Hitchin Hill [1873 2855], where Hill (1908) observed samples of Gault being brought up from beneath 104 m of mostly sandy glacial deposits at 20 m below OD.

Apparently, this borehole was drilled above an enclosed hollow in the Hitchin Channel (Figure 24). The gravity interpretation for Line 1 suggests that a western tributary channel also extends well below sea level, but there is insufficient evidence to be sure whether this is in another enclosed hollow or if the base of the tributary slopes continuously east into the main channel (Aldiss, 1992a).

From Hitchin, the Hitchin Channel continues south and then south-east past Langley (Figure 23) but there the floor of the channel is at about 55 m above OD, with only some 35 m of fill (Raines and Chacksfield, 1991): the deeply incised section probably ends about 3 km south of Hitchin.

South-east of Langley, the Hitchin Channel passes into a tributary of the Stevenage Channel. This lies to the east of the Hitchin Channel in the Hitchin–Stevenage Gap, passing south-east into the Vale of St Albans in the Hertford district (Figure 23). Several boreholes within the Stevenage Channel prove the base of the Anglian at less than 50 m above OD, the deepest level being at about 36 m above OD at a borehole near Hanginghill Wood [3079 1893], Watton at Stone. There is no indication that closed hollows occur in the Stevenage Channel, but data is too sparse to confirm this at present. Up to 50 m of drift deposits may be present in the Stevenage Channel between Stevenage and Little Wymondley.

Links between the Stevenage Channel and the Hitchin Channel to the west of Little Wymondley shown to lie at less than 45 m above OD in the interpretations of Brown (1959) and Woodland (1970), cannot be substantiated. Recent evidence from boreholes and field survey shows that the Stevenage Channel can continue at less than 60 m above OD only due north of Little Wymondley [216 274], towards Letchworth (Figures 23 and 24). Indeed, Hill (1912) points out that the valley at Stevenage appears not to end 'at the present watershed, but may have extended northward for a considerable distance'. The presence of the preglacial Letchworth Gravel north of Letchworth (Figure 23) suggests that during the early Anglian the Stevenage valley passed through the Chiltern escarpment at less than 63 m above OD, taking drainage from the Midlands to form a north bank tributary of the proto-Thames. However, the northward continuation of the Stevenage Channel at this level beneath Letchworth has not been proved (Figure 23).

Bloom and Harper (1938) observe that although the Ash Brook rises in a consequent, southwards draining valley near Graveley, it then turns west and becomes obsequent (Figure 23). They suggest that in preglacial times it continued in a southerly course to join the Beane south-east of Stevenage. A similar phenomenon is seen near Langley, where a south-eastwards sloping dry valley south of the Hitchin Channel turns first to the north-east, then to the north-west, joining the flow towards Hitchin. Before the glaciation, this valley would have continued down the regional dip slope into the Beane.

In the Stevenage Channel and its tributaries, the shape of the sub-Anglian surface broadly resembles that of present-day, southwards draining, dry valleys, and was probably modified little by glacial erosion. The Hitchin Channel and the Ash Brook Channel are narrower and more steeply sided (Figure 24), presumably because of erosion during the Anglian.

The probable preglacial existence of the Stevenage Channel, together with its modest depth compared with the Hitchin Channel, its resemblance to modern chalklands valleys and the occurrence of till in the base (see below) all indicate that it did not form as a subglacial tunnel valley.

Sedimentary sequences in the Hitchin–Stevenage Gap

Details of the sedimentary sequences deposited within the Hitchin buried channel have been obtained mainly from boreholes logged by BGS on behalf of the NRA, together with site investigation records from southern Hitchin (Figures 25 and 26). Site investigation boreholes from the line of the Little Wymondley bypass provide a detailed section across part of the Stevenage Channel (Figure 26).

For ease of reference, the tills occurring between Hitchin and Stevenage have been given local names (Table 12). Although tills in each of the two large channels can be assigned to the same four phases of deposition, the bottom and top till in each sequence are not necessarily directly correlated with each other and so have been named separately (Aldiss, 1992a, 1992b). Some of the tills and other deposits can be correlated with named units recognised in the Vale of St Albans by Gibbard (1977).

The presence of two till units in the same section or borehole can be demonstrated in only a few places, the thickness of the tills varies considerably and lithological descriptions in borehole records are often inadequate to distinguish them. The local correlations which are implied by naming the tills depend on the assumptions that the tills were deposited over fairly wide areas and that within the channels they were mostly subhorizontal.

CHANNEL-FILL SEQUENCE AT HITCHIN   Borehole records and the interpretation of the gravity and electromagnetic data from the five geophysical traverse lines across the buried channel (Figures 24 and 25) indicates that the

channel-fill near Hitchin is dominated by glaciofluvial deposits, with till being virtually absent from the eastern side of the channel (Aldiss, 1992a; Chacksfield and Raines, 1992).

No evidence from sedimentary structures for transport direction in the Hitchin Channel has been recorded, but it is assumed that subglacial drainage would have been towards the south, away from the ice sheet. This is consistent with the inferred source of the sedimentary infill at Hitchin, which includes relatively local material, derived from the channel walls to the north, including fossilised wood from the Woburn Sands and rare phosphatic pebbles from the Cambridge Greensand or Gault.

Pre-Priory Till   The sequence in the deepest parts of the Hitchin Channel is seen only in two boreholes (Figure 25a). The Gosmore Borehole [1867 2759] penetrated a metre of medium- to fine-grained, bedded sands and silts with sparse gravel of chalk and flint just above final depth. The lowest 44 m of the Ransom's Brickyard Borehole [1873 2855] proved sands and gravels, some clayey, with intercalations of 'stony clay' which may be till. Geophysical interpretations suggest that these records are representative of a predominantly arenaceous sequence (Figure 25b).

Geophysical surveys at Langley showed that the floor of the channel is at only about 55 m above OD (Raines and Chacksfield, 1991). If the drainage in the Hitchin Channel was indeed to the south, erosion below the level of the Langley outfall must have occurred subglacially, in the manner described by Woodland (1970) and Ehlers et al. (1984). Deposition of the basal glaciofluvial sequence would have followed soon after and was also subglacial.

Table 12 Summary of Anglian deposits in the Hitchin–Stevenage Gap.

Hitchin Channel	Stevenage Channel	Main genetic lithofacies	Deposition phase	Vale of St Albans*
Glaciofluvial outwash and postglacial fluvial deposits			Retreat, with periglacial lakes	
VICARSGROVE TILL	GRAVELEY TILL	Waterlain and flow tills		
MAYDENCROFT TILL		Lodgement till	Main ice advance	Eastend Green Till
Glaciofluvial outwash				Westmill Upper Gravel
CHARLTON TILL		Waterlain and flow tills, some lodgement till	Retreat, with proglacial lakes	
Glaciolacustrine deposits. Subglacial fluvial deposits in the Hitchin Channel				
PRIORY TILL	STEVENAGE TILL	Lodgement till	First ice advance	Ware Till
Glaciofluvial outwash. Subglacial fluvial deposits in the Hitchin Channel				Westmill Lower Gravel (part)

* Vale of St Albans sequence after Gibbard (1977).

Figure 25a   An interpretation of lithofacies in boreholes near Charlton.

b   Geological interpretation of the Hitchin Channel near Charlton based on an interpretation of the residual Bouguer gravity anomaly profile shown (x-x′ is equivalent to Line 2, Figure 24: see also Figure 27 for location) (Chacksfield and Raines, 1992).

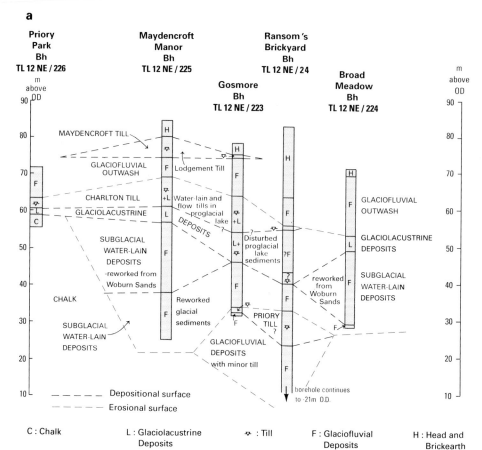

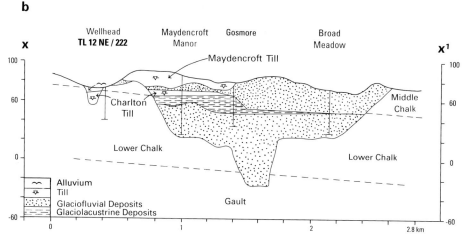

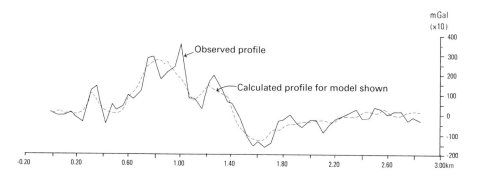

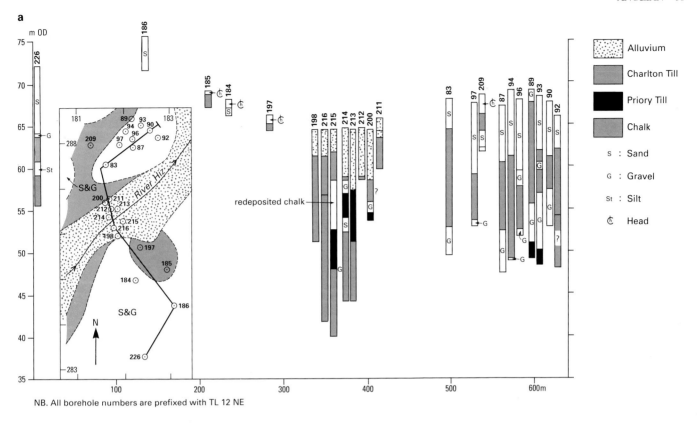

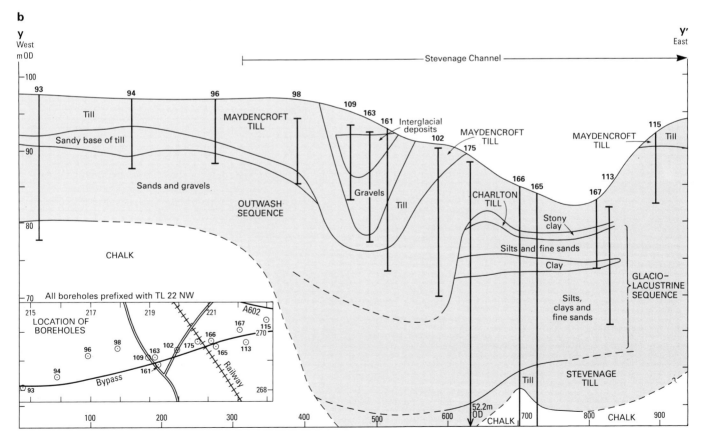

Figure 26a The sequence of channel-fill deposits in the Hitchin Channel, south of Hitchin.

b A section across the Stevenage Channel south of Little Wymondley demonstrating the relationship of the channel-fill deposits (see Figure 27 for line of section y-y′).

Priory Till   The Priory Till is named from occurrences of lodgement till in boreholes to the north of the River Hiz in southern Hitchin (Aldiss, 1992a), where it locally rests on the Chalk at the channel edge (Figure 26).

In the deepest levels of the Hitchin Channel, glacio-fluvial deposits are overlain by till which occurs as stiff clay with stones between 33 and 23.2 m above OD in the Ransom's Brickyard Borehole, and in the Gosmore Borehole as sandy till between 32.5 and 31.1 m above OD (Figure 25a). In the last-named borehole, the sandy till rests with a sharp basal contact on disturbed bedded sands. This and the uniform composition of the till suggests that it is a lodgement till. Both occurrences are included with the Priory Till, although it is possible that they may be somewhat older.

An alternative correlation of the Priory Till with other levels in the sequences in the Ransom's Brickyard and Gosmore boreholes is suggested below (see discussion under Charlton Till).

Two tills crop out in a valley north of Almshoe Bury [203 261], separated by glaciofluvial deposits. The lower one is possibly part of the Priory Till (Aldiss, 1992b). No other outcrops are known. To the south the Priory Till is cut out of the sequence between Hitchin and Langley. There is insufficient evidence to suggest its northwards extent.

Post-Priory Till–pre-Charlton Till   Near the line of the Hitchin Priory bypass, which is close to the western channel margin, boreholes show that the Priory Till is overlain by several metres of gravel. In a borehole off Charlton Road, Hitchin [1820 2863], adjacent to the Chalk sub-crop, some 6 m of rubbly chalk are presumably rede-posited by mass movement or ice transport (Figure 26).

In the boreholes closer to the centre of the channel (Figure 25a), the Priory Till has been largely removed by subglacial erosion thought to have created the 'terraces' between 15 and 25 m above OD (Figure 25b), well below the level of the Langley outfall. The erosion surface is overlain by waterlain silty gravelly sands and sandy gravels containing clasts of chalk, flint and a variety of other lithologies typical of Anglian glacial erratics. In the Gosmore Borehole, these deposits (12.4 m thick) are cyclic and coarsen upwards overall. Similar deposits occur in Broad Meadow [1932 2773] (1.2 m) and May-dencroft Manor [1829 2760] (13 m) boreholes, where they are overlain by almost 20 m of more uniform, bedded, fine silts and silty sands with thin interbeds of clayey silt. Gravel (mainly chalk or flint) is rare in these deposits, but fragments of fossilised wood occur at some levels. This closely resembles wood preserved in the Woburn Sands, which crops out in the channel floor below 40 m above OD about 4 km to the north of Hitchin. Indeed, much of the sand in this deposit could itself have been reworked from that formation.

The glaciofluvial deposits pass rapidly upwards into glaciolacustrine deposits, up to 18 m thick. These are thought to have been laid down after the hydrostatic load of ice became insufficient to force the subglacial waters over the outfall at Langley, allowing a proglacial lake to form. At least partial ice cover probably remained

Plate 9   Representative cores from the Gosmore (CH2) [1867 2759] and Maydencroft Manor (CH4) [1829 2760] boreholes within the glaciogenic fill of the Hitchin Channel. The highly variable nature of the channel fill is demonstrated with representatives of the till, glaciofluvial and glaciolacustrine deposits. (GS 113)

Note that in each case, with the sample number upright, the top of the core sample is to the left. Each sample is about 0.45 m long.

CH2 U36
Till; silty pebbly clay, resting on glaciolacustrine pebbly, clayey silt (part of Charlton Till sequence).

CH2 U32
Glaciolacustrine pebbly, clayey silt, with pale grey silt intraclasts (interbedded with Charlton Till).

CH2 U22
Glaciofluvial laminated fine sands, silts and clays; slumped and faulted in lower part (interbedded with Charlton Till).

CH2 U2
Post-Anglian brickearth/head: poorly sorted pebbly, clayey sand.

CH2 U38
Glaciolacustrine thinly bedded to laminated silty sands enclosing silt intraclasts and slightly disrupted, interbedded with thin pebbly silty clays (waterlain tills) (part of Charlton Till sequence).

CH2 U34
Glaciolacustrine slumped fine sandy, silt and clayey silt, over-lying slightly pebbly clayey silt (interbedded with Charlton Till).

CH2 U30
Flow till: very silty, sandy, pebbly clay (part of Charlton Till sequence).

CH2 U20
Glaciofluvial very fine and fine laminated sands and sandy silts (interbedded with Charlton Till).

CH4 U31
Glaciolacustrine, slumped clayey silts with silt and clay intra-clasts and a large dark grey till intraclast at the base (interbedded with Charlton Till sequence).

CH4 U27
Glaciolacustrine slumped interbedded sandy silts, clayey silts and silty clays with silt intraclasts and interbedded dark grey pebbly sandy silty clay (waterlain or flow till) (interbedded with Charlton Till sequence).

on this lake, indicated by dropstones, till intraclasts and waterlain tills within the glaciolacustrine sequence (Plate 9). In the Broad Meadow Borehole, this deposit is repre-sented by 4 m of slumped, fine-grained sands and silts, including some silts with microbreccia texture, indicat-ing that the sediment was once frozen. Slumping is seen in several other boreholes where it is confined to discrete beds (Plate 9).

The glaciolacustrine sequence aggraded to about 64 m above OD, as proved in the Maydencroft Manor Borehole, implying that the channel at Langley was still blocked to at least that level.

Charlton Till   In the Maydencroft Manor Borehole, the glaciolacustrine sequence is overlain by 2.2 m of sandy gravel, passing up into 2.7 m of weakly bedded diamicton

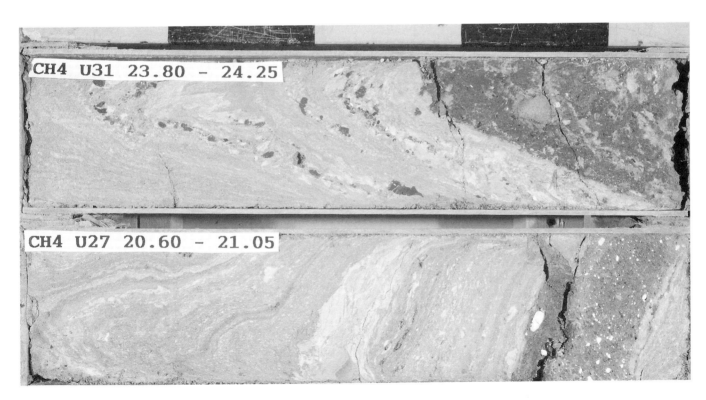

with silt laminae, interpreted as a water-laid till. This is correlated with the Charlton Till, which crops out at a similar level (65 to 70 m above OD) along the River Hiz [181 286]. Near Wellhead [1755 2770], the till was shown to be about 15 m thick by gravity and electromagnetic traverses across the valley (Figure 25b; Chacksfield and Raines, 1992).

Several other boreholes at Hitchin proved probable representatives of the Charlton Till at several levels between about 50 and 70 m above OD. The till comprises thin water-lain or flow tills composed mainly of sandy clay, with some thin seams of sand. It extends locally below 48 m above OD, apparently cutting out the underlying gravel and the Priory Till towards the centre of the channel (Aldiss, 1992a). The sparse evidence from north of Hitchin town centre shows that the Charlton Till probably also crops out there.

Tills between 50 and 40 m above OD in boreholes at Ransom's Brickyard and Gosmore could have been deposited during the same phase of deposition as the Charlton Till, as shown in Figure 25a, but might instead represent the Priory Till. In that case, till occurring at a lower level in the same boreholes would have been deposited during an earlier phase.

The composition of the deposits assigned to the Charlton Till, and their association with glaciolacustrine sediments, suggests that they were deposited in and immediately around a proglacial lake.

Post-Charlton Till–pre-Maydencroft Till   No likely correlative of the Charlton Till appears in the Broad Meadow Borehole. The glaciolacustrine sequence instead gives way abruptly to 15.8 m of glaciofluvial deposits. This sharp break seemingly represents on an erosion surface. These deposits comprise gravelly sand and sandy gravel, with thin intercalations of stoneless silty clay, in crude upward-fining cycles. Cross-bedding is present. The gravel is composed variously of chalk, flint and other Anglian glacial erratics, with a few occurrences of phosphatic nodules and fossilised wood which were probably derived from the nearby Lower Cretaceous outcrops, either directly by subglacial erosion to the north of Hitchin or by redistribution of existing glacial deposits.

Similar deposits occur in the nearby boreholes (Figure 25a) and also crop out widely within the Hitchin Channel, representing outwash from the readvancing ice sheet. Outcrop patterns and borehole records in southern Hitchin show that the top of the Charlton Till was deeply incised below the deposition of glaciofluvial sands, with gravel in the deepest part of the incision, for example two boreholes at The Priory [1825 2884]. The 5.4 m of glaciofluvial deposits in the Maydencroft Manor Borehole include thin, clast-supported gravels (pebble lags) draped with clay, at three levels.

Maydencroft Till   The Maydencroft Till is seen north of Maydencroft Manor [1819 2743] and was proved in the nearby borehole. It consists of hard, dark grey till between 74.7 and 80.1 m above OD. It was also proved in two nearby boreholes where the base of the till lies between 74.5 and 75 m above OD.

Small outcrops of till, close to the channel margin to the north-west, are probably also part of the Maydencroft Till. Till recorded in borehole TL12NE/22 [1727 2899], between about 84 m and 41 m above OD, may represent both the Maydencroft Till and the Charlton Till.

Some 3.5 m of massive till in the disused Vicarsgrove Pit [1925 2590], composed of dark grey pebbly silty clay, altered to pale grey and brown colours at the top and base, is tentatively correlated with the Maydencroft Till because of its similar lithology and comparable elevation.

The Maydencroft Till is interpreted as a lodgement till and is taken to be the local equivalent of the till deposited over a wide area outside the channel. It reaches about 16 m in thickness near Maydencroft Manor (Figure 25b).

Vicarsgrove Till   In the Vicarsgrove Pit (Figure 23), the Maydencroft Till is locally overlain by greyish brown, very chalky till with a thin gravelly sand at the base. This upper till is the Vicarsgrove Till (Aldiss, 1992a). It wedges-out against the side of the buried channel to the west and south of the pit. To the east it passes laterally into bedded glaciolacustrine silts.

The Vicarsgrove Till is interpreted as one of the deposits associated with the retreat of the Anglian ice, perhaps representing debris flow from the channel sides into the margin of a proglacial lake.

CHANNEL-FILL SEQUENCES NEAR STEVENAGE   Sequences proved in the Stevenage Channel are broadly similar to those at Hitchin, except that the thick subglacial outwash deposits are not seen. A basal glaciofluvial deposit does occur in places, but it is thin.

In the south, boreholes near Watton-at-Stone show that there are two tills in the Stevenage Channel, each underlain by glaciofluvial deposits. These can be correlated with the Eastend Green Till and the Ware Till of the Vale of St Albans (Table 12; Gibbard, 1977).

Up the channel to the north-west, the regional Bouguer gravity anomaly map (Figure 4) shows a small positive anomaly in the vicinity of Stevenage [22 25]. This is probably caused by a density contrast between till (and other clay-rich deposits) within the channel and the Chalk in the channel walls. By contrast, the fill in the Hitchin Channel is dominated by sands and gravels, and the resultant anomalies are difficult to detect in the regional gravity field.

Most evidence for the glacial sequences in the Stevenage Channel comes from the Little Wymondley area. Equivalents of some of the named deposits in the Vale of St Albans can be recognised there (Table 12).

Pre-Stevenage Till   Some 17 m of gravel and 'very chalky drift' resting on the Chalk at about 44 m above OD in a borehole near the railway bridge, Wymondley [214 274], and 5.5 m of sandy gravel on the Chalk at 65 m above OD in the Bury Farm Borehole [216 270], can be correlated with the Westmill Lower Gravel, which predates the earliest till in the Vale of St Albans. These glacial outwash deposits probably continue throughout the channel, but there is no evidence for very thick glaciofluvial sequences like those seen at Hitchin.

Stevenage Till   The Stevenage Till is the oldest till in the Stevenage Channel. It is seen only in a few of the deepest boreholes, where it overlies either the Chalk (Figure 26) or the basal glaciofluvial deposits (Table 12). It is a uniform, dark grey, silty, slightly sandy clay with chalk gravel, but presumably also contains flint and erratic pebbles. It ranges from 1.4 to 9.1 m in thickness and was found between 55 m and 71 m above OD. It cannot be correlated with any outcrops with certainty, but is possibly represented in the Purwell valley [200 295].

The Stevenage Till is cut out against the sides of channel and only one till appears on the interfluve area to the west (in a borehole north of Titmore Green [2147 2682]) (Figure 26). It is analogous to the Priory Till of the Hitchin area (Aldiss, 1992b) and to the Ware Till of the Vale of St Albans (Gibbard, 1977), but there is no evidence that these are all parts of a single deposit, so they are named separately.

Post-Stevenage Till–pre-Charlton Till   Boreholes at the eastern end of the Little Wymondley bypass (Figure 26) prove a thick glaciolacustrine sequence above the Stevenage Till. This is composed of fairly well-sorted bedded and laminated fine sands, silts and clays, some slightly stony. There is much lateral variation, however, and only one bed (composed of silty clay) can be traced between all the boreholes. The sequence is up to 26.5 m thick (in a borehole north of Margaret's Wood [2208 2695]), where it aggraded to 83.6 m above OD. Mostly it rests on the Stevenage Till at about 60 m OD, but its base lies at 70.5 m above OD in borehole TL22NW/106 [2212 2707] consistent with the sequence wedging-out rapidly towards the channel margins (Figure 26).

The glaciolacustrine sequence crops out between Little Wymondley and Letchworth in two series of lensoid bodies intimately interbedded with sands, gravels and diamictons, with which they seem to be intergradational in places.

Charlton Till   The glaciolacustrine deposits seen in the Little Wymondley bypass boreholes are overlain by a diamicton, up to 2.2 m thick, (Figure 26). This is generally composed of orangish, yellowish or greyish brown sandy, silty clay with fine to medium chalk and flint gravel. In borehole TL22NW/165 [2213 2695], the clay contains laminae of silt and sand, with some gravel laminae, and passes down into sand. The diamicton is of fairly uniform thickness but drapes the underlying surface, so its position varies from about 75 to 86 m above OD. It is overlain by sandy, gravelly glaciofluvial deposits and so occupies an analogous position to the Charlton Till at Hitchin.

Till, much of which could have been waterlain, interdigitates with glaciolacustrine deposits, between 65 and 85 m above OD, north and north-west of Little Wymondley. This is also thought to be equivalent to the Charlton Till.

Post-Charlton Till–pre-Maydencroft Till   Outwash deposits underlying the Maydencroft Till of the district can be correlated with the Westmill Upper Gravel in the Vale of St Albans (Gibbard, 1977; Aldiss, 1992a). The same phase of deposition is apparent in the Stevenage Channel and accounts for most of the outcrops of glaciofluvial deposits shown on the face of the map.

Boreholes at the east end of the Little Wymondley bypass prove a thick sequence of poorly sorted sands and gravels which overlie the glaciolacustrine sequence and, in the deepest part of the channel, cut across it. These glaciofluvial deposits continue west beneath the Maydencroft Till (Figure 26).

Maydencroft Till   The lodgement till deposited during the second and main ice advance in the Hitchin–Stevenage Gap was named the Maydencroft Till in the Hitchin area (Aldiss, 1992a). It can be traced into the Stevenage Channel and is widespread elsewhere in the district (Figure 26). It is composed of homogeneous 'chalky boulder clay', although it may be sandier at the base.

Outcrop patterns suggest that the Maydencroft Till partly drapes a pre-existing topography. In boreholes it is at least 9 m thick in places in the Stevenage Channel, but probably rarely exceeds 10 m.

Post-Maydencroft Till   There are some glaciofluvial deposits which overlie the Maydencroft Till and so can be inferred to have been laid down during or after the retreat of the Anglian ice sheet.

Excavations for bridge works on the Little Wymondley bypass [2195 2688] show that the glaciofluvial deposits at Todd's Green [220 265] overlie the Maydencroft Till and are locally overlain by Hoxnian interglacial deposits. Boreholes and outcrop patterns suggest that these glaciofluvial deposits lie within a narrow hollow above the deepest part of the Stevenage Channel (Figures 24 and 26). This hollow could be a result of subsidence, possibly coupled with some erosion of the Maydencroft Till. The elongated outcrop of the glaciofluvial deposits above the Maydencroft Till indicates that the subsidence is likely to have been caused by compaction of the thick outwash sequence in the channel, whereas the localisation of the Hoxnian sediments suggests that melting of 'dead' ice within the sequence probably also played a part.

Graveley Till   To the west of Graveley, boreholes on the line of the A1(M) (for example, a borehole near Pinch Lane [2285 2826]) proved a sequence of till, resting on glaciofluvial deposits, and overlying the Maydencroft Till. The till, named the Graveley Till (Aldiss, 1992b) is laminated in part and is composed of heterogeneous, sandy, silty clays containing chalk and flint gravel. It is up to 16.8 m thick and the base of the deposit lies at more than 95 m above OD.

In the north, the Graveley Till is probably intergradational with glaciolacustrine deposits, composed of silts, fine sands and stony clays. Their position at more than 106 m above OD suggests that they are one of the last sequences to be laid down as the Anglian glaciers retreated. An auger hole [2270 2871] proved bedded silty clay, sandy clay and shelly silt with a trace of peaty clay. These organic deposits possibly represent the early part of the Hoxnian interglacial, by analogy with deposits at Fisher's Green and Maydencroft (p.106 and 104).

The Graveley Till is thought to have been deposited as waterlain and flow till in a proglacial or periglacial lake during the retreat of the ice sheet and as such it is analogous to the Vicarsgrove Till in the Hitchin Channel.

Ash Brook Channel   The glaciolacustrine sequence above the Stevenage Till near Little Wymondley is mostly replaced by till in the southern part of the Ash Brook Channel [20 27]. Boreholes show that it is underlain by poorly-sorted glaciofluvial deposits in the channel but excavation of a cutting on the east side of the Ash Brook [203 276] exposed a steeply dipping (1 in 8) contact between the till and underlying Chalk. In the cutting, the till is overlain on a dipping surface by glaciofluvial deposits, so that a 25 m width of till at the base of the cutting has been entirely cut out at the top, although it crops out just to the north. To the south-east, the glaciofluvial deposits are themselves overlain by the Mayden-croft Till (Table 12) and so the till in the cutting is correlated with the Charlton Till.

The base of Anglian in the Ash Brook Channel has been proved as deep as 56.3 m above OD. Although till is present in the channel, its fill is dominated by glaciofluvial sand and gravel. It was probably initiated as an ice-margin channel and then deepened by subglacial erosion.

Formation of buried channels in the Hitchin–Stevenage Gap The sequences demonstrated in these buried glacial channels can be interpreted by reference to the glacial history of the Vale of St Albans described by Gibbard (1977).

Before the Anglian ice sheet reached the Chilterns, it is probable that only the Stevenage Channel existed in the Hitchin–Stevenage Gap, carrying a river draining from the Midlands south to the proto-Thames (Figure 27a). The Hitchin Channel probably existed only as minor valleys, if at all, some draining south to the Stevenage Channel and some north, off the escarpment. The Letchworth Gravel was deposited during this phase and is approximately equivalent to the Leavesden Green Gravel in the Vale of St Albans.

When the front of the ice sheet met the Chilterns escarpment, approaching from the north or north-east (Perrin et al., 1979), a glacier began to flow into the Stevenage Channel. As it did so, ice-margin drainage was progressively diverted to the west, cutting into the western side of the valley (Figure 27b, c). The subsidiary channels to the west of the Stevenage Channel, including the Ash Brook Channel, are taken to represent successive stages of ice-margin or subglacial erosion at this time. As each channel was abandoned, it was filled with glaciofluvial deposits or till.

Ultimately, the main axis of drainage moved to the position of the Hitchin Channel. As the ice sheet moved south, a major subglacial channel had developed, progressing in stages down the Ouse valley, through the Sandy Gap and down the Ivel valley towards Hitchin. This line of approach would have met the escarpment somewhat to the west of the preglacial Stevenage Channel. When the advancing valley glacier had sufficiently blocked the northern end of the Hitchin–Stevenage Gap, meltwater could no longer escape along the ice margin into the Stevenage Channel at Stevenage, nor could this line of drainage shift further westwards by cutting into the scarp. Meltwater in the subglacial channel was therefore forced southwards, breaching the escarpment to form the Hitchin Channel and escaping through the spillway at Langley (Figure 27d).

The deepest parts of the Hitchin Channel were eroded by meltwater during this initial advance of the Anglian ice into the Hitchin–Stevenage Gap. They were then filled by glaciofluvial deposits and minor tills as the ice advanced to block the spillway at Langley. The main ice mass would have been held back by the Chalk escarpment, and possibly was becoming colder and thicker, so that eventually meltwater ponded beneath the ice sheet would be left too far from the ice front to escape sub-glacially. Southwards propagation of the deep subglacial channel was thus arrested.

Glaciofluvial outwash during this phase formed parts of the Westmill Lower Gravel in the north of the Vale of St Albans, together with equivalents upstream in the Hitchin–Stevenage Gap. The Anglian ice appears not to have surmounted the Chalk escarpment at this time. The glacier which moved through the Hitchin–Stevenage Gap deposited the Stevenage Till in the Stevenage Channel and the Priory Till at Hitchin (Figure 27e). It eventually reached the Vale of St Albans, where it deposited the Ware Till (Gibbard, 1977).

The climate then appears to have ameliorated and the ice front retreated. Subglacial erosion by meltwater in the Hitchin Channel could resume, down-cutting below 20 m above OD at the site of Maydencroft Manor Borehole (Figure 25a) and broadening the channel at about that level (Figure 25b), although leaving remnants of the Priory Till (e.g. in Ransom's Brickyard and Gosmore boreholes).

The hollows thus created were then filled with thick sequences of sand and gravel, probably also subglacially. With further retreat, the hydrostatic load became insufficient to force the subglacial meltwater stream over the lip of the channel at Langley, and eventually a proglacial lake formed between the ice front and the Langley outfall (Figure 27f). The glaciofluvial deposits thus pass rapidly upwards into glaciolacustrine deposits.

Proglacial lakes also formed in the Stevenage Channel between Stevenage and Hitchin, presumably held back to the north by the ice sheet and to the south by moraines. Up to 25 m of low-energy sediments were laid down in these lakes, aggrading to at least 83.6 m above OD north of Stevenage. The equivalents at Hitchin aggraded to only 69 m above OD, so the lakes in the two channels were probably not connected.

Part of the Ash Brook Channel [20 27] remained blocked by ice or drift at this time, and a thick glaciolacustrine sequence apparently did not accumulate there. Glaciofluvial deposits were laid down, about the same time in southern Hitchin, which seemingly lay at the margin of the proglacial lake, or beyond it. The waterlain tills and flow tills comprising the Charlton Till reflect the continued presence of floating ice, and of mass-movement from the channel sides. The distribution of glaciolacustrine deposits in the Stevenage Channel suggests that the glacier retreated as far as Letchworth at this time. It presumably reached a similar position just north of Hitchin.

The barriers which dammed the proglacial lakes eventually failed, the lakes drained and the glaciolacustrine deposits and the Charlton Till were dissected to a level less than 70 m above OD in the axis of the Stevenage Channel and 53 m above OD in the Hitchin Channel. This is sufficiently close to the inferred level of the Langley outfall for the drainage to have occurred there.

As the glacier began to re-advance, the glaciolacustrine deposits were overlain first by glaciofluvial deposits representing proglacial outwash and then by a widespread lodgement till, the Maydencroft Till. At its peak, this ice advance over-topped the Chalk escarpment and seems to have extended over most of the district, reaching down into the Vale of St Albans to deposit the Eastend Green Till (Gibbard, 1977).

The glacial sequences in the other buried channels in the district formed during this main glacial advance. Ice lobes blocked the Lilley Bottom/Mimram valley, forming an ice-margin lake south-east of Whitwell and creating southwards drainage diversions (Figure 27g).

The Vicarsgrove Till, the Graveley Till and associated glaciolacustrine sediments are taken to represent the retreat phase of this glaciation, when sufficient ice still remained to dam the Hitchin–Stevenage Gap, allowing the reformation of proglacial or periglacial lakes (Figure 27h).

BURIED CHANNELS IN THE WEST OF THE DISTRICT

This section describes the three glacial channels to the west of the Hitchin–Stevenage Gap, the sole local examples of Types 4, 5 and 6.

Offley Grange (Type 4) A line of elongated outliers of mixed glacial deposits occurs on hill tops a few kilometres to the west of Hitchin (Figure 23). Near Offley Grange [15 28] these outliers are composed of glaciofluvial deposits, some very gravelly, with interbedded silts and small lenses of till. They are about 5 to 10 m thick and extend as low as 95 m above OD. To the north-west, near Pirton, the assemblage becomes dominated by till. The outliers are somewhat thicker, perhaps up to 20 m, and mostly lie above 115 m above OD.

The complexity of the assemblage and the presence of bedded silts suggest that these outliers are remnants of a channel-fill sequence, perched above the Hitchin Channel. It seems probable that they mark a glacial channel draining towards the south-east, between the ice sheet and the contemporary Chalk escarpment. As such this would be the only example of a tangential ice-margin channel identified within the district.

The isolation of these outliers makes it difficult to determine their place in the local sequence, but it seems probable that the till near Pirton is part of the Maydencroft Till and that the channel developed during the final retreat of the Anglian ice, as an approximate contemporary of the Vicarsgrove Till (Figure 27h).

Mimram Valley (Type 5) Outcrop patterns of the glacial deposits in and near the River Mimram and its headwaters (Figure 23), including Lilley Bottom, reveal a buried channel which differs from those in the east of the district in two important respects: in several places the channel fill seems to consist entirely of till, and in these places the postglacial stream has not exhumed the preglacial channel, but has been diverted and eroded a new one.

In the district this is seen best between Whitwell and Kings Walden (Figure 23). There, two sections of the old channel have been plugged by till and for about 4 km north-west of Whitwell the valley lies to the south of the buried channel, entirely within the Chalk outcrop. The till 'plug' was apparently breached by drainage from the Offley valley, marked by glaciofluvial deposits. The

presence of ice near King's Walden seems to have initiated the southwards drainage diversion (Brown, 1959).

A similar diversion of the Mimram from its preglacial channel has occurred south-east of Whitwell, starting only a few hundred metres from the edge of the district [1965 1925] and continuing south, then east in the neighbouring Hertford district. This diversion was caused by till (and ice) blocking the valley at Codicote [21 18] (Sherlock, 1919b; Wooldridge, 1953). The till gives way abruptly upstream to a thick sequence of glaciofluvial sands and gravels. These continue north-west into the district where they are interbedded with a lens of glaciolacustrine, stoneless silts and silty clays, up to about 12 m thick.

Wooldridge (1953) concluded that during the Anglian glaciation a lobe of the ice sheet entered the Mimram valley at Codicote from the north-east, so impeding the drainage. A small ice-margin lake could have formed in the Mimram valley at that time. Laminated sediments have also been recorded a few kilometres south-east of Lilley [142 245], suggesting that similar ice-dammed lakes formed above the blockage at King's Walden (Brown, 1959).

There is no evidence that any part of the preglacial Mimram channel was deeply eroded during the Anglian, although there are very few boreholes in the area. In some sections, more than 30 m of glacial fill may be present.

River Lea (Type 6) The Lea Gap, which carries the River Lea south-east from Luton through the Chiltern escarpment, crosses the south-west of the district (Figure 23). There is a narrow outcrop of glaciofluvial sands and gravels in the valley floor, shown by boreholes (for example near Luton Lodge [1023 2001]) to be at least 5.4 m thick. Till occurs in the upper part of the Lea catchment only in the north of Luton [05 26], about 8 km north-west of where the Lea enters the district (Shephard-Thorn et al., 1994). There is none downstream until the Lea enters the Vale of St Albans (Wooldridge, 1953).

It is most probable that the ice sheet ceased its advance at Luton but that its outwash was carried through the Lea Gap. Tills in the Vale of St Albans were deposited by ice which advanced into that area from the north and north-east (Gibbard, 1977).

POST-ANGLIAN

Hoxnian deposits

In the district, deposits thought to date from the Hoxnian interglacial stage are preserved only in parts of the Hitchin–Stevenage Gap, where remnants of the Hoxnian land surface have survived dissection of the buried channel infill sequences during the later Quaternary (Figure 28). Between Fisher's Green and the west of Hitchin, these remnants form the highest ground, which is gently undulating and lies between 85 m and about 110 m above OD. They are separated from the sloping

Figure 27   Glacial
history of the Hitchin–
Stevenage Gap.

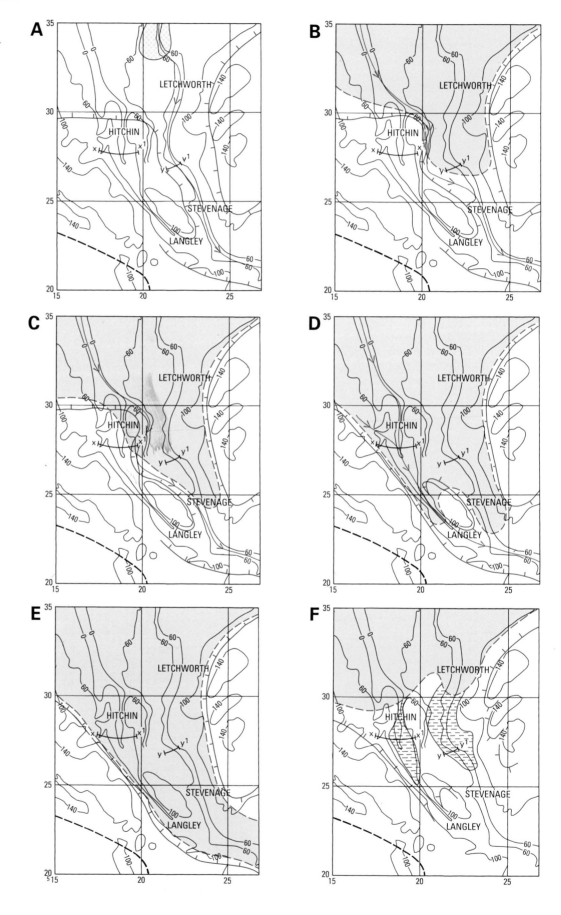

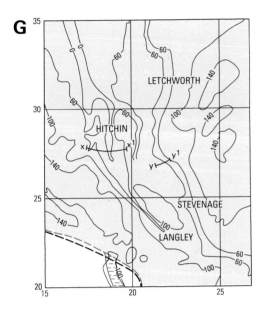

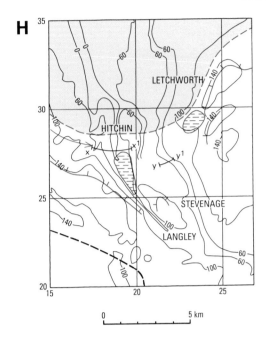

Base map shows contours on present-day 'base of Anglian' surface at 0, 60, 100, and 140 m above OD.

├──┤ : Sections shown in Figures 25b and 26b

– – – – – : Approximate maximum limit of Anglian ice-sheet

A: Pre-glaciation

Anglian ice lies to the north, advancing from the Wash. Only one channel passes through the Chilterns at the Hitchin–Stevenage Gap.

⬭ : Letchworth Gravels

⟶ : Pre-glacial river draining south from the Midlands

⊥⊥⊥⊥ : Chalk escarpment

B, C, D: Advance of the Anglian ice into Hitchin–Stevenage Gap

───── : Successive positions of the ice margin

⟶ : Corresponding principal axes of glacial drainage, partly between the ice margin and the Chalk escarpment and partly subglacial

⊥⊥⊥⊥ : Corresponding positions of the retreating Chalk escarpment

E: Anglian glacier completes first advance through Hitchin–Stevenage Gap

───── : Ice margin

At the maximum, the ice is confined below about 120 m above OD. As ice advances and becomes colder and thicker, sub-glacial drainage wanes.

F: Anglian glacier retreats to north end of Hitchin–Stevenage Gap

───── : Ice margin

⬭ : Proglacial lake

G: Main advance of Anglian ice sheet

H: Final retreat of Anglian ice sheet

⟶ : Ice margin channel

sides of the river valleys by a break of slope, although this is not everywhere well defined. These elevated remnants are further marked by areas of decalcified till, believed to reflect Hoxnian weathering (Aldiss, 1992a). South-east of Fisher's Green, the Hoxnian land surface is hidden beneath increasing thicknesses of head in the low ground of the Stevenage Channel (Figure 23) and has probably been eroded from the rising ground to the east and west.

The Hoxnian deposits comprise sequences up to 8.5 m thick, of lacustrine or fluviolacustrine clays and silts with some interbedded organic-rich clays and thin peats, and overlain in some areas by shelly calcareous silt. Each of the deposits is underlain by glacial sediments of inferred Anglian age. Each is almost entirely obscured by post-Hoxnian head or brickearth and was exposed only in excavations, boreholes or auger holes.

At Stevenage, the Hoxnian deposits were laid down in a cluster of small depressions, probably 'kettle-holes' (small depressions formed by subsidence over melting rafts of 'dead ice' in the glacial channel-fill sequence). These kettle-holes lie close to the axis of the Stevenage Channel

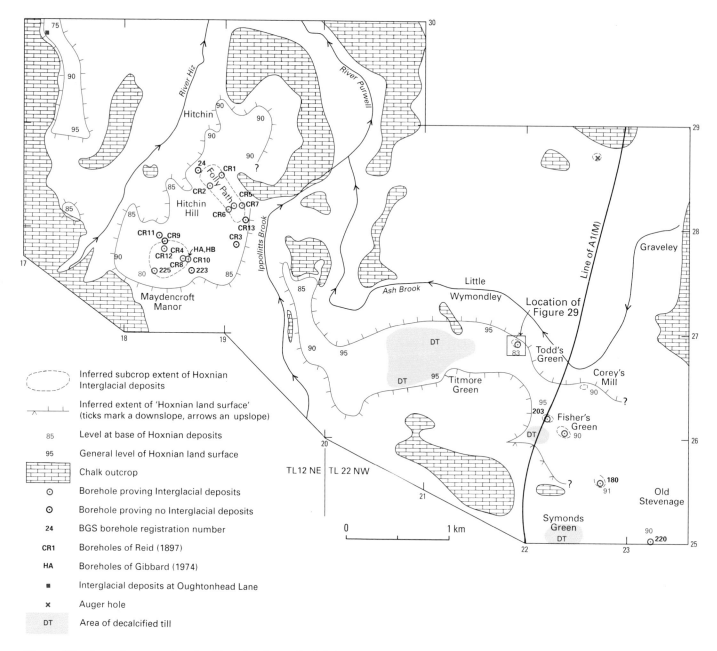

Figure 28 Location map for the Hoxnian interglacial deposits.

(Figure 23) and in at least one instance probably also on a line of post-Hoxnian drainage. At Hitchin, two major deposits mark larger lakes, which probably received some fluvial inflow. They perhaps formed where drainage was impeded by banks of moraine. The other occurrences are of unknown extent, but are apparently much smaller. One lies just to the west of Hitchin, on Oughtonhead Lane, and the other near Graveley (Figure 28).

Details

South Hitchin: Folly Path and Maydencroft

Hoxnian fluviolacustrine deposits were discovered during the 19th century in brickearth workings in two areas of south Hitchin, along the 'Folly Path' between the cemetery and Black Horse Lane, and between Brick Kiln Lane and Maydencroft Manor. A series of shallow boreholes were drilled to investigate the nature and relationships of these deposits (Hill, 1891; Reid, 1897, 1901; Gibbard, 1974) (Figure 28). The Maydencroft Manor Borehole, drilled by BGS for the National Rivers Authority during this survey, was sited on the margin of the same deposit.

The same general sequence is seen in both areas. The brick-earth rests on calcareous clayey silt or sand, 1 m to 2.74 m thick. This is evenly bedded and varies in colour from white to brown. Locally, the top appears to have been decalcified (Plate 10; Hill, 1891). It contains abundant fossil remains, notably of plants, freshwater molluscs, fish teeth and mammals, and is described in the literature variously as the 'Chara Marl', the

Plate 10 Section in a brickearth working near the Folly Path, southern Hitchin.

No contemporary description of this section is known. It appears to show 1 to 3 m of stony brickearth resting on a very irregular surface of well-bedded and laminated lacustrine sediments. The white card is reputed to mark the place where a flint implement (see inset) (GS 07) was found, although the literature states that such implements were discovered within the brickearth itself. The figure is said to be William Hill, the celebrated geologist. (Photograph by T B Latchmore, c.1885. Reproduced by courtesy of the North Hertfordshire Museum Services; inset by T Cullen, BGS from the collection of the Letchworth Museum, North Herts. District Council.) (GS 11)

'shell marl', or the 'freshwater bed'. This passes down, with a gradational contact, into clays and silts, but locally it rests sharply on 'gravelly brickearth' or glaciofluvial gravel (Hill, 1891; Hill and Monckton, 1896; Reid, 1897).

The underlying clays and silts are up to 8.2 m in thickness, and are well bedded or laminated (Reid, 1897). Some are sandy or gravelly and some are carbonaceous, with thin interbedded lignites or peats. They vary between white, yellow, brown and black in colour, and contain the fossil remains of freshwater molluscs, fish and plants (Hill, 1891; Reid, 1897, 1901; Chapman, 1901; Kennard and Woodward, 1922; Kennard, 1943; Gibbard, 1974). The clays and silts overlie sands and gravels which are probably glaciofluvial deposits or, in some places, till.

Interglacial sediments were proved between 2.9 and 4.8 m depth in the Maydencroft Manor Borehole. The sequence encountered is given below:

	Thickness m
Head, gravelly and clayey, with brickearth	2.9
Interglacial deposits	
Disturbed clay-rich lacustrine deposits	0.6
Clay, waxy, mottled brown and grey	0.3
Sand, fine, clayey, passing down into laminated sandy clay then waxy, purplish grey clay	0.4
Peat and organic-rich clay	0.6
These beds rest on chalky till.	

Earlier workers concluded that the sequences between the glaciogenic sediments and the brickearth were of temperate lacustrine or fluviolacustrine origin and Reid (1897) noted their similarity to the interglacial deposits at Hoxne. Gibbard (1974, 1977) concluded, on the basis of pollen analysis and lithology, that the sediments were indeed deposited in a temperate lacustrine environment, probably with a fluvial inflow, with marginal marshy ground and nearby dry grassland with trees, and that they are of Hoxnian age. Pollen and spore assemblages from the organic sediments in the Maydencroft Manor borehole found an assemblage dominated by grasses with birch (*Betula* sp.) and sea buckthorn (*Hippophaë rhamnoides*), indicating that the sequence is of late Anglian to early Hoxnian age (Gibbard and Boreham, written communication, 1993).

Oughtonhead Lane

A tufa deposit was discovered west of Hitchin in 1943 during the excavation of a trench for a water pipe along Oughtonhead Lane [1721 2985] (Figure 28). Kennard (1943) recorded 11 species of nonmarine molluscs from this section. He concluded that the deposit dated from the same temperate period as those in south Hitchin (p.104).

The deposit was re-excavated by Kerney (1959) who described four units from the trench:

	Thickness m
Gravel, flint, coarse, sandy, including many erratics	0.46
Calcareous tufa, very variable in texture, with a rich olluscan fauna	0.2 to 0.4
Clay, sandy, light brown, highly calcareous, or brickearth, with occasional flints and chalk pellets, molluscan fauna similar to bed above	0.6
Sandy gravels, fine, with glacial erratics and brown and grey calcareous loams	less than 3.0

Kerney classified the lowest gravels as glaciofluvial deposits of Anglian age. He considered that the overlying clay or brickearth is a fluviatile interglacial deposit, although it contains fossils only of terrestrial species. The brickearth becomes increasingly calcareous towards the top, and grades into the overlying tufa. The tufa is somewhat disturbed, with minor folding and faulting. It contains a variety of identifiable mammalian and

nonmarine molluscan remains. The topmost gravel includes a flint artefact at the base and is regarded as Devensian head.

The species present in the brickearth and tufa suggested to Kerney (1959) that the deposit formed in spring-fed marshy ground in woodland, during a temperate climate, possibly warmer than at present. He assigned it to the Hoxnian, albeit on grounds that might now be considered inconclusive. Holyoak et al. (1983) discuss further evidence from this deposit, concluding that it is of Hoxnian age or older.

There are obvious similarities between this Oughtonhead Lane sequence and the Folly Path and Maydencroft Hoxnian subcrops. In addition, the position of the Oughtonhead Lane deposit on the inferred 'Hoxnian land surface' is compatible with Kerney's conclusion. If this deposit was indeed formed at the site of a spring then it would be expected to be fairly small, but there could be similar deposits nearby in analogous situations.

Fisher's Green

Lacustrine deposits discovered during construction of a pedestrian underpass at Fisher's Green (Figure 28) in 1974 were described by Gibbard and Aalto (1977). A borehole sunk just east of the road at this site [2240 2605] (surface c.96 m OD) proved the following sequence:

	Thickness m	Depth m
Made Ground	0.30	0.30
Head		
Sand, silty, clayey, light grey, with some pebbles; cryoturbated	1.20	1.50
Alluvium		
Cryoturbated sandy gravel and sand, orangish brown; passing downwards into brown silty sand	1.95	3.45
Hoxnian lacustrine deposit		
Clay, grey or greyish brown, silty, with organic flints and plant fragments, passing down into	1.00	4.45
Black organic mud containing plant fragments, passing down into	0.90	5.35
Clay, silty, grey, calcareous and shelly	0.66	6.01
Anglian		
Chalky till	0.19	6.20

At Fisher's Green, organic deposits probably extend over an area of about 150 m in diameter (P L Gibbard and S Boreham, written communication, 1992). The associated silts continue at least 110 m west-north-west of the original underpass site, close to the motorway (Figure 28). Borehole TL22NW/203 [2221 2620] on the site of the nearby bridge over the motorway proved 1.8 m clay and gravel (head), over 0.3 m peat, resting on chalky till.

Following palaeobotanical analysis, the lower part of the Fisher's Green sequence was interpreted as late glacial to early interglacial deposits, laid down in a shallow pool, in an area of sea buckthorn (*Hippophaë*), birch (*Betula*) and willow (*Salix*) scrub. The organic-rich sediments above were taken to represent the second half of the interglacial, when coniferous woodland was established in the area (Gibbard and Aalto, 1977).

The sand and gravel overlying the interglacial deposits at Fisher's Green displays current bedding, indicating deposition by a north-westwards flowing stream. The cryoturbated sandy head at the top of the sequence marks a post-Hoxnian cold period.

Todd's Green

Excavations during 1991 for the construction of the Little Wymondley bypass, north-west of Todd's Green [2193 2693], exposed up to 7.5 m of sandy clayey head resting on lacustrine clays and peat which in turn overlies glaciofluvial sand and gravel and till (Figure 29). The lacustrine sequence occupies a basin about 50 m in diameter (P L Gibbard and S Boreham, written communication, 1992). Most of this deposit, including the section described here, will have been removed as construction proceeded.

Pollen analysis indicates that the Todd's Green organic sediments are of Hoxnian age, with an early birch zone, followed by a period of mixed oak woodland and finally by a period with silver fir (P L Gibbard and S Boreham, written communication, 1993).

Corey's Mill

A temporary section, almost 100 m long and up to 4 m high, was created in 1992 on a construction site between Corey's Mill and the A1(M) [2256 2652] (Figure 28). In the middle of an east–west-trending part of the section, a lacustrine deposit up to 3 m thick was exposed, which wedged-out completely at either end between sloping surfaces on underlying till and the subhorizontal surface of the overlying sandy gravelly head. The exposed width of about 50 m is probably close to its maximum extent (P L Gibbard and S Boreham, written communication, 1992).

The lowest part of this dish-shaped deposit lies at about 90 m above OD, where about 1 m of pale grey to grey laminated clays rest on massive chalky till. There are traces of organic material at the contact. The clays are overlain in turn by about 1 m of dark brown organic clay, which is peaty in parts, then about 1 m of slightly organic pale grey to brown clays containing rootlets. The similarity of this sequence to that proved nearby at Fisher's Green and its position overlying un-weathered till suggests that it too is of Hoxnian age (P L Gibbard and S Boreham, written communication, 1993).

Graveley

An occurrence of shelly silts and a trace of organic clay was found by hand-augering within an outcrop of Anglian glacio-lacustrine deposits north-west of Graveley [2270 2871]. As with the lower part of the Fisher's Green deposit (Gibbard and Aalto, 1977) these may be deposits of the late glacial to early interglacial period.

Gunnel's Wood Road

There are a few occurrences of probable lacustrine sediments in boreholes in north-west Stevenage (Figure 28). Borehole TL22NW/180 [2274 2559], just south of Gunnel's Wood Road, proved 3.6 m clayey head overlying 0.8 m soft, brown, organic, silty clay above 1 m grey, slightly organic, silty clay and silt with scattered shell debris to 90.6 m above OD, lying on 0.5 m sand and gravel over till. The organic sediments are probably Hoxnian deposits.

Borehole TL22NW/220 [2324 2501], between Old Stevenage and the railway line, records 2.7 m of brown clayey sand and gravel (head), above 1 m of brown and grey mottled silty clay with lenses of sand and traces of decayed plant matter, overlying sand and gravel at about 90 m above OD.

Culpin (1921) refers to evidence for the formation of a lake, 3.2 km (2 miles) long and 1.6 km (1 mile) wide, rising up to 97.5 m above OD within the Stevenage valley. He states that 'Pleistocene shells' were found on the north-west boundary,

and that sewer excavations in 1898 proved widespread bands of 'peaty soil' 0.10 to 0.15 m (4 to 6 inches) thick and 1.8 to 2.4 m (6 to 8 feet) below the surface.

Brickearth

Post-Hoxnian brickearths, composed of sparsely gravelly, clayey sandy silts, form relatively large deposits in south Hitchin. Similar brickearths occur elsewhere in the area, in association with clay-with-flints or head, but these deposits have not been differentiated on the maps. As noted in Chapter 8, brick-making material has also been taken from other formations, both solid and drift, in the district; these are described in Chapter 8.

There are numerous shallow pits in the southern part of Hitchin which were exploited for brickearth, mainly during the nineteenth century. They are now disused and mostly backfilled or built over. The largest were Ransom's pits, which lay between the cemetery and the Stevenage Road, on either side of the 'Folly Path' [189 285]. Jeeves' pit was nearby, just south of the Stevenage Road [191 281]. There was another group of pits north-east of Maydencroft Manor [185 277].

The term 'brickearth' is notoriously inexact, as in the past it seems to have been used indiscriminately to describe virtually any 'material used to make bricks'. The Hitchin brickearth deposits are described as yellow, reddish brown or brown clayey or sandy silts (loams), containing small stones (including angular flints) in irregular and discontinuous layers and particularly concentrated at the base (Hill, 1891; Reid, 1897). The brickearth is generally rather homogeneous and only obscurely bedded, if at all, but Reid (1897) recorded a few metres of 'bedded brickearth with seams of sand' at the bottom of the thickest proved section.

The brickearth deposits contain flint implements, mostly found in the gravelly basal layer (Reid, 1897). Examples are illustrated by Evans (1896) and briefly described by Oakley (1947a, b) and Roe (1968a, b).

Boreholes and excavated sections show that in Ransom's pits the brickearth is at least 11.6 m thick in places, which seems to be close to the maximum thickness of the deposit, but to the south in Jeeves' pit it is barely 1 m. Near Maydencroft Manor, the thickest section recorded is 4.6 m (Hill, 1891; Reid, 1897). The brickearth generally rests on the interglacial deposits (Plate 10) but in two boreholes (Reid, 1897) it lies directly on glaciofluvial deposits.

The brickearth at Hitchin is thought to have been deposited by a combination of wind action and solifluction (cf. Reid, 1897), as inferred for similar brickearths elsewhere in the Chilterns (Avery et al., 1982), and therefore to have accumulated preferentially in topographic depressions. Avery et al. (1982) present evidence for post-Anglian brickearth formation in the Chilterns both before and during the Devensian.

Details

An exposure on the north side of the cemetery, beside Standhill Road [1865 2860], showed 0.8 m of gravelly sand

Figure 29
Hoxnian
interglacial
deposits near
Todd's Green
incorporating the
pollen analysis of
samples collected
by Cambridge
University.

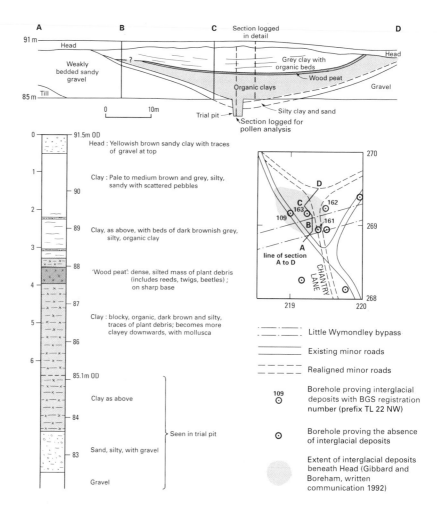

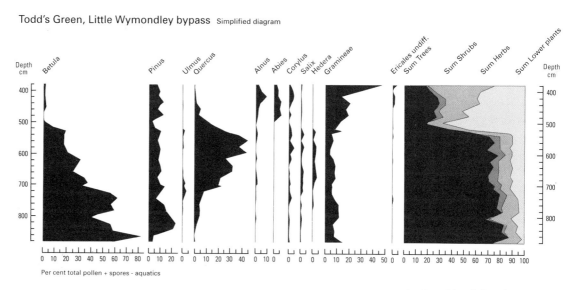

Todd's Green, Little Wymondley bypass   Simplified diagram

Per cent total pollen + spores - aquatics

Analysed by S Boreham 1992

(head) overlying at least 3 m of pale brown slightly gravelly and sandy silt. This lies at the same topographic height as part of the previous workings of Ransom's pits, nearby.

Two exposures in the brickearth, observed by Gibbard (1974) close to Ransom's pits [188284] and [187 285], showed up to 6.5 m of decalcified, sandy, clayey silt with narrow irregular and impersistent pebbly and sandy horizons.

Coombe deposits

Occurrences of coombe deposits have been recorded in the bottom of dry valleys (coombes) in the Middle and Upper Chalk escarpment in the west of the district. They are a special category of head confined to this situation, and are composed of chalky loams, locally with flint gravel and clay. Their formation is discussed by Shephard-Thorn et al. (1994). Similar deposits elsewhere in the district have not been differentiated from head and dry valley deposits.

Head

In general, head deposits are taken to have formed by mass-movement processes under periglacial conditions, but also include elements of recent soil creep and hill wash. Their composition therefore reflects that of the source material and is correspondingly variable. Thin head is present in most parts of the area. Only the thicker deposits on lower valley sides and in the bottom of minor valleys have been recorded, particularly where they form a separate topographic feature. Valley-bottom deposits forming a shallow, concave cross-profile are generally regarded as head, whereas flat valley floors are thought to be underlain mainly by alluvium, or by dry valley deposits.

In the district, head typically comprises brown, or brown and grey mottled, silty, sandy clays and sandy silts with variable amounts of flint gravel. The gravel is normally concentrated at the base of the deposit but can also define crude bedding within it. On outcrops of the Chalk, head is more likely to comprise a brown clayey silt with chalk fragments but little sand or gravel, while sandy gravelly heads occur on outcrops of glaciofluvial deposits. In general, head is likely to be less consolidated than its source. Its thickness ranges up to about 5 m.

Head is particularly widespread and voluminous in the dry valleys in the south-west of the district, where material from the clay-with-flints has spread downhill. These valleys lay beyond the maximum ice-limit during the Anglian glaciation, and so head predating that time was not removed by glacial erosion. In the rest of the area, head is assumed to postdate the retreat of the Anglian ice sheet.

Small sections of head are commonly exposed in streams, quarries, ditches and temporary excavations. Many borehole records, especially those from modern site investigations, show head deposits, although in some instances it is not possible to identify the gradational boundary with the underlying formations. Incidental details have been included in some descriptions of other deposits.

River terrace deposits

River terrace deposits, representing the remnants of eroded former floodplain aggradations, are of limited extent, occurring only in sections of the larger, north-flowing streams. Terraces formed at two levels may be present in some places in the north, but they could not be separated consistently.

The river terraces are underlain by brown or grey silts, sands and gravels with varying proportions of clay. Thin interbeds of organic silts, shelly sand or peat occur locally. Most of the gravel is composed of flint but some chalk or erratic clasts are present. It is not everywhere possible to distinguish river terrace deposits from glaciofluvial deposits reliably. Up to 3.8 m of river terrace deposits have been proved in the Hiz valley.

The flat, gravelly terrace surfaces are separated from the adjacent alluvial plain by a low bluff 0.5 to 1.0 m high. Corresponding knick-points occur in the courses of the Ash Brook and the Ippollitts Brook, just upstream from their confluence [2026 2867], but deposits in those valleys are treated as alluvium.

The terrace deposits are post-Hoxnian in age and probably date from the Devensian glacial stage, but no direct evidence for the age is available.

Dry valley deposits

Dry valley deposits occur in the bottom of the dry valleys in the Chilterns, typically forming flat-topped spreads up to 100 m wide. They pass laterally into head or alluvium, in places across a break of slope.

The dry valley deposits are rarely exposed and have been seen only in a few drainage ditches, temporary excavations or boreholes. Their composition is variable and is not known in detail, but generally they seem to comprise brown sandy silty clays or silty sands with sandy flint gravel and some chalk detritus. Typically, the gravel is in the lower part of the sequence or just at the base. The dry valley deposits are generally less than 3 m in thickness.

As mapped, the dry valley deposits probably include water-lain sediments deposited by ephemeral streams, particularly at past times of higher water tables, together with hill wash and solifluction deposits (head) from the valley sides. It can be argued that the greater part of these deposits dates from post-Anglian periods of cold climate, when permafrost rendered the Chalk impermeable and there was abundant frost-shattered detritus on poorly vegetated slopes nearby.

Alluvial fan deposits

In the district, the dissected remnants of low-angle alluvial fans occur along the sides of dry valleys and on minor interfluves below the Upper Chalk escarpment east and south of Baldock and below the Middle Chalk escarpment west of Letchworth (Figure 23). These remnants tend to be rather elongated, in some instances extending downslope for several kilometres. They are separated from adjacent outcrops of dry valley deposits by breaks of slope, but form low mounds rather than flat-topped terraces.

The alluvial fan deposits are typically composed of orangish brown to pale brown, sparsely gravelly, silty medium to fine sands with some sandy clayey silts and thin sandy gravels. The gravel is composed of soft chalk or subangular pieces of flint, in some places with erratic quartz and quartzite pebbles. Cryoturbation structures at the base of the deposit have been noted in trial pits (e.g. TL23SE/13 [2659 3479]). The greatest proved thickness is 4 m.

The alluvial fan deposits pass upslope into head deposits and laterally into thin spreads of gravelly hillwash, which have not been mapped. Their distribution and composition indicates that they were laid down from flowing water. Similar deposits in Cambridgeshire display cross-bedding (White and Edmunds, 1932). The components of sand, silt and hard gravel were presumably derived from the glaciofluvial deposits, till, and clay-with-flints on top of the escarpment. The occurrence of pebbles of soft chalk suggests that transport took place in a periglacial regime, when fragments of frost-shattered chalk would have been available on an impermeable, permafrost land surface, and could have been carried downslope by waters from seasonally melting snow. Rapid transport and deposition would have enabled the preservation of fragments of soft chalk, particularly if they had been frozen when picked up by the meltwaters.

The similar deposits in Cambridgeshire were described as 'taele gravels' (White and Edmunds, 1932; Chatwin, 1961), but sediments grouped under this term were later found to include river terrace deposits and glaciofluvial deposits (Edmonds and Dinham, 1965). The term has thus fallen into disuse (Aldiss, 1991).

Alluvium

Alluvium forms ribbon-like outcrops, up to about 300 m wide, in the floors of each of the valleys with flowing streams. On or near the Chalk outcrop, valley bottom deposits downstream from the headwater springs of the Rivers Lea, Mimram and Hiz and their tributaries have been mapped as alluvium, but similar deposits upstream are classified as dry valley deposits. In the north of the area, alluvium rests in channels cut into, or through, the river terrace deposits. It is usually less than 3 m in thickness, but is over 7 m in places.

The composition varies considerably, including brown or grey sandy or silty clays, sands and gravels, with some shelly sands, organic muds and peats in places. The gravel is mostly composed of flint, but clasts of chalk or of erratic rock types also occur. The gravel is commonly concentrated in a basal layer, up to 1 m thick in places.

Alluvium is commonly exposed in river banks, in places perched above the present stream where the underlying Chalk has been incised. Several borehole records from modern site investigations show alluvium, but it is not always possible to distinguish it from underlying glaciofluvial deposits.

Peat and calcareous tufa

Small deposits of peat or tufa are sparsely distributed in the district. The oldest occurrences are of Hoxnian age and have already been noted. Post-Hoxnian peat occurs with alluvium on the floodplains in the north of the district and has also formed at springs in the glacial sequences, in some places together with calcareous tufa.

Much of the floodplain of the River Oughton at Oughtonhead Common, north-west of Hitchin [168 303], is underlain by dark brown to black fibrous wood and sedge peat, between 0.5 and 1.0 m thick. The peat lies on saturated alluvial gravel and probably passes laterally into alluvium.

Similar but less extensive deposits, in places interbedded with organic muds, occur beside the River Ivel, north of Baldock [240 349], and by the River Hiz, north of Ickleford [186 337], [179 347], [180 352] and near Arlesey [190 370].

At Ridlins Marsh, which is a small county nature reserve in the south of Stevenage [263 222], a small domed peat bog (90 m by 70 m) has developed at a seepage from glaciofluvial deposits onto till. The deposit consists of dark brown peat up to 1.8 m thick. Concentrations of lime (Tilia) pollen occur in the basal peat. Borings found a number of worked flints at the base of the deposit. The peat is thought to be younger than 7000 years BP (Tinsley and Cosgrove, 1991).

At Biggin Moor, which is about 2 km east of Buckland [380 336], there is an elongated outcrop of peat associated with head in the bottom of a minor valley in the headwaters of the River Quin. The dark brown to black fibrous reed and wood peat is interbedded with dark brown (speckled white or cream) sandy or peaty silts and fine sands with calcareous nodules, which in some instances develop into calcareous tufa. The peat overlies till, in places with an intervening bed of gravel.

Calcareous tufa has also been observed at Norton Common, Letchworth [218 333]. Less than 1 m of white to yellowish calcareous tufa is known to occur. It rests on till in the shallow valley of the River Pix, about 3 m above the level of the stream. Thirty-six species of mollusca have been found in the tufa, including some species which became extinct in Britain by about 4000 years BP (Kerney, 1955).

Note on Palaeolithic finds in the district

Dr J J Wymer

Palaeolithic activity is well represented by the discovery of flint hand-axes at several places in the area of the Hitchin Gap. Some of the sites are of considerable archaeological importance, as the artifacts are found sealed under the Hitchin brickearth apparently where they were discarded. Material of this age in such a primary context is very rare, for fluvial agencies, solifluction or permafrost have generally destroyed the actual land surfaces of the time and, for the most part, palaeoliths upon them have been dispersed into river terrace deposits. Such have been found in gravel which was exposed by the Great Northern

Railway cutting in 1887, at Knebworth in the Stevenage Valley. Others come from gravels which used to be dug north of Hitchin between the Rivers Oughton and Hiz. They include flakes, and pointed and ovate forms of hand-axes. All are rolled to varying degrees by their transportation, and generally stained from iron oxides in the gravel. A few more were found at Henlow to the north of the Gap, but nothing is known of their concepts except that at least one was a surface find.

The hand-axes found associated with the base of the Hitchin brickearth are mainly as fresh and sharp as the day they were made, having been gently covered by fine sediments. The majority were found in two pits, south of the town: Ransom's Brickyard [TL 189 285], which was south of the present cemetery, and in Jeeve's Pit (otherwise known as the Folly Pit [TL 192 281]) just south of the Stevenage Road. Both pits are now landscaped, levelled or built over. The discoveries were made in the late 19th century and the Folly Pit was examined by Clement Reid in 1896. He established the sequence of brickearth overlying alluvial, freshwater deposits containing shells, insects, vegetable remains and some mammalian fauna, comprising bones of elephant and rhinoceros, bear teeth and red deer antler fragments. The same sequence was probably exposed in some of the many brickearth pits which opened up in and around Hitchin at this time, for hand-axes have been recorded in a few of them. Those hand-axes which were in primary context were not found in the alluvial deposits but at the gravelly base of the brickearth or within the body of it. This suggests that they lay on a land surface which existed after the lake or abandoned river channel represented by the alluvial interglacial deposits had lowered its water table or been drained. Those hand-axes found within the brickearth tend to be rather worn, patinated and frost-cracked, indicating that they had been exposed to long, surface exposure. On the basis of the shells, mammalian fauna and the typology of the hand-axes, it is likely that they date from the latter part of the Hoxnian Interglacial stage and into the following cooler period. The hand-axes from the Hitchin brickearth have been examined by Dr D A Roe (1968a) and metrical analyses place them in the same group as those from Hoxne.

This district lies just to the east of numerous palaeolithic discoveries made by Worthington Smith (1894) within brickearth in the neighbourhood of Luton. Although these could be contemporary with those from the Hitchin brickearth, the brickearth of the Luton area tends to fill sink-holes in the Chalk and not rest conformably on interglacial deposits.

A few hand-axes have also been found on the modern surface at Letchworth and in the Mimram Valley at St Pauls Walden and Langley. Others at Ippollitts and Fisher's Green, Stevenage, may be contemporary with the Hitchin brickearth material. References to Palaeoliths in Hertfordshire may be found in a paper by Oakley (1947) and the Gazetteer of British Lower and Middle Palaeolithic sites by Roe (1968b).

SEVEN

Structure

The main elements of the structure of the concealed formations are discussed in Chapter 2. The nature of this sub-Mesozoic 'basement' is largely inferred from the regional Bouguer gravity anomaly and aeromagnetic fields whose interpretation is controlled by borehole evidence from outside the district.

This chapter first summarises the main lineaments interpreted from the regional geophysical data sets. This is followed by a description of the structural features of the Mesozoic formations, principally of the Chalk. These have been observed directly, or inferred from field mapping surveys, and interpretation of borehole data, or are expressed as lineaments on satellite images (Figure 30c). A brief review of the structure as it effects the Palaeogene and Quaternary strata is also given.

GEOPHYSICAL LINEAMENTS

As noted in Chapter 2, major lineaments on maps of the potential field data are likely to mark geological structures. Much of the medium- to small-scale variation in the gravity field is probably related to near-surface formations, whereas the aeromagnetic map shows the influence primarily of deeper-seated bodies (small anomalies, for example at [513 221] on Figure 4b are probably related to the influence of towns). Therefore features on the Bouguer gravity anomaly map which coincide with those on the aeromagnetic map probably represent basement structures which have been reactivated within the Upper Palaeozoic and Mesozoic cover (Allsop, 1985; Lee et al., 1990). Four structural trends influence the

Figure 30a Bouguer anomaly gravity pseudo-relief map (illuminated at 45° from north).

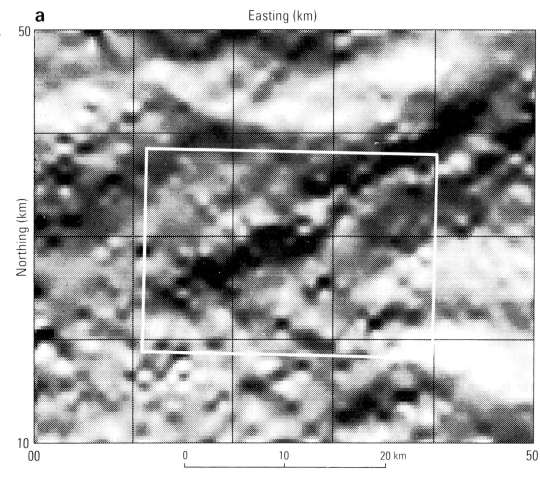

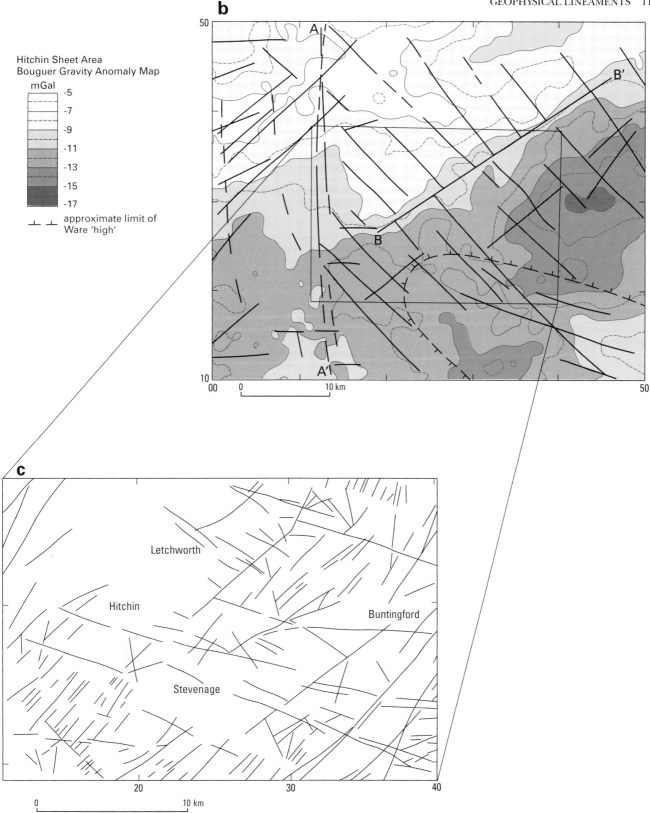

b

Hitchin Sheet Area
Bouguer Gravity Anomaly Map

mGal

-5
-7
-9
-11
-13
-15
-17

⊥—⊥ approximate limit of
Ware 'high'

Figure 30b Bouguer anomaly gravity contours and geophysical lineaments. Lineaments interpreted from various plots of regional gravity and aeromagnetic data shown in Figures 4a and b.

c Satellite image lineaments in the district.

district (north–south, ENE–WSW, ESE–WNW and NW–SE), although minor structures of other orientations, such as east–west, are also present.

NORTH–SOUTH TRENDS

North–south geophysical lineaments thought to mark faults in the sub-Mesozoic basement are present in the west of the district (Figure 30b, A–A′), further to the west near Leighton Buzzard (Shephard-Thorn et al., 1994), and elsewhere in the Midlands Microcraton (Lee et al., 1990). The residual gravity data (Figure 4c) indicate a density contrast between sub-Mesozoic rocks on either side of the lineament in the west of the district, suggesting that it could mark a fault juxtaposing Devonian strata of the Luton–Cambridge Basin against the Silurian to the west. The major north–south lineament in the Leighton Buzzard area coincides with the limit of the Woburn Sands outcrop, suggesting that faulting on this line (and perhaps on others of similar orientation) resumed during the Mesozoic.

ENE–WSW TRENDS

The district is bisected by a major linear east-north-east-trending feature (B–B′), which is a zone of increased Bouguer gravity anomaly gradient (Figures 30a and b, and 4a). This is superimposed on a general decrease in the gravity field towards the south-east, thought to be partly a consequence of the progressive increase in relative thickness of the Mesozoic but also of the lateral variations in the Palaeozoic sequences already noted. Minor subparallel lineaments are also apparent on a pseudo-relief plot of the Bouguer gravity anomaly map (Figure 30a).

The feature (B–B′) approximately coincides with the Chalk escarpment. Its characteristics suggest that it could be caused by a density contrast at a relatively shallow level, as would arise if the base of the Mesozoic sequence were faulted down to the south-east against the Devonian. There is, however, no geological evidence for a significant displacement of the Cretaceous across this gradient (although there is very little relevant borehole information about the thickness of the Lower Chalk and the Gault). It is more likely that the gravity gradient reflects density variations across east-north-east-trending structures at several depths, possibly fractures which have propagated upward from the Devonian.

Faulting in this position could have controlled the south-eastern extent of the Woburn Sands and Lower Gault between the 'Bedfordshire Straits' (Chapter 3) and the Ware high, although this would imply that the Devonian was downthrown to the north-west.

North-easterly lineaments, some more than 10 km long, are visible throughout the Chalk outcrop on satellite images of the district (Figure 30c). The Charlton Axis, is noted to have influenced Mesozoic deposition to the west (Shephard-Thorn et al., 1994). Expressed as a broad positive Bouguer gravity anomaly, the Charlton Axis trends south-west–north-east, passing just north of the district (Figure 5b), and appears to terminate in the Cambridge area (Horton et al., 1994; Shephard-Thorn et al., 1994). This axis approximately coincides with the 'Cambridge Line' of Woodcock (1991), which separates contrasting domains in the sub-Mesozoic formations of both the microcraton and the Lower Palaeozoic basin to the east and which is thought to mark a major basement fault or fold-belt. However, the Charlton Axis has no discernible effect on the potential fields within the district itself and little apparent effect on the local geology.

ESE–WNW TRENDS

The Ware high is likely to be bounded by faults of this orientation. Although it lies well to the north of the Variscan Front (Lee et al., 1990), the Ware high is thought to be a small Variscan flexure in which the region magnetic basement has been brought closer to the surface (Allsop and Smith, 1988). While the aeromagnetic evidence suggests that the Ware high is generally elongated in an east–west direction (Figure 4), a more precise orientation is indicated by east-south-east-trending lineaments on the Bouguer gravity anomaly map (Figure 30). The presence in the district of several sets of persistent lineaments of the same orientation recognised from satellite images suggests that there are faults on that trend which also influence the surface geology (Figure 30).

NW–SE TRENDS

The main east-north-east–west-south-west regional gravity gradient is interrupted by several north-west-trending *en-échelon* deflections, which are taken to mark faults at depth. Lineaments of this orientation occur throughout the area (Figure 30c). They are parallel to structures in the Lower Palaeozoic of the eastern Caledonides, and the postulated north-eastern boundary of the Midlands Microcraton (Lee et al., 1990). Lee et al. (1991) note that south-easterly and east-south-easterly structural trends are widespread in eastern England and suggest that these mark the reactivation of major structures in concealed Precambrian and Lower Palaeozoic basement.

EAST–WEST TRENDS

Relatively short east–west geophysical lineaments (of unidentified cause) also occur widely in the eastern Caledonides (Lee et al., 1991). In the district, east–west trends are visible as closures in both Bouguer gravity anomaly and aeromagnetic maps (Figures 4 and 30).

STRUCTURES IN THE EXPOSED FORMATIONS

Cretaceous

Although the Cretaceous formations of the district broadly conform to the uniform undisturbed sequence expected on the London Platform, there are some minor perturbations arising from local tectonic activity, seen both in the structure and the sedimentary sequences, chiefly in the Chalk.

The late Aptian to early Albian transgressions overlapped an eroded surface of Upper Jurassic rocks and, presumably, the Devonian subcrop in the south (Chapter

Figure 31a Structure contours on the base of the Middle Chalk.

b Structure contours on the base of the Upper Chalk.

c Structure contours on the base of the Palaeogene and the clay-with-flints.

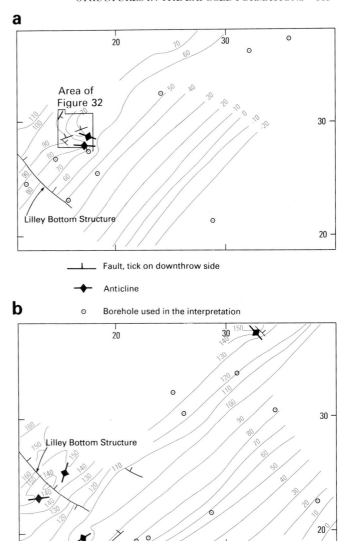

a

Area of Figure 32

Lilley Bottom Structure

⊥ Fault, tick on downthrow side

◆ Anticline

○ Borehole used in the interpretation

b

Lilley Bottom Structure

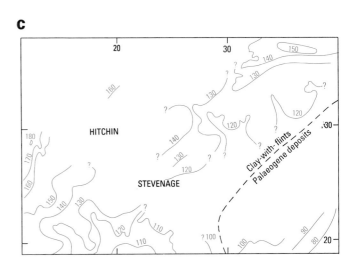

c

HITCHIN

STEVENAGE

Clay-with-flints Palaeogene deposits

3). Their south-eastern limit against the London Platform is not known with any precision, but a linear gradient in the gravity data indicates a zone of faulting near the position of the Chalk escarpment which possibly controlled the extent of the Woburn Sands and of the succeeding Lower Gault. The data are insufficient to reveal any other possible structural control of the thickness of the Woburn Sands (cf. Shephard-Thorn et al., 1994).

Borehole information for the Mesozoic formation boundaries is sparse and of rather variable quality. Structure contours are presented only for the base of the Upper Chalk and of the Middle Chalk and even these are generalised and partly speculative, particularly in the subcrop region (Figures 31a and b). Most of the data are compatible with a model in which the regional dip of all the Cretaceous strata is south-eastwards at about half a degree. It is not known whether the borehole data which do not conform to this model indicate perturbations in the regional structure or are merely inaccurate.

Small faults are commonly seen in the larger exposures of the Chalk, but in unexposed ground the outcrop patterns are usually insufficiently well defined to demonstrate displacements of less than about 5 m. Very gentle folding and some faulting of the Melbourn Rock and Chalk Rock can, however, be observed at outcrop, causing local deflections of the regional dip to inclinations of 2° or more. Syndepositional movements can be demonstrated in a few places. Similar structures are assumed to be present in the Chalk subcrop and in the Lower Cretaceous formations but this cannot be proved from the data available. Although the outcrop of the base of the Chalk is locally contorted no consistent pattern of folding has emerged and it is suspected that this deformation is a result of ice-loading during the Anglian, or of post-Anglian cambering.

Satellite lineaments on the Chalk outcrop mostly follow trends between west-north-west and east-west or north-east and north-north-east (Figure 30c), which are subparallel to geophysical lineaments and suspected basement structural trends. The orientation of joints and faults observed at exposures was not recorded systematically.

The structure contours (Figure 31) indicate that there is a north-west-trending dislocation of the Chalk in the Lilley Bottom buried valley in the west of the district. This extends into the Leighton Buzzard district, where it intersects the Chalk escarpment near Barton-le-Clay. Coincident geophysical lineaments support the interpretation (Figures 4 and 30b). This dislocation is named the Lilley Bottom structure (Shephard-Thorn et al., 1994). On most of its length, it has the appearance of a normal fault downthrown to the north-east by up to 10 m, although on present evidence it could instead be a

monoclinal roll of the same orientation. It is therefore not shown on the face of the map. Displacements in the structure contours close to the south-eastern end of the Lilley Bottom structure (around Whitwell) suggest that the throw is reversed but these might instead be the consequence of strike-parallel faulting or folding: there is insufficient evidence to show which is the case.

As noted by Shephard-Thorn et al. (1994), the Lilley Bottom structure appears to have exerted a significant control on sedimentation at several times during the Upper Cretaceous. It coincides with the south-western limit of the Cambridge Greensand (Hart, 1973b) and also appears to mark the south-western limit of the 'Anglian Trough', which is the sector of maximum development of the Plenus Marls in the Chilterns (Jefferies, 1963). Conversely, it separates an area to the west with a thick Lower Chalk sequence (of about 75 m) from one to the east where the Lower Chalk seems to be only 60 m or less in thickness. If real, the cause of this reduction is problematical.

There is no discernible change in the thickness of the Middle Chalk in the vicinity of the Lilley Bottom structure, but it increases from between 60 and 80 m in the west of the district to between 80 and 100 m in the east, probably reaching a maximum south of Royston, just east of the district [45 30], where there is a negative Bouguer gravity anomaly (Figure 30b). This is close to the centre of Jefferies' (1963) 'Anglian Trough'. The Chalk Rock displays a comparable increase from west to east. A relatively abrupt change in its facies in the vicinity of Clothall (Chapter 4) suggests some element of structural control.

With the exception of the variation in the Lower Chalk, these changes in thickness of the Chalk are all consistent with the effects of regional subsidence towards the Caledonide fold-belt, presumably accompanied by basement faulting parallel to the north-east edge of the Midlands Microcraton.

Superimposed on this eastwards thickening of the Chalk, the small number of relevant gamma-ray logs from Chalk boreholes suggests that from the south-east to the north-east of the district the lower part of the Middle Chalk decreases in thickness by some 10 to 20 m while the upper part thickens by a similar amount (Chapter 4).

Details

Mapped outcrop patterns of the Melbourn Rock in an area just west of Hitchin [29 16] (Figure 32) show that the Chalk is there gently folded on easterly trending axes, so that the dip of the Melbourn Rock varies between horizontal and about 1.5° and between south and north-north-east in azimuth. The flexures seem to be parasitic minor folds at the southern closure of a regional-scale fold-pair (Figures 31 and 32).

In the same area, displacements of the Melbourn Rock show that the Chalk is also faulted. Although the orientation of the faults is usually not very well defined, the largest seem to trend east-north-east and are downthrown by up to 5 m (Figure 32). North-westerly and north-north-easterly faults are also present.

The Melbourn Rock outcrop marks a very gentle east–west-trending syncline a short distance north of Hitchin [197 307]. Nearby, to the north of Cadwell Farm [189 327], the Melbourn Rock is disrupted by several small faults mostly trending north-west. The occurrence of these disturbances in the Chalk at the mouth of the Hitchin–Stevenage gap, in an area which would have been subjected to considerable ice pressure during the Anglian, suggests that they might be of glaciotectonic origin. If

so, this has occurred by crumpling in situ: there is no repetition of the stratigraphy, intercalation of Chalk rafts with till, or other evidence for thrusting (cf. description of glaciotectonic thrusting in Chapter 6). It is here considered more likely that both folds and faults mark rejuvenated basement structures. Zones of fracturing above such structures might have been exploited during erosion in the Hitchin–Stevenage Gap.

Exposures of the lowest part of the Middle Chalk at Steeple Morden Quarry [300 405], which lies just north of the district, reveal a low amplitude upright fold-pair, plunging gently south-eastwards. Local variations in the Chalk sequence, notably a restricted development of flint over the anticline, indicate syn-sedimentary tectonism. The western limb of a gently south-south-east-plunging syncline is seen in the outcrop pattern of the Melbourn Rock nearby to the south. Any south-eastwards continuation of the anticline at Steeple Morden is not obvious within the Middle Chalk sequence, but flexures in the Chalk Rock near Therfield [330 375] are thought to reflect the same structure (Figure 31).

Very gentle folding of the Chalk on north-east-trending axes can be demonstrated locally, for example around Great Offley [14 27], where the Chalk Rock marks a very gently undulating surface at about 150 m above OD. The outcrop pattern of the Melbourn Rock in the Claybush Hill area [269 385] suggests a very low amplitude fold with its axis trending approximately north-west–south-east.

In some instances, it is not possible to be sure whether minor perturbations of the regional strike are due to gentle folding or to faulting. However, strike-parallel faulting can be inferred south-east of Whitwell [19 19], where a north-westerly down-throw of the Chalk Rock by about 5 m is indicated by displacements of the outcrop and of structural contours, which coincide with a north-east-trending satellite lineament. North-east-trending faults at Therfield [340 380] and between Reed and Barkway [371 372] throw down to the south-east by 10 to 20 m.

Palaeogene

The distribution of Palaeogene strata and of the clay-with-flints within the district suggests that the north-western limit of the London Basin lay beyond the present-day Chalk escarpment (Chapter 5). Only rather generalised and incomplete structure contours for the base of these deposits can be constructed from the localised information available (Figure 31c). These indicate a regional south-easterly dip of only 0.2° (rather less than for the Chalk), but there is considerable variation from this, reflecting a tendency for the base of the clay-with-flints to slope into major valleys and towards the Chalk escarpment (Chapter 6).

The slight difference between the regional inclination of the Chalk and of the Palaeogene supports indications from elsewhere in the region that tectonic inversion on the London Platform commenced in late Upper Cretaceous times, but the main south-eastwards tilting of the Palaeogene in the northern part of the London Basin probably occurred much later, during the Miocene (Chadwick, 1985d).

Quaternary

Faulting of Quaternary sediments has been observed in a few places, all within the Hitchin–Stevenage Gap. Salter (1866) observed that faults exposed within a quarry beside Hitchin railway station [196 294] displaced both the Chalk and overlying glacial sediments. Bloom and Wooldridge (1930) record that well-bedded glaciofluvial sands and gravels exposed in the Vicarsgrove Pit [1925 2590] are displaced by 'step-faulting'.

It is thought that these displacements are most likely to mark subsidence following solution of the Chalk, stress relief at the margins of glacial channels (Chapter 6), or settlement within glacial sequences, perhaps following the melting of buried ice.

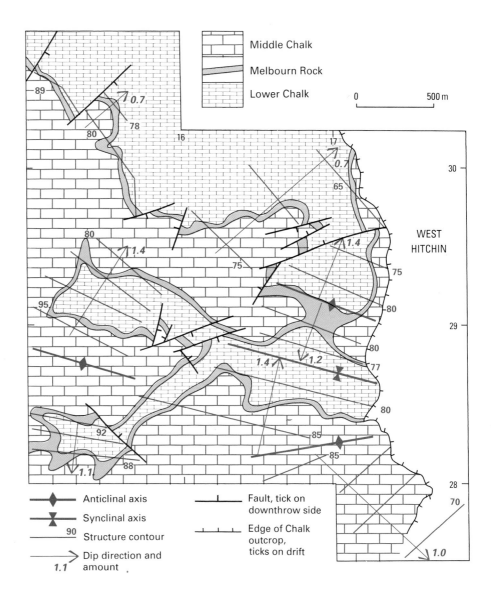

Figure 32 Folds in the Melbourn Rock west of Hitchin.

EIGHT

Economic geology

The exploitation of the geological resources of the district has been spasmodic, depending more on the vagaries of local and national markets than on the availability of materials. This is particularly true of brick clays, chalk and aggregate which are the only 'bulk mineral' resources available locally. Most of the deposits identified in the district have been utilised in the past, mainly on a local basis. At present only two deposits, the Gault at Arlesey and the Middle Chalk at Steeple Morden (Station Pit), which produce bricks and high-quality chalk whiting respectively, satisfy an inter-regional market. Aggregate and agricultural lime are won from deposits at a number of localities to satisfy local requirements.

Prior to the nineteenth century no large-scale exploitation of geological resources occurred and small communities used locally available materials wherever possible. Deposits of limited extent and thickness and of variable quality were often sufficient to supply the demand for building stone, chalk, tile and brick clays and aggregate. Shallow degraded pits of this vintage abound although modern farming practice is fast destroying even these remnants. To some extent such 'borrow pitting' still occurs today, particularly for aggregate to maintain 'metalled' tracks on farms capable of carrying the heavy machinery employed in modern farming.

With the rapid expansion of urban communities in the mid-nineteenth century, the demand for durable building materials increased dramatically and many of the former industries expanded to satisfy the new markets. Areas with limited resources, however, often in deposits of marginal quality were soon exhausted or abandoned and production became centralised around thicker and more extensive deposits with a longer life. Better road and rail transport allowed larger producers to expand their markets even for low-value 'bulk' minerals. Thus the use of glacial and alluvial silts and clays for brick and tile manufacture declined, initially in favour of the more dependable Palaeogene clays and the Gault, but later for the even larger resources and production units based on the Oxford Clay in Bedfordshire to the north.

The soils and land use of the area are directly related to the underlying solid and drift geology of the district. A brief account is given below.

Large areas of worked-out or made ground have been mapped in the district; they are the result of the extraction of chalk, clay and aggregate resources. Many of these sites are being, or have been, used as landfill sites for the disposal of domestic and industrial waste.

The most significant economic resource of the district at present is groundwater. The public supply is predominantly derived from the Chalk aquifer and to a lesser extent from the Woburn Sands in the north-west.

Groundwater is also obtained, for individual supplies, from drift deposits throughout the district, but many of these are in hydraulic continuity with the Chalk aquifer.

In the mid-1960s regional investigations suggested that rocks of Carboniferous age might be found at shallow depth within the district. Two boreholes at Ashwell (see Appendix 1) and Little Chishill (Lake and Wilson, 1990) were sunk in 1964 by Superior Oil (UK) Ltd to investigate the potential for hydrocarbons. Both were barren and proved Devonian rocks beneath the Permo-Triassic.

Major planned construction projects for the A10 Colliers End bypass, the A505 Baldock bypass, the widening of the A1(M) and the, as yet unspecified, east–west trunk route between the M1 and the east coast will increase significantly the local demand for aggregate in the future.

BRICK CLAY

Clay from the Gault is the only deposit now dug for brickmaking in the district. Past and present workings occupy only a small part of the outcrop, and there are ample resources available here and in adjoining districts for possible future use.

The clay is very calcareous and produces a characteristic porous and creamy white or yellow 'gault brick' (Bonnell and Butterworth, 1950). It is usually fired at the low temperature of 900°C which is about 100°C above the temperature of rapid shrinkage when the free lime reacts with the clay minerals, but still below the unusually low and sudden vitrification temperature when the brick would fuse (Freeman, 1964). Recent whole-rock analyses of the Gault Clay from the Arlesey Borehole (Prior et al., 1993) show that in the worked material near the top of the formation clay minerals predominate, and calcite makes up to about 30 per cent; minor quartz and traces of pyrite and organic matter are also present. The clay content of the fine (less than 2 microns) fraction comprises abundant smectite, (60–80 per cent), subordinate kaolinite (20–40 per cent) and minor illite (10 per cent).

The Gault has been dug in this area since 1852 when Robert Beart opened the first brickworks at Arlesey (A Cox, 1979). Sited alongside the Great Northern Railway, it employed the railway both to bring in coal fuel for firing and to distribute its products in supplying the heavy demand from London, the Home Counties and the Midlands. It exploited the latest mechanisation and rapidly became the most important brickworks in Bedfordshire producing machine-made perforated 'Beart' bricks and land drains. Three other brickworks were opened nearby including the Great Northern Brick

Company, a wholly owned subsidiary of the railway company, which supplied bricks for building railway stations, bridges and viaducts along the Great Northern Railway line. Later closures and mergers have left just one company, now Butterley Brick Limited, situated on the original site [185 353]. In 1992, the operators estimated that up to 6000 tonnes of Gault clay were dug per year and blended with imported clays to vary the colour. A maximum of 12 million bricks were produced, most by the soft mudbrick process but hand made 'specials' were supplied on demand. At the time of writing lack of demand has forced a (?temporary) shutdown.

Just to the north of the district another brickworks was established later, alongside the same railway line, at Stotfold Road [192 381]; it exploited Gault clay but had closed by 1907. Elsewhere, at Upper Stondon [160 360] and at Meppershall Hoo [158 372], brick and tile works had closed by 1914 and 1940 respectively. A small and possibly ancient disused clay pit is found to the west of Campton [115 379].

Other clayey strata which have been dug in the past include the Palaeogene (Woolwich and Reading formations and Thames Group) and the drift deposits: clay-with-flints, till, glaciolacustrine silts and clays, and brick-earth. Till and clay-with-flints are quite widespread but they are of inferior quality because of the pebble content. For the most part they were dug in small workings, scattered across the district and wood was used for firing. In places, the only evidence remaining of this industry is in the use of place names such as 'brickfield' or 'kiln'.

The Palaeogene beds are confined to the south-east where they have been dug at Colliers End [370 201 and 369 203], Standon Green End [357 193] and near Barwick [377 197]. Clay-with-flints comprising material derived from the Palaeogene formations was formerly dug at Rableyheath [239 190] to make red bricks and tiles, the clay here being mixed with sand from Hitchin.

Glacial till was widely exploited throughout the district on a small scale for use in local buildings. The bricks were usually of inferior quality because any included chalk pebbles produced concentrations of calcium oxide (quicklime) on firing which were likely to crack the brick on expansion when rehydrated. The clay mineralogy of the till reflects that of the clay bedrock from which it has been derived; thus tills with a Jurassic component are likely to be higher in illite and lower in smectite (Perrin, 1957). Till was dug for brick and tile manufacture at Stotfold [227 372] until about 1920, and at Kiln Wood [185 245] near Preston.

Either glacial till or a clayey glaciofluvial deposit was dug near Weston [256 308] where shallow workings mark the site of brick kilns.

Glaciolacustrine deposits have been worked near High Heath [198 194], Walkern [293 257], Chipping Hall [355 319] and Hare Street [383 297 and 387 295].

Brickearth was worked in the nineteenth century in two large pits at Hitchin [189 284 and 191 281] and a group of smaller pits near Gosmore [around 184 276]. Brickworks in Luton at Old Eaton Green [115 216] may have exploited brickearth in a solution collapse feature.

CALCIUM PHOSPHATE

From about 1850 to 1900 beds of phosphatic nodules or 'coprolites' were exploited by a small but vigorous industry in the country's first extensive opencast mining operation, for use as the raw material in the manufacture of the world's first chemical fertiliser, 'superphosphate'.

In this district most nodules were extracted from the Cambridge Greensand, with minor amounts coming from the base of the Gault. The distinctive glauconitic marl of the Cambridge Greensand has phosphatic nodules concentrated in its lowest 0.1–0.3 m (see Plate 2). These nodules of phosphorite (rock phosphate) are of mainly calcium phosphate, probably the variety of carbonate fluorapatite known as francolite (McClellan, 1980) with appreciable CO_2 (up to 5–6 per cent) and more than 1 per cent fluorine. Most nodules are moulds of whole or fossil fragments and the phosphate usually contains glauconite, quartz and unreplaced micrite.

General accounts of the industry have been given by Seeley (1866), Jenyns (1867), Strahan et al. (1917) and Oakley (1941); its development in Cambridgeshire has been documented more recently by Grove (1976). It probably followed a similar course in the district where it became particularly important in the Shillington area. John Lawes, a Hertfordshire farmer, successfully dissolved the phosphatic nodules in sulphuric acid and so produced a soluble fertiliser, (Cook et al., 1990). He patented the process in 1842, following which the industry expanded rapidly, producing at its peak over 250 000 tons a year. John Lawes used his superphosphate fortune to found the Rothamsted Experimental Station. The decline of the industry was precipitated by the large-scale import of cheap foreign phosphates and the exhaustion of the best reserves.

Extensive areas of the outcrop were dug by hand, the nodules screened out, washed and then carted to a nearby mill. The crushed nodules were then transported to the nearest processing works for mixing with acid to make superphosphate fertiliser or 'coprolite manure'. As the deposits were worked down-dip up to about 6 m of overburden were removed before it became uneconomic to proceed further. On steep slopes this limit was quickly reached and the workings were only about 50 m wide, as at Meppershall [138 355]. On flatter ground, where the increase in overburden was more gradual, the workings were as much as 200–500 m wide. Virtually total extraction took place and it is hard to detect evidence for the former presence of nodules in the worked areas.

Most of the workings were progressively backfilled and reinstated with topsoil, and 'coproliting' may not be suspected from looking at the field surface. When such areas are augered, however, there is invariably some evidence of disturbance with traces of glauconitic marl brought up to the surface, and surface sand and soil deeply buried with the marl bedrock. Elsewhere less care was taken and the soil is mixed with much grey marl, or the fields may retain a hummocky surface, though modern ploughing is progressively destroying this evidence. Aerial photographs are useful for detecting workings, and in favourable conditions show intricate trenching patterns which should not be confused with ancient field systems.

Oakley (1941) in a wartime pamphlet on British phosphates listed the known occurrences of phosphate in the region. He recognised two areas of former workings in the Woburn Sands within Bedfordshire, Ampthill to the west and Potton to the north, but omitted the extensive workings along the Cambridge Greensand.

Nodule workings have been traced for about 10 km along most of the Cambridge Greensand outcrop and near-surface subcrop from Apsley End through Shillington, Upper and Lower Stondon, then east of the Hitchin buried channel from Arlesey to Clifton and across to the north of Stotfold.

At Upper Stondon large areas of low ground were worked with scattered grey marl spoil lightening the surface soil. Around Lower Stondon the entire outcrop was worked along the gentle slope north of the village southeastwards until it disappears under the till near the buried channel margin. On the other side of the channel, 2 km to the east, a small outlier of basal Chalk [182 358] has been worked, probably through a thin cover of till in parts. To the east of the railway line in Arlesey, workings can be traced northwards to Chase Farm [194 371] where the Cambridge Greensand swings eastwards beneath glaciofluvial deposits, through which it continues to be worked in places such as to the east of Waterloo Farm [208 376] and north of Stotfold [219 380].

Nodules were dug at Campton near Shefford (Jukes-Browne and Hill, 1900) from near the base of the Gault, the exact site is uncertain.

CHALK

Chalk has a variety of end uses and has been exploited throughout the district as a source of agricultural lime, building stone and more importantly for the production of high-purity whiting and for the manufacture of cement. Practically every outcrop of Chalk has evidence of either small pits or shallow surface terracing from which chalk has been won in the past. Its extraction has been aided by its softness or 'workability' or in the harder beds by the close jointing, both of which have permitted exploitation without recourse to machinery.

Agricultural lime

Chalk has been used in agriculture at least since the last century. Its main function is to reduce soil acidity but in areas where soils are severely leached, such as over dry sands its application adds essential calcium to the soil. In some cases, particularly on deep sandy soils, very chalky till may also be used to add body to the soil.

National output reached a peak in 1959 when government subsidies encouraged its use (Harris, 1982). Many medium-sized chalk pits were then active in the district supplying local markets with chalk of various size grades. These pits supplemented the ad hoc farm-by-farm exploitation of the Chalk outcrop. Pits at Standon [396 227], Westmill [372 278], Anstey [395 329], Steeple Morden [302 389], Grove Mill [191 310], Arlesey (two pits) [198 348, 197 344] and a number in and around Letchworth and Luton are known to have been active during the peak years of production. At some of these pits agricultural lime was a by-product of extraction mainly dedicated to cement and whiting production.

Only the Anstey and Steeple Morden pits still supply lime today and these only on a seasonal basis.

Cement manufacture

In this district raw material for cement manufacture was formerly won from the Lower Chalk, principally from the Chalk Marl. This material has an advantage over other parts of the Chalk sequence in that it naturally contains appreciable amounts of silica and alumina and therefore only minimal admixture of additional clay is required. Cement was formerly produced at Arlesey, using Chalk Marl from the sites now known as the Green [198 348] and Blue [197 344] Lagoons. Both were abandoned in the 1960s as the industry concentrated its production on larger sites elsewhere in the Chilterns.

Whiting

Two quarries [298 401, 302 389] at Steeple Morden on the northern margin of the district produce high-purity whiting (over 97 per cent calcium carbonate) powder from the 20 m or so of the Middle Chalk immediately above the Melbourn Rock. Their annual production of approximately 100 000 tonnes is used mainly in the paper, rubber and plastic, paint, pharmaceutical and food industries as a filler and vehicle. There is an abundant resource of this Chalk regionally and the principal constraints on its wider development are planning controls and market economics.

Building stone

An early, localised use of chalk as a type of 'cement' was in the production of 'clunch; a chalk slurry, clay and straw mix producing crude concrete-like blocks. Such blocks were of low strength and required a protective plaster, tile or thatch cover to prevent the penetration of water. This usage of clunch was quickly discontinued in the nineteenth century in favour of more durable building materials but some examples of its use can still be seen.

The Totternhoe Stone, Melbourn Rock and Chalk Rock have provided durable building stone in the past and numerous small pits are found in their respective outcrops. None of these pits are worked commercially today.

TOTTERNHOE STONE

This pale brown or fawn coloured calcarenite from the Lower Chalk has been used in the walls of churches on a local basis near to outcrops. The deposit is generally only 1 to 2 m thick over much of the region but ranges up to 6 m in channel sequences (see Chapter 4). These thicker deposits contain an even-textured soft massive calcarenite rock which can be easily worked into dimensional stone blocks and mouldings, but which also has the property of hardening on exposure. Its main drawback is that it suffers from spalling with constant wetting and drying, and this acted as a constraint to its continued use as a facing stone. This effect can be seen on Ashwell village church just north of the district.

The only known commercial operation within the district was at the small pit [158 325] north-east of Pirton which was reopened for a short time after World War 2 to repair the bomb-damaged Pirton church. It is not known whether the Totternhoe Stone extracted from the Green Lagoon [198 348] at Arlesey was sold for building purposes but it is within a thick channel sequence of the sort extracted elsewhere. The Totternhoe Stone is still worked at Totternhoe to the west of this district, where a small-scale operation supplies dimensional stone for the renovation of existing buildings (Shephard-Thorn et al., 1994).

MELBOURN AND CHALK ROCKS

These hard, creamy white, durable limestones have been quarried at many sites but their brittleness and close jointing, resulting in a rubbly rock, makes them generally unsuitable for dimensional stone. Their use has been limited therefore to the fortuitous and ad hoc extraction of crudely shaped blocks most frequently seen incorporated into walls as random masonry between dressed corner stones, as at Pirton Church. Their rubbly nature and durability has allowed them to be used locally to maintain farm tracks and roads in the past.

FLINT

Flint derived as a by-product of the extraction of chalk, from 'field picking' on Chalk outcrops, and from sand and gravel deposits has been used extensively in the past as a decorative building stone. Flint-built churches are one of the characteristic features of the north Hertfordshire landscape. It is little used today other than for renovation and it is not marketed. Small stockpiles are kept at Steeple Morden and Anstey for occasional users.

SAND AND GRAVEL

The aggregate resources within the Vale of St Albans immediately to the south of this district have been quantified to resource level by the work of the former Industrial Minerals Assessment Unit of the British Geological Survey. These results are embodied within Mineral Assessment Reports numbered 67, 69, 71 and 112, of which the last three cover the southern margin of the district up to northing grid line 20. These reports adopted the following physical criteria to define sand and gravel as a resource:

a) the deposit should average at least 1 m in thickness,
b) the ratio of overburden to sand and gravel should be no more than 3:1,
c) the proportion of fines should not exceed 40 per cent (fines, that is silt and clay grade material, comprise particles less than 0.063 mm mean diameter),
d) the deposit should lie within 25 m of the surface.

No consistent aggregate resource information based on these criteria exists for the remainder of the district and the quantity and quality of the resources within the mapped sands and gravels is poorly known. The summary below, and in Figure 33, is at the inferred, indicated level of resource assessment based on an interpretation of the above criteria, on observations of individual exposures and from information held in the BGS archives.

Sand and gravel is not dug on a large scale within the district, much of the demand being satisfied at the moment (1993) by large-scale commercial operations in the Vale of St Albans. Small-scale production has been mainly from the glaciofluvial deposits and to a lesser extent from river terrace and suballuvial deposits. Resources also exist within the Kesgrave Sands and Gravels and Letchworth Gravel but these are of limited extent in the district.

Glaciofluvial deposits

These deposits are the largest resource of sand and gravel in the district. Their origin as outwash from the Anglian ice sheet is discussed in the Quaternary chapter of this memoir. The variety of depositional processes has a marked affect on the quantity and quality of the deposits now seen at any one site. They are the most variable of aggregate resources; they grade from sand to gravel and from 'very clayey' (20 to 40 per cent fines) to clean (less than 10 per cent fines); in composition they range from a pure chalk gravel to a deposit composed entirely of durable materials; and in quantity they range from thin impersistent beds to thick deposits of considerable lateral extent.

In general, the gravel (between 4 and 64 mm) components of these deposits are composed chiefly of flint, both angular and well rounded, with quartz and quartzite as secondary constituents. Chalk is also a major constituent but its occurrence can be affected significantly by postdepositional solution. Other rare rock fragments include Jurassic and Cretaceous fossil debris, Carboniferous Limestone, septaria, igneous and metamorphic rocks, carbonaceous material and shale.

Of these constituents only the chalk is present in sufficient quantity to seriously affect the end use of the aggregate. Only moderate proportions of included chalk are deleterious in concrete mixes and therefore relegate a deposit to one used only as general fill.

The sand fraction is composed of subequal proportions of quartz and flint, with the former dominant in the finer grades. Chalk is also common but is more readily removed by solution than that contained in the gravel fraction.

Terrace and suballuvial deposits

These deposits are mainly confined to the larger river valleys, notably the rivers Ivel, Purwell and Hiz. The sand and gravel is less variable than that contained in the glaciogenic deposits having suffered another cycle of deposition, and is generally less 'clayey'. The deposits are of limited thickness (up to 5 m in the River Ivel) and lateral extent, but in places they rest on glaciogenic

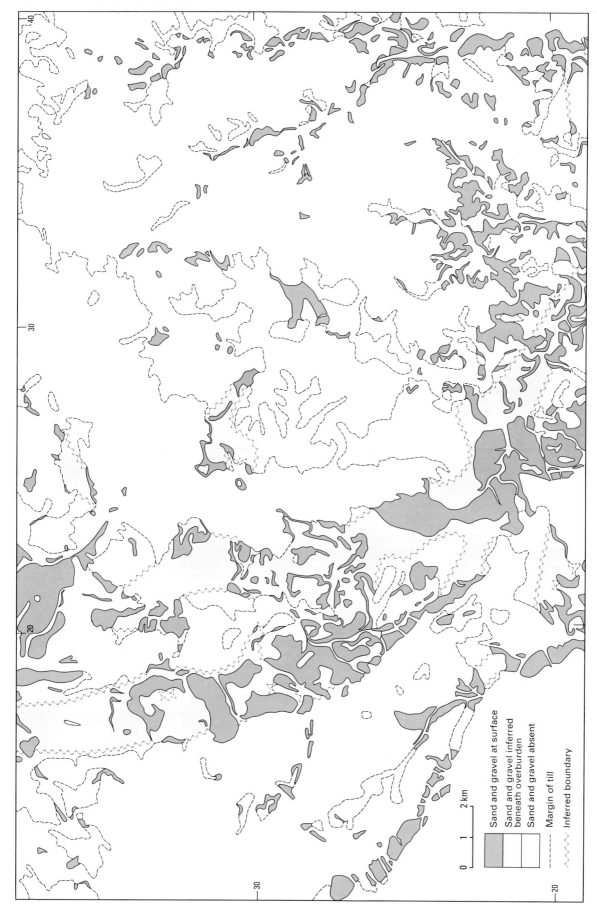

Figure 33 The distribution of sand- and gravel-bearing deposits and their inferred extent beneath overburden in the district.

Sand and gravel at surface

Sand and gravel inferred beneath overburden

Sand and gravel absent

Margin of till

Inferred boundary

0 1 2 km

deposits of wider distribution. The gravel and sand compositions are very similar to those for the glaciofluvial deposits from which they must have been principally derived.

Kesgrave Sands and Gravels

As with the Letchworth Gravels these deposits are of limited extent. Small outcrops in the east represent the western margin of a more extensive spread around Westland Green [422 220], in the Great Dunmow district. Elsewhere in East Anglia, the Kesgrave Sands and Gravels represent a major aggregate resource, with thick deposits composed of durable rock fragments, and with low fines contents ideal for concrete mixes.

The limited outcrops around Braughing [395 250] and further north in the river Quin valley east of Dassels [393 274] show a surface brash composed of quartz and flint gravel in a pale yellow, fine to medium sand matrix. The deposits in this district are estimated to be only a few metres thick. They are unlikely to be of commercial interest but may provide a useful local resource.

Letchworth Gravel

These gravels are of limited extent being found only in the vicinity of Fairfield Hospital [203 347]. Their pre-Anglian origin is discussed in Chapter 6.

The deposit has a maximum proven thickness of 3.55 m and is thought to be no thicker than 3 to 4 m. It ranges in grade from pebbly sand to 'very clayey' gravel, and is composed in the gravel fraction of up to 75 per cent rounded quartzite and quartz with some subangular to subrounded flint. The fine gravel (4 to 8 mm) also contains appreciable amounts of ironstone.

The sand is mainly medium to coarse, but with some very coarse grade, and composed predominantly of quartzose material. Appreciable quantities of other lithic fragments were also noted in the coarser fractions, and are similar in composition to the fine gravel fraction.

Although composed predominantly of very durable materials, its limited distribution, ironstone content and 'clayeyness' limit its resource value.

SOILS

The district is covered by two maps and accompanying reports of the Soil Survey of Great Britain. These maps, at the 1:50 000 scale, cover the area around Saffron Walden in the east (Thomasson, 1969) and Luton and Bedford in the west (King, 1969). The results of these surveys are summarised in the Soils of Hertfordshire by Thomasson and Avery (1970).

As the district is predominantly a rural agricultural area the soils, which owe their character to the underlying geology, probably represent the greatest economic resource after groundwater.

In general, the clay formations such as the Gault, those in the Palaeogene, the till and the clay-with-flints give rise to heavy variably calcareous and pebbly poorly drained soils. Although some areas still retain the traditional pasture or beech woodland, improved drainage and modern mechanical farming methods have encouraged arable farming and much of the ground is now given over to cereal production.

Sandy and gravelly deposits such as the Woburn Sands and the aggregate-rich drift deposits give rise to lighter free-draining sandy soils which are acidic, and on steeper slopes liable to erosion. These easily worked soils are used for arable farming and small-scale market gardening, but frequently require irrigation during seasonal droughts. Because of their free-draining character, they are considered to be 'hungry' soils and demand high inputs of organic matter to maintain fertility.

The Chalk develops light, very shallow, calcareous soils which are easily worked and free draining. The soil is thin, 0.2 to 0.4 m thick, requires only shallow ploughing to prevent the incorporation of the underlying shattered chalk. Despite this drawback much of the Chalk outcrop, with the exception of the steepest slopes has been under cultivation for a long time.

LANDFILL

Many of the former pits for sand and gravel, chalk and clay are or have been used as landfill sites. Many important sites are now lost to geology.

A simple listing of those sites known to the Hertfordshire and Bedfordshire County Councils are given in Table 13. The list does not include all unnotified sites prior to 1974 nor small areas reclaimed by farmers.

LANDFILL GAS

The only site currently developed as a source of landfill gas is that at the Arlesey brickworks [185 351], where the potentially hazardous gases are drained by a series of capped boreholes. The gas derived from these boreholes provides the fuel for the nearby brick kilns.

The working brickpit is being backfilled cell by cell as the face advances; the cells being lined and capped by an impervious mixture of locally dug Chalk Marl and weathered Gault. Each enclosed cell generates principally methane and carbon dioxide gas from the breakdown of the household putrescible waste in anaerobic moist conditions.

The potential for other landfill gas sites within the district is unknown and beyond the subject of this memoir, but other sites (see Table 13) within which putrescible material has or is being lodged are likely to produce hydrocarbon gases.

ENGINEERING GEOLOGY

The physical parameters affecting the engineering characteristics of the formations in the district are unknown from specific studies in the area. Bulk figures for these physical characteristics derived from regional studies are

Table 13   Notified landfill sites in the Hitchin district.

Site name	National Grid reference	Waste type	Status
Church Fm., Lilley	117 269	inert	closed
Clarks Hill, Pegsden	118 299	inert	closed
Luton Airport	125 218	inert/difficult/putrescible	closed
Chiltern Green	135 191	inert	closed
Wandon End Fm., Luton	130 226	inert	granted
Meppershall	133 354	inert/putrescible	closed
Upton End Fm., Shillington	135 356	inert	dormant
Tyne Hill	149 346	inert/putrescible	closed
Lower Stondon	151 347	inert/semi-inert/putrescible	closed
Stondon Manor	153 354	inert/putrescible	closed
Airman, Meppershall	156 374	inert/semi-inert/putrescible	closed
Holwell Gravels, Holwell	167 323	putrescible	closed
Hambridge Way, Hitchin	173 315	putrescible	closed
Maydencroft Manor, Gosmore	184 277	inert	closed
Cadwell Lane, Hitchin	187 315	putrescible	active
Ickleford Lower Green, Ickleford	187 323	general non-putrescible	closed
Arlesey Brickworks	186 352	inert/semi-inert/putrescible	active
Vicars Grove Pit, St Ippollitts	193 257	inert/general non-putrescible	active
Blue Lagoon, Arlesey	196 343	inert/putrescible	closed
Chapel Foot Gravel pit, Hitchin	201 252	general non-putrescible	closed
Tittendell, St Ippollitts	200 264	inert	closed
Titmore Green Rd., Little Wymondley	204 271	putrescible	closed
Wymondley Quarry, Little Wymondley	206 273	inert/general non-putrescible	active
Bungalow Farm, Little Wymondley	213 272	inert	closed
Norton Green Tip, Stevenage	225 273	inert	active
Stotfold	228 372	inert	closed
Rookery pit, Watton-at-Stone	291 203	inert	closed
Walnut Tree Farm, Luffenhall	290 284	general non-putrescible	closed
			closed
Throcking Lane, Buntingford	354 304	inert	closed
Westmill	371 275	not known	closed

to be found in the literature. Forster (1991) includes data on the Lower Greensand (cf. Woburn Sands), Gault and the Lower Chalk derived from information held on the Thame district (Sheet 237). Carter and Mallard (1974) discuss the Chalk and include data from the Chiltern area west of this district. Burnett and Fookes (1974) investigated the regional relationship between the geology and engineering index properties of the London Clay. The engineering properties of the till are discussed in a number of papers generally applicable to East Anglia, most notable amongst these are Boulton and Paul (1976), Denness (1974) and Little and Atkinson (1988).

Apart from the usual considerations with respect to the engineering aspects of the formations present in the district, the presence of numerous small quarries, of solution pipes affecting the Chalk and the volume variability characteristics of expandable clays may also influence the design of site investigations or engineering works.

Subsidence and the associated ground heave are the principal geological hazards likely to be encountered in the district. It must be emphasised that they are not considered to be a significant problem being neither generally common nor widespread throughout the district.

The term subsidence used in its general sense applies to all areas which have suffered collapse or lateral and vertical movement of the underlying strata. The reasons for subsidence vary, and may be due to, for example, progressive settling as unconsolidated strata compress (a problem associated with landfill and recent deposits, particularly peat), to lateral movement of weak strata on steep slopes (landslip), or to catastrophic collapse into underground caverns and solution pipes in the Chalk. The other major cause of subsidence (or ground heave) is related to the presence of 'expandable' clay minerals which cause marked volume changes, between periods of normal rainfall and drought conditions, in clay formations.

Gault

The Gault is, for the most part, a highly shrinkable clay with a high smectite content (Driscoll, 1983). Much of the Gault in this district is concealed beneath drift deposits and poses no serious threat. Where Gault does come to the surface it has been largely avoided for building purposes, with the exception of parts of Church End and Arlesey. Future developments on the Gault should certainly take the appropriate precautions to ensure foundation stability.

Chalk

The Chalk may be affected by solution phenomena which result in small surface depressions (dolines), that range in size up to 50 m across and commonly up to 6 m deep. As a consequence of this solution, fractures naturally occurring in the Chalk are enlarged. The resultant pipes, commonly filled with superficial deposits, continue to provide sumps for excess surface water up to the present day. During periods of heavy rainfall, or when attempts are made to fill the depressions for construction purposes, they may be liable to further subsidence.

The solution pipes are most frequently encountered where thin veneers of Palaeogene deposits or clay-with-flints are also found but they also occur on bare Chalk outcrops.

Edmonds (1983) in a preliminary analysis of known surface expressions shows that this part of the Chilterns has intermediate incidences of solution features between 11 and 30 per 100 km^2. The incidence increases where thin clay-with-flints is prevalent, where the upper part of the quoted range (between 21 to 30 per 100 km^2) pertains. The solution features are distributed randomly across the area although locally concentrations in groups or along well-defined lines may reflect weaknesses (?joints) in the underlying Chalk.

Features of this type are notoriously difficult to identify, particularly in areas under the plough, and are commonly indistinguishable from small disused pits or indeed from bomb craters dating from the 1940s. Some are indicated on the 1:10 000 scale maps of the district, and further details are given in the relevant Technical Reports.

Swallow holes, where surface streams go underground, are found, particularly in the headwater valleys on the scarp backslope. They are most common where streams cut down through drift to unsaturated chalk. A number of swallow holes may occur in these valleys; their development being related to the intersection of ephemeral streams and open joints.

Palaeogene

The Palaeogene deposits are actively incorporated into these Chalk solution features along the feather edge of their outcrop. Elsewhere, in the south-east around Colliers End, clays within the Thames Group (London Clay) contain appreciable amounts of expandable clay minerals and can be expected to suffer shrinkage during drought conditions where they are exposed.

Water seepage from the sandy base of the Palaeogene outcrops has initiated landslip on steep slopes at four localities within minor east–west valleys. At these localities, [371 226 (two slips) and 372 221] near St Edmunds College and west of Barwick at [377 199], the slips affect the overlying drift deposits and indeed at the first three sites the Palaeogene strata are not seen at the surface.

Quaternary

The drift sequence of the district in itself poses little threat of subsidence, although care should be taken in these highly variable deposits to avoid differential subsidence where geological boundaries are crossed by foundations. None of the clay beds within the drift contain appreciable quantities of expandable clays, and subsidence related to this phenomena is not expected.

Made and landscaped ground

Apart from the known landfill sites given in Table 13 many small pits are known to exist in the district. They have been used to dump all manner of materials from farm refuse and redundant farm machinery to industrial inert wastes. For the most part, these areas are reasonably obvious but some have been filled and the surface contours restored. In these cases the site may only be marked by extraneous materials such as brick or wood incorporated into the soil.

A number of small pits in and around Letchworth were used for dumping fly ash and foundry slag from the originally coal-fired power station and the major steel foundry (now demolished) to the east of the town.

The major urban expansion of the 1950s and 1960s, and the development of industrial estates throughout the district, led to a large number of sites being levelled by a cut-and-fill process. Thus appreciable areas around the old urban centres were considerably reshaped. In places, up to 5 m of fill material are known to exist on these cut-and-fill sites but its distribution is not known in detail.

HYDROGEOLOGY

The southern and eastern sections of the district are drained towards the south by the Rivers Mimram, Beane, Rib and Quin, tributaries of the River Lea. The Ivel and Hiz, tributaries of the River Ouse, drain the area to the north of the surface water divide (Figure 34).

Average annual rainfall exceeds 600 mm over much of the district, rising to over 650 mm on the high ground between the river catchments but falling to as little as 550 mm at the north-western edge of the district. Mean annual evaporation is about 460 mm over most of the district, possibly a little lower on the high Chalk areas, leaving a potential for infiltration of between 100 and 200 mm/a. A water resource study for the Hitchin area carried out by the University of Birmingham (1989) reported an assumed recharge component of 209 mm/yr to the Chalk outcrop but only 56 mm/yr where till is present.

The Chalk is the main aquifer in the district. The thin Cambridge Greensand at the base of the Lower Chalk is not recognised as a separate aquifer. The Woburn Sands beneath the Gault and Lower Chalk has a limited outcrop area in the district, but it provides appreciable amounts of groundwater, with the Gault acting as an aquiclude between the two aquifers. The superficial deposits do not contain enough groundwater to be of economic value.

Licensed groundwater abstraction from the Chalk and the Woburn Sands, together with the uses to which the water is put, is shown in Table 14. Surface water flows are maintained through much of the year by baseflow from the Chalk aquifer and in consequence licensed abstraction from this source has also been included in Table 14 for comparative purposes. The Chalk and to a lesser extent the Woburn Sands aquifer provide large quantities of water for public supply (82 per cent of the total licensed groundwater abstraction is from the Chalk) as well as water for growing watercress, for spray irrigation and general agricultural purposes.

A group of boreholes, of which only one (at Barkway [3880 3790]) is located in the district, are jointly licenced for abstraction to augment the River Rhee

Table 14   Water abstraction licence data for the Hitchin district.

Water use / Water source	Public supply		Private supply		River augmentation		Agriculture						Industry		Totals	
							General		Horticulture		Spray irrigation					
	m³/a	No. licences	m³/a	No. licences	m³/a	No. licences	m³/a	No. licences	m³/a	No. licences	m³/a	No. licences	m³/a	No. licences	m³/a	No. licences
Chalk	32 521 449	15	26 501	6	3 000 000	1	231 959	60	3 350 066	3*	158 997	13	23 550	3	39 312 522	101
Woburn Sands	2 045 000	1	—	—	—	—	55 784	4	—	—	120 277	3	3 409	1	2 224 470	9
Surface water (rivers, streams, lakes etc.)	—	—	—	—	—	—	6 045	1	—	—	260 217	27	271 895	3	538 157	31
Totals	34 566 449	16	26 501	6	3 000 000	1	293 788	65	3 350 066	3	539 491	43	298 854	7	42 075 149	141

Derived from base data provided by the National Rivers Authority, Anglian and Thames regions.

* Total included one licence for 3 341 310 m³/a for watercress growing.

springheads and river flows. The licenced annual abstraction for the Barkway sources is shown in Table 14 but the actual maximum abstraction is likely to be significantly less than that licenced because in many years river support is not required.

In contrast to groundwater usage, surface waters are predominantly used for spray irrigation and industry although 218 213 m³/a licensed for use by industry comprises a single licence used for washing sands and gravels, and a further 48 000 m³/a is used for non-consumptive cooling purposes. There are no licences to abstract water from any of the superficial deposits.

Woburn Sands

The Woburn Sands aquifer consists of a series of fine- to coarse-grained, loosely cemented or unconsolidated (apart from some ferruginous bands), cross-bedded, poorly sorted sandstones. Lateral and vertical variations in lithology give rise to a range of hydraulic properties and vertical changes in cementation can lead to the perching of aquifer horizons (Anon, 1982). Generally, the thickness of the aquifer is variable; the upper surface is nearly planar, but the lower surface is uneven and rests on an erosion surface cut in Jurassic formations. Within the district, the minimum known thickness of about 20 m occurs in the area of outcrop and to the south-east diagonally across the centre of the district where the aquifer is confined beneath the Gault and overlain by the Chalk aquifer. It is probable that the aquifer continues to thin towards the south-east. Near the western margin of the district, to the north of Luton, the confined aquifer attains a maximum thickness of between 45 and 70 m (Monkhouse, 1974).

The predominantly loosely cemented nature of the aquifer precludes fissure flow and groundwater movement is almost entirely intergranular. Despite this, many older boreholes were constructed with solid linings through the Gault into the upper part of the Woburn Sands, with open hole below. Boreholes with low rates of abstraction were often operated successfully whereas those with higher rates sometimes silted up; for example, at the Old Brewery, Stotfold, [2191 3701] it was necessary to clean the borehole on three occasions over a 20 year period to maintain the original yield. Most successful high-yielding boreholes were constructed with solid linings through the Gault and into the upper part of the aquifer with suitable sand screens installed below to prevent the ingress of sand. In a few cases a gravel pack has also been inserted behind the well screen.

At Meppershall Pumping Station [150 370], the only major licensed abstraction from the Woburn Sands in the district, there are six borehole sources. Three of them are 500 mm in diameter and contain only well screens whilst the other three are 380 mm in diameter but were completed with screens and gravel packs. At this location the presence or absence of the gravel pack appears to have very little effect on the borehole yield/drawdown relationship and specific capacities range between 5 and 6.5 l/s/m. The largest recorded yield of 53 l/s for a drawdown of 10.7 m, was obtained from one of the larger-diameter boreholes. Surprisingly sand did prove to be a problem in one of the smaller-diameter boreholes despite the presence of both screen and an artificial filter pack; this was only overcome by a substantial reduction in abstraction rate. Specific capacities are generally of a similar order in other large-diameter boreholes in the district, but much lower (as are yields) in small-diameter boreholes. It would appear however that this may not be entirely due to the reduced diameter as many of these boreholes penetrate a smaller thickness of aquifer.

The regional hydraulic gradient falls gently to the east and south-east. Groundwater elevations are at about 40 m above OD and seasonal variations are small, often less than 1 m (British Geological Survey, 1984). Limited recharge may occur to the Woburn Sands in the small area of drift-free outcrop where till is thin or absent. Recharge occurring elsewhere on the narrow aquifer outcrop to the north-west will however, migrate down gradient into the district and there may be recharge from the drift-filled buried channel beneath Henlow.

No detailed aquifer tests have been carried out in the district and there are few in adjoining areas. Locally, however, the transmissivity of the Woburn Sands may attain 500 m^2/d (Monkhouse, 1974).

Groundwater from the Woburn Sands is potable and of calcium-bicarbonate type. Chloride concentrations are low, rarely exceeding 15 mg/l but sulphate concentrations range up to about 30 mg/l. The groundwater is iron-rich in some locations probably due to the dissolution of pyrite or ferruginous cement which is often present in the upper part of the aquifer. At Meppershall, the iron concentrations are 1 to 1.5 mg/l, and the raw water has to be treated before use for public supply. A typical water analysis from Meppershall is included in Table 15. An analysis from Bygrave Plantation [2559 3655] where the aquifer is deeply confined beneath the Gault and Lower Chalk, is also included for comparison.

Chalk

The Chalk, the major aquifer underlying much of the district, is a microporous limestone formation in which groundwater predominantly flows along fissures and joints (on both the micro and macro scale). Matrix porosity is commonly in the range of 25 to 45 per cent but makes a minimal contribution to total groundwater flow. A considerable number of fissures and joints orientated both at right angles and parallel to the bedding planes cut the Chalk strata, but investigations have shown that the majority of groundwater flow occurs only along a few discrete horizons termed 'secondary fissures' (Price et al., 1982; Foster and Milton, 1974). These 'secondary fissures' result from the enlargement of joints, usually bedding-plane joints, by solution and weathering pro-

cesses. There is evidence to suggest that in places they may develop a preferred orientation (Price, 1987) producing a significant enhanced permeability in that direction. It is generally considered that the density of fissures is greatest in lower topographic areas as the result of stress release from the removal of overburden. Consequent solution enlargement of fissures and relatively shallow water tables in such locations provides the best hydrogeological conditions for high-yielding boreholes.

The Chalk aquifer, as a whole, is unconfined in the district but minor, perhaps locally, confined conditions may occur due to the presence of impermeable marl horizons within the Chalk. Such a marl may be responsible for the seasonal artesian conditions at Nine Wells, Whitwell [1800 2124]. The hydraulic properties of the Chalk also vary according to the marl content. The Upper Chalk generally provides higher yields than the more marly Middle and Lower Chalk. The Lower Chalk in particular contains large amounts of marl; the lowest subunit, the massive, poorly fissured Chalk Marl, commonly has such a low permeability that the top of this horizon is often considered to constitute the effective base of the Chalk aquifer (Longstaff et al., 1992; Grout et al., 1992).

The water table tends to assume the form of a subdued version of the surface topography. The highest elevation of the water table in 1976 was 110 m above OD to the east of Luton in the south-west of the district, and 100 m above OD in the north-east. A groundwater ridge stretches between the two areas constituting a major groundwater divide across the district. Groundwater elevations decline to the north and north-east towards the feather edge of the Chalk, as well as in a downdip direction to the south and south-east (British Geological Survey, 1984). Contours on the potentiometric surface (water table) of the Chalk aquifer in autumn 1976, when water-level elevations were close to or at a minimum, are shown in Figure 34.

Table 15 Typical chemical analyses of groundwater in the Hitchin district.

Location		Meppershall Pumping Station	Bygrave Plantation	Buckland	Offley Bottom Pumping Station	Jack's Hill	Hare Street Pumping Station	Watton Road Pumping Station	Sacombe Pumping Station
National Grid reference		TL 1489 3700	TL 2589 3655	TL 345 339	TL 1607 2886	TL 2327 2908	TL 394 292	TL 255 203	TL 3300 1879
Aquifer		Woburn Sand	Woburn Sand	U/M Chalk	L Chalk	M? Chalk	U Chalk	U/M Chalk	U/M Chalk
Analysis date		21.2.1963	26.11.1962	22.5.1974	28.1.1959	1.8.1991	6.8.1992	29.6.1992	30.6.1992
pH		7.2	NA	7.2	7.3	7.6	7.2	7.0	7.0
Conductivity	μS	390	NA	690	445	636	584	569	561
Calcium (Ca^{2+})	mg/l	66	110	132	90	119	102	110	102
Magnesium (Mg^{2+})	mg/l	9	3	4	2	2	3	3	3
Sodium (Na$^+$)	mg/l	9	20	12	4	7	8	11	8
Potassium (K$^+$)	mg/l	4	NA	2	1	<1	2	1	1
Bicarbonate (HCO$_3^-$)	mg/l	214	293	293	268	339	312	310	315
Sulphate (SO$_4^{2-}$)	mg/l	26	19	58	7	15	35	19	20
Chloride (Cl$^-$)	mg/l	14	18	28	12	16	19	23	18
Nitrate (NO$_3^-$)	mg/l	1	22	42	23	NA	24	24	25

NA = not available.

Figure 34a   Contours (in metres relative to Ordnance Datum) on the potentiometric surface of the Chalk aquifer in the autumn of 1976.

b   Hydrograph for the period 1988–1992 for the Holt, Kimpton.

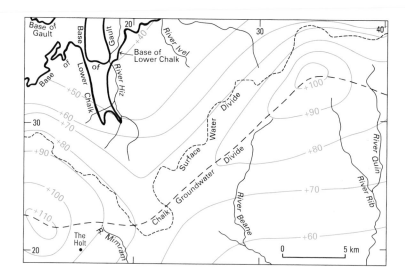

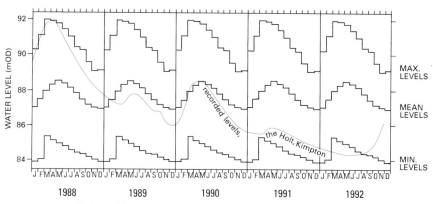

Maximum, Minimum and Mean values calculated from years 1964 to 1989

The deep buried channel, oriented approximately north–south through Hitchin, in a similar direction to the groundwater gradient, appears to have little or no discernible effect on regional groundwater flow (Mott MacDonald, 1992). Evidence from boreholes and wells penetrating the valley fill would, in fact, suggest that the drift groundwater is in direct hydraulic continuity with the Chalk aquifer and does not act as a barrier to groundwater flow except perhaps where the valley fill is predominantly of till.

Rest water levels are regularly monitored in a number of wells and boreholes in the district. Particularly long, fairly continuous records are available for The Holt, Kimpton [1692 1965] (1964 to present), and Therfield Rectory [3355 3697] (1883 to present) (British Geological Survey, in press). The borehole hydrographs show regular seasonal water-level fluctuations in response to recharge, the largest fluctuations being for boreholes located on high ground remote from surface water courses. In many boreholes water levels were at, or near to, maximum early in 1988. Falling water levels, often to below the previous minimum, in response to the period of drought which commenced in 1989 are particularly noticeable as is the rapid rise in the latter part of 1992 due to recharge caused by particularly heavy rainfall. These effects are well illustrated by the hydrograph for The Holt for the period 1988 to 1992 (Figure 34).

Yield drawdown characteristics of Chalk boreholes are highly variable, depending on the intersection of suitable fissures, depth of penetration below the water table and, to a degree, borehole diameter. Rapid variations in fissure size and distribution can cause significant variations in yield even over very short distances.

The highest yield recorded in the district (145 l/s for a drawdown of 12.3 m), was obtained from a 910 mm-diameter borehole penetrating the Middle and Lower Chalk at Wittenhall Pumping Station [2863 2161]. This and two other nearby boreholes at the station gave specific capacities of between 7 and 12 l/s/m but a fourth borehole initially gave only 3 l/s/m. Shots were fired at three levels in this borehole which was then surged. This gave an improved but still inferior specific capacity of 6 l/s/m. Although not carried out within the district, develop-ment using hydrochloric acid was shown to be beneficial near Royston [3570 4000] to the north-east. An initial yield of 8.6 l/s for a drawdown of 23.8 m was improved after development by acid treatment to 18.7 l/s for a drawdown of only 14.6 m. Boreholes of up to 200 mm diameter, penetrating only a limited thickness of the saturated zone, generally provide yields of less than 1 l/s with specific capacities less than 1 l/s/m.

The highest specific capacity of 135 l/s/m in the district was recorded for a 460 mm diameter borehole yielding 20 l/s from the Upper and Middle Chalk at Watton Road Pumping Station, Knebworth [2551 2030]. It was reported that, after an initial unsuccessful test, it was necessary to raise the casing from 31 to 26 m below surface to allow water from the high-yielding Melbourne Rock to enter the borehole. A second borehole at the station [2556 2023] was completed at the larger diameter of 490 mm having penetrated 45 m deeper but was cased to a depth of 32 m and obtained a specific capacity of only 8 l/s/m although for the larger yield of about 63 l/s.

The yield of many sources varies according to regional water level conditions and may, in some cases, preclude the full licensed quantity being abstracted except in periods of high regional water levels (Grout et al., 1992). Drought conditions cause water levels to fall below the normal seasonal average levels. As the water table falls the aquifer saturated thickness declines as, in consequence, does the transmissivity. This leads to declining yields and increasing amounts of drawdown. In extreme drought conditions it may become necessary to reduce yield further in order to prevent the source drying out. At Willian Road Pumping Station [2416 3248] the effective saturated thickness above the low permeability Chalk Marl is only about 35 m. In October 1958 when the rest water was at 25.9 m below ground level (bgl) pumping at a rate of 101 l/s produced a drawdown of 8.2 m, whereas in October 1964 when the rest water level was at 31.7 m bgl pumping at a rate of 86 l/s produced a drawdown of 16.5 m. In the autumn of 1965, under severe drought conditions, it became necessary to reduce the yield in order to hold the pumping water level at about 50 m bgl (Grout et al., 1992).

Chalk groundwater is generally potable although hard and, like the Woburn Sands, of calcium-bicarbonate type although generally more mineralised. Groundwater chemistry does not vary greatly, as illustrated by the analyses from representative boreholes and wells spread across the district (Table 15). Nitrate concentrations are commonly high in Chalk groundwater in the district.

In common with other industrialised areas, groundwater contamination by organic chlorinated solvents has been detected in the district. The solvents are a particu-larly insidious groundwater contaminant due to their physico-chemical properties. They are only sparingly soluble in water, do not readily degrade under natural conditions and are persistent in the subsurface. The immiscible phase is significantly more dense and less viscous than water. These properties result in rapid deep penetration to the effective base of the aquifer where solvent can provide a long-term source of contamination. The solvents are widely used for dry cleaning in laundries, cleaning and degreasing in heavy engineering, metal working and new 'high technology' industries of which many exist in the district.

Longstaff et al. (1992) provided details of a case study of solvent contamination of the Chalk aquifer in Dunstable and Luton. Two sites (Crescent Road and Albert Road Pumping Stations) specifically mentioned are located immediately west of the district. Air-stripping water treatment equipment has been installed at the former site to reduce the concentration of solvents in the abstracted water to below the prescribed concentration for supply. Within the district pumping has been suspended at two public supply sources located on the margins of urban industrialised areas due to contamination by solvents. As at Crescent Road Pumping Station, water treatment would be necessary before these sources could recommence pumping to supply.

REFERENCES

Most of the references listed below are held and available for consultation in the libraries of the British Geological Survey at Keyworth, Nottingham and Murchison House, Edinburgh. Copies of the references can be purchased from the Keyworth Library subject to the current copyright legislation.

ALDISS, D T. 1990. Geological notes and local details for 1:10 000 sheet SP92SE (Totternhoe), and part of sheet SP91NE. *British Geological Survey Technical Report*, WA/91/51.

— 1991. Geological notes and local details for 1:10 000 sheet TL23SE (Weston). *British Geological Survey Technical Report*, WA/91/51.

— 1992a. Geological notes and local details for 1:10 000 sheet TL12NE (Hitchin). *British Geological Survey Technical Report*, WA/92/61.

— 1992b. Geological notes and local details for 1:10 000 sheet TL22NW (Little Wymondley). *British Geological Survey Technical Report*, WA/92/62.

— and SHEPHARD-THORN, E R. 1992. Geological notes and local details for part of 1:10 000 sheets TL01NE (Caddington), TL11NW (Luton Hoo), and TL11NE (Kimpton). *British Geological Survey Technical Report*, WA/92/58.

ALLEN, J R L. 1982. Mud drapes in sand-wave deposits: a physical model with application to the Folkestone Beds (early Cretaceous, southeast England). *Philosophical Transactions of the Royal Society of London*, Series A, Vol. 306, 291–345.

ALLEN, P. 1955. Age of the Wealden in North-Western Europe. *Geological Magazine*, Vol. 92, 265–281.

— 1959. The Wealden environment: Anglo-Paris Basin. *Philosophical Transactions of the Royal Society*, B 242, 283–346.

ALLSOP, J M. 1985. Geophysical investigations into the extent of the Devonian rocks beneath East Anglia. *Proceedings of the Geologists' Association*, Vol. 96, 371–379.

— and SMITH, N J P. 1988. The deep geology of Essex. *Proceedings of the Geologists' Association*, Vol. 99, 249–260.

ANON. 1883. Field meeting, 15th July 1882. Royston. *Transactions of the Hertfordshire Natural History Society*, Vol. 2, 30–33.

— 1982. *Report on the hydrogeology of the Lower Greensand aquifer (Leighton Buzzard–Ely).* (London: Binnie and Partners.)

AVERY, B W, BULLOCK, P, CATT, J A, RAYNER, J H, and WEIR, A H. 1982. Composition and origin of some brickearths on the Chilterns Hills, England. *Catena*, Vol. 9, 153–174.

BADEN-POWELL, D F W. 1948. The chalky boulder clays of Norfolk and Suffolk. *Geological Magazine*, Vol. 35, 279–296.

— 1950. Field meeting to Lowestoft district. *Proceedings of the Geologists' Association*, Vol. 61, 191–197.

BAILEY, H W, GALE, A S, MORTIMORE, R N, SWIECICKI, A, and WOOD, C J. 1983. The Coniacian–Maastrichtian stages of the United Kingdom, with particular reference to southern England. *Newsletters in Stratigraphy*, Vol. 12, 29–42.

BANHAM, P H. 1971. Pleistocene beds at Corton, Suffolk. *Geological Magazine*, Vol. 108, 281–285.

— 1975. Glacitectonic structures: a general discussion with particular reference to the contorted drift of Norfolk. 69–94 *in* Ice ages: ancient and modern. WRIGHT, A E, and MOSELEY, F (editors). *Special Issue of the Geological Journal*, No. 6.

BARKER, R D, and HARKER, D. 1984. The location of the Stour buried tunnel-valley using geophysical techniques. *Quarterly Journal of Engineering Geology*, Vol. 17, 103–115.

BATEMAN, R M. 1988. Relationship of the Woolwich and Reading Formation (Late Palaeocene) to the Upper Chalk (Late Cretaceous) and Clay-with-flints *sensu lato* (Quaternary) in the Chiltern Hills, southern England. *Tertiary Research*, Vol. 10, 53–63.

— and MOFFAT, A J. 1987. Petrography of the Woolwich and Reading formation (late Palaeocene) of the Chiltern Hills, southern England. *Tertiary Research*, Vol. 8, 75–103.

BECK, R B, FUNNELL, B M, and LORD, A R. 1972. Correlation of the Lower Pleistocene Crag at depth in Suffolk. *Geological Magazine*, Vol. 109, 137–139.

BERGGREN, W A, and 11 others. 1980. Towards a Quaternary time scale. *Quaternary Research*, Vol. 13, 277–302.

— KENT, D V, and FLYNN, J J. 1985. Jurassic to Palaeogene: Part 2. Palaeogene geochronology and chronostratigraphy. 141–195 in *The chronology of the geological record*. SNELLING, N J (editor). *Memoir of the Geological Society of London*, No. 10.

BILLINGHURST, S A. 1927. On some new Ammonoidea from the Chalk Rock. *Geological Magazine*, Vol. 64, 511–518.

BLEZARD, R G, BROMLEY, R G, HANCOCK, J M, HESTER, S W, HEY, R W, and KIRKALDY, J F. 1967. The London region (north of the Thames). *Geologists' Association Guide*, No. 30A.

BLOOM, E F D. 1930. Report of field meeting at Hitchin. *Proceedings of the Geologists' Association*, Vol. 41, 441–442.

— 1934. Geology. 26–52 in *The natural history of the Hitchin region*. HINE, R L (editor). (Hitchin: Hitchin and District Regional Survey Association.)

— and HARPER, A R C S. 1938. Field meeting in the Hitchin district. *Proceedings of the Geologists' Association*, Vol. 49, 415–419.

— and WOOLDRIDGE, S W. 1930. Field meeting in the Hitchin District. *Proceedings of the Geologists' Association*, Vol. 41, 87–91.

BONNELL, D G R, and BUTTERWORTH, B. 1950. Clay building bricks of the United Kingdom. *Ministry of Works National Brick Advisory Council, paper five.* (London: HMSO.)

BONNEY, T G. 1872. On the Upper Greensand or Chloritic Marl of Cambridgeshire. *Proceedings of the Geologists' Association*, Vol. 3, 1–20.

— 1906. On the relations of the Chalk and Boulder Clay near Royston (Hertfordshire). *Quarterly Journal of the Geological Society*, Vol. 62, 491–498.

BOSWELL, P G H. 1914. On the age of the Suffolk valleys and the buried channels of drift. *Quarterly Journal of the Geological Society*, Vol. 69, 581–620.

— 1931. The stratigraphy of the glacial deposits in East Anglia in relation to early man. *Proceedings of the Geologists' Association*, Vol. 42, 87–111.

BOULTON, G S. 1979. Processes of glacier erosion on different substrata. *Journal of Glaciology*, Vol. 23, 15–38.

— and PAUL, M A. 1976. The influence of genetic processes on geotechnical properties of glacial tills. *Quarterly Journal of Engineering Geology*, Vol. 9, 159–194.

BRIDGES, P J. 1982. Sedimentology of a tidal sea: the Lower Greensand of southern England. 183–188 in *Offshore tidal sands*. STRIDE, A H (editor). (London: Chapman and Hall.)

BRISTOW, C R. 1990. Geology of the Berwick St John (Wiltshire), 1:10 000 sheet ST92SW, with contribution on the macropalaeontology of the Chalk by C J Wood. *British Geological Survey Technical Report*, WA/90/49.

BRITISH GEOLOGICAL SURVEY. 1984. Hydrogeological map of the area between Cambridge and Maidenhead including parts of hydrometric areas 33, 38 and 39. 1:100 000. (Southampton: Ordnance Survey for British Geological Survey.)

— 1985. Pre-Permian geology of the United Kingdom (South). Maps 1 and 2. 1:1 000 000 scale.

— In press. Therfield Rectory hydrograph. BGS, Keyworth.

BROMLEY, R G. 1966. Field meeting on the Chalk of Cambridgeshire and Hertfordshire. *Proceedings of the Geologists' Association*, Vol. 77, 277–279.

— 1967. Some observations on burrows of thalassinidean Crustacea in chalk hardgrounds. *Quarterly Journal of the Geological Society of London*, Vol. 123, 157–182.

— and GALE, A S. 1982. The lithostratigraphy of the English Chalk Rock. *Cretaceous Research*, Vol. 3, 273–306.

BROWN, J C. 1959. The sub-glacial surface in east Hertfordshire and its relation to the valley pattern. *Transactions and Papers of the Institute of British Geographers*, Vol. 26, 37–50.

BUCK, S G. 1985. Sand-flow cross strata in tidal sands of the Lower Greensand (Early Cretaceous), southern England. *Journal of Sedimentary Petrology*, Vol. 55, 895–906.

BURNETT, A D, and FOOKES, P G. 1974. A regional engineering geological study of the London Clay in the London and Hampshire basins. *Quarterly Journal of Engineering Geology*, Vol. 7, 257–295.

BUSBY, J P, KIMBELL, G S, and PHARAOH, T C. 1993. Integrated geophysical/geological modelling of the Caledonian and Precambrian basement of southern Britain. *Geological Magazine*, Vol. 130, 593–604.

BUTLER, D E. 1975. Preliminary report by D E Butler on Devonian faunas from the Ashwell borehole (Superior Oil No. 4). *Report of the Palaeontology Unit, Institute of Geological Sciences*, No. PD 75/14.

— 1981. Marine faunas from concealed Devonian rocks of southern England and their reflection of the Frasnian transgression. *Geological Magazine*, Vol. 118, 679–697.

BUURMAN, P. 1980. Palaeosols in the Reading Beds (Paleocene) of Alum Bay, Isle of Wight, UK. *Sedimentology*, Vol. 27, 593–606.

CARTER, D J, and HART, M B. 1977. Aspects of mid-Cretaceous stratigraphical micropalaeontology. *Bulletin of the British Museum (Natural History), Geology*, Vol. 29, 1–135.

CARTER, P G, and MALLARD, D J. 1974. A study of the strength, compressibility and density trends within the Chalk of southeast England. *Quarterly Journal of Engineering Geology*, Vol. 7, 43–55.

CASEY, R. 1961. The stratigraphical palaeontology of the Lower Greensand. *Palaeontology*, Vol. 3, 487–621.

— and RAWSON, P F. 1973. A review of the boreal Lower Cretaceous. 415–430 in The boreal Lower Cretaceous. CASEY, R, and RAWSON, P F (editors). *Special Issue of the Geological Journal*, No. 5.

CATT, J A. 1983. Cenozoic pedogenesis and landform development in south-east England. 251–258 in Residual deposits: surface related weathering processes and materials. WILSON, R C L (editor). *Special Publication of the Geological Society of London*, No. 11.

— 1986. The nature, origin and geomorphological significance of clay-with-flints. 151–159 in *The scientific study of flint and chert: proceedings of the Fourth International Flint Symposium held at Brighton Polytechnic 10–15 April 1983*. SIEVEKING, G de G, and HART, M B (editors). (Cambridge: Cambridge University Press.)

— and HODGSON, J M. 1976. Soils and geomorphology of the Chalk in south-east England. *Earth Surface Processes and Landforms*, Vol. 1, 181–193.

CAYEUX, L. 1897. Contribution à l'étude micrographique des terrains sédimentaires. I Études de quelques dépôts siliceux secondaires et tertiaires du Bassin de Paris et de la Belgique. II Craie du Bassin de Paris. *Mémoires de la Société Géologique du Nord*, Vol. 4, No. 2, 589 pp. [In French]

CHACKSFIELD, B C, and RAINES, M G. 1992. Further geophysical surveys across a buried valley at Hitchin, Hertfordshire. *British Geological Survey Technical Report*, WK/92/2R.

CHADWICK, R A. 1985a. Permian, Mesozoic and Cenozoic structural evolution of England and Wales in relation to the principles of extension and inversion tectonics. 9–25 in *Atlas of onshore sedimentary basins in England and Wales. Post Carboniferous tectonics and stratigraphy*. WHITTAKER, A (editor). (Glasgow: Blackie.)

— 1985b. Upper Jurassic: late Oxfordian to early Portlandian. 49–51 in *Atlas of onshore sedimentary basins in England and Wales. Post Carboniferous tectonics and stratigraphy*. WHITTAKER, A (editor). (Glasgow: Blackie.)

— 1985c. End Jurassic–early Cretaceous sedimentation and subsidence (late Portlandian to Barremian), and the late-Cimmerian unconformity. 52–56 in *Atlas of onshore sedimentary basins in England and Wales. Post Carboniferous tectonics and stratigraphy*. WHITTAKER, A (editor). (Glasgow: Blackie.)

— 1985d. Cenozoic sedimentation, subsidence and tectonic inversion. 61–63 in *Atlas of onshore sedimentary basins in England and Wales. Post Carboniferous tectonics and stratigraphy*. WHITTAKER, A (editor). (Glasgow: Blackie.)

CHAPMAN, F. 1901. Ostracoda from the Chara-Marl of Hitchin. *Transactions of the Hertfordshire Natural History Society*, Vol. 11, 60–62.

CHATWIN, C P. 1961. *British regional geology: East Anglia and adjoining areas* (4th edition). (London: HMSO for the Institute of Geological Sciences.)

CHESHIRE, D A. 1983. Till lithology in Hertfordshire and west Essex. 50–59 in *Diversion of the Thames Field Guide*. ROSE, J (editor). (Cambridge: Quaternary Research Association.)

CHRISTIANSEN, E A, and WHITAKER, S H. 1976. Glacial thrusting of drift and bedrock. 121–130 in Glacial till. An interdisciplinary study. LEGGET, R F (editor). *Royal Society of Canada, Special Publication, Natural Resources Council of Canada, Ottawa*, No. 12.

CLAYTON C J. 1986. The chemical environment of flint formation in Upper Cretaceous chalks. 43–54 in *The scientific study of flint and chert: Proceedings of the Fourth International Flint*

Symposium held at Brighton Polytechnic 10–15 April 1983. SIEVEKING, G de G, and HART, M B (editors). (Cambridge: Cambridge University Press.)

CLAYTON, L, and MORAN, S R. 1974. A glacial process-form model. 89–119 in *Glacial geomorphology.* COATES, D R (editor). (Binghamton: University of New York State.)

COCKS, L R M, HOLLAND, C H, and RICKARDS, R B. 1992. A revised correlation of Silurian rocks in the British Isles. *Special Report of the Geological Society of London,* Vol. 21, 1–32.

COLLINSON, M E. 1983. Fossil plants of the London Clay. *Palaeontological Association field guide to fossils, No. 1.* (London: The Palaeontological Association.)

COOK, P J, SHERGOLD, J H, BURNETT, W C, and RIGGS, S R. 1990. Phosphorite research: a historical overview. 1–22 in *Phoshorite research and development.* NOTHOLT, A J G, and JARVIS, I (editors). *Special Publication of the Geological Society of London,* No. 52.

COOPER, J. 1976. British Tertiary stratigraphical and rock terms formal and informal, additional to Curry 1958, *Lexique Stratigraphique International;* with a stratigraphical table. *Tertiary Research Special Paper,* No. 1.

COPE, J C W, INGHAM, J K, and RAWSON, P F (editors). 1992. Atlas of palaeogeography and lithofacies. *Memoirs of the Geological Society of London,* No. 13.

COSTA, L, and DOWNIE, C. 1976. The distribution of the dinoflagellate *Wetzeliella* in the Palaeogene of North Western Europe. *Palaeontology,* Vol. 19, 591–614.

— and MÜLLER, C. 1978. Correlation of Cenozoic dinoflagellate zones from the NE Atlantic and NW Europe. *Newsletters on Stratigraphy,* Vol. 7, 65–72.

COWPERTHWAITE, I A, FITCH, F J, MILLER, J A, MITCHELL, J G, and ROBERTSON, R H. 1972. Sedimentation, petrogenesis and radioisotopic age of the Cretaceous fuller's earth of southern England. *Clay Minerals,* Vol. 9, 309–327.

COX, A. 1979. *Survey of Bedfordshire brickmaking, a history and gazeteer.* (Bedford: Bedfordshire County Council, Royal Commission on Historical Monuments.)

COX, B M. 1984. Jurassic strata immediately below the Cretaceous unconformity in the Ashwell borehole (Superior Oil Co. No. 4), Hertfordshire. *Report of the Palaeontology Unit, British Geological Survey,* No. PDL/84/4.

— 1990. Lower Greensand ammonoids from Clophill, Bedfordshire. *British Geological Survey Technical Report,* WH/90/276R.

COX, F C. 1985. The tunnel-valleys of Norfolk, East Anglia. *Proceedings of the Geologists' Association,* Vol. 96, 357–369.

CROOT, D G. 1987. Glacio-tectonic structures: a mesoscale model of thin skinned thrust sheets. *Journal of Structural Geology,* Vol. 9, 797–808.

CRUX, J A. 1991. Albian calcareous nannofossils from the Gault Clay of Munday's Hill (Bedfordshire, England). *Journal of Micropalaeontology,* Vol. 10, 203–222.

CULPIN, B E L. 1921. Excursion to Stevenage, Herts. Part I. *Proceedings of the Geologists' Association,* Vol. 32, 20–25.

DENNESS, B. 1974. Engineering aspects of the chalky boulder clay at the new town of Milton Keynes in Buckinghamshire. *Quarterly Journal of Engineering Geology,* Vol. 7, 297–309.

DESTOMBES, J-P, and SHEPHARD-THORN, E R. 1971. Geological results of the Channel Tunnel site investigation 1964–65. *Report of the Institute of Geological Sciences,* No. 71/11.

DE RANCE, C E. 1868. On the Albian, or Gault, of Folkestone. *Geological Magazine,* Vol. 5, 163–171.

DINES, H G, and CHATWIN, C P. 1930. Pliocene sandstone from Rothamsted (Hertfordshire). 1–7 in *Summary of Progress for 1929, Pt III.* Geological Survey of Great Britain. (London: HMSO.)

DIXON, J E, FITTON, J G, and FROST, R T C. 1981. The tectonic significance of post-Carboniferous igneous activity in the North Sea Basin. 121–137 in Petroleum geology of the continental shelf of North-West Europe. ILLING, L V, and HOBSON, G D (editors). *Proceedings of the second conference on petroleum geology of the continental shelf of north-west europe organised by The Institute of Petroleum and held in London 4–6 March 1980.* (London: Heyden and Son.)

DONOVAN, D T, HORTON, A, and IVIMEY-COOK, H C. 1979. The transgression of the Lower Lias over the northern flank of the London Platform. *Journal of the Geological Society of London,* Vol. 136, 165–173.

DRISCOLL, R. 1983. The influence of vegetation on the swelling and shrinking of clay soils in Britain. *Geotechnique,* Vol. 33, 93–105.

DRUMMOND, P V O. 1983. The Micraster biostratigraphy of the senonian White Chalk of Sussex, southern England. *Géologie Méditerranéene,* 10, 177–182.

EDMONDS, C N. 1983. Towards the prediction of subsidence risk upon the Chalk outcrop. *Quarterly Journal of Engineering Geology,* Vol. 16, 261–266.

EDMONDS, E A, and DINHAM, C H. 1965. Geology of the country around Huntingdon and Biggleswade. *Memoir of the Geological Survey of Great Britain,* Sheets 187 and 204 (England and Wales).

EHLERS, J, GIBBARD, P L, and WHITEMAN, C A. 1986. Recent investigations of the Marly Drift of northwest Norfolk, England. In *INQUA Symposium on the Genesis and Lithology of Glacial Deposits.* (Rotterdam: Balkema.)

— MEYER, K-D, and STEPHAN, H-J. 1984. The Pre-Weichselian glaciation of north-west Europe. *Quaternary Science Reviews,* Vol. 3, 1–40.

ELLISON, R A. 1983. Facies distribution in the Woolwich and Reading Beds of the London Basin, England. *Proceedings of the Geologists' Association,* Vol. 94, 311–319.

— KNOX, R W O'B, JOLLEY, D W, and KING, C. 1994. A revision of the lithostratigraphical classification of the early Palaeogene strata of the London Basin and East Anglia. *Proceedings of the Geologists' Association,* Vol. 105, 187–198.

EVANS, J. 1896. The Stone Age in Hertfordshire. *Transactions of the Hertfordshire Natural History Society,* Vol. 8, 169–187.

EYERS, J. 1991. The influence of tectonics on early Cretaceous sedimentation in Bedfordshire, England. *Journal of the Geological Society of London,* Vol. 148, 405–414.

— 1992. Sedimentology and palaeoenvironment of the Shenley Limestone (Albian, Lower Cretaceous): an unusual shallow-water carbonate. *Proceedings of the Geologists' Association,* Vol. 103, 293–302.

FISHER, O. 1873. On the phosphatic nodules of the Cretaceous rock of Cambridgeshire. *Quarterly Journal of the Geological Society of London,* Vol. 29, 52–63.

FORDHAM, H G. 1874. Notes on the structure sometimes developed in Chalk. *Quarterly Journal of the Geological Society of London,* Vol. 30, 43–44.

FORSTER, A. 1991. The engineering geology of the country around Thame, Oxfordshire. 1:50 000 Geological map sheet 237. *British Geological Survey Technical Report*, WN/91/14.

FOSTER, S S D, and MILTON, V A. 1974. The permeability and storage of an unconfined chalk aquifer. *Hydrology Science Bulletin*, Vol. 19, 485–500.

FREEMAN, I L. 1964. Mineralogy of ten British brick clays. *Clay Minerals Bulletin*, Vol. 5, 474–486.

FUNNELL, B M. 1962. The Palaeogene and Early Pleistocene of Norfolk. *Transactions of the Norfolk and Norwich Naturalists' Society*, Vol. 19, 340–364.

GALE, A S. 1989a. A Milankovitch scale for Cenomanian time. *Terra Nova*, Vol. 1, 420–425.

— 1989b. Field meeting at Folkestone Warren, 29 November, 1987. *Proceedings of the Geologists' Association*, Vol. 100, 73–82.

— JENKYNS, H C, KENNEDY, W J, and CORFIELD, R M. 1993. Chemostratigraphy versus biostratigraphy: data from around the Cenomanian–Turonian boundary. *Journal of the Geological Society of London*, Vol. 150, 29–32.

— WOOD, C J, and BROMLEY, R G. 1987. The lithostratigraphy and marker bed correlation of the White Chalk (Late Cenomanian–Campanian) in southern England. *Mesozoic Research*, Vol. 1, 107–118.

GALLOIS, R W, and MORTER, A A. 1982. The stratigraphy of the Gault of East Anglia. *Proceedings of the Geologists' Association*, Vol. 93, 351–368.

GARDEN, I R. 1991. Changes in the provenance of pebbly detritus in southern Britain and northern France associated with basin rifting. 273–289 in Developments in sedimentary provenance studies. MORTON, A C, TODD, S P and HAUGHTON, P D W (editors). *Special Publication of the Geological Society of London*, No. 57.

GAUNT, G D, FLETCHER, T P, and WOOD, C J. 1992. Geology of the country around Kingston upon Hull and Brigg. *Memoir of the British Geological Survey*, Sheets 80 and 89 (England and Wales).

GIBBARD, P L. 1974. Pleistocene stratigraphy and vegetational history of Hertfordshire. Unpublished PhD thesis, University of Cambridge.

— 1977. The Pleistocene history of the Vale of St Albans. *Philosophical Transactions of the Royal Society of London, Series B*, Vol. 280, 445–483.

— 1983. The diversion of the Thames — a review. 8–23 in *Diversion of the Thames field guide*. ROSE, J (editor). (Cambridge: Quaternary Research Association.)

— 1985. *Pleistocene history of the middle Thames valley.* (Cambridge: Cambridge University Press.)

— 1986. Flint gravels in the Quaternary of southeast England. 141–149 in *The scientific study of flint and chert: Proceedings of the Fourth International Flint Symposium held at Brighton Polytechnic 10–15 April 1983.* SIEVEKING, G de G, and HART, M B (editors). (Cambridge: Cambridge University Press.)

— and AALTO, M M. 1977. A Hoxnian interglacial site at Fishers Green, Stevenage, Hertfordshire. *New Phytologist*, Vol. 78, 505–523.

— and 16 others. 1991. Early and early Middle Pleistocene correlations in the southern North Sea Basin. *Quaternary Science Reviews*, Vol. 10, 23–52.

GREEN, C P, and McGREGOR, D F M. 1978. Pleistocene gravel trains of the River Thames. *Proceedings of the Geologists' Association*, Vol. 89, 143–156.

— — and EVANS, A H. 1982. Development of the Thames drainage system in Early and Middle Pleistocene times. *Geological Magazine*, Vol. 119, 281–290.

GROUT, M W, ALEXANDER, D W, and SIMPSON, R J. 1992. Practical aspects of yield investigations of groundwater sources. *Journal of the Institute of Water and Environmental Management*, Vol. 6, No. 4, 397–407.

GROVE, R. 1976. *The Cambridgeshire coprolite mining rush.* (Cambridge: Oleander Press.)

GRUBE, F. 1983. Tunnel valleys. 257–258 in *Glacial deposits in North-West Europe.* EHLERS, J (editor). (Rotterdam: A A Balkema.)

HALLSWORTH, C R. 1986. Grain size profiles through two BGS boreholes in the Lower Cretaceous Woburn Sands and the mineralogy of the clay horizons. *BGS Stratigraphy and Sedimentology Research Group Report*, No. SRG/86/19.

HANCOCK, J M. 1958. Itinerary 12. The Lower Cretaceous near Leighton Buzzard. 36–41 in The London region. *Geologists' Association Guide*, No. 30.

— 1967. Itinerary 2. The Lower Cretaceous around Leighton Buzzard. 8–15 in The London region (north of the Thames). *Geologists' Association Guide*, No. 30A.

— 1989. Sea-level changes in the British region during the Late Cretaceous. *Proceedings of the Geologists' Association*, Vol. 100, 565–594.

— and KAUFFMAN, E G. 1979. The great transgressions of the Late Cretaceous. *Journal of the Geological Society of London*, Vol. 136, 175–186.

HAQ, B U, HARDENBOL, J, and VAIL, P R. 1987. Chronology of fluctuating sea levels since the Triassic. *Science*, Vol. 235, 1156–1167.

HARE, F K. 1947. The geomorphology of a part of the Middle Thames. *Proceedings of the Geologists' Association*, Vol. 58, 294–339.

HARLAND, W B, ARMSTRONG, R L, COX, A V, CRAIG, L E, SMITH, A G, and SMITH, D G. 1990. *A geologic time scale 1989.* (Cambridge: Cambridge University Press.)

HARMER, F W. 1902. A sketch of the later Tertiary history of East Anglia. *Proceedings of the Geologists' Association*, Vol. 17, 416–479.

HARRIS, P M. 1982. Limestone and dolomite. *Mineral Dossier Mineral Resources Consultative Committee*, No. 23.

HART, M B. 1973a. A correlation of the macrofaunal and microfaunal zonations of the Gault Clay in southeast England. 267–288 in The boreal Lower Cretaceous. CASEY, R, and RAWSON, P F (editors). *Special Issue of the Geological Journal*, No. 5.

— 1973b. Foraminiferal evidence for the age of the Cambridge Greensand. *Proceedings of the Geologists' Association*, Vol. 84, 65–82.

— 1987. Orbitally induced cycles in the Chalk facies of the United Kingdom. *Cretaceous Research*, Vol. 8, 335–348.

— BAILEY, H W, CRITTENDEN, S, FLETCHER, B N, PRICE, R J, and SWIECICKI, A. 1989. Cretaceous. 273–315 in *Stratigraphical atlas of fossil foraminifera* (2nd edition). JENKINS, D G, and MURRAY, J W (editors). (Chichester: British Micropalaeontological Society/Ellis Horwood.)

HAWKES, L. 1943. The erratics of the Cambridge Greensand — their nature, provenance and mode of transport. *Quarterly Journal of the Geological Society of London*, Vol. 99, 93–104.

HAWKINS, H L. 1946. Field meeting at Reading. *Proceedings of the Geologists' Association*, Vol. 57, 164–171.

HESTER, S W. 1965. Stratigraphy and palaeogeography of the Woolwich and Reading Beds. *Bulletin of the Geological Survey of Great Britain*, Vol. 23, 117–137.

HEY, R W. 1965. Highly quartzose Pebble Gravels in the London Basin. *Proceedings of the Geologists' Association*, Vol. 76, 403–420.

HILL, W. 1886. On the beds between the Upper and Lower Chalk of Dover, and their comparison with the Middle Chalk of Cambridgeshire. *Quarterly Journal of the Geological Society of London*, Vol. 42, 232–248.

— 1891. Our forgotten lake. *Journal of the Hitchin Natural History Club*, No. 12, 93–97.

— 1900. Excursion to Hitchin and Arlesey. *Proceedings of the Geologists' Association*, Vol. 16, 446–447.

— 1908. On a deep channel of drift at Hitchin (Hertfordshire). *Quarterly Journal of the Geological Society of London*, Vol. 64, 8–26.

— 1911. Excursion to Arlesey and Letchworth. *Proceedings of the Geologists' Association*, Vol. 22, 8–10.

— 1912. Report of an excursion to the Hitchin and Stevenage Gap. *Proceedings of the Geologists' Association*, Vol. 23, 217–224.

— and JUKES-BROWNE, A J. 1886. The Melbourn Rock and the zone of Belemnitella plena from Cambridge to the Chiltern Hills. *Quarterly Journal of the Geological Society of London*, Vol. 42, 216–231.

— and MONCKTON, H W. 1896. Excursion to Hitchin. Saturday, 20th June, 1896. *Proceedings of the Geologists' Association*, Vol. 14, 415–419.

HOLLOWAY, S. 1985. Lower Jurassic: the Lias. 37–40 in *Atlas of onshore sedimentary basins in England and Wales. Post Carboniferous tectonics and stratigraphy*. WHITTAKER, A (editor). (Glasgow: Blackie.)

HOLYOAK, D T, IVANOVICH, M, and PREECE, R C. 1983. Additional fossil and isotopic evidence for the age of the interglacial tufas at Hitchin and Icklingham. *Journal of Conchology*, Vol. 31, 260–261.

HOPE MACDONALD, H A. 1965. Mineral analyses of four samples of sand from the Woolwich and Reading Beds. *Bulletin of the Geological Survey of Great Britain*, Vol. 23, 139–143.

HOPKINSON, J. 1886. List of works on the geology of Hertfordshire, 1874–83. *Transactions of the Hertfordshire Natural History Society*, Vol. 3, 165–171.

— 1902. Geology. 1–31 in *The Victoria history of the counties of England, Hertfordshire, Vol. 1*. (London: Archibald Constable, Westminster.)

— 1903. List of works on the geology of Hertfordshire, 1884–1900. *Transactions of the Hertfordshire Natural History Society*, Vol. 11, 87–104.

— and SAUNDERS, J. 1904. The geology of Bedfordshire. 1–32 in *The Victoria histories of the counties of England, Bedfordshire. Vol.1*. (London: Archibald Constable, Westminster.)

HOPSON, P M. 1979. The sand and gravel resources of the country north of Harlow, Essex; description of 1:25 000 resource sheet TL41. *Mineral Assessment Report Institute of Geological Sciences*, No. 46.

— 1982. The basal London Clay and Lower London Tertiaries of sheet TL41 (Harlow, Essex). *Report of the Institute of Geological Sciences*, No. 82/1, 19–22.

— 1990. Geology of the Buntingford, Little Munden, Puckeridge and Wyddial district. *British Geological Survey Technical Report*, WA/90/73.

— 1992. Geology of the Letchworth, north-west Hitchin and Holwell district, Hertfordshire. *British Geological Survey Technical Report*, WA/92/42.

— 1995. Chalk rafts in Anglian till in north Hertfordshire. *Proceedings of the Geologists' Association*, Vol. 106, 151–158.

— and SAMUEL, M D A. 1982. The sand and gravel resources of the country around Hertford, Hertfordshire; description of 1:25 000 resource sheet TL31. *Mineral Assessment Report Institute of Geological Sciences*, No. 112.

HORTON, A. 1970. The drift sequence and subglacial topography in parts of the Ouse and Nene basin. *Report Institute of Geological Sciences*, No. 70/9.

— 1988. Geological notes and local details for 1:25 000 sheet TL43. *British Geological Survey Technical Report*, WA/88/46.

— SUMBLER, M G, and COX, B M. 1994. Geology of the country between Oxford and Aylesbury. *Memoir of the British Geological Survey*, Sheet 237 (England and Wales).

HUGHES, T McK. 1868. On the two plains of Hertfordshire and their gravels. *Quarterly Journal of the Geological Society of London*, Vol. 24, 283–287.

INSTITUTE OF GEOLOGICAL SCIENCES. 1978. IGS Boreholes 1976. *Report of the Institute of Geological Sciences*, No. 77/10.

IVIMEY-COOK, H C. 1982. Outline of Middle Jurassic stratigraphy of the Superior Oil Company's Ashwell borehole. *Report of the Palaeontology Unit, Institute of Geological Sciences*, No. PD/82/26.

JARVIS, I. 1992. Sedimentology, geochemistry and origin of phosphatic chalks: the Upper Cretaceous deposits of NW Europe. *Sedimentology*, Vol. 39, 55–97.

— CARSON, G A, COOPER, M K E, HART, M B, LEARY, P, TOCHER, B A, HORNE, D, and ROSENFELD, A. 1988. Microfossil Assemblages and the Cenomanian–Turonian (late Cretaceous) Oceanic Anoxic Event. *Cretaceous Research*, Vol. 9, 3–103.

JEANS, C V, LONG, D, HALL, M A, BLAND, D J, and CORNFORD, C. 1991. The geochemistry of the Plenus Marls at Dover, England: evidence of fluctuating oceanographic conditions and of glacial control during the development of the Cenomanian–Turonion $\delta^{13}C$ anomaly. *Geological Magazine*, Vol. 128, 603–632.

— MERRIMAN, R J, and MITCHELL, J G. 1977. Origin of Middle Jurassic and Lower Cretaceous fuller's earths in England. *Clay Minerals*, Vol. 12, 11–44.

JEFFERIES, R P S. 1963. The stratigraphy of the Actinocamax plenus Subzone (Turonian) in the Anglo-Paris Basin. *Proceedings of the Geologists' Association*, Vol. 74, 1–33.

JENYNS, L. 1867. On the phosphatic nodules obtained in the eastern counties, and used in agriculture. *Proceedings of the Bath Natural History and Antiquarian Field Club*, Vol. 1, 9–24.

JOHNSON, H D, and LEVELL, B K. 1980. Sedimentology of Lower Cretaceous subtidal sand complex, Woburn Sands, Southern England. *Bulletin of the American Association of Petroleum Geologists*, Vol. 64, 728–729.

JOLLEY, D W, and SPINNER, E. 1992. Spore-pollen associations from the lower London Clay (Eocene), East Anglia, England. *Tertiary Research*, Vol. 13, 11–25.

JONES, D K C. 1981. *The geomorphology of the British Isles: southeast and southern England.* (London: Methuen.)

JONES, O T. 1938. Report of visit to the Sedgwick Museum, Cambridge, and field meeting at Royston. *Proceedings of the Geologists' Association*, Vol. 49, 405–406.

JUKES-BROWNE, A J. 1875. On the relations of the Cambridge Gault and Greensand. *Quarterly Journal of the Geological Society of London*, Vol. 31, 256–316.

— 1880. The subdivision of the Chalk. *Geological Magazine*, Vol. 17 [decade 2, Vol. 7], 248–257.

— and HILL, W. 1900. The Cretaceous rocks of Britain. Vol. 1. The Gault and Upper Greensand of England. *Memoir of the Geological Survey of the United Kingdom.*

— — 1903. The Cretaceous rocks of Britain. Vol. 2. The Lower and Middle Chalk of England. *Memoir of the Geological Survey of the United Kingdom.*

— — 1904. The Cretaceous rocks of Britain. Vol. 3. The Upper Chalk of England. *Memoir of the Geological Survey of the United Kingdom.*

KAPLAN, U, KENNEDY, W J, and WRIGHT, C W. 1987. Turonian and Coniacian Scaphitidae from England and north-west Germany. *Geologisches Jahrbuch*, Reihe A103, 5–39.

KEEN, M. 1978. The Tertiary. Palaeogene. 385–450 *in* A stratigraphical index of British Ostracoda. BATE, R H, and ROBINSON, E (editors). Special Issue of the Geological Journal, No. 8.

KEEPING, W. 1880. On the included pebbles of the upper Neocomian sands of the south-east of England, especially those of the Upware and Potton pebble beds. *Geological Magazine*, Vol. 17 [decade 2, vol. 7], 414–421.

KENNARD, A S. 1943. The post-Pliocene non-marine mollusca of Hertfordshire. *Transactions of the Hertfordshire Natural History Society*, Vol. 22, 1–18.

— and WOODWARD, B. 1922. The post-Pliocene mollusca of the east of England. *Proceedings of the Geologists' Association*, Vol. 33, 104–142.

KENNEDY, W J, and GARRISON, R E. 1975a. Morphology and genesis of nodular chalks and hardgrounds in the Upper Cretaceous of southern England. *Sedimentology*, Vol. 22, 311–386.

— — 1975b. Morphology and genesis of nodular phosphates in the Cenomanian Glauconitic Marl of south-east England. *Lethaia*, Vol. 8, 339–360.

— and JUIGNET, P. 1974. Carbonate banks and slump beds in the Upper Cretaceous (Upper Turonian-Santonian) of Haute Normandie, France. *Sedimentology*, Vol. 21, 1–42.

KERNEY, M P. 1955. On the former occurrence of *Vertigo parcedentata* (Al. Braun) in Hertfordshire. *Journal of Conchology*, Vol. 24, 55–58.

— 1959. An interglacial tufa near Hitchin, Hertfordshire. *Proceedings of the Geologists' Association*, Vol. 70, 322–337.

KING, C. 1981. The stratigraphy of the London Clay and associated deposits. *Tertiary Research Special Paper*, No. 6, 1–158.

KING, D W. 1969. Soils of the Luton and Bedford district. A reconnaissance survey. *Soil Survey Special Survey*, No. 1.

KIRKALDY, J F. 1939. The history of the Lower Cretaceous period in England. *Proceedings of the Geologists' Association*, Vol. 50, 379–417.

— 1947. The provenance of the pebbles in the Lower Cretaceous rocks. *Proceedings of the Geologists' Association*, Vol. 58, 223–241.

— 1963. The Wealden and marine Lower Cretaceous beds of England. *Proceedings of the Geologists' Association*, Vol. 74, 127–146.

KNOX, R W O'B. 1984. Nannoplankton zonation and the Palaeocene/Eocene boundary beds of NW Europe: an indirect correlation by means of volcanic ash layers. *Journal of the Geological Society of London*, Vol. 141, 993–999.

— 1990. Thanetian and early Ypresian chronostratigraphy in south-east England. *Tertiary Research*, Vol. 11, 57–64.

— and ELLISON, R A. 1979. A Lower Eocene ash sequence in SE England. *Journal of the Geological Society of London*, Vol. 136, 251–253.

— and MORTON, A C. 1988. The record of early Tertiary N. Atlantic volcanism in sediments of the North Sea Basin. 407–419 *in* Early Tertiary volcanism and the opening of the NE Atlantic. MORTON, A C, and PARSEN, L M (editors). *Special Publication of the Geological Society of London*, No. 39.

LAKE, R D, and WILSON, D. 1990. Geology of the country around Great Dunmow. *Memoir of the British Geological Survey*, Sheet 222 (England and Wales).

LAMPLUGH, G W. 1922. On the junction of Gault and Lower Greensand near Leighton Buzzard (Bedfordshire). *Quarterly Journal of the Geological Society of London*, Vol. 78, 1–81.

— and WALKER, J F. 1903. On a fossiliferous band at the top of the Lower Greensand near Leighton Buzzard (Bedfordshire). *Quarterly Journal of the Geological Society of London*, Vol. 59, 234–265.

LEE, M K, PHARAOH, T C, and SOPER, N J. 1990. Structural trends in central Britain from images of gravity and aeromagnetic fields. *Journal of the Geological Society of London*, Vol. 147, 241–258.

— — and GREEN, C A. 1991. Structural trends in the concealed basement of eastern England from images of regional potential field data. *Annales de la Société Géologique de Belgique*, 114, 45–62.

LITTLE, J A, and ATKINSON, J H. 1988. Some geological and engineering characteristics of lodgement tills from the Vale of St Albans, Hertfordshire. *Quarterly Journal of Engineering Geology*, Vol. 21, 185–199.

LONGSTAFF, S L, ALDOUS, P J, CLARK, L, FLAVIN, R J, and PARTINGTON, J. 1992. Contamination of the Chalk aquifer by chlorinated solvents: a case study of the Luton and Dunstable area. *Journal of the Institute of Water and Environmental Management*, Vol. 6, 541–550.

LOTT, G K. 1992. A note on the petrography and depositional environment of a stromatolitic limestone sample from the Lower Cretaceous of the Arlesey borehole, Hitchin sheet. *British Geological Survey Technical Report*, WH/92/252.

McCLELLAN, G H. 1980. Mineralogy of carbonate fluorapatites. *Journal of the Geological Society of London*, Vol. 137, 675–681.

MARTINI, E. 1971. Standard Tertiary and Quaternary calcareous nannoplankton zonation. 739–785 in *Tecnoscienza Proceedings of the Second Planktonic Conference, Rome.* FARINACCI, G (editor). Vol. 2.

MATHERS, S J, and ZALASIEWICZ, J A. 1986. A sedimentation pattern in Anglian marginal meltwater channels from Suffolk, England. *Sedimentology*, Vol. 33, 559–573.

MIDDLEMISS, F A. 1962. Brachiopod ecology and Lower Greensand palaeogeography. *Palaeontology*, Vol. 5, 253–267.

MITCHELL, G F, PENNY, L F, SHOTTON, F W, and WEST, R G. 1973. A correlation of Quaternary deposits in the British Isles. *Special Report of the Geological Society of London*, No. 4.

MOFFATT, A J and CATT, J A. 1986a. A re-examination of the evidence for a Plio-Pleistocene marine transgression on the Chiltern Hills. 2: Drainage patterns. *Earth Surface Processes and Landforms*, Vol. 11, 169–180.

— — 1986b. A re-examination of the evidence for a Plio-Pleistocene marine transgression on the Chiltern Hills. 3: Deposits. *Earth Surface Processes and Landforms*, Vol. 11, 233–247.

— — WEBSTER, R, and BROWN, E H. 1986. A re-examination of the evidence for a Plio-Pleistocene marine transgression on the Chiltern Hills. 1. Structures and surfaces. *Earth Surface Processes and Landforms*, Vol. 11, 95–106.

MONKHOUSE, R A. 1974. An assessment of the groundwater resources of the Lower Greensand in the Cambridge–Bedford area. Report of the Water Resources Board, Reading.

MOORLOCK, B S P, LAKE, R D, and WYATT, R J. 1987. The Leighton Buzzard area (phase 2): Geological report on 1:10 000 sheets SP92NE, TL02NW, TL03NW, NE, SW, SE, TL13NW. (Keyworth, Nottinghamshire: British Geological Survey.)

MORTER, A A. 1986. Regional stratigraphy of the Lower Greensand. 72–78 *in* An outline study of the Lower Greensand of parts of south-east England. SHEPHARD-THORN, E R, HARRIS, P M, HIGHLEY, D E, and THORNTON, M H. *Technical Report of the British Geological Survey*, WF/MN/86/1.

— and WOOD, C J. 1983. The biostratigraphy of Upper Albian–Lower Cenomanian *Aucellina* in Europe. *Zitteliana*, Vol. 10, 515–529.

MORTIMORE, R N. 1979. The relationship of stratigraphy and tectonofacies to the physical properties of the White Chalk of Sussex. Unpublished PhD thesis, Brighton Polytechnic.

— 1983. The stratigraphy and sedimentation of the Turonian-Campanian in the southern province of England. *Zitteliana*, Vol. 10, 27–41.

— 1986. Stratigraphy of the Upper Cretaceous White Chalk of Sussex. *Proceedings of the Geologists' Assocation*, Vol. 97, 97–139.

— 1987. Upper Cretaceous Chalk in the North and South Downs, England: a correlation. *Proceedings of the Geologists' Association*, Vol. 98, 77–86.

— 1988. Upper Cretaceous White Chalk of the Anglo-Paris Basin: a discussion of the lithostatigraphical units. *Proceedings of the Geologists' Association*, Vol. 99, 67–70.

— and POMEROL, B. 1991. Upper Cretaceous tectonic disruptions in a placid Chalk sequence in the Anglo-Paris Basin. *Journal of the Geological Society of London*, Vol. 148, 391–404.

— and WOOD, C J. 1986. The distribution of flint in the English Chalk, with particular reference to the 'Brandon Flint Series' and the high Turonian flint maximum. 7–20 in *The scientific study of flint and chert: proceedings of the Fourth International Flint Symposium held at Brighton Polytechnic 10–15 April 1983*. SIEVEKING, G de G, and HART, M B (editors). (Cambridge: Cambridge University Press.)

MORTON, A C. 1982. The provenance and diagenesis of Palaeogene sandstones of southeast England as indicated by heavy mineral analysis. *Proceedings of the Geologists' Association*, Vol. 93, 263–274.

Mott Macdonald. 1992. River Hiz regulation scheme investigation and feasibility study. Final Report to the National Rivers Authority, Anglian Region.

MURRAY, K H. 1986. Correlation of electrical resistivity marker bands in the Cenomanian and Turonian Chalk from the London Basin to east Yorkshire. *Report British Geological Survey*, Vol. 17, No. 8.

MURRAY, J W, CURRY, D, HAYNES, J R, and KING, C. 1989. Palaeogene. 490–536 in *Stratigraphical atlas of fossil foraminifera* (2nd edition). JENKINS, D G, and MURRAY, J W (editors). (Chichester: Ellis Horwood.)

NARAYAN, J. 1963. Cross-stratification and palaeogeography of the Lower Greensand of south-east England and Bas-Boulonnais, France. *Nature, London*, Vol. 199, 1246–1247.

NORTON, P E P. 1967. Marine molluscan assemblages in the Early Pleistocene of Sidestrand, Bramerton and the Royal Society borehole at Ludham, Norfolk. *Philosophical Transactions of the Royal Society of London, Series B*, Vol 253, 161–200.

NOTHOLT, A J G. 1980. Economic phosphatic sediments: mode of occurrence and stratigraphical distribution. *Journal of the Geological Society of London*, Vol. 137, 793–805.

— and JARVIS, I (editors). 1990. Phoshorite research and development. *Special Publication of the Geological Society of London*, No. 52.

OAKLEY, K P. 1941. British phosphates. Part 3. Lower Cretaceous phosphorites, Isle of Wight to Yorkshire, with supplementary notes on Lincolnshire. *Wartime Pamphlet of the Geological Survey of Great Britain*, No. 8.

— 1947a. Fossil and sub-fossil vertebrates. *Transactions of the Hertfordshire Natural History Society*, Vol. 22, 239–246.

— 1947b. Early man in Hertfordshire. *Transactions of the Hertfordshire Natural History Society*, Vol. 22, 247–257.

ODIN, G S, and LETOLLE, E. 1980. Glauconitization and phosphatization environments: a tentative comparison. *Special Publication of the Society of Economic Palaeontologists and Mineralogists*, No. 29, 227–237.

OLLIER, C D, and THOMASSON, A J. 1957. Asymmetrical valleys of the Chiltern Hills. *Geographical Journal*, Vol. 123, 71–80.

OWEN, H G. 1971. Middle Albian stratigraphy in the Anglo-Paris basin. *Bulletin of the British Museum (Natural History): Geology*, Supp. 8, 1–164.

— 1972. The Gault and its junction with the Woburn Sands in the Leighton Buzzard area, Bedfordshire and Buckinghamshire. *Proceedings of the Geologists' Association*, Vol. 83, 287–312.

— 1975. The stratigraphy of the Gault and Upper Greensand of the Weald. *Proceedings of the Geologists' Association*, Vol. 86, 475–498.

— 1988a. The ammonite zonal sequence and ammonite taxonomy in the *Douvilleiceras mammillatum* Superzone (Lower Albian) in Europe. *Bulletin of the British Museum (Natural History), Geology*, Vol. 44, 177–231.

— 1988b. Correlation of ammonite faunal provinces in the Lower Albian. 477–489 in *Cephalopods past and present*. WIRDMANN, J, and KULLMANN, J (editors). (Schweizerbartische Verlag.)

PATTISON, J, BERRIDGE, N G, ALLSOP, J M, and WILKINSON, I P. 1993. Geology of the country around Sudbury (Suffolk). *Memoir of the British Geological Survey*, Sheet 206 (England and Wales).

PENNING, W H. 1876. Notes on the physical geology of East Anglia during the glacial period. *Quarterly Journal of the Geological Society of London*, Vol. 32, 191–204.

— and JUKES-BROWNE, A J. 1881. Geology of the neighbourhood of Cambridge. *Memoir of the Geological Survey of Great Britain*, Old Series sheets 51SW and part 51NW (England and Wales).

PERRIN, R M S. 1957. The clay mineralogy of some tills in the Cambridge district. *Clay Minerals Bulletin*, Vol. 3, 193–205.

— ROSE, J, and DAVIES, H. 1979. The distribution, variation and origins of pre-Devensian tills in eastern England. *Philosophical Transactions of the Royal Society of London, Series B*, Vol. 287, 535–570.

PHARAOH, T C, MERRIMAN, R J, WEBB, P C, and BECKINSALE, R D. 1987. The concealed Caledonides of eastern England: preliminary results of a multidisciplinary study. *Proceedings of the Yorkshire Geological Society*, Vol. 46, 355–369.

— — EVANS, J A, BREWER, T S, WEBB, P C, and SMITH, N J P. 1991. Early Palaeozoic arc-related volcanism in the concealed Caledonides of southern Britain. *Annales de la Société Géologique de Belgique*, Vol. 114, 63–91.

PRESTWICH, J. 1850. On the structure of the strata between the London Clay and the Chalk in the London and Hampshire Tertiary Systems. Part 1 The Basement Bed of the London Clay. *Quarterly Journal of the Geological Society of London*, Vol. 6, 252–281.

— 1852. On the structure of the strata between the London Clay and the Chalk in the London and Hampshire Tertiary Systems. Part 3, The Thanet Sands. *Quartely Journal of the Geological Society of London*, Vol. 8, 235–268.

— 1854. On the structure of the strata between the London Clay and the Chalk in the London and Hampshire Tertiary Systems. Part 2, The Woolwich and Reading Series. *Quarterly Journal of the Geological Society of London*, Vol. 10, 75–170.

— 1890. On the relation of the Westleton Beds or pebbly sands of Suffolk, to those of Norfolk and their extension inland; with some observations of the period of final elevation and denudation of the Weald and of the Thames valley etc. *Quarterly Journal of the Geological Society of London*, Vol. 46, 120–154.

PRICE, F G H. 1874. On the Gault of Folkestone. *Quarterly Journal of the Geological Society of London*, Vol. 30, 342–368.

PRICE, M. 1987. Fluid flow in the Chalk of England. 141–156 *in* Fluid flow in sedimentary basins and aquifers. GOFF, J C, and WILLIAMS, B P J (editors). *Special Publication of the Geological Society of London*, No. 34.

— MORRIS, B L, and ROBERTSON, A S. 1982. Recharge mechanisms and groundwater flow in the Chalk and Permian aquifers using double packer injection testing. *Journal of Hydrology*, Vol. 54, 401–423.

PRIEST, S. 1921. Excursion to Stevenage, Herts. Part II. *Proceedings of the Geologists' Association*, Vol. 32, 25–27.

PRIOR, S V, KEMP, S J, PEARCE, J M, and INGLETHORPE, S D J. 1993. Mineralogy of the Gault from the Arlesey and Klondyke Farm boreholes. *British Geological Survey Technical Report*, WG/93/17.

RAINES, M G. 1992. Magnetic properties of the Arlesey and Klondyke Farm boreholes (interim report). *British Geological Survey Technical Report*, WN/92/15R.

— and CHACKSFIELD, B C. 1991. Geophysical survey across a buried valley at Langley near Stevenage, Hertfordshire. *British Geological Survey Project Note*, PN/91/3.

RASTALL, R H. 1919. The mineral composition of the Lower Greensand strata of eastern England. *Geological Magazine*, Vol. 56, 211–220 & 265–272.

— 1925. On the tectonics of the southern Midlands. *Geological Magazine*, Vol. 62, 193–222.

RAWSON, P F. 1992. The Cretaceous. 355–388 in *Geology of England and Wales*. DUFF, P McL D, and SMITH, A J (editors). (London: The Geological Society.)

— CURRY, D, DILLEY, F C, HANCOCK, J M, KENNEDY, W J, NEALE, J W, WOOD, C J, and WORSSAM, B C. 1978. A correlation of Cretaceous rocks in the British Isles. *Special Report of the Geological Society of London*, No. 9.

REID, C. 1890. The Pliocene deposits of Britain. *Memoir of the Geological Survey of the United Kingdom*.

— 1897. The Palaeolithic deposits at Hitchin and their relation to the glacial epoch. *Proceedings of the Royal Society of London*, Vol. 61, 40–49.

— 1901. Further note on the palaeolithic deposits at Hitchin. *Transactions of the Hertfordshire Natural History Society*, Vol. 2, 63–64.

REID, R E H. 1962. Sponges and the Chalk Rock. *Geological Magazine*, Vol. 99, 273–278.

— 1973. The Chalk sea. *Irish Naturalists' Journal*, Vol. 17, 357–375.

RINGBERG, B. 1983. Till stratigraphy and glacial rafts of chalk at Kvarnby, southern Sweden. 151–154 in *Glacial deposits in north-west Europe*. EHLERS, J (editor). (Rotterdam: Balkema.)

ROBINSON, N D. 1986. Lithostratigraphy of the Chalk Group of the North Downs, southeast England. *Proceedings of the Geologists' Association*, Vol. 97, 141–170.

— 1987. Upper Cretaceous Chalk in the North and South Downs, England. *Proceedings of the Geologists' Association*, Vol. 98, 87–93.

ROE, D A. 1968a. British Lower and Middle Palaeolithic hand-axe groups. *Proceedings of the Prehistorical Society*, Vol. 34, 1–82.

— 1968b. A gazetteer of British Lower and Middle Palaeolithic sites. *Research Report of the Council for British Archaeology*, Vol. 8.

ROSE, J. 1991. Stratigraphic basis of the 'Wolstonian Glaciation', and retention of the term 'Wolstonian' as a chronostratigraphic stage name — a discussion. 15–20 in *Central East Anglia and the Fen Basin field guide*. LEWIS, S G, WHITEMAN, C A, and BRIDGLAND, D R (editors). (London: Quaternary Research Association.)

— and ALLEN, P. 1977. Middle Pleistocene stratigraphy in south-east Suffolk. *Journal of the Geological Society of London*, Vol. 133, 85–102.

— — and HEY, R W. 1976. Middle Pleistocene stratigraphy in northern East Anglia. *Nature, London*, Vol. 263, 492–494.

RUFFELL, A H. 1992. Correlation of the Hythe Beds Formation (Lower Greensand Group: early-mid-Aptian), southern England. *Proceedings of the Geologists' Association*, Vol. 103, 273–291.

— and WIGNALL, P B. 1990. Depositional trends in the Upper Jurassic–Lower Cretaceous of the northern margin of the Wessex Basin. *Proceedings of the Geologists' Association*, Vol. 101, 279–288.

SALTER, A E. 1896. Pebbly Gravel from Goring Gap to the Norfolk coast. *Proceedings of the Geologists' Association*, Vol. 14, 389–404.

— 1905. On the superficial deposits of central and parts of southern England. *Proceedings of the Geologists' Association,* Vol. 19, 1–56.

SALTER, J W. 1866. On faults in the drift-gravel at Hitchin, Herts. *Proceedings of the Geological Society of London,* Vol. 22, 565–567.

SAUNDERS, J. 1890. Notes on the geology of south Bedfordshire. *Geological Magazine,* Vol. 7, 117–127.

SCHWARZACHER, W. 1953. Cross-bedding and grain size in the Lower Cretaceous sands of East Anglia. *Geological Magazine,* Vol. 90, 322–330.

SEALY, K R, and SEALY, C E. 1956. The terraces of the middle Thames. *Proceedings of the Geologists' Association,* Vol. 67, 369–392.

SEELEY, H. 1866. The rock of the Cambridge Greensand. *Geological Magazine,* Vol. 3, 302–307.

SHACKLETON, N J, and OPDYKE, N D. 1976. Oxygen isotope and palaeomagnetic stratigraphy of Equatorial Pacific core V28-239, Late Pliocene to latest Pleistocene. 449–464 in *Investigation of Late Quaternary palaeoceanography and palaeoclimate.* CLINE, R M, and HAYS, J D (editors). *Memoir of the Geological Society of America,* No. 145.

SHEPHARD-THORN, E R. 1988. Geology of the country around Ramsgate and Dover. *Memoir of the British Geological Survey,* Sheets 274 and 290 (England and Wales).

— 1993. Geological notes and local details for 1:10 000 sheets TL02SE (Luton), TL12SW (Luton east) and TL12SE (Kings Walden). *British Geological Survey Technical Report,* WA/93/12.

— MOORLOCK, B S P, COX, B M, ALLSOP, J M, and WOOD, C J. 1994. Geology of the country around Leighton Buzzard. *Memoir of the British Geological Survey,* Sheet 220 (England and Wales).

SHERLOCK, R L. 1919a. Excursion to Datchworth and Welwyn. *Proceedings of the Geologists' Association,* Vol. 30, 69–70.

— 1919b. Excursion to Codicote, Herts. *Proceedings of the Geologists' Association,* Vol. 30, 92–93.

— 1924. The superficial deposits of south Buckinghamshire and south Hertfordshire and the old course of the Thames. *Proceedings of the Geologists' Association,* Vol. 35, 1–28.

SHOTTON, F W. 1953. Pleistocene deposits of the area between Coventry, Rugby and Leamington and their bearing on the topographic development of the Midlands. *Philosophical Transactions of the Royal Society of London, Series B,* Vol. 237, 209–260.

— 1977. The Devensian Stage: its development, limit and substages. *Philosophical Transactions of the Royal Society of London, Series B,* Vol. 280, 107–118.

ŠIBRAVE, V. 1992. Should the Pliocene–Pleistocene boundary be lowered? *Sveriges Geologiska Undersökning,* Vol. 81, 327–332.

SMART, J G O, BISSON, G, and WORSSAM, B C. 1966. Geology of the country around Canterbury and Folkestone. *Memoir of the Geological Survey of Great Britain,* Sheets 289, 305 and 306 (England and Wales).

SMELLIE, D W. 1956. Elementary approximations in aeromagnetic interpretations. *Geophysics,* Vol. 21, 1021–1040.

SMITH, A. 1992. Geology of the Henlow, Stotfold and Ashwell districts. *British Geological Survey Technical Report,* WA/92/22.

SMITH, N J P, ALLSOP, J M, CHADWICK, R A, HOLLIDAY, D W, HOLLOWAY, S, KIRBY, G A, ARMSTRONG, E J, AULD, H A, BULAT, J, JACKSON, D I, JONES, S M, MULHOLLAND, P, OATES, N K, QUINN,

M F, SWALLOW, J L, and BENNETT, J R P. 1985a. Map 1. Pre-Permian geology of the United Kingdom (South). British Geological Survey.

SMITH, W G. 1894. *Man the primeval savage: his haunts and relics from the hill-tops of Bedfordshire to Blackwall.* (London: Edward Stanford.)

SOLLAS, W J. 1873a. On the Ventriculidae of the Cambridge Upper Greensand. *Quarterly Journal of the Geological Society of London,* Vol. 29, 63–70.

— 1873b. On the coprolites of the Upper Greensand Formation, and on flints. *Quarterly Journal of the Geological Society of London,* Vol. 29, 76–81.

— 1876. On the glauconitic granules of the Cambridge Greensand. *Geological Magazine,* Vol. 13, 539–544.

— and JUKES-BROWNE, A J. 1873. On the included rock-fragments of the Cambridge Upper Greensand. *Quarterly Journal of the Geological Society of London,* Vol. 29, 11–16.

SPAETH, C. 1971. Untersuchungen an Belemniten des Formenkreises um Neohibolites minimus (Miller, 1826) aus dem Mirrel-und Ober-Alb Nordwestdutschlands. *Beihefte zum Geologischen Jahrbach,* Vol. 100, 7–127.

SPATH, L F. 1923a. Excursion to Folkestone. Saturday, September 30th, 1922. With notes on the zones of the Gault. *Proceedings of the Geologists' Association,* Vol. 34, 70–76. [In German.]

— 1923b. On the ammonite horizons of the Gault and contiguous deposits. Appendix II. 139–149 in *Summary of progress of the Geological Survey of Great Britain and the Museum of Practical Geology for 1922.* (London: HMSO.)

— 1923–1943. A monograph of the Ammonoidea of the Gault. 16 parts. *Monograph of the Palaeontographical Society of London.*

SPECTOR, A, and GRANT, F S. 1970. Statistical models for interpreting aeromagnetic data. *Geophysics,* Vol. 35, 293–302.

STRAHAN, A, FLETT, J S, and DINHAM, C H. 1917. Potash-felspar–phosphate of lime–alum shales–plumbago or graphite–molybdenite–chromite–talc and steatite (soapstone, soap-rock and potstone)–diatomite (2nd edition). *Memoir of the Geological Survey, Special Report on the Mineral Resources of Great Britain,* Vol. 5.

THOMASSON, A J. 1961. Some aspects of the drift deposits and geomorphology of south-east Hertfordshire. *Proceedings of the Geologists' Association,* Vol. 72, 287–302.

— 1969. Soils of the Saffron Walden district. A reconnaissance survey. *Soil Survey Special Survey,* No. 2.

— and AVERY, B W. 1970. The soils of Hertfordshire. *Soil Survey Special Survey,* No. 3.

TINSLEY, H M, and COSGROVE, T P. 1991. The peat deposits at Ridlins Mire, Stevenage, Hertfordshire. *Transactions of the Hertfordshire Natural History Society,* Vol 31, 53–57.

TOWNSEND, H A, and HAILWOOD, E A. 1985. Magneto-stratigraphic correlation of Palaeogene sediments in the Hampshire and London Basin, southern UK. *Journal of the Geological Society of London,* Vol. 142, 957–982.

TURNER, C. 1970. The Middle Pleistocene deposits at Marks Tey, Essex. *Philosophical Transactions of the Royal Society of London, Series B,* Vol. 257, 373–440.

— and WEST, R G. 1968. The subdivision and zonation of interglacial periods. *Eiszeitalter und Gegenwart,* Vol. 19, 93–101.

UNIVERSITY OF BIRMINGHAM. 1989. TVWC water resources study. School of Civil Engineering, University of Birmingham.

VACQUIER, V, STREELAND, N C, HENDERSON, R G, and ZEITZ, I. 1957. Interpretation of aeromagnetic maps. *Memoir of the Geological Society of America*, No. 47.

WATEREN, D F M van der. 1985. A model of glacial tectonics, applied to the ice-push ridges in the Central Netherlands. *Bulletin of the Geological Society of Denmark*, Vol. 34, 55–74.

WEST, R G. 1956. The Quaternary deposits at Hoxne, Suffolk. *Philosophical Transactions of the Royal Society of London, Series B*, Vol. 241, 1–31.

— 1957. Interglacial deposits at Bobbitshole, Ipswich. *Philosophical Transactions of the Royal Society, Series B*, Vol. 241, 1–31.

— 1961. Vegetational history of the Early Pleistocene at the Royal Society borehole at Ludham, Norfolk. *Proceedings of the Royal Society of London, Series B*, Vol. 155, 437–453.

— 1980. *The pre-glacial Pleistocene of the Norfolk and Suffolk coasts.* (Cambridge: Cambridge University Press.)

— and DONNER, J J. 1956. The glaciations of East Anglia and the East Midlands: a differentiation based on stone orientation measurements of the tills. *Quarterly Journal of the Geological Society of London*, Vol. 112, 69–91.

WHITAKER, W. 1866. On the 'Lower London Tertiaries' of Kent. *Quarterly Journal of the Geological Society of London*, Vol. 22, 404–435.

— 1872. The geology of the London Basin, I. *Memoir of the Geological Survey of Great Britain.*

— 1876. List of works on the geology of Hertfordshire. *Transactions of the Watford Natural History Society*, Vol. 2, 78–82.

— 1889. The geology of London and part of the Thames Basin. *Memoir of the Geological Survey of Great Britain.*

— PENNING, W H, DALTON, W H, and BENNETT, F J. 1878. The Geology of the N.W. part of Essex and the N.E. part of Herts. with parts of Cambridgeshire and Suffolk. *Memoir of the Geological Survey of Great Britain*, Old Series Sheet 47 (England and Wales).

WHITE, H J O. 1909. The geology of the country around Basingstoke. *Memoir of the Geological Survey of Great Britain*, Sheet 284 (England and Wales).

— and EDMUNDS, F H. 1932. The geology of the country near Saffron Walden. *Memoir of the Geological Survey of Great Britain*, Sheet 205 (England and Wales).

WHITEMAN, C A. 1987. Till lithology and genesis near the southern margin of the Anglian ice-sheet in Essex, England. 55–66 in *Tills and glaciotectonics*. MEER, J J M van der (editor). Proceedings INQUA Symposium on the genesis and lithology of glacial deposits, 1986, Amsterdam. (Rotterdam: Balkema.)

— and ROSE, J. 1992. Thames river sediments of the British Early and Middle Pleistocene. *Quaternary Science Reviews*, Vol. 11, 363–375.

WHITTAKER, A (editor). 1985. Atlas of onshore sedimentary basins in England and Wales. *Post Carboniferous tectonics and stratigraphy.* (Glasgow: Blackie.)

WILKINSON, I P. 1988a. Ostracoda across the Albian/Cenomanian boundary in Cambridgeshire and western Suffolk, eastern England. 1229–1244 *in* Evolutionary biology of Ostracoda, its fundamentals and applications. HANAI, T, IKEYA, N, and ISHIZAKI, K. *Developments in Paleontology and Stratigraphy*, No. 11.

— 1988b. Calcareous microfaunas from a suite of samples from Shillington. *British Geological Survey Technical Report*, WH/88/239R.

— 1990a. Foraminifera from the Anstey Chalk quarry. *British Geological Survey Technical Report*, WH/90/170R.

— 1990b. The biostratigraphical application of Ostracoda to the Albian of eastern England. *Courier Forschungsinstitut Senckenberg*, Vol. 123 239–258.

— 1991. Calcareous micropalaeontology of the Shefford Hardwick Borehole (TL 1387 3949). *British Geological Survey Technical Report*, WH/91/35C.

— 1992a. The biostratigraphical distribution of microfaunas from the Albian and Cenomanian of the Arlesey borehole. *British Geological Survey Technical Report*, WH/92/20R.

— 1992b. Calcareous microfossils from the 72.76–72.96 m interval of the Arlesey Borehole. *British Geological Survey Technical Report*, WH/92/294R.

— 1993a. Calcareous microfaunas from the Green Lagoon, Arlesey. *British Geological Survey Technical Report*, WH/93/94R.

— 1993b. Calcareous microfaunas from the Chalk at Cadwell Farm, Arlesey. *British Geological Survey Technical Report*, WH/93/105R.

— 1993c. Calcareous microfaunas from the Blue Lagoon, Arlesey. *British Geological Survey Technical Report*, WH/93/106R.

— 1993d. Calcareous microfaunas from the Dallow Road borehole, Luton (TL 06412208). *British Geological Survey Technical Report*, WH/93/203R.

— In press. Palaeoenvironmental controls on British ostracoda between 112.5 and 108 MA. In the 2nd European Ostracodologists meeting, University of Glasgow, Scotland, 23–27 July 1993.

— and MORTER, A A. 1981. The biostratigraphical zonation of the East Anglian Gault by Ostracoda. 163–176 in *Microfossils from Recent and fossil shelf seas*. NEALE, J W, and BRASIER, M D (editors). (Chichester: Ellis Horwood.)

WINGFIELD, R T R. 1990. The origin of major incisions within the Pleistocene deposits of the North Sea. *Marine Geology*, Vol. 91, 31–52.

WOOD, C J. 1990. The stratigraphy of the Middle and Upper Chalk of the Rugby Portland Cement Co. working quarry at Kensworth. *British Geological Survey Technical Report*, WH/90/99R.

— 1991. The stratigraphy of the Upper Chalk of Anstey quarry, Herts. *British Geological Survey Technical Report*, WH/91/124R.

— 1993. The Plenus Marls and Melbourn Rock of the Chilterns and north Hertfordshire in the context of successions in southern England. *British Geological Survey Technical Report*, WH/93/120R.

WOODCOCK, N H. 1991. The Welsh, Anglian and Belgian Caledonides compared. *Annales de la Société Géologique de Belgique*, Vol. 114, 5–17.

— 1993. Silurian facies beneath East Anglia. *Geological Magazine*, Vol. 130, 681–690.

WOODLAND, A W. 1970. The buried tunnel-valleys of East Anglia. *Proceedings of the Yorkshire Geological Society*, Vol. 37, 521–578.

WOODS, H. 1896. The Mollusca of the Chalk Rock. 1. *Quarterly Journal of the Geological Society of London*, Vol. 52, 68–98.

— 1897. The Mollusca of the Chalk Rock. 2. *Quarterly Journal of the Geological Society of London*, Vol. 53, 377–404.

WOODS, M A. 1992a.   Biostratigraphical interpretation of the Cretaceous macrofaunas of the Arlesey Borehole.   *British Geological Survey Technical Report*, WH/92/83R.

— 1992b.   Chalk macrofaunas from Ashwell quarry, Herts. *British Geological Survey Technical Report*, WH/92/158R.

— 1992c.   Macrofaunas from the Lower Chalk (Chalk Marl and Totternhoe Stone) of the Green Lagoon and Blue Lagoon, Arlesey, Beds.   *British Geological Survey Technical Report*, WH/92/213R.

— 1992d.   Identification and interpretation of macrofaunas from the Gault, Cambridge Greensand and Chalk Marl of Arlesey Brickpit, Bedfordshire.   *British Geological Survey Technical Report*, WH/92/218R.

— 1992e.   Biostratigraphical interpretation of the Gault of the BGS Klondyke Farm Borehole, Cambridgeshire.   *British Geological Survey Technical Report*, WH/92/264R.

— 1992f.   Biostratigraphical interpretation of Lower and Middle Chalk macrofaunas from the Dallow Road (Luton) boreholes, (Nos. 21 & 22).   *British Geological Survey Technical Report*, WH/92/341R.

— 1993.   A palaeontological review of the Chalk of the Hitchin area based on BGS fossil collections.   *British Geological Survey Technical Report*, WH/93/49R.

— WILKINSON, I P, and HOPSON, P M. 1995.   The stratigraphy of the Gault Formation (Middle and Upper Albian) in the BGS Arlesey Borehole, Bedfordshire.   *Proceedings of the Geologists' Association*, Vol. 106, 271–280.

WOODWARD, H B. 1903a.   On some disturbances in the Chalk near Royston (Hertfordshire).   *Quarterly Journal of the Geological Society of London*, Vol. 59, 362–374.

— 1903b.   Excursion to Royston, Hertfordshire.   *Proceedings of the Geologists' Association*, Vol. 18, 166–170.

— 1903c.   Geology.   1–30 in *The Victoria history of the counties of England, Essex*. Vol. 1. (London: Archibald Constable.)

WOOLDRIDGE, S W. 1953.   Some marginal drainage features of the chalky boulder clay ice-sheet in Hertfordshire.   *Proceedings of the Geologists' Association*, Vol. 64, 208–231.

— and LINTON, D L. 1955.   Structure, surface and drainage in south-east England (2nd edition).   (London: G Philip and Sons.)

WRAY, D S, and GALE, A S. 1993.   Geochemical correlation of marl bands in Turonian chalks of the Anglo-Paris basin. 221–226 *in* High resolution stratigraphy. KIDD, R V, and HAILWOOD, E A (editors). *Special Publication of the Geological Society of London*, No. 70.

WRIGHT, C W. 1979.   The ammonites of the English Chalk Rock.   *Bulletin of the British Museum (Natural History)*, Vol. 31, 281–332.

APPENDIX 1

Key boreholes of the Hitchin district

At the time of going to press, 1856 borehole records of the Hitchin district are held in BGS archives, and additional information is constantly being added to the database as it becomes available.

Abstracts of selected boreholes are shown in this appendix, together with a list of all the boreholes mentioned in the text. Each borehole is given a unique registered number in the BGS archives and this number should be quoted with any enquiries on individual boreholes.

The full borehole records are held in the National Geological Records Centre, BGS, Keyworth. Most are available in full for inspection by prior appointment, and copies of records may be made; a charge is made for these services, which reflects the storage and maintenance of the archive.

An index to all BGS borehole records is available on workstation computers at each of the BGS offices and provides rapid access to the location of individual boreholes or to a set of boreholes for any defined area. A list of boreholes can be retrieved either by a place name, National Grid reference or map sheet number. The index contains information on the location and depth of the boreholes and the method of drilling. Plans to add to this data base are at an advanced stage.

Abstracts of selected borehole logs referred to in the text

Dallow Road, Luton   TL02SE/240   [0641 2208]
Surface level c.+141.69 m OD

	Thickness m	Depth m
Middle Chalk	33.18	33.18
Lower Chalk		
Plenus Marls	0.97	34.15
'Grey Chalk'	19.71	53.86
Totternhoe Stone	3.49	57.35
Chalk Marl	19.35	76.70

The following five boreholes were drilled for BGS with support from the National Rivers Authority (NRA):

Wellhead (BGS)   TL12NE/222   [1770 2770]
Surface level 75.2 m OD

	Thickness m	Depth m
Soil	0.45	0.45
MIDDLE CHALK:		
Chalk, weathered fragments in soft putty matrix	0.55	1.00
Chalk, very hard, fractured, brownish white and nodular	1.20	2.20
MELBOURN ROCK (top uncertain)		
Chalk, hard, nodular, with pale green wispy marls	2.00	4.20

LOWER CHALK:

PLENUS MARLS	Thickness	Depth
Marl, thin, interbedded with very hard chalks (?J4–8)	1.10	5.30
Chalk, hard, nodular (?J3)	0.30	5.60
Marl, pale yellowish grey, with marly chalk (?J1–2)	0.70	6.30
GREY CHALK		
Chalk, soft to firm, pale brownish white or pale grey, with brown iron staining at top and black manganese dioxide spots on blocky fracturing. Rare shell fragments, pyritic trace fossils and burrow mottling	13.20	19.50
Chalk, marly, soft, yellowish grey, with 0.1–0.2 m grey anastomosing marls at 21.1 m	4.40	23.90
TOTTERNHOE STONE		
Chalk, hard, brownish grey, slightly coarser, burrow mottled, with sparse phosphatic vertebrate debris. Rests on burrowed surface	1.00	24.90
CHALK MARL		
Chalk marl and marly chalk, soft, pale yellowish or brownish grey or pale grey, burrow mottled, cemented in parts. Minor concentrations of fish scales and traces of shell fragments	10.00	34.90

Gosmore (BGS)   TL12NE/223   [1867 2759]
Surface level 78.8 m OD

	Thickness m	Depth m
Head	1.1	1.1
Brickearth	2.4	3.5
Glaciofluvial deposits and till	43.7	47.2

Broad Meadow (BGS)   TL12NE/224   [1932 2773]
Surface level 71.4 m OD

	Thickness m	Depth m
Glaciofluvial deposits and till	43.0	43.0

Maydencroft Manor (BGS)   TL12NE/225   [1829 2760]
Surface level 84.9 m OD

	Thickness m	Depth m
Head and brickearth	2.9	2.9
Interglacial deposits	1.9	4.8
Till	5.4	10.2
Glaciofluvial deposits and till	49.8	60.0

Priory Park (BGS)   TL12NE/226   [1825 2832]
Surface level 71.9 m OD

	Thickness m	Depth m
Glaciofluvial deposits and till	12.9	12.9
Middle Chalk	3.5	16.4

Arlesey (BGS)   TL13SE/45   [1887 3463]
Surface level c.+44.0 m OD

	Thickness m	Depth m
Lower Chalk		
Chalk Marl	14.38	14.38
Cambridge Greensand	1.07	15.45
Gault		
Upper Gault	52.85	68.30
Lower Gault	4.50	72.80
Junction Beds	0.16	72.96
Woburn Sands	10.26	83.49

Fairfield Hospital (Augerhole) (BGS)   TL23NW/113
[2048 3540]   Surface level c.70 m OD

	Thickness m	Depth m
SOIL		
Sand, humic, grey to brown, very slightly clayey, with rootlets and a few pebbles of mainly quartzose components as found in underlying gravels with traces of coal and ash or slag contaminants	0.20	0.20
LETCHWORTH GRAVEL		
Gravel, clayey. Gravel 48%: fine to coarse pebbles of rounded quartzite with quartz and sandstone, subangular flint, minor rounded ironstone and traces of igneous and metamorphic rocks. Traces of ash and coal contaminants at top. Sand 40%: fine to very coarse quartz and quartzose fragments. Fines 12%: orange-brown clay matrix, probably illuviation product	1.25	1.45
Gravel, sandy. Gravel 28%: fine to medium pebbles of rounded quartzite and subangular flint with ironstone, especially in the fine fraction, rounded quartz and sandstone, and traces of igneous and metamorphic rocks. Sand 64%: medium to coarse quartz and quartzose grains, some very coarse rock fragments. Fines 8%: some orange-brown clay in matrix	0.50	1.95
Gravel, very clayey, sandy. Gravel 27%: fine subangular flint and rounded ironstone, quartz and quartzite with minor igneous and metamorphic pebbles. Sand 51%: fine quartz with some medium to coarse grains. Fines 22%: sample 'clean' with little clay but much silt-size material	0.20	2.15
Gravel, very clayey. Gravel 50%: fine and medium rounded quartzite and subangular flint with rounded quartz, sandstone and ironstone, especially in the fine fraction, with trace of igneous and metamorphic pebbles. Sand 25%: coarse to very coarse		

quartzose rock fragments with finer quartz grains. Fines 25%: orange-brown clay in matrix — 0.90 3.05

Sand, pebbly. Gravel: fine rounded quartzite with subangular flint, rounded quartz, sandstone and ironstone, traces of igneous and metamorphic rocks, and ?Jurassic shell fragments and limestone pebbles. Sand: medium to very coarse lithic fragments as for gravel and finer quartz grains. Fines: minor component only	0.50	3.55

LOWER CHALK:
Chalk, very pale brown to off-white, soft, marly with a few pieces of hard arenitic chalk (?Totternhoe Stone) at top. Traces of phosphatic granules throughout. Patches of orange, medium sand and minor gravel at top caused by cryoturbation and contamination by augered sampling	0.43	3.98

Ashwell (Superior Oil No. 4)   TL23NE/1   [286 390]
Surface level +59.4 m OD

	Thickness m	Depth m
Lower Chalk	51.80	51.80
Gault	54.90	106.70
Woburn Sands	27.87	134.57
Cornbrash	3.81	138.38
?Blisworth Clay	0.38	138.76
Blisworth Limestone	1.45	140.21
?Rutland Formation	0.68	140.89
Core loss	0.13	141.02
?Grantham Formation	11.68	152.70
Devonian (undivided)	33.84	186.54

Letchworth Obs 1 (BGS)   TL23SW/135   [2318 3299]
Surface level c.+81.0 m OD

	Thickness m	Depth m
Made ground	4.80	4.80
Middle Chalk	14.20	19.00
Lower Chalk		
'Grey Chalk' (inc Plenus Marls)	30.00	49.00
Totternhoe Stone	2.00	51.00
Chalk Marl	6.00	57.00

Letchworth Obs 2 (BGS)   TL23SW/136   [2336 3328]
Surface level c.+77.0 m OD

	Thickness m	Depth m
Made ground	2.91	2.91
Middle Chalk	14.20	19.00
Lower Chalk		
'Grey Chalk' (inc Plenus Marls)	28.00	45.50
Totternhoe Stone	2.00	47.50
Chalk Marl	8.50	56.00

Worsted Lane, Hare Street   **TL32NE/18**   [3987 2920]
Surface level +90.02 m OD

	Thickness m	Depth m
Alluvium	3.50	3.50
Upper Chalk	37.50	41.00
Middle Chalk	93.50	134.50
Lower Chalk	15.50	150.00

Hamels Mill   **TL32SE/23**   [3860 2468]
Surface level +68.59 m OD

	Thickness m	Depth m
Alluvium	2.44	2.44
Glaciofluvial deposits	2.44	4.88
Upper Chalk	42.40	47.28
Middle Chalk	91.40	138.68
Lower Chalk	21.34	160.02

Dowsett's Farm (BGS), Colliers End   **TL32SE/38**
[3806 2079]   Surface level +113.36 m OD

	Thickness m	Depth m
Soil	0.75	0.75
Glaciofluvial deposits	1.41	2.16
Thames Group (undivided, principally Harwich Formation)	16.28	18.44
Woolwich and Reading formations (undivided)	6.06	24.50
Upnor Formation	2.90	27.40
Upper Chalk	3.60	31.00

The following is a listing of boreholes referred to in the text, together with their unique reference number by which they may be identified within the records system of the National Geological Records Centre at the British Geological Survey, Keyworth.

Boreholes outside the district

Name	National Grid reference	Registered number
Tattenhoe	SU 8289 3437	SP83SW/1
Little Missenden	SU 9009 9818	SU99NW/9
Dallow Road, Luton	0641 2208	TL02SE/240
Elstow	0463 4428	TL04SE/317
Ashwell	286 390	TL23NE/1
Turnford	3600 0444	TL30SE/109
Ware	3531 1397	TL31SE/57
Royston	3570 4000	TL34SE/4
Gilston	4417 1349	TL41SW/35
Little Chishill	4528 3637	TL43NE/1
Meesden Hall	4384 3247	TL43SW/4
Saffron Walden	5386 3840	TL53NW/50
Soham	5928 7448	TL57SE/1
Klondyke Farm	5940 7010	TL57SE/29
Clare	7834 4536	TL74NE/15
Lakenheath	748 830	TL78SW/1
Bushey	TQ 1195 9577	TQ19NW/29
Willesden	TQ 2086 8477	TQ28SW/88

Boreholes within the district

Name	National Grid Reference	Registered Number
The Holt, Kimpton	1692 1965	TL11NE/18
Wain Wood	1832 2558	TL12NE/17
Hitchin Brewery	184 288	TL12NE/20
St Michael's School	1727 2899	TL12NE/22
Ransom's Brickyard, Hitchin	1873 2855	TL12NE/24
Temple End	1723 2760	TL12NE/25d
West of Oughton Head	1590 2980	TL12NE/29
West of Oughton Head	1591 2982	TL12NE/30
Offley Bottom	1607 2886	TL12NE/48
The Priory	1825 2884	TL12NE/93
The Priory	1825 2884	TL12NE/96
Off Charlton Road, Hitchin	1820 2863	TL12NE/215
Wellhead	1775 2770	TL12NE/222
Gosmore	1867 2759	TL12NE/223
Broad Meadow	1932 2773	TL12NE/224
Maydencroft Manor	1829 2760	TL12NE/225
Priory Park	1825 2832	TL12NE/226
Luton Lodge	1023 2001	TL12SW/105
King's Walden	1546 2338	TL12SE/5
Nine Wells, Whitwell	1800 2124	TL12SE/35
Meppershall	1494 3705	TL13NW/20
Rectory Road, Campton	1285 3817	TL13NW/56
Henlow	164 356	TL13NE/1
Pollard's Nurseries	1616 3506	TL13NE/9
Hitchin Road, Arlesey	1899 3513	TL13NE/11
Meppershall	1504 3706	TL13NE/13
Church End	1934 3783	TL13NE/78
Pirton Pumping Station	1406 3818	TL13SW/11
Pirton Hall	1255 3289	TL13SW/12
Old Rectory, Holwell	165 330	TL13SE/2
Pollard's Nurseries	1653 3493	TL13SE/5
The Rectory, Ickleford	1823 3169	TL13SE/6
Arlesey	1887 3463	TL13SE/45
Hornbeam Spring, Welwyn	2432 1921	TL21NW/67
Pinch Lane, Graveley	2285 2826	TL22NW/12
Railway Bridge, Wymondley	214 274	TL22NW/38
Bury Farm, Wymondley	216 270	TL22NW/39
Near Wymondley Bury	2150 2702	TL22NW/41
North of Titmore Green	2147 2682	TL22NW/93
Near Wymondley Bury	2212 2707	TL22NW/106
Near Wymondley Bury	2213 2695	TL22NW/165
North of Margaret's Wood	2208 2695	TL22NW/176
Off Gunnel's Wood Road, Symonds Green	2274 2559	TL22NW/180
Fishers Green	2221 2620	TL22NW/203
Lytton Way, Stevenage	2324 2501	TL22NW/220
Wymondley Bury	2213 2712	TL22NW/239
Victoria Brewery, Walkern	287 257	TL22NE/6
Walkern Mill	2858 2545	TL22NE/8
Watton Road, Knebworth	2551 2030	TL22SE/17
Watton Road, Knebworth	2556 2023	TL22SE/18
Wittenhall Pumping Station	2863 2161	TL22SE/24
Off A1, Radwell	2337 3636	TL23NW/18
St Mary's Church, Stotfold	221 366	TL23NW/33
Fairfield Hospital	2043 3526	TL23NW/34
The Mill, Radwell	2288 3592	TL23NW/35
Old Brewery, Stotfold	2191 3701	TL23NW/36
Newnham Hall	2466 3762	TL23NW/38
Baldock Road, Radwell	2308 3618	TL23NW/49
Stotfold Road, Church End	2011 3710	TL23NW/68
Hitchin Road, Stotfold	2051 3631	TL23NW/78

Name	National Grid Reference	Registered Number
Norton Road, Stotfold	2215 3617	TL23NW/98
Letchworth Gravel Type Site	2048 3540	TL23NW/113
Bygrave Plantation	2559 3655	TL23NE/17
William Road Pumping Station	2417 3248	TL23SW/61
William Road Pumping Station	2416 3248	TL23SW/61
Avenue One, Letchworth Obs 1	2318 3299	TL23SW/135
Letchworth Obs 2	2336 3328	TL23SW/136
Off A505, Baldock	2659 3479	TL23SE/13
Newfield Hill, Weston	2532 3234	TL23SE/56
Newfield Hill, Weston	2530 3234	TL23SE/70
Sacombe Hill Farm	3221 1970	TL31NW/12
Sacombe Green	3424 1940	TL31NW/19
Hangingwood Hill, Watton	3079 1893	TL31NW/52
Standon Green End	3590 1968	TL31NE/1
Haven End, Standon	3573 1840	TL31NE/8
Cromer Windmill	3031 2857	TL32NW/1
Bury Grange	3017 2764	TL32NW/10
Walkern Park Farm	3151 2474	TL32SW/8
North-west of Dowsett's Farm	3768 2124	TL32SE/43
Therfield Rectory	3355 3697	TL33NW/7
Barkway	3880 3790	TL33NE/9
Bury Farm, Wyddial	3741 3171	TL33SE/3

APPENDIX 2

1:10 000 maps and open-file reports

The following is a list of 1:10 000 geological maps included in the area of 1:50 000 geological sheet 221, with the names of the surveyors and the dates of survey of each map. The surveyors were D T Aldiss (DTA), J P Colleran (JPC), P M Hopson (PMH), A Horton (AH), R D Lake (RDL), B S P Moorlock (BSPM), G Richardson (GR), E R Shephard-Thorn (ERST) and A Smith (AS). Manuscript copies of the maps are deposited for public reference in the library of the British Geological Survey at Keyworth. Uncoloured dyeline copies of these maps are available for purchase from the British Geological Survey, Keyworth, Nottingham, NG12 5GG.

TL11NW*	Luton Hoo	ERST	1987–88
TL11NE*	Kimpton	DTA	1992
TL12NW	Great Offley	JPC	1987
TL12NE	Hitchin	DTA	1991–92
TL12SW	Luton East	ERST	1987–88
TL12SE	Kings Walden	ERST	1988
TL13NW	Shefford	BSPM	1986
TL13NE	Henlow	AS	1991–92
TL13SW	Shillington	JPC	1987–88
TL13SE	Holwell	PMH	1991
TL21NW*	Codicote	AS	1992
TL21NE*	Datchworth	AS	1992
TL22NW	Little Wymondley	DTA	1991
TL22NE	Walkern	RDL	1988
TL22SW	Stevenage South-west	BSPM/ERST	1988–89
TL22SE	Stevenage South-east	BSPM	1988
TL23NW	Stotfold	AS	1991
TL23NE	Ashwell	AS	1990
TL23SW	Letchworth	PMH	1991
TL23SE	Weston	DTA	990
TL31NW*	Watton at Stone	PMH	1992
TL31NE*	Thundridge	PMH	1992
TL32NW	Cottered, Ardeley and Wood End	ERST	1989
TL32NE	Buntingford	PMH	1989
TL32SW	Little Munden	PMH/BSPM	1989
TL32SE	Puckeridge	PMH/BSPM	1989
TL33NW	Therfield	PMH	1989–90
TL33NE	Barkway	PMH	1989–90
TL33SW	Rushden and Sandon	ERST	1989
TL33SE	Wyddial	PMH	1989
TL42NW	Furneux Pelham	GR/AH	1982–85
TL42SW	Little Hadham	GR	1982–85
TL43NW	Great Chishill	AH	1983
TL43SW	Brent Pelham	AH	1983

* denotes that part only of this sheet was surveyed.

Technical Reports

1:10 000 LAND SURVEY SERIES

The Technical Reports listed below are detailed accounts of the geology of selected 1:10 000 sheets which form part of the Hitchin (221) 1:50 000 Geological Sheet. Copies of the reports may be ordered from the British Geological Survey, Keyworth, Nottingham, NG12 5GG.

TL01NE, 11NW and 11NE	WA/92/58	Caddington, Luton Hoo and Kimpton	DTA/ ERST
TL02SE, 12SW and 12SE	WA/93/17	Luton, Luton East and Kings Walden	ERST
TL12NE	WA/92/61	Hitchin	DTA
TL13NE, 23NW and 23NE	WA/92/22	Henlow, Stotfold and Ashwell	AS
TL13SE and 23SW	WA/92/42	Letchworth, north-west Hitchin and Holwell	PMH
TL21NW and 21NE	WA/92/73	Codicote and Datchworth	AS
TL22NW	WA/92/62	Little Wymondley	DTA
TL22NE	WA/92/29	Walkern	RDL
TL23SE	WA/91/51	Weston	DTA
TL31NW and 31NE	WA/92/41	Watton at Stone, Sacombe and High Cross	PMH
TL32NW and 33SW	WA/93/19	Cottered, Ardeley, Wood End, Rushden and Sandon	ERST
TL32NE, 32SW, 32SE and 33SE	WA/90/73	Buntingford, Little Munden, Puckeridge and Wyddial	PMH
TL33NW and 33NE	WA/91/06	Barkway, Reed, Therfield and Kelshall	PMH
TL42NW and 42SW	WA/86/15	Ferneux Pelham and Little Hadham	GR
TL43NW, 43NE, 43SW and 43SE	WA/88/46	Great Chishill, Elmdon, Chrishall, Anstey, Nuthampstead and Clavering	AH

AUTHOR CITATIONS FOR FOSSIL SPECIES

To satisfy the rules and recommendations of the international codes of botanical and zoological nomenclature, authors of cited species are listed below.

Chapter 1 (Introduction)
Meristina obtusa (J Sowerby, 1818)

Chapter 2 (Concealed formations)
Cyrtospirifer verneuili (Murchison, 1840)
Leptodesma (*L.*) *disparile* Hall, 1884
L. (*L.*) *spinigerum* (Conrad, 1842)
Modiolus imbricatus (J Sowerby, 1818)
Palaeoneilo constricta (Conrad, 1842)
Placunopsis socialis Morris & Lycett, 1853
Retichonetes armatus (Bouchard-Chantereaux in de Verneuil, 1845)
Ripidiorhynchus ferquensis (Gosselet, 1887)

Chapter 3 (Lower Cretaceous)
Anahoplites picteti Spath, 1926
A. planus (Mantell, 1822)
Arenobulimina chapmani Cushman, 1936
A. frankei Cushman, 1936
A. sabulosa (Chapman, 1892)
Aucellina coquandiana (d'Orbigny, 1846)
Birostrina concentrica (Parkinson, 1819)
B. concentrica gryphaeoides (J de C Sowerby, 1828)
B. sulcata (Parkinson, 1819)
Dimorphoplites alternatus (S Woodward, 1833)
Entolium orbiculare (J Sowerby, 1817)
Epihoplites compressus (Parona & Bonarelli, 1896)
Euhoplites alphalautus Spath, 1928
Gavelinella cenomanica (Brotzen, 1945)
Hysteroceras bucklandi (Spath, 1922)
H. orbignyi (Spath, 1922)

'Inoceramus' lissa (Seeley, 1866)
Ostrea papyracea Sinzow

Chapter 4 (Upper Cretaceous: Chalk)
Actinocamax plenus (Blainville, 1825)
'Aequipecten' arlesiensis (Woods, 1902)
Arenobulimina advena (Cushman, 1936)
A. anglica Cushman, 1936
Aucellina gryphaeoides (J de C Sowerby, 1836)
Belemnitella plena (Blainville, 1825)
Belemnites minimus Lister, 1678
Cardiaster pygmaeus Forbes, 1850
Collignoniceras woollgari (Mantell, 1822)
Cremnoceramus? rotundatus (Fiege, 1930) sensu Tröger (1967)
C.? waltersdorfensis hannoverensis (Heinz, 1932)
Cretirhynchia cuneiformis Pettitt, 1950
Cytherelloidea globosa Kaye, 1964
Dicarinella hagni (Scheibnerova, 1962)
Dimyodon nilssoni (Hagenow, 1842)
Discoidea minima (Agassiz, 1840)
Fagesia catinus (Mantell, 1822)
Filograna avita (J de C Sowerby, 1844)
Flourensina intermedia Ten Dam, 1950
Galerites castanea (Brongniart, 1822)
G. subrotundus (Mantell, 1822)
Gavelinella baltica Brotzen, 1942
G. intermedia (Berthelin, 1880)
Gibbithyris ellipsoidalis Sahni, 1929
Hedbergella brittonensis Loeblich & Tappan, 1961
Hirudocidaris hirudo (Sorignet, 1850)
Hyphantoceras reussianum (d'Orbigny, 1850)
Inoceramus apicalis Woods, 1912
'I.' concentricus Parkinson, 1819
I. cuvieri J Sowerby, 1814
I. mytiloides Mantell, 1822
I. pictus J de C Sowerby, 1829
Kingena elegans Owen, 1970
Marssonella trochus (d'Orbigny, 1840)
Metaptychoceras smithi (Woods, 1896)
Metoicoceras geslinianum (d'Orbigny, 1850)
Micraster corbovis Forbes, 1850
M. cortestudinarium (Goldfuss, 1826)
M. leskei (Desmoulins, 1837)

M. precursor Rowe, 1899 sensu Drummond (1983)
Monticlarella jefferiesi Owen, 1968
Mytiloides columbianus (Heinz, 1935)
M. hattini Elder, 1991
M. labiatus (Schlotheim, 1813) sensu Seitz (1934)
M. mytiloides (Mantell, 1822)
M. subhercynicus (Seitz, 1934)
Neohibolites preaultimus Spaeth, 1971
Orbirhynchia cuvieri (d'Orbigny, 1847)
O. mantelliana (J de C Sowerby, 1826)
O. multicostata Pettitt, 1954
O. reedensis (Etheridge, 1881)
Ornatothyris sulcifera (Morris & Davidson, 1847)
Ostrea vesicularis Lamarck, 1806
Praeglobotruncana stephani (Gandolfi, 1942)
Pseudopuzosia marlowense (Noble, 1911)
Pseudotexulariella cretosa (Cushman, 1932)
Ptychodus decurrens Agassiz, 1836
Pycnodonte (*Phygraea*) *vesiculare* (Lamarck, 1806)
Reussella kelleri Vasilenko, 1961
Rhynchonella cuvieri d'Orbigny, 1847
R. plicatilis (J Sowerby, 1816)
Rotalipora cushmani (Morrow, 1934)
R. greenhornensis (Morrow, 1934)
R. reicheli Mornod, 1950
Sciponoceras bohemicus anterius Wright & Kennedy, 1981
Spondylus spinosus (J Sowerby, 1814)
Sternotaxis plana (Mantell, 1822)
Terebratula biplicata J Sowerby, 1815
Terebratula semiglobosa J Sowerby, 1813
Terebratulina gracilis var *lata* Etheridge, 1881
T. lata Etheridge, 1881

Chapter 5 (Palaeogene)
Ammodiscus cretaceus (Reuss, 1845)
Clithrocytheridea faboides (Bosquet, 1852)
Cytheretta nerva Apostolescu, 1956
Cytheridea unispinae Eagar, 1965

Chapter 6 (Quaternary)
Hippophae rhamnoides Linnaeus, 1753

INDEX

BRITISH GEOLOGICAL SURVEY

Keyworth, Nottingham NG12 5GG
0115-936 3100

Murchison House, West Mains Road, Edinburgh
EH9 3LA   0131-667 1000

London Information Office, Natural History Museum
Earth Galleries, Exhibition Road, London SW7 2DE
0171-589 4090

The full range of Survey publications is available through the
Sales Desks at Keyworth and at Murchison House, Edinburgh,
and in the BGS London Information Office in the Natural
History Museum (Earth Galleries). The adjacent bookshop
stocks the more popular books for sale over the counter. Most
BGS books and reports can be bought from HMSO and
through HMSO agents and retailers. Maps are listed in the
BGS Map Catalogue, and can be bought together with books
and reports through BGS-approved stockists and agents as well
as direct from BGS.

*The British Geological Survey carries out the geological survey of Great
Britain and Northern Ireland (the latter as an agency service for the
government of Northern Ireland), and of the surrounding continental
shelf, as well as its basic research projects. It also undertakes
programmes of British technical aid in geology in developing countries
as arranged by the Overseas Development Administration.*

*The British Geological Survey is a component body of the Natural
Environment Research Council.*

HMSO publications are available from:

HMSO Publications Centre
(Mail, fax and telephone orders only)
PO Box 276, London SW8 5DT
Telephone orders 0171-873 9090
General enquiries 0171-873 0011
Queuing system in operation for both numbers
Fax orders 0171-873 8200

HMSO Bookshops
49 High Holborn, London WC1V 6HB
(counter service only)
0171-873 0011   Fax 0171-831 1326
68–69 Bull Street, Birmingham B4 6AD
0121-236 9696   Fax 0121-236 9699
33 Wine Street, Bristol BS1 2BQ
0117-9264306   Fax 0117-9294515
9 Princess Street, Manchester M60 8AS
0161-834 7201   Fax 0161-833 0634
16 Arthur Street, Belfast BT1 4GD
01232-238451   Fax 01232-235401
71 Lothian Road, Edinburgh EH3 9AZ
0131-228 4181   Fax 0131-229 2734
HMSO Oriel Bookshop,
The Friary, Cardiff CF1 4AA
01222-395548   Fax 01222-384347

HMSO's Accredited Agents
(see Yellow Pages)

And through good booksellers